WESTERN CIVILIZATION SINCE 1500

FROM A 17TH CENTURY WOODCUT

THE BETTMANN ARCHIVE

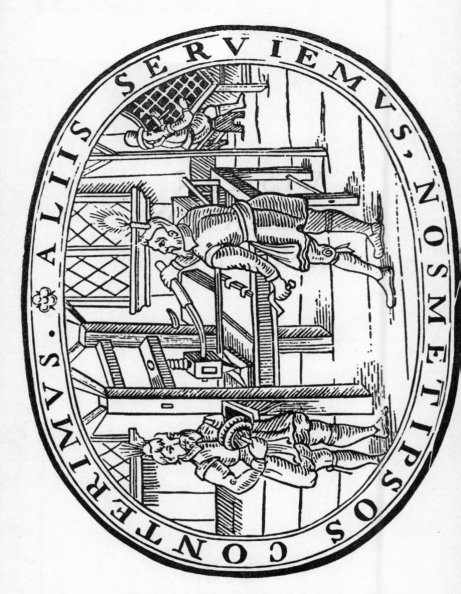

SERVIEMVS · NOSMETIPSOS CONTERIMVS · ALIIS

FROM A 17TH CENTURY WOODCUT

COLLEGE OUTLINE SERIES

WESTERN

CIVILIZATION
SINCE 1500

WALTHER KIRCHNER
University of Delaware

BARNES & NOBLE, PUBLISHERS
NEW YORK
FOUNDED 1873

Library of Congress Catalog Card Number: 66–22196

ISBN 389 00133 3

Distributed

In Canada
    by McGraw-Hill Company of Canada Ltd.,
    Toronto

In Australia and New Zealand
    by Hicks, Smith & Sons Pty. Ltd.,
    Sydney and Wellington

In the United Kingdom, Europe,
and South Africa
    by Chapman & Hall Ltd., London

Published in the United States of America
by Barnes & Noble, Publishers
A Division of Amtel, Inc.

ABOUT THE AUTHOR

Walther Kirchner is Professor of History at the University of Delaware. He received his B.A., M.A., and Ph.D. degrees from the University of California at Los Angeles. He has held teaching positions at the University of California at Los Angeles, the University of Pennsylvania, and Lehigh University. Dr. Kirchner, a research specialist in Russian history, has written *Rise of the Baltic Question, Jacob Fries' Journey through Siberia,* and *History of Russia* (in the College Outline Series). He has also written *Middle Ages 375– 1492* (in the College Outline Series) and contributed numerous articles to leading history periodicals. Professor Kirchner has traveled extensively throughout the world and has spent a Fulbright year in Denmark. For the years 1955– 1956 he was appointed a member of the Institute for Advanced Study at Princeton.

PREFACE

In former times, history meant essentially a narrative of events and included primarily political, legal, military, and biographical data. In more recent times, the scope of historical writing has been steadily broadened. We have added the history of ideas, history of science, economic history, psychological and sociological history, etc. Only future generations will be able to judge whether or not we have served "the truth" and presented a clearer image of life as reflected in history. As a whole, we have enriched historical writing, but we have also infinitely complicated the picture. A vast amount of new work and clear thinking will be needed to integrate the various areas of history into an understandable whole, to appreciate their interrelationships, and to evaluate their relative importance.

While trying to relate soberly in chronological order "what has happened," I have attempted in the present volume to examine—in line with modern historical concepts—the manifold aspects of Western Civilization. The extent to which I may have succeeded in this task, I owe to past and living historians, to chance and purposeful conversations, to studies in the "ivory tower" and to concrete impressions on travels in many lands. My special thanks are due to several colleagues, in particular to Professor Walter Woodfill of the University of Delaware. My wife has been, as usual, the first, the second, the most critical, and the most appreciated of readers.

W. K.

TABLE OF CONTENTS

MAPS AND CHARTS

CHAPTER I

THE ANCIENT HERITAGE

THE MODERN AGE begins around 1500. Historians generally date it from the year 1492. By then, Western civilization had undergone an evolution of more than five thousand years. Great empires and civilizations had arisen—and had disappeared. Egyptians, Babylonians, Hittites, Assyrians, Persians, Hebrews, Phoenicians, Etruscans, Greeks, and Romans had passed over the stage of Western history. All of them had flourished in the same comparatively small area, which was restricted to lands surrounding the eastern Mediterranean basin and extending eastward not farther than the valley of the rivers Euphrates and Tigris. Geographic links connected the various peoples: the commercial enterprises, the religious beliefs, the artistic creations, and the political fates of the peoples were interwoven. The inventions, the achievements, of each older civilization fructified the thought and the work of civilizations which came after it. But time has annihilated most of what they produced. Although our knowledge of the oldest precursors of Western civilization has increased owing to the recent work of archaeologists and epigraphists, any direct impact of the Egyptians and Babylonians, the Persians and Phoenicians, or the Hittites and Etruscans is hard to perceive because of the paucity of surviving monuments. Only indirectly— by affecting Greeks and Romans and, through these, modern Western civilization—has their legacy been preserved. Even the influence of the Hebrews has been limited in its direct effect chiefly to those ethical principles which have come down to us through Christianity.

1

GREEK CONTRIBUTIONS TO MODERN
WESTERN CIVILIZATION

It is different with Greece and Rome. Grecian influence has been felt directly in almost all facets of modern life, and most potently has it shaped Western civilization.

Language. A first indication of Greece's significance can be derived from the treasure of words the modern world has taken over. Examples are such English terms as "philosophy," "history," "mathematics," "aesthetics," "mysticism," "architecture," "poetry," "choir," "monarchy," "democracy," "barbarism," "theory," "paper," and "atom." Such words are not important simply for having entered our vocabulary. Rather, their importance lies in the fact that the concepts for which they stand have kept a meaning for modern man; the thought behind them has enriched his thinking; the ideas they represent have retained validity throughout the ages.

Philosophy. Greek thought roamed widely and freely, restrained by clear and logical minds but unimpeded by a written set of values, by an enforced creed, or by a dogma. This was perhaps one of the most important factors which have helped to make the concepts of ancient Greece a permanent, usable tool. The Greeks loved wisdom and sought a path to wise living. They studied the reality that surrounded them and tried first to understand it, then to master it. To achieve such mastery, they looked to manly qualities in human nature, to self-control, fortitude, and temperance. They studied themselves, both as individuals with individual aspirations and as members of a community with a common fate, and they searched for a compromise between the ideal state of man and the limited status imposed upon him by nature. Various philosophical schools were initiated by them, such as the Sophists, the Epicureans, the Stoics, and the Cynics. Socrates, Plato, and Aristotle (fourth century B.C.) created systems of logic and concepts of ethics which have remained guides ever since. They thought through the various paths which may direct man in his search for knowledge and drive to action; and they recognized and established limits, within which philosophical investigation could move throughout the history of Western civilization.

Science. With their rational procedures and their reliance upon logical deduction, the Greeks achieved a remarkable insight into the works of nature. They arrived at it by speculation rather than by observation and experimentation. This, to be sure, limited their achievement. Since they failed to evolve physical instruments which could have supplemented their methods and measured their results, they formed numerous erroneous conclusions. These, too, contributed a lasting heritage; for, as the errors played an important role in the Greek view of the universe, so to a large extent they dominated Western thought and interpretations deep into the nineteenth century. Simultaneously, however, the Greeks developed views which modern investigations have to an astounding degree proved to be correct. By means of logical deduction, they anticipated many findings acceptable to modern man, and they prepared the way for fundamental procedures and discoveries. Among the achievements which were of such significance were those of Pythagoras, Archimedes, and Euclid in mathematics; of Democritus, who postulated an atomic theory, and of Thales, who taught that the earth is a sphere. In medicine, views assigned to Asclepiades or principles recognized by Hippocrates and Galen have guided the medical profession into the present; they set forth fundamental concepts of the duties of a doctor, and they recognized the value of sanitariums and healing springs, of hygiene and physical exercise. Moreover, recent psychological trends were anticipated by philosophers like Plato, who insisted on the interconnection of mind and body. In zoology, data on the animal world were compiled by Aristotle. In geography, on the basis of philosophical speculation and travel accounts, a picture of the globe was drawn which, notwithstanding all its faults, has determined the views of geographers deep into the Modern Age and has given direction to almost two thousand years of map making. In the field of education, a special contribution was made by Greek philosophers. The Socratic method of teaching by questioning (and demanding logical answers) has become an integral part of modern pedagogy. Invariably the modern world has been forced to go back to Greek models in its search for a satisfactory path to learning. Even in military tactics, Greek principles have survived. Though weapons have changed, wedgelike formations for attack and oblique arrangement of battle forces, as used and described by the Greeks, have retained usefulness.

Art. Greek civilization was marked by devotion to beauty. Their sense of harmony induced the Greeks, not only to seek an understandable picture of man and universe, but also to express their thoughts and feelings in a form which would inspire generations to come. Nowhere is this striving for harmony of form and content more vividly expressed than in their architecture. The Greek temple has remained the best example of serene "classical" beauty. Hardly a town exists in the entire modern Western world where the Greek temple has not been copied outright or has not at least affected the style of public and private buildings. The simplicity and vigor of the Doric column, the grace of the Ionian, and the restrained exuberance of the Corinthian have never ceased to charm and inspire builders and architects. They have imitated Greek friezes, gables, and porticoes, seeking eternally to achieve a similar clarity of line and simplicity of concept. The use of mathematical forms may explain in some degree the marvelous proportions of Greek architecture, but it was the meaningful ideas created by the great masters which gave their work its overwhelming appeal throughout the ages. And as in architecture, so it has been in sculpture, with the statues of Phidias, Praxiteles, and others. Greek sculpture has often been praised for its trueness to life. However, it was not this aspect that gave it lasting value; it was the fact that an abstract concept of beauty and a thoughtful approach to life were expressed in a lifelike form. Unfortunately, we know too little to make similar assertions about Greek painting, music, and dance. Many indications exist that in these arts, too, the Greeks created works of unsurpassed beauty; and some of their instruments, such as the flute and lyre, have been inherited by later ages. But being more perishable than stone and marble, painting and music could not be passed on to future generations like buildings and sculpture.

Literature. Time has taken a similar toll of the written works of Greece. Only a small fraction of what the Greeks composed has come down to the Modern Age. Surprising is the unparalleled influence which Greek literature has exercised. The very words for different poetic forms—"tragedy," "comedy," "lyric," "epic"—or for different verse meters—"iamb," "dactyl," "hexameter"—bear witness to its importance. What schoolboy of modern times has not heard of Homer, has not dreamed of the mighty deeds of his heroes? What modern reader would not be awed by the breadth of Homer's vision of the human race, his insight into human emotions, the charm and meaningfulness of his parables? What poet or lover of poetry would not be captured by the infinite warmth and tenderness of the lyrics of Sappho, Pindar, or Anacreon? Their names may be less familiar than Homer's, but their influence has been felt, consciously and unconsciously; and their poetry has given direction to the form and content of songs and poems in all subsequent ages. Equally potent has been the influence of the great Greek dramatists, of Sophocles, Aeschylus, and Aristophanes. Their individual topics, whether mythological or political, have lost much pertinence, but their general significance has remained undiminished. Antigone's appeal to unwritten laws which may be higher than any man-made rules; Oedipus' tragic involvement in predestined guilt; Orestes' battle against the Furies persecuting him for a crime though it was one which was necessary and ordained—never have these problems lost their hold over man's life and imagination. Man's relationship to necessity, to a fate which is ever interwoven with all his actions, which is buried in his own nature as well as imposed by external forces—this problem, which persistently engaged the attention of Greek thinkers and which has brought forth the deepest passages of the great dramatists, has captured, puzzled, shaken, and inspired the modern mind.

History. Greek civilization has often been described as unconcerned with history or as hostile to it, yet it produced some of the greatest historians. Among them were Herodotus, Xenophon, and, especially, Thucydides. The latter was perhaps even more conscious of the permanent significance of his work than were the poets (who, while giving expression to lasting thought, addressed themselves to contemporary audiences). As he himself states, he set out to write a history which was to be a treasure for all times. His method of presenting historical events has set no standards; but, with his artistic genius, the perfection of his treatment, the range of his presentation, and the scope of his insight into the human drama, he left a work that has proved to be the treasure which he aspired to create.

Statecraft. The political problems of little Greece were in many ways very different from those which the modern, eventually industrialized, nation-states have had to face. But what has made the political achievements of Athens, Sparta, Thebes, and others so imposing has been that they did not merely adjust themselves pragmatically to a given political form. Rather, the fundamental issues confronting any human community were thought through by the Greeks. They did not, like others, unthinkingly take over the despotic models or priest-dominated systems of their Oriental neighbors. Instead, they experimented with monarchy, aristocracy, oligarchy, democracy, and tyranny. Seeking independence, law, and order, and—at least in Athens—the free development of the citizen, they worked out constitutions of the most varied types. Although they experienced, like others, the weaknesses of any form of human government, their philosophers set themselves to the task of investigating the various aspects of all these forms, evaluating the merits and dangers. In poems, tragedies, and comedies, or in philosophical treatises, they set forth the conflicts between civic duties and personal aspirations, between society and individual. Thus, a body of political writings emerged in which the realistic everyday setting was described where government and citizenship operate, as well as the ideal of an Utopian state where the conflicting forces might ultimately be reconciled.

Sports. The same sense of harmony which inspired Greek art and the Greek search for political order caused the Greeks to strive for the development of individual man not only as a vehicle of spiritual aspirations, but also as a being proud of his physical body. The beauty of the human body was a cherished ideal; valor was expected of a man, and strength, fleetness, and grace. It was in order to further such ideals that the Greeks favored sports and instituted sporting competitions. Regularly, they held great festivals at Olympia, Corinth, and Delphi. True to the tradition of harmonious development of spirit, mind, and body, they generally started these events with religious rites, with a dedication to the gods. Then, during several days they held sports competitions, wherein racing, discus throwing, and wrestling played prominent roles. They concluded with musical and literary performances in which composers, writers, and artists vied for the laurel. Separate festivals with similar programs were held for women. So vital a part did these occasions play in Greek life that the very calendar of Greece was dated according to the Olympic games.

Surviving Greek Civilization. Enthusiasm for Greek life has induced many historians to idealize Greek institutions, Greek thought, and Greek habits to such an extent that they have neglected the darker aspects of conditions in Greece. They have said little of the degrading reality forming the background against which Greek artistic and philosophical achievements have to be viewed. They have forgotten that the Greeks were vain and arrogant. The entire world, outside their borders, the Greeks considered "barbaric." They were hard dealing and apt at cheating, prone to perjury and to treason. Of all peoples, they were the ones who unhesitatingly made one of their gods the protector of liars. They were quarrelsome, dishonest, greedy, brutal, and oppressive. Slavery was an integral part of their social institutions, they had little respect for laws, and politicians and demagogues sacrificed the welfare of the state to personal ambitions. Homosexuality was a commonly accepted phenomenon, and prostitutes were praised in song while wives and daughters of the best were little regarded and generally oppressed. But the events in the market place, the evil quarrels of daily living, and the abject, ugly condition of the masses have disappeared as completely as the individual citizen. What have survived are the immortal works of the few; the depth of thought of the greatest minds; the longing for freedom and free development of nation and individual, as expressed in deeds; the artistic creations which Grecian sensitivity to beauty made possible; the penetration of nature's secrets and the understanding of man—these have become a guide for all Western civilization.

THE ROMAN CONTRIBUTIONS

If the Greek heritage has been praised for its legacy of rationality, truth, and beauty, the Roman heritage has been extolled for its practical usefulness. Scant justice, however, has been thus done to Rome. For Rome, too, left in its innumerable monuments a large spiritual heritage to future generations; and this can well challenge that of Greece.

Language. Like the Greek language, so has Latin made inestimable contributions to the civilization of the modern world. Just as many Greek terms, so did numerous Latin terms find entrance into modern vocabularies, and with them the concepts and institutions for which they stand. Among Latin-English words are "citizen," "family," "census," "senate," "monument," and "arch." Others which originally were Greek entered the Latin and were preserved by the Romans; and the Western world thus owes to Rome a vast store of experience, embodied in language, which otherwise would have had to be painfully worked out anew and independently.

History. Most important among the legacies of Rome are those contributions which have taught the modern world a rational, reasonable approach to political conduct and nation building. The political genius of Rome, her ability to rule herself and others, to adapt herself to changing conditions, to invent checks and balances in order to avoid excesses, to overcome the threats of social challenges, to regulate "the relationship of man to man"—this, though worked out under infinite pains, has constituted an unequaled lesson for future Western civilization. Preserved and evaluated by Livius, Tacitus, and others, the history of Rome furnishes insight into the evolution not only of Rome, but also of any other great people. It is embodied in the lives and traditions of the entire Mediterranean world, in monuments erected in the most varied countries, in their languages, law codes, and institutions. These Roman achievements, unlike those of Greece in her time of glory, were less the work of a few individuals with outstanding genius than (as the German historian Mommsen once wrote) the result of "extraordinary deeds" by "ordinary men."

Law. Underlying the structure of the mighty empire that eventually was built, was a concept of law which had many roots in Greek philosophical thought and derived from many examples of other Mediterranean nations, but which stood unique in the ancient world. Roman law was a living procedure, adaptable to constantly changing situations. Only toward the very end of the Empire, when decay of the state had progessed far, was it codified in its various aspects. Roman law embraced the relationship between individuals, and it progressively defined civic rights and the membership of the citizen within the common republic. Its vocabulary is still used; its procedures serve as models: its stipulations in regard to property, the conduct of business, matters of inheritance, marriage, and divorce, and numerous other fields have fructified the codes of justice among all Western nations. Moreover, international rules worked out by Rome have constituted the beginning of endeavors on a long path toward a universal organization which would do justice to all members of the society of nations.

Architecture and Public Construction. In architecture, the Romans showed less originality than genius at adaptation. To a large extent, they adopted the artistic concepts which Greece had evolved. They built temples which, following the styles of Greece, inspire through harmony of form and elegance of structure. But what they took over they also applied to different sorts of architectural projects, to types of construction which reflect an enterprising spirit and an inventive genius that Greece had not developed. To these buildings Rome gave much of that beauty which had flourished in Greece. Mighty waterworks were completed, aqueducts

[margin handwritten note: Romans borrowed from Greeks]

were installed, bridges with noble spans were thrown across rivers and canals, viaducts were laid across valleys, and a *Cloaca Maxima* (sewer system) was built which has astounded modern engineers. The most distant parts of the Empire were connected by a remarkable system of roads, many of them still in use, and for hundreds of miles walls and forts were erected along endangered borders. Beyond such necessities—witnesses of the practical inclinations of an empire-building society—the Romans also created remarkable public monuments for the beautification and glory of their state. Such projects served simultaneously the solution of social problems, the providing of work for the unemployed, and the entertainment of the discontented classes. They erected triumphal arches, constructed columns celebrating victories, and adorned these structures with inscriptions and representations of Rome's deeds of glory. They built public baths, a Colosseum and, in numerous cities, large arenas. The private houses of the rich, such as those found in long-buried Pompeii, were embellished with beautiful frescoes, reliefs, mosaics, and fountains.

Literature. As in the field of building, so in that of literature Rome did not initiate many new styles, did not think of many new approaches, and thus did not show much originality. For her epics, she borrowed the hexameter from Greece; for her lyrics, she used and adapted the verse meters of Sappho, Alcaeus, and others; for her prose, she took Herodotus' and Thucydides' histories or Aesop's fables as models; and in the form and content of her drama she reflected the tragedies and comedies of Greece. One of the most important Roman literary masterpieces, Vergil's *Aeneid,* a work of lasting grandeur, would have been impossible without the model of Homer's *Iliad* and *Odyssey.* Nevertheless, at certain times (especially during the Renaissance) the literature of Rome has meant more to Western civilization than that of Greece. The writings of Cicero (which embody the author's eclectic philosophical views and possess little of the genius of Plato and Aristotle) and the orations of Cicero (which hardly equal those of Demosthenes) have been praised again and again as the embodiment of worldly wisdom and have exercised a profound influence. Stoic philosophy has become known chiefly through the writings of Seneca and Marcus Aurelius, and Epicureanism found a home and tradition in the wealthy Roman Empire rather than in Greece. Among the poets, Ovid and Horace are better known to the modern world than most of the

Greeks (to be sure, the greater quantity of Latin poetry which has survived may partially account for its popularity). For the stage, Rome produced the plays of Plautus, Terence, and Juvenal. To these lasting contributions can be added the works of the great Roman historians—Livy, Caesar, Tacitus, and many others—who by transmitting the deeds of their compatriots have helped to shape Western civilization. It is through their eyes that Rome's history is viewed, that Rome's glory is appraised, and that Rome's mistakes and vices are recognized. Roman moral judgment has ineradicably affected the attitude of the West, has impressed upon it standards which have become an inseparable part of the civilization within which modern man acts.

Surviving Rome. Like all great empires Rome fell. She, too, showed human weaknesses in all their diversity. Like the Greeks, Romans were arrogant and brutal; ruthless toward their enemies, they were also fickle friends. Corruption was rampant among the bureaucracy, greed animated those who should have dispensed justice, arbitrariness marked those who should have looked after the welfare of the state and its citizens. The Romans extolled bravery and, wading in blood, spread their sway. They immoderately extorted from the subjected, they exploited the lands and peoples which they had conquered, and at home they kept the masses in servitude by brute force. They never achieved a stable societal structure: a constantly reviving revolutionary element, produced by war and misery, had to be kept in check by force, gifts, bribes, or costly amusements. Ethical principles were seldom heeded except insofar as they served the ruling classes of the Empire. And disillusioned men longing for a peaceful and pure life turned away from public affairs and sought refuge in the stern, solitary atmosphere of Stoicism. Yet, Rome, like Greece, left an unparalleled heritage. The stories of Lucretia, of Fabius Cunctator, and of Brutus have taught lessons of devotion and fulfillment of duty which have never been forgotten. Roman fortitude in adversity during the war against Hannibal, Roman rectitude as tragically exemplified by the two Catos, Roman statesmanship as proved by Augustus, and the Roman peace, as it prevailed under a Trajan, Hadrian, or Marcus Aurelius, have remained treasures of Western civilization and symbols of a conquest greater than armies could achieve.

CHAPTER II

THE MEDIEVAL HERITAGE

THE STORY OF Greece and Rome is ended. The empires have disappeared; the societies they represented are dead; a cycle was completed. The heritage which they left can be summed up. Most of the areas where they once flourished passed into the hands of different kinds of people; and Western civilization found new centers in France, Germany, England, Spain, and other parts of the world. Not only in the Mediterranean area, but also in the center of Europe and along Europe's Atlantic borders, as well as in Italy, the story of Western civilization continued. Whether it was in the fourth, fifth, or as late as the seventh and eighth centuries that the ancient world made room for medieval civilization is a fascinating question. On our answer to this question may depend our whole attitude toward the problem of survival of civilizations, including our own. In any case, sometime between A.D. 375 and 732, a new age began. This new age, which is called the "Middle Ages," does not represent so much of a closed book, a finished story, as do ancient times. The centers of medieval civilization, unlike most of those of the ancient world, and many institutions of medieval society live on. No break has since occurred, but almost imperceptibly did the Middle Ages merge during the fourteenth, fifteenth, and sixteenth centuries into modern times. In East, West, and North new areas were added to old-established centers, which carried on along traditional paths.

MEDIEVAL CONTRIBUTIONS

Four factors especially demark the fundamental departure of Western medieval civilization from that of ancient times: (1) a

11

geographic shift of the centers of power and civilization from the eastern Mediterranean basin northward to all Europe; (2) an influx of Germanic races into the Roman world and the emergence of a number of new political and social units carrying forward not only the Roman, but also the young, fresh, "barbarian" German, heritage; (3) an economic transformation which followed the decline of the commercial markets in the wide Mediterranean Empire and the transition from a slave-owning, capitalistic society to an organization based on a feudal, local economy; and (4) the introduction and impact of Christianity.

Language. At the beginning of the medieval epoch, not a single modern Western language existed. At its end, almost every one of the Western national languages, as they have survived until today, had emerged. Latin was preserved throughout the Middle Ages as a means of international communication. But when modern times began, there had been shaped the linguistic tools which we use today and which form our thinking. Vocabularies and grammars of present-day languages had developed from Latin and Germanic roots and, in the East, from Slavic sources. They had been enriched, moreover, by numerous new words, either coined in order to express new thoughts and designate new instruments or taken over from other civilizations. By then, the vulgar tongues of the various nations predominated not only in daily life, but also in popular literature; and they began to invade the realms of religion and scholarship. Thus, modern languages constitute one of the chief legacies of the Middle Ages.

Religion. In addition to the development of languages, the most outstanding contributions of the Middle Ages include the preservation and propagation of Christianity. The introduction of Christianity in the Western world as the official religion with monopolistic rights coincides with the beginnings of medieval times. By then, the creed of all major Christian churches had been formulated at Nicea, and ever since it has prevailed. The Bible was translated into Latin, and it has become the property of all succeeding generations. Christian ethics were imposed upon pagan views; even if at no time triumphant, they have remained the ideal toward which the Western world has been striving. The Church, Catholic or Orthodox throughout the Middle Ages, became the dominant social influence upon all inhabitants. It permeated every facet of life and thought; and with its artistic and educational tenets, its calendar, its law, and its services as well as its political and economic power, it set the pattern for secular and spiritual conditions that have given direction to all subsequent ages. The Church imposed an order and a unity which even a later division into nations has never entirely effaced. The Catholic Church created, with its papacy and hierarchy, an organization which has survived as a potent factor in modern times. Even so-called "heresies" made their contributions. For through their challenge a constant process of purification has been forced upon the Christian church, and the Christian faith has been kept as the guiding code through almost two thousand years. This has been enriched by rebellious and defending forces alike.

Philosophy. Naturally, Christian thought dominated all speculation about transcendental questions. Its influence has caused philosophy to engage in a search for ultimate goals and standards of logic and ethics different from those of the ancient world. Church fathers, such as Augustine, Ambrose, Jerome, John Chrysostom, and others, especially in the fourth century, started medieval philosophy on the new path. But it was only in the twelfth and thirteenth centuries that a complete system of Christian philosophy emerged. Under the guidance of the universities and of so-called "schoolmen," among whom Peter Abelard, Albertus Magnus, and Thomas Aquinas stand out, an attempt was made to preserve or revive the Greek heritage, to follow the Greeks on the path of logic and rationality, yet not to sacrifice any part of the Christian and Church tradition, or any of its mysteries and transcendental teachings. During the thirteenth century, which has been called "the greatest of centuries," the scholastic attempt was carried forward by two schools, the "Realists" and the "Nominalists." The former were closer in their thinking to Plato; the latter relied more on Aristotle. Though neither challenged the Christian foundations, the Realists insisted on the primacy of universal ideas and their exclusive "reality," whereas the Nominalists emphasized the role of the "particular" evidences of God's creation in nature and their significance. The Nominalists paved the way for a future naturalistic, scientific approach. The long struggle of the two sides forced them to make the greatest intellectual efforts, and these have again and again fructified modern thinking and investigation. But also outside of scholastic philosophy did the Middle Ages produce a mighty impulse for modern philosophical pursuits. Scientific speculations about cosmos and nature by men such as Roger Bacon and, more important for philosophical developments, the mystical views and "experiences," which were expressed or witnessed by St. Francis and Meister Eckart, have stimulated again and again the speculations of modern man. Indeed, the various forces of Scholasticism, of science, of mysticism, and of a revived classical philosophy constitute one of the most lasting contributions of the Middle Ages.

Learning. Religious thought and philosophical speculation gave direction to all forms of education in medieval times. After several centuries of stagnation during the early Middle Ages, secular knowledge resumed its path toward broader enlightenment of man. The Middle Ages created gradually an educational system, whose aspirations could, at least in part, form a basis and offer inspiration for developments in the modern world. Medieval primary schooling with its emphasis on discipline, considered necessary for the formation of character, for the learning of reading and writing, and for Bible studies, was perhaps of wide significance only in the early period of modern times. The more advanced curriculum, which provided training in grammar, astronomy, music, etc., also did not find permanent imitation. But the university, a creation of the eleventh century, has been of unique importance. Professors and students began to meet in "universities." Within an atmosphere free from outside interference, they devoted themselves to the study of the universe and of mankind in its manifold aspects. Their studies embraced the four faculties of theology, law, philosophy, and medicine. Jews and, particularly, Arabs contributed to these studies by their accumulated wisdom in such fields as astronomy, agriculture, classics, science, and medicine. The four faculties of the universities as well as their rites and forms have proved to be of fundamental importance for the progress of Western civilization ever since. It was largely in the universities that the striving "Faustian" spirit which has characterized Western civilization was fostered. It was through them that the training in logical thought was provided which, in many instances, made possible the flowering of all secular activity outside their walls. Thus, receptivity was also created for many scientific considerations. Interest grew in the accomplishments of other civilizations; paper, the compass, and glass were adopted from them; and this heritage, in turn, stimulated original contributions, such as the invention of gunpowder and, toward the end of the medieval period, the printing press with movable type. The Faustian spirit was carried on and grew throughout the Renais-

sance, the transitional period from the Middle Ages to modern
times.

Art. Faced by the enormous scope and significance of the medieval legacy, the historian is at a loss to put into adequate relief all the
different facets of this heritage. Certainly, medieval art challenges
all other medieval accomplishments in its importance for later times.
It has exercised an influence not inferior to that of art created in
the ancient world. Just as there is hardly a community in the West,
in which imitations of Greek temples and columns cannot be found,
so there is hardly one in which the round Romanesque arch or,
more frequently, the pointed arch of the Gothic cathedral and town
hall, the stained window, the imagery of Mary and the Christ child,
and the paintings of the early Renaissance are not represented,
copied, or imitated. The countless wonders of the Gothic style have,
indeed, found duplication, often incongruously, in such a variety
of modern buildings—churches, universities, private homes, stations,
office buildings—that they have become an integral part of our lives.
The unthinking modern man is seldom aware of their origin.
Cathedrals, which show Gothic style in its ultimate beauty, were,
it has been said, "built before God, not before man." But also the
more humble artistic achievements of the Middle Ages, those
evinced by articles made for daily household use, have left an inde-
structible heritage. The small arts, the handicrafts in all trades, have
excited the imagination of Western man ever since. And mosaics and
paintings, successively in Byzantine, Romanesque, Gothic, and,
finally, Renaissance style, are not only on display in museums, where
they are the pride of town and nation; they also live in homes, often
as transformed in the work of later generations of artists. Each
medieval creation bears witness to the individual genius and detailed, loving care of the individual master. Even if the creations of
the early medieval periods with their special beauty and symbolism
are not always meaningful to the uninitiated, those of the Renaissance, of Giotto, Fra Angelico, Botticelli, van Eyck, Memling, and
hundreds of others, have become part of the lives of millions, who
may not be conscious of the names of painting or artist.

Literature. Another medieval contribution that has never ceased
to be of importance was made in literature. Twofold was the merit
of the medieval scholar and writer. He preserved what Greece and
Rome had done, copying with infinite patience, and commenting
and interpreting. And then, he added to the ancient heritage his

own creative work. Early during the medieval period, a minuscule was developed. This rendered easier the labor of writing and helped to increase the treasury of great thought which could be preserved. Many of the books then written or reproduced were, moreover, done in beautiful lettering, and innumerable manuscripts with their splendid illuminations are witnesses to medieval interest in literature and an inspiration to modern endeavors. We possess, in Latin and in later vernacular tongues, Church translations and commentaries; mighty hymns, such as *Ave Maria* and *Dies Irae;* great epos, like *Parzival, Tristan and Iseult,* the *Nibelungenlied,* and *La Chanson de Roland*; histories, chronicles, and scientific treatises; the love songs of Troubadours and Minnesänger; a vast heritage of folk songs; and a not yet sufficiently appreciated body of prose works. In the late Middle Ages, individual masterpieces stand out. Towering among them are the works of three Italians: those of Dante, Petrarch, and Boccaccio.

Music. Much of the writing and folklore was originally destined to be accompanied by music. The sound has long passed; the voices are dead. We know little more of it than parchment or paper can preserve with notations for music, or than instruments which have survived and been adapted to modern use can tell us. Yet, the oral tradition has not been entirely lost. Through it, the sonorous Gregorian chant has come down to us across the centuries, and so have thousands of lovely and mysterious folk songs and dances, which have never ceased to be repeated by generation after generation. Significantly, in many regions of the West, folklore did not become a conscious heritage until rediscovered during the past two centuries.

Statecraft. During the Middle Ages, all of the great modern nations emerged as separate entities and within territorial limits which approximate those they still inhabit today. France and Germany became the common heirs of Charlemagne's empire; England, conquered and settled by numerous invaders, was fused into the unit which she still represents. Russia emerged as a nation centering around Moscow. By the end of the Middle Ages the Italians, though not finding independent statehood, possessed a common language and common national aspirations. The Scandinavian countries were formed; and a basis was laid for Switzerland, Hungary, and other nations. As a whole, medieval times put an end to the unity which the Western world under Roman rule had once possessed. Notwithstanding the attempts of the Catholic Church to preserve at least a spiritual unity, a multiplicity of states emerged with those separate and identifiable characteristics which are known to modern times.

Law and Legislation. Besides the evolution of nations, the Middle Ages made other important political contributions. To be sure, feudal ethics and economics have found no acceptance in later times. But certain aspects of medieval legal developments have been of great significance. The Middle Ages left in the field of law a three-fold legacy: they preserved the heritage of ancient Rome; they evolved Church canons which have retained validity in the Catholic world and have influenced other areas; and they developed what became known as "common law." Originating with chiefly Germanic concepts of justice, native in northern and eastern Europe and distinct from those of ancient Rome, this common law gradually expanded through oral tradition and through usage, until it came to constitute, though uncodified, an integral part of the mores, ethics, and laws of the modern age. Courts and judges through their decisions, as well as lawyers and professors of law through their opinions, have established certain principles in conformity with an old spiritual heritage. Closely interwoven with this growth of the medieval system of law was that of a number of political legal institutions. Most important among them were "diets" and "parliaments," which assumed rights of public legislation. They have left their mark upon all subsequent ages. They were composed of representatives of "estates" or classes; to a large extent, modern class stratification is based on medieval organization. The surviving aristocracy and many of the ruling families of modern times have derived their pretensions from their medieval status. Titles and privileges go back to medieval patterns, but medieval times anticipated also the broader constitutional rights which were later claimed by the bourgeoisie.

Commerce and Discoveries. The medieval inheritance in the economic field has been least investigated and is for this reason, and for lack of sources, least known. Yet, both in economic theory and in practical matters of commerce, the Middle Ages passed on a rich inheritance. Christian scholars as well as historians and chroniclers left treatises to posterity which reflect deep insight into questions of just price, interest-taking, monopoly, and profit. Economic theory forms part of as fundamental a work as St. Thomas Aquinas' *Summa Theologica*. He and others sought to direct natural human urges, such as ambition and greed, into channels where they would not conflict with the ethical demands of Christianity. Their theories have retained importance throughout the ages. Likewise, practical aspects of medieval economic life and economic organization have been influential. Guilds, developed in the Middle Ages, have remained meaningful. Envisaging certain principles of morality, they sought to limit competition, which was considered a vice, and they promoted high standards of quality in workmanship. The Middle Ages also experimented with organization of communal labor, communal property, and planned production. During medieval times, many principles of banking, credit, exchange, and capital formation were taken over from the East or worked out independently. Numerous achievements of this kind gave direction to later entrepreneurial activity and exercised an influence on various political experiments—even in the Industrial Age. Perhaps one of the chief reasons for the continued importance of some parts of the medieval economic system was that a vast expansion of the European trade system took place during the Middle Ages. Commerce had to adapt itself to world-wide markets. The enterprises of the Italian towns in the Mediterranean area, of the Hanseatic League in the Baltic, the Portuguese ventures to the Far East, and the Spanish explorations into the Atlantic regions were not merely precursors, leading to modern business activities, but in many respects they represented undertakings of the same order as modern entrepreneurship and therefore were subject to very similar conditions. They thus could teach important lessons.

Cities. Lastly, the Middle Ages saw the founding or, after Roman beginnings the refounding, of almost all the great cities of Europe. By 1500 had been established almost all the great commercial centers of Italy, Germany and France, Spain, England, Scandinavia, and Russia which have played a role in modern times. The establishment of towns necessitated their organization. People had to be attracted, shifts of population had to be dealt with, special laws and privileges had to be worked out, and a division of labor had to be introduced, all of which was bound to set patterns for later times.

THE "DARK AGES"

The "Dark Ages," as the Middle Ages have sometimes been called, like all other periods in history were full of misery. Pestilence.

war, and starvation were man's constant companions. Intolerance of man toward man, often in the name of religion, was greater almost than ever before. Those who did not share the beliefs of the powerful were declared heretics, were outlawed and persecuted; some were burned at the stake. The oppressed poor, tied to the soil and, as serfs, deprived of the right to move, had no recourse against the arbitrariness of their local masters. Though standards of honor were established and extolled in heroic poetry, treachery and falsehood prevailed. Pride in clean and healthy bodies, as it had existed once in Greece, was lost; disease and suffering were rampant, owing to a wide disdain of nature and body and to an otherworldly orientation of the mind. Praise of womanhood was sung, the cult of Mary was initiated; yet women were maltreated and held in contempt as the begetters of evil. Superstitions were widespread, and the age, like most of the preceding ones, was marked by insecurity and fear. Yet, the "Dark Ages" have also illuminated the modern world with their faith, scholarship, and the beauty they created. They brought forth ideas, and they established ideals which have remained meaningful. The faith and ethics of Christianity, the standards set in learning and philosophy, the works in art and literature stand unique and have enriched the modern world no less than did the highest achievements of Greece and Rome.

CHAPTER III

THE BEGINNING OF
"THE MODERN AGE" (1492–1517)

N<small>OT</small> <small>ARBITRARILY</small> is the Modern Age dated from about 1500. The historical period from then until now possesses cohesion and a common outlook. Naturalism, individualism, and nationalism give it a special meaning. Moreover, the global expansion of Western civilization constitutes a distinguishing characteristic. Whereas the Classical Period had embraced the evolution of civilizations around the Mediterranean Sea and in the Near East and whereas the Medieval Period had enlarged man's horizon by including all Europe as well as most of the Old World, the Modern Age takes in the entire globe.

The Modern Age was introduced by one of the most glorious epochs in Western civilization. Justly does Preserved Smith write:

> Though in some sense every age is one of transition and every generation sees the world remodelled, there sometimes comes a change so startling and profound that it seems like the beginning of a new season in the world's great year. . . . Spring has come.[1]

That is what happened. Within "the span of a single life" (for convenience's sake, Smith takes the life of Luther, 1483–1546, as his measure) there appeared a great number of the most memorable personalities in history. And in all fields of human endeavor and human understanding—exploration and enterprise, science, art, music, literature, religion, and state-building—there were created some of the most momentous works. This first generation of mod-

[1] *The Age of the Reformation* (New York: Henry Holt, 1920), p. 3.

ern times was "great in what it achieved, sublime in what it dreamed; abounding in ripe wisdom and heroic deeds; full of light and of beauty and of life."

WESTERN SOCIETY AROUND 1500

The society which brought forth such accomplishments was a true child of the Renaissance. It was devoted to beauty; it was enterprising and skeptical; it rejected many of the past religious traditions and past authorities and yet was itself religious and reverent. It undertook to penetrate the secrets of nature with unaccustomed curiosity and confidence. Youth played so important and leading a role as never again: men, and sometimes women, of thirty, twenty-five, twenty, and even sixteen years of age occupied many of the most influential posts and achieved feats of lasting significance. Truly could the young German poet and humanist Ulrich von Hutten sing: "It is a joy to live!"

Social Aspirations. Unlike the cultural atmosphere of medieval times, when the longings toward otherworldliness gave direction to many of the greatest achievements, the spirit of the Renaissance tended toward worldly things—toward a full development of the natural gifts of man and a full gratification of his senses through the attractions offered by this world. Among all layers of society do we witness a thirst to enjoy life and all it could offer in meaningful experience and in transient pleasure. It was a time of great moral, cultural, and spiritual achievement, albeit it was also an age of pleasure-seeking, of intemperate eating, drinking, dressing, and love-making. Men and women risked life and limb in adventure and enterprise. Behind this lust for life stood the expectation of pain and early death; for great perils threatened from wars, murders, pestilences, unsanitary surroundings, disasters on the seas, and persecutions by political antagonists or religious fanatics.

Social Stratification. The changes in the attitudes of man toward his surroundings had a very slow, yet distinct, effect upon societal structure. Classes or "estates" remained essentially as they had been in the past, but interest in secular matters and, with it, attention to worldly tasks changed their outlook and occupations.

CLERGY. The first estate, the clergy, continued to play in the early sixteenth century the prominent role it had enjoyed throughout the Middle Ages. A change in this role, however, was in prospect, for, although there were thousands of higher prelates and humble priests and monks who devoted themselves with unabated zeal and piety to the service of Christianity, a vast number indulged in the most varied mundane undertakings. They expanded their economic activities and participated in political struggles and secular pleasures and ambitions. A pope such as Alexander VI of the Borgia family (d. 1503), with his greed, his politics, his mistresses and children, and his poisons, may have constituted an extreme of clerical depravity; but only too many showed greater interest in art, devotion to science, ability in languages, perfection in Renaissance manners, and participation in humanistic endeavors than in the performance of their duties. Soon, low morals, lack of training, and neglect of duty characterized also certain reforming groups, and thus the clergy as a whole lost in respect and importance.

NOBILITY. The second estate, the nobility, rivaled the first in the promotion of the new aspirations. As the medieval code of honor came to mean little when gunpowder and other inventions had undermined the standards formerly set for the conduct of a nobleman, his military occupations began to play a lesser role. In order to retain his prestige in society, he turned his mind increasingly to the pursuit of industry and trade. Many among the nobles acquired land and used it for the production of industrial crops, exploited its mineral resources, and participated in mercantile ventures. With the wealth thus acquired, they indulged in the entertainments of the age and the furtherance of secular interests in scholarship, art, literature, and science. A new ideal for the cultured nobleman was set up, originating in Italy: the ideal of *virtù*, i.e., of manly activity, intelligence, achievement, and conduct, devoted to all facets of Renaissance life. Significantly, women shared in the interests and activities of the upper classes. Though they were in some respects, and in many instances, still held down, treated with cruelty, and abused as the "begetters of evil," some of them attained prominent positions, exercising a greater influence upon political and cultural developments than in most other periods. Women ruled as queens, served as regents, diplomats, and administrators of estates, and engaged in professions as doctors, lawyers, and teachers. They excelled as scholars, poets, and arbiters of arts and manners. Unchastity was as common among them as among men; and power and luxury were as much craved by them.

THE BURGHER. In the age of discovery, the townsman or burgher, who, together with the free peasant, formed the "third estate," necessarily acquired increased prestige. Everywhere, merchants and bankers rose to prominence. Owing to the wealth of the burghers, not only ports such as Cadiz, Lisbon, Antwerp, and London, but also trading cities and centers of crafts such as Augsburg and Nuremberg in southern Germany gained far-reaching influence. The Fugger family of Augsburg—whose interests extended to textile industries, silver and copper mining, wholesale trade, and banking—with its influence on emperors and kings of Germany, England, Spain, and Portugal, was exceptionally powerful; but other businessmen with less wealth than the Fuggers could also influence the political fate of great commonwealths. Moreover, as a result of the demand for manifold objects useful for beautification or for new production methods, artisans gained in influence. Within the burgher class, however, there developed an increasing differentiation between the standards of the wealthy and those of the poor. The rich took the nobility as their model and participated in Renaissance pleasures and aspirations. The poor were more limited in their search for pleasure. Among them, new standards of morality, with emphasis upon restraint, sobriety, frugality, and duty, began to emerge. This trend was accelerated in the course of the century by the influence of religious reform movements and by the gradual worsening of the economic conditions of the lower classes, brought about by unemployment, rising prices, and nascent capitalism which in its early form deprived them of security and imposed new burdens.

THE PEASANT. Around 1500, the vast majority of the populations was still composed of the peasantry. This was true even in a small country as active in trade as the Netherlands. However, considerable changes also occurred within this class. In the East, especially in Poland and Russia, a tendency toward greater enslavement of the peasantry was noticeable, but serfdom in Central and Western Europe continued to diminish. With the growth of towns and trade, the need for free labor increased further, while simultaneously changes in agricultural production methods reduced the usefulness of the institution of serfdom. As a result, many serfs were released and left the villages; others, who stayed, gained at least partial freedom. It should be noted that this emancipation movement benefited the peasants to a limited degree only. Although, as the canvases of Pieter Brueghel the Elder and other masters show, many of them indulged in licentiousness (for which the upper classes set an example) and sought special enjoyment in feasting (something made possible because the food supply had become more ample than ever before), social evolution at this time brought new hardships for them. Deprived of security, peasants in various lands revolted. But they failed to stem the tide.

ECONOMIC CONDITIONS

The most significant factor shaping Western society around 1500 was the expansion of its horizon. New technical means had become available; there were new types of ships, maps, nautical instruments, and superior weapons. Wealth was accumulated with which to equip expeditions; political authority was established which could give protection to them; scientific experience was gained which made success possible; and an economic organization was achieved which not only provided financial backing but also enabled men of various specializations to combine in common undertakings.

Geographic Explorations. With the material necessities available, men of genius, animated by the enterprising spirit of the age, could undertake to turn long-held dreams into reality. Threefold were their incentives, the three ever-present "G's": Gospel, Gold, and Glory—the desire to convert others, to enrich themselves, and to win fame. So they set out in search of new shores: Columbus reached America in 1492. Vasco da Gama sailed to India via the Cape of Good Hope in 1498. Amerigo Vespucci gave his name to the continent which he saw. Balboa crossed this continent and in 1513 sighted the Pacific Ocean. The Portuguese Magellan, with incredible courage and perseverance, performed perhaps the most heroic feat of all; he undertook the first circumnavigation of the earth, and one of his five ships actually accomplished the round trip. John Cabot touched the North American continent. Cortes in 1521 conquered the Aztec Empire in Mexico; and Pizarro, somewhat later, conquered for the Spanish the Inca Empire in Peru. The Portuguese, in addition, built an empire of their own in the East Indies. Strife over the new possessions was avoided by a Line of Demarcation established by the pope in 1493 and amended one year later by the Treaty of Tordesillas, which assigned to Portugal most of the eastern, and to Spain most of the western, colonies.

The discoveries had far-reaching influence upon European life.

Economically, they provided enormous quantities of coveted gold and silver; they also secured vast new sources of food, especially fish. Soon, the value of the agricultural resources, game, and fish of many colonies overshadowed that of mining. Many new products, such as maize and potatoes, were introduced in Europe and changed prevailing food habits. Politically, the discoveries strengthened the monarchs, who enlarged their personal dominions and augmented their wealth. A shift of power from old trade centers to new ones in different countries occurred. Eventually, the Atlantic sea routes grew in importance compared with traditional Mediterranean and Baltic trade routes, and the redistribution of power resulting from the acquisition of colonies led to new struggles for trade supremacy and to new wars. Socially, the discoveries benefited merchants of the burgher class, who gained prestige through similar acquisition of new wealth. Discoveries affected the poor, for, by providing them with new means of sustenance, they made possible enormous population growth. They encouraged emigration. Moreover, increased knowledge about the earth changed thinking habits. Lastly, discoveries led to the transformation not only of the Old World, but also of the new lands, which had to change their own ways of life in accordance with European desires and customs.

Economic Reorganization. Geographical discoveries, combined with the individualistic enterprising spirit of Renaissance man, fundamentally influenced economic developments.

BUSINESS ORGANIZATION. The enormous expansion of markets and development of a money economy, strengthened by an ample supply of precious metals flowing from the New World as well as from Europe herself (for example, from Hungary), laid the basis for the rise of modern capitalism and private enterprise. Thus, the Fugger family of Augsburg represented entrepreneurial activity of a new magnitude and importance. A sharp competitive spirit aiming at personal monopolistic advantages in production and internal and external trade replaced former social attitudes and economic morals. Greater leniency of the Church toward interest-taking aided a rapid formation of capital in the modern business sense, and this, in turn, led to the organization of new business structures. Best-known among these were the so-called "joint-stock companies," which were corporations of merchant adventurers who pooled their resources—at first temporarily for one specific undertaking, later permanently for repeated ventures. They chose directors and sea

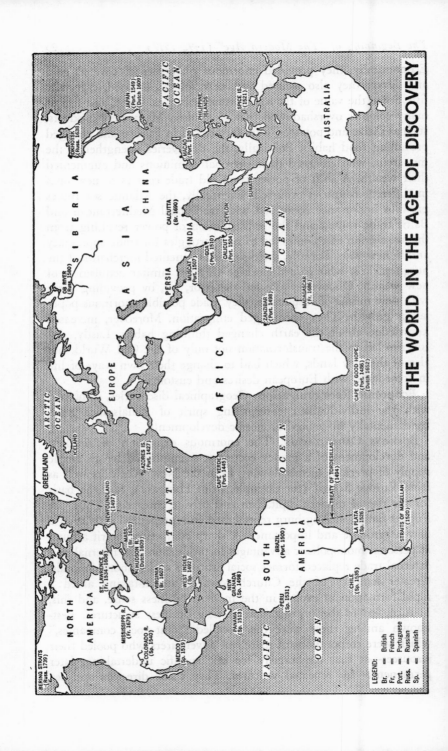

THE WORLD IN THE AGE OF DISCOVERY

LEGEND:
Br. = British
Fr. = French
Port. = Portuguese
Russ. = Russian
Sp. = Spanish

NORTH AMERICA
BERING STRAITS (Russ. 1739)
GREENLAND
ICELAND
NEWFOUNDLAND (1497)
ST. LAWRENCE R. (Fr. 1534-1608)
MASS. (Br. 1620)
HUDSON R. (Dutch 1609)
MISSISSIPPI R. (Fr. 1679)
COLORADO R. (Sp. 1540)
VIRGINIA (Br. 1607)
MEXICO (Sp. 1519)
WEST INDIES (Sp. 1492)
PANAMA (Sp. 1513)
NEW GRANADA (Sp. 1498)
PERU (Sp. 1531)
CHILE (Sp. 1535)

SOUTH AMERICA
BRAZIL (Port. 1500)
LA PLATA (Sp. 1526)
STRAITS OF MAGELLAN (1520)
TREATY OF TORDESILLAS (1494)

ARCTIC OCEAN
ATLANTIC OCEAN
PACIFIC OCEAN
AZORES IS. (Port. 1427)
CAPE VERDE (Port. 1445)

EUROPE
AFRICA
ZANZIBAR (Port. 1498)
CAPE OF GOOD HOPE (Port. 1486) (Dutch 1652)
MADAGASCAR (Fr. 1686)

SIBERIA
OB RIVER (Russ. 1580)
OKHOTSK (Russ. 1638)

ASIA
PERSIA
CHINA
INDIA
CALCUTTA (Br. 1690)
GOA (Port. 1510)
MUSCAT (Port. 1507)
CALICUT (Port. 1504)
CEYLON
INDIAN OCEAN

JAPAN (1549) (Dutch 1609)
MACÃO (Port. 1520)
PHILIPPINE ISLANDS
SPICE IS. (1521)
SUMATRA

AUSTRALIA

PACIFIC OCEAN

captains to transact the actual business for them, and they restricted their own activities to accumulating gains from investments. They often secured charters from their governments granting them monopolies in certain areas or on certain commodities. The necessary capital was raised for extensive, though often very risky, enterprises. One of the most famous joint-stock companies was the Muscovy Company in England, which toward the middle of the sixteenth century secured a monopoly over the Russian trade. Later, various Levant and East and West Indies companies of different countries were founded. Provisions for greater credit facilities (for bills of exchange and for paper certificates), new tools used in the mining or the textile industries, as well as more rational division of labor through specialization in production methods further augmented Europe's economic potential.

EXPANSION OF MARKETS. With the help of the newly created facilities, European producers and traders could reach out for untouched markets. They exported horses, cattle, and agricultural products; they established new overseas production centers for Old World products, such as sugar. They introduced such hitherto unknown produce as potatoes, tomatoes, tobacco, maize, and quinine, or they increased the imports of familiar produce such as coffee, rice, silk, and cotton. From Newfoundland they brought fish; from China, tea. Gold and silver provided not only for monetary funds, but also for a greatly expanded jewelry trade which made use of Indian pearls and rubies. New "needs" were artificially created. A commodity of special importance contributed to the wealth of the European countries: the slaves who, transported from Africa, were used as a labor supply for the New World. Spanish, Portuguese, and, later, English traders specialized in slave traffic.

PHILOSOPHY OF MERCANTILISM. Through the new economic practices conditions were evolved which underlie the system known to economists as "mercantilism." While some aspects of mercantilism can be traced in ancient and medieval economies, others depended upon conditions evolving in the early modern period. The ideal of the mercantilist philosopher was to strengthen the position of his nation. Believing that the position of a nation depends upon the "bullion"—gold, silver, precious stones—amassed by it, he held that the nation should export more than it imported. This he sought to achieve through increased industrial production, through establishment and exploitation of colonies, through monopolization of crucial raw materials, and through building up a merchant marine and a carrying trade which would be able to exclude competitors. Such measures could, of course, be utilized only with the help of a powerful government, which backed the commercial enterprises. Mercantilism thus implied a measure of government interference in economic affairs. But, since the bourgeoisie was in any case favorable to firm central governmental control, government interference was tolerated; and those nations in which centralization under strong rulers had advanced most took the lead.

AGRICULTURAL CONDITIONS. Inasmuch as mercantilism favored trade and required increased productivity, agriculture had to adapt itself to changed conditions. Commercial farming of industrial products which yielded higher returns replaced—insofar as tools and organization permitted—subsistence farming. Once many peasants had begun to migrate to cities, their lands were sold for profit, and large farms were established and worked by an impoverished laboring class. Common lands were appropriated by landlords, and in countries such as Spain and England, many of them were enclosed and used for sheep-grazing and wool production.

THE ARTS AND SCIENCES

Some historians have been inclined to see in the economic shifts, which brought wealth and leisure to the upper groups of the population, the chief reason for the marvelous artistic achievement which the early sixteenth century, following the example of the preceding age, still witnessed. However, such a view cannot be accepted. As always, the primary factor was the genius of individual men. Fortunately, men of outstanding genius were produced by the age, and this good chance was not lost, for the available genius was accorded appreciation by a cultivated society. Other times, equally prosperous, have failed to show similar appreciation.

Painting and Sculpture. Encouraged by popes, princes, and wealthy burghers, Renaissance Italy especially continued to bring forth an astounding number of the greatest masters in the fine arts. It suffices to mention the painters Leonardo da Vinci ("Mona Lisa," "Last Supper"); Raphael ("Sistine Madonna," "Madonna of the Chair"); Michelangelo (ceiling of the Sistine Chapel, "Moses"), equally great as sculptor, architect, and thinker; Titian ("Charles V"); and the sculptor and goldsmith Cellini. But not less amazing are the great Germans Dürer ("Holzschuher," "Trent," "Knight, Devil, and Death"), Cranach ("Luther"), and Holbein ("Erasmus," "Anne of Cleves"). England had little to offer; but in France there were eminent artists, among them Jean Clouet ("Francis I"). And there were in most countries many minor painters who, had they lived in times less overshadowed by the greatest, would have been considered unique.

Music. The early sixteenth century, outstanding in art, is known also for its music. As a "Golden Age of Song," it saw the flourishing of the motet and, after 1520, the madrigal—both polyphonic compositions for voices, the former on sacred, the latter on secular, texts. In many countries, popular song festivals were held and the art of singing was promoted by guilds (Hans Sachs and the Meistersinger). The Catholic Church and religious reformers—especially Luther himself, who composed enduring hymns—competed in beautifying Church services by organ music and encouraged singing among the community. Netherland composers taught their art and style in many countries, and with previously unknown perfection their works for voice and for instruments were performed at the courts of princes and nobility as well as in the houses of wealthy burghers.

Literature. Owing to the mid-fifteenth-century invention of printing with movable type, popular education became more widespread and new educational ideals arose. Luther, in particular, favored widespread teaching of the fundamentals of reading and writing and advocated kindness toward children and understanding of pupils in addition to discipline. With the increase in literacy, the demand for books accelerated. The great controversies of the age brought forth a stream of pamphlets, tracts, and brilliant works on classics, history, criticism, education, and politics. The intellectual trend known as *humanism,* with its interest in classical studies and in things human rather than otherworldly, penetrated from the southern into the northern countries. One of the greatest humanists of the age was Erasmus of Rotterdam (d. 1536), a scholar, a promoter of classical erudition, editor of the Greek text of the Bible, and author of *The Praise of Folly* (which ridiculed such human weaknesses as avariciousness, credulity, pedantry, and gluttony). As an advocate of peace and reason, Erasmus opposed the excesses, violence, and coarseness of the age and admonished princes and churchmen to abandon evil traditions, to reform, be tolerant, and

devote themselves to the true service of Christ. Other leading northern humanists were the statesman Thomas More, the pamphleteer
and poet Ulrich von Hutten, and Johann Reuchlin, who compiled
a Hebrew grammar for Bible studies and vigorously took part in
the controversies of the age. Numerous French and Scandinavian
writers, as well as some Spanish writers, followed the Italian, German, and English example. They combined the pagan and Christian
(the classical and medieval) heritage and published widely read
works of lasting merit. Permanently important histories and biog-
raphies of many sorts appeared: Guicciardini's history of Italy,
Gomara's history of America, Vasari's lives of Italian artists, and
Benvenuto Cellini's famous autobiography. A special place in literary achievement belongs to Luther, who with his translation of the
Bible into German created a work of almost unparalleled beauty
and majesty. The dialect which he used prepared the way for the
modern High German tongue as generally spoken today. On his
edition the English Bible translation by Tyndale was based.

Compared with the great religious and humanistic literature,
however, poetry and drama attained lesser heights. Besides the
Italian Ariosto (d. 1533), who was by no means one of the greatest
of writers, yet was appreciated widely and served as a model for
several generations, there were few who excelled in literary works
of imagination. Popular drama, miracle plays, and poems in the
classical style became sterile.

Natural Sciences. Western man's broadening horizon, his in-
quisitiveness, and his secular interests directed his attention to closer
observation and investigation of natural phenomena. Moreover, his
geographical discoveries stirred his mind and enlarged his scientific
understanding. A great amount of new knowledge was gained in
geography and anthropology. Discoveries brought new inventions
and improvements in technique. But also in other areas, which had
no direct connection with geographical discoveries, outstanding advances were made. The greatest was perhaps that of Copernicus
(d. 1543), who showed that the earth circles about the sun; and
man came, rather unwillingly, to realize the relative insignificance
of his own world within the larger scheme of nature. Of comparable importance was the growing understanding of human physiology. Vesalius (d. 1564) dissected and described the human body;
Leonardo da Vinci (d. 1519) examined and charted many of its
organs; Servetus (d. 1553) investigated the pulmonary circulation

of the blood; and Paracelsus (d. 1541) sought new therapeutic methods. Similar interests led Gesner (d. 1565) to compose a history of animals and Agricola (d. 1555) to study mineralogy. To be sure, the exact sciences—which in the tradition of Peter Abelard were to lead through doubt and inquiry to the truth and which were based on rational deduction and observation—were still intermingled with pseudo sciences based on acceptance of authority or superstition. Standards set for scientific work by Leonardo da Vinci, who called for mathematical thinking and experimentation, were not yet generally accepted; and man continued to attempt to solve the mysteries of life and nature with the help of astrology, alchemy, and plain magic. But since these unscientific methods did not stand the test of time, historians have been inclined to pass over in their descriptions this important part of man's interests during the sixteenth century.

Political Science. A special place in the scientific endeavors of the age belongs to the numerous political writings which, despite widespread adherence to the theoretical propositions of medieval thinkers, evince a clear, realistic approach to political problems. Many works appeared discussing the duties of princes and of highborn ladies. Erasmus wrote such a book; more influential was the internationally used *Courtier* by Castiglioni, the standard work on courtly manners and on Christian behavior in public affairs. The English humanist and statesman Thomas More (d. 1535) wrote *Utopia,* which describes (despite a rather moralistic insular point of departure) an "ideal commonwealth" that through the nobility of its conception exercised a strong influence on later political thought. But none of these works compare in historical influence with that of Machiavelli (d. 1527), author of *The Prince.* In this book, Machiavelli, who as a humanist was well acquainted with classical literature, analyzes with penetrating insight into human psychology the sources of political power and its "demoniac" nature. Drawing upon experience and showing no concern with morality, he counsels the princes how best to gain, maintain, and use power. Self-interest alone, he holds, should dictate their actions. His work has remained unique in the field of rational statecraft.

CHAPTER IV

THE NEW MONARCHIES

T HE ATMOSPHERE created by the new interests and directions of the active forces in society brought forth a new political organization of Europe. For several centuries, feudal traits had been on the wane, and tendencies toward greater cohesion within the territories of various national groups had appeared. These tendencies were supported by rulers who sought to extend their personal power; they were also promoted by economic necessities, by the increase of productivity and expansion of commerce. Both favored the development of new centralizing, absolutist monarchical forms; and thus came into being what is known as the "New Monarchies." In a "New Monarchy," the ruling prince, having practically overcome the challenge of a feudal nobility, succeeded in concentrating decisive power in his own hands, in reducing the influence of estates, parliaments, or diets, and in controlling the military forces, the jurisdiction, and the finances of his realms. In his endeavors, which put an end to much of the strife of the feudal age, he was usually supported by the burgher class whose wealth and whose jealousy of the privileges of the nobility provided him with the means to strengthen his own monarchical position.

WESTERN EUROPE

The development of "New Monarchies" was much more rapid in the West of Europe than in other parts. Owing to the recent discoveries and the opportunities they offered, a shift of the center of authority and power from Empire and Papacy in Germany and Italy to the western areas took place. This was paralleled by a corresponding shift in initiative and leadership. Indeed, the western regions of Europe bordering on the Atlantic and profiting from the new trade-routes to the wealth of Asia and America adapted their political organization more speedily to the demands of modern times.

Portugal. A "New Monarchy" developed early in Portugal. It gained strength owing to the acquisition of colonies in the Indies and in Brazil. It benefited from the influx of Oriental products, from spices and jewels, from the income from the slave trade, from the national strength gained through sea power, and from support by the merchants and bankers interested in colonial expansion. Lisbon in Portugal soon surpassed the greatest older trading city, Venice; and the Portuguese king assumed a virtual trade monopoly. Concentrating in his hands the lucrative Indian spice trade (a monopoly which, even after Portugal's early decline, he could still maintain) and avoiding conflict with England by allowing foreign participation in Portuguese trade ventures, he firmly established his power and could dominate nobility and burghers alike.

Spain. The acquisition of colonies determined the new greatness of Spain under Ferdinand and Isabella, as it did that of Portugal. Gold and silver flowed into the treasury of the rulers, who since 1503 had held a monopoly on trade with America, a monopoly conferred by them upon a *Casa de Contratación* and controlled by the ports of Seville and Cadiz. Annually from these ports ships sailed in convoys to bring colonial products safely home. However, unlike the ruler of Portugal, the Spanish royal house used its position less for accumulation of bullion than for dynastic aggrandizement. After Queen Isabella's death, the king secured—in addition to the large territories of the New World—domination of southern Italy and of trade routes in the western Mediterranean. He built the most powerful and effective army in the world, commanded by some of the greatest generals of all times. Piracy and brigandage were checked, and firm order under strong monarchical supervision was maintained. He carried forward the unification of the country, which had started with his marriage. A common, royally supervised, but essentially weak parliament (*Cortes*) was created; religious dissidents were suppressed; and a generally valid law code based on Roman law was introduced. Arts were protected; and law studies flourished. Unfortunately for Spain, commercial interests had generally been the domain of existing brotherhoods of towns (*hermandades*); and the king continued to give these conservative forces his protection, so that a vigorous, enterprising, independent middle class could not develop.

France. France had progressed under King Louis XI on the road toward the status of a "New Monarchy." Under Louis' successors Charles VIII, Louis XII, and (after 1515) Francis I—all of whom belonged to the House of Valois—she continued on the same path. The representative body, the Estates-General, whose functions paralleled those of diets and parliaments elsewhere, was kept weak while royal power was augmented in jurisdictional, administrative, and financial matters. Yet, France's development was slower than that of Spain, for neither did she succeed in securing colonies—despite Cartier's discoveries in the St. Lawrence region—nor did she sufficiently encourage modern economic tendencies. Instead she pursued wars against the Empire in Italy, which Charles VIII, out of expansionist desires, greed, or fear of Hapsburg power, had begun in 1494. Francis I, a generous and cultured, but also an outmoded, treacherous, and inefficient ruler, continued the struggle and wasted the resources needed for improving France's internal conditions.

England. Like other Atlantic seaboard countries, England, too, entered a stage in which the establishment of a modern nation became possible. Henry VII of the House of Tudor had already re-established respect for law and order, had favored the merchant class, had amassed a large treasury, and had secured control of the judiciary. The nobility, decimated in the preceding times of trouble, was deprived of its military power and compelled to obey his wishes. His successor Henry VIII adhered to the same policy; Parliament, however, continued to function, even though its potential was greater than its actual influence, for the initiative rested with the Crown. England, too, thus exemplified the "New Monarchies."

CENTRAL AND EASTERN EUROPE

In the regions of Europe which did not border on the Atlantic Ocean, the traditions of the past remained strong. As the politically dominant powers of Central Europe benefited little from the economic shifts occurring in the age of discoveries, they were forced into a defensive position; this caused them to seek the preservation of the existing social organization. Moreover, their attention was increasingly directed eastward, where two new great powers, Turkey and Russia, had emerged. Neither of these shared in the political evolution of the West, and thus neither could set an example of political modernization. Yet, with the vigor of rising nations, both began to make their influence felt on the European political scene, and principally on the neighboring German Empire.

The German Empire. At the beginning of modern times, the Empire was still an international organization, extending beyond Germany into areas inhabited by diverse national groups, such as the Dutch, Burgundians, Swiss, Italians, Czechs, and others. It was composed of seven electorates, many smaller states, hundreds of towns, and other areas governed by independent knights; and it was held together by imperial authority which, though the office of emperor was elective, remained in the hands of the House of Hapsburg. It had a few federal institutions, such as a diet (which decided questions of finance and common organization that affected all members) and a federal court. But it did not offer a fertile soil for the evolution of a strong centralized state. Nevertheless, "new" monarchical trends were not entirely absent. While they did not pervade the Empire as a whole, they could be found within the larger member states, such as Saxony, Brandenburg, Bavaria, Austria, and others. It would therefore be incorrect to speak of the political development of Germany as differing radically from that of the Atlantic nations; but it was on a more restricted, local rather than national, scale that the trends toward "New Monarchies" appeared.

Despite its lack of modern political evolution, the German Empire as a whole was to achieve early in the sixteenth century a position of power in the world almost unequaled in any earlier or later period. This was achieved through the shrewd diplomacy of the House of Hapsburg, which concluded numerous advantageous marriage alliances; through the enterprising spirit of some individuals, especially the merchants of southern Germany and of the Low Countries; and through the economic opportunities afforded by the proximity of rising Eastern Europe with its resources of grain in Poland-Lithuania and of metals in Tyrol and Hungary, and with its export markets in Russia and the Balkans. Dominating the central areas connecting East and West as well as North and South, the Hapsburgs undertook to exploit the situation. The Emperor Maximilian I (1489–1519)—an intelligent, chivalrous, well-educated, but weak-spirited man—did not succeed in enforcing his will upon the Empire, in improving its cumbersome, outdated judicial and administrative machinery, or in leading the whole country toward unification. But he strengthened its position enormously by securing as dowry the rich Burgundian and Netherland domains and then marrying his son to a Spanish princess, through whom his grandson Charles was enabled to claim the entire Spanish Empire. In 1517, upon the death of his grandfather Ferdinand, this Charles, born in Ghent in the Netherlands in 1500, actually became king of Spain and all her colonies; and in 1519, upon the death of his grandfather Maximilian, the same Charles was elected German emperor. To win the election, however, it was necessary for him to engage in a bitter contest with Francis I of France, and this forced him not only to distribute lavish bribes to the electors, but also to make sweeping promises (contrary to the trends toward "New Monarchies") to maintain "German liberties." As Charles V, he was to rule for almost forty years over an empire on which the sun never set—a man of high moral standards, earnestly devoted to his task, slow and wise in decision, and shrewd in his judgment of men, but facing a task surpassing his strength as it would have surpassed that of any other man.

Italy. The only country in which the new absolutist monarchical form of government made no progress, either on a national or a city-state level, was Italy. No central authority existed there, and individual attempts at making the inhabitants conscious of common links remained without practical effect. Emperor, pope, and French and Spanish kings shared with the Medici, Sforza, Este, Gonzaga, and other famous Renaissance princes the domination of the area which only centuries later was to form the Italian nation; and almost all sectors retained the accustomed forms of government. Moreover, wars fought by the Valois and the Hapsburgs over the disunited country desolated the land, and the rivalries of the great powers checked the growth of a modern state system. The commercial importance of the country (formerly based on Italian business connections with the Moslems in the Near East) was diminished by the advance of the Turks and the opening of the direct seaway from western Europe to India.

Russia and Turkey. Centralization and absolutism, toward which the European national states developed, had long existed in the two Eastern empires; but owing to Oriental concepts of des-

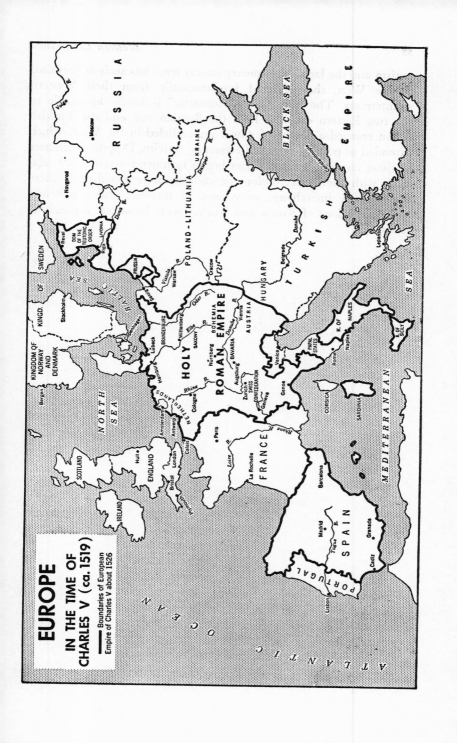

EUROPE
IN THE TIME OF CHARLES V (ca. 1519)

Boundaries of European
Empire of Charles V about 1526

potism and the lack of customary ethical restraints such as prevailed in the West, they differed fundamentally from their Western counterparts. The term "New Monarchy" is hardly applicable to the two Eastern empires. Both the Russian tsar and the Turkish sultan enjoyed a degree of power unparalleled in the West, which extended to politics, law, and economic activity. Despite differences in these respects, both countries began to move toward closer relations with the West: diplomatic contacts were established; there was a lively interchange of visitors, of travelers and merchants; and descriptions of Russia and Turkey were broadcast throughout Europe.

CHAPTER V

THE AGE OF THE REFORMATION
(1517–1555)

B Y FAR THE MOST momentous event of the early modern period
was the Reformation. It started as a reform movement within
the Catholic Church and its original objective was not more than a
purification of the Christian church and a revivification of Christian
morals in European life. Indeed, the leading men of the Reformation were, and remained, theologians and considered all their proposals for reform only from the theological point of view. But the
effect of their work was soon felt in all areas of European life—
in politics, social relationships, sciences, and arts, and also in the
economic arena. Historians have for this reason been tempted to
speak of the Reformation as a broad, international revolution—a
term which certainly misrepresents the work and aims of the reformers, but which may have a measure of justification on the basis
of the wide effects of the Reformation.

THE REFORMATION

The urgent need of a reform in existing religious institutions was
generally recognized outside as well as within the Catholic Church.
In the course of the centuries, doctrinal views had arisen which
seemed to many to be in need of revision; but, more important,
numerous practical abuses had penetrated all parts and layers of the
institutions of the Catholic Church and threatened its entire structure. Therefore, many of the most devoted Church members concerned with a Christian way of life joined in demanding re-

form with those who sought reform for selfish economic advantages.

Church Abuses. Manifold, indeed, were the sins of the Church and of churchmen.[1] Anarchy reigned within the Church. Central authority had been weakened and had made it possible for kings and nations to assume rights and duties which belonged to the Church. Among popes and bishops, corruption of morals existed. Many followed worldly policies, allowed nepotism and simony, and proved greedy and venal. Among the clergy, a shocking lack of training existed; the rank and file found themselves in desperate economic circumstances, while the hierarchy lived in unequaled luxury. Immorality and sexual promiscuity were correctly charged to many of the churchmen. Church services and the care of church buildings were neglected by the priests. A large portion of the clergy interested themselves in secular affairs, in science, art, and economics, rather than in the salvation of souls. To all this should be added constant rivalries and jealousies among the members of the hierarchy, among various monastic orders, and between monks and priests. Bishops tried to hold as many lucrative Church offices as possible without fulfilling the corresponding duties. Moreover, errors of faith had developed, which led to errors in conduct. Popes misused indulgences and abused their power to censure and excommunicate. The Church maintained economic views derived from a period with an entirely different economic system and needs; she insisted on exemption from taxation and refused to divest herself of "unproductive" lands.

As always, to be sure, there were many forces at work within the Church to improve external conditions, purify the hearts of its members, and reconcile Christian tasks with the humanistic trends of the age. But these forces proved weak; their effects came too late.

Early Reform Movements. The greatest figure of the Reformation was Luther. Today, hundreds of years later, the immediate and direct influence of his work is continuously felt. Luther was not, however, a great originator: he was a great accomplisher. Many men before him had urged reform of the organization of the Church and some had attacked the same dogmas which Luther challenged; Ockham, Marsilius, Bradwardine, Wycliffe, Wessel, Huss, and many a humanist were among them. The last of their number was

[1] A Catholic author, Pierre Janelle, S.J., in *The Catholic Reformation* (Milwaukee. 1949), has given a comprehensive account of conditions in the Church.

Savonarola, a Florentine who, shocked by the corruption of the Roman Court under the Borgia pope and by the widespread secular interests of the clergy, preached purification and repentance. When he became involved in Florentine political quarrels, his enemies succeeded (in 1498) in having him hanged and burned as a heretic.

Luther. Martin Luther was, in a sense, Savonarola's immediate successor. He was born in 1483, the son of a miner. At first he studied law, then turned to theology and became an Augustine monk. He took his duties most seriously, prayed, fasted, castigated himself, and made a pilgrimage to Rome. When a new university was founded in Wittenberg, Saxony, his superiors sent him there to teach. Terrified by the corruption he had seen in Rome, doubtful as to many teachings of the Church, and convinced that only faith and the grace of God can lead to man's salvation, he posted (in 1517) ninety-five theses on the church door in Wittenberg, attacking one of the worst abuses, the sale of indulgences.[2]

NINETY-FIVE THESES (1517). The publication of theses was a rather customary procedure. Luther's act, however, had extreme repercussions because of the logic and vigor of his statements and his implied challenge of papal authority. Pious Christians everywhere saw in it the long-desired beginning of reform, and numerous worldly interests saw in it a means to escape some of the tutelage or financial impositions of the popes. Princes saw in his act a basis for stopping the flow of money to Rome and for channeling it, instead, into their own pockets. They used it as an appeal to German national consciousness, and sensed in it an opportunity to break entirely with a degraded papacy absorbed in politics, whose heirs they themselves wanted to become. Rome therefore reacted vigorously, and a number of disputations were sponsored between Luther and some of the leading Catholic scholars. These, however, led only to a widening of the breach.

DOCTRINARY TRACTS AND LUTHER'S EXCOMMUNICATION. In 1520, Luther took a further decisive step by publishing three pamphlets. Again he described Rome's abuses, demanded reforms in morals and in dogma, attacked some of the sacraments, transubstantiation, and worship of saints, and again insisted that the Bible alone, with

[2] Indulgences were to bring remittance of sins if the sinner showed a contrite heart, confessed, accepted due penalty, and performed good works. But they were granted and often sold without demanding repentance or good works, and the profits of the resulting big business flowed into the pockets of bankers and bishops, or were used for the beautification of Rome.

no additional precepts of the Church, constituted the final authority for a Christian. He emphasized that, on the foundation of God's Word, everyone could be his own priest and master and need be nobody's servant. The pope threatened a ban of excommunication against Luther; but, in the presence of applauding Wittenberg students, Luther publicly burned the pope's bull and thereby protested in behalf of the individual's inalienable right, as a Christian, to be subject to God alone.

DIET OF WORMS (1521); TRANSLATION OF THE BIBLE. The rebellion against established Church authority, thus started by Luther, led to a quick reaction on the part of political authority, for emperor and kings began to fear for their own position. Charles V, a devout Catholic, invited Luther to attend a diet of the German estates which was to be held in Worms in 1521. Under safe-conduct, Luther appeared and before the assembled princes courageously restated his position, as "it is neither safe nor right to act against one's conscience." Charles honored the safe-conduct, but Luther was put under the ban of the German Empire, and his political friends had to give him asylum in one of their castles, the Wartburg. There, Luther composed hymns, studied educational methods, and, particularly, worked on his translation of the Bible. But within a year, grave disturbances called him back to Wittenberg.

Social Consequences. Luther's attack on authority and tradition had released manifold revolutionary forces. Numerous preachers and theologians felt that he had not gone far enough. Groups arose which demanded the abolition of, or substitutions for, all dogmas and sacraments, images, and traditional worships. Often they also rejected worldly authorities, princely powers, and existing economic and behavior patterns. Some wanted to introduce free love and a completely free, communistic society. Luther, who himself had rejected celibacy and who had married in 1525, fought such extreme trends. But the stream could not be stopped. Anabaptists and other religious radicals caused widespread disturbances. Rebellions of knights against their overlords occurred, and eventually—as in Wycliffe's and Huss's times—a great peasant revolt broke out. In "Twelve Articles," the peasants protested against serfdom, illegal and extravagant taxes, restriction of their rights to common lands, and the abolition of customary law in favor of Roman law with its property concepts. They demanded emancipation and the right to worship God in their own chosen ways. Luther had exhorted the lords to deal fairly with their peasants and to yield to justified de-mands. Anticipating John Locke, he had advocated the peasants' rights to defend themselves against unjust government; but he was shocked by the violence that the resulting peasant uprising brought. He gradually became more conservative, turned with a crudity customary to his age against the pillaging peasants (a change which cost him the support of many) and insisted on the right of the God-ordained secular powers to re-establish order and worldly authority by fire and sword. Yet, the entire social fabric of past ages remained shattered.

Political Consequences. The political effect of Luther's work was no less significant than the social consequences. In the German Empire, the forces of disintegration were strengthened; many princes, foreseeing an opportunity to confiscate the wealth of the churches and monasteries located in their realms, adhered to the new religion and rebelled against the emperor. In England, on the other hand, the king himself took advantage of religious controversies to strengthen his personal rule. In Scandinavia, the conflict caused the Swedes, under the leadership of Gustavus Vasa, to break the links with Denmark and establish an independent kingdom. In most regions, strife and internecine war resulted. On the international stage, the French used the newly developing dissensions for territorial aggrandizement; and the papacy was torn by political ambitions and the desire to see Catholicism everywhere restored.

Effects on Imperial Policies. Of special consequence was the effect of the Reform movement on the position of the German Empire and on the role of empire and papacy in the Western world. Despite numerous struggles, the two powers had always been inter-dependent. But at this critical moment, when the survival of both was threatened and unity would have been the first necessity, Charles V was deserted by the pope, who feared imperial might more than heresy. The emperor was forced to meet the problems alone, and with fortitude he sought to stem the tide. He turned, first, against the French, who had once more invaded his possessions in Italy. His Spanish armies decisively defeated them and took their king prisoner. Francis was not released until he had promised to keep the peace and to make restitution of conquered lands—a promise which, with the connivance of the pope, he soon broke. Next, Charles had to use force against the pope himself, the ambitious and luxury-loving Medici, Clement VII. In 1527, Spanish, German, and Swiss mercenaries, commanded by a French duke, seized Rome, which they sacked, destroying untold works of art and stripping it of much of its riches. For the time being, papal opposition was eliminated and a measure of co-operation between empire and papacy could be established. Then, Charles had to deal with the Turks, the arch enemy of Christendom, with whom the king of France had entered into close relations and whom he had enticed to invade the empire from the rear. In 1529, the Turks reached the gates of Vienna, where they were repulsed; but they did gain domination over Hungary. Lastly, the emperor had to contend with the German princes. Toward them he tried a policy of moderation. In 1529, a diet was held in Spires, which, however, produced no concession by the Catholic princes, so that the Lutherans protested against the decision. (From this protest the name "Protestants" is derived.) In the following year, they drew up a statement of their faith, the famous "Augsburg Confession," which reaffirmed their creed. But owing to the mediation of the emperor, a *modus vivendi* for Catholics and Protestants was worked out.

THE SPREADING OF THE REFORMATION

Soon, Luther's religious reform movement turned from a principally German development into a European movement. In doing so, it lost some of the parochial character which, notwithstanding its universal religious meaning, it had possessed owing to its incorporation of specifically German grievances.

Expansion on the Continent. In Switzerland, the first country affected by the Reformation in Germany, Luther's initial steps in 1518 had promptly induced the priest Ulrich Zwingli of Zurich to advocate similar reforms. Zwingli, like other humanists, recognized only the authority of sources; he therefore followed Luther in turning for theological interpretation to the Bible itself rather than to Church traditions. But he went further in regard to purification of dogma and did not hesitate to include even the sacraments of baptism and communion, whereby he created a breach between his own adherents and those of Luther. Theological disputations between the two men failed to resolve the dogmatic differences, whereupon an early split among the Protestants resulted. Zwingli himself was killed in 1531 while accompanying Zurich troops in battle, but his work was carried on by others.

In Sweden and Denmark, too, Lutheranism spread early. The Swedes, once they had freed themselves from Denmark, which was ruled by Christian II (brother-in-law of Charles V), introduced Lutheranism; shortly thereafter the Danes themselves revolted against their king, mainly because of his economic policies and arbitrary rule. Having driven Christian out of the country, they, too, accepted the Lutheran faith and introduced it into Norway also. The new faith was likewise accepted by large segments of the population, especially townspeople, in Hungary, Lithuania, Livonia, and the Netherlands, and even by some converts in France, Spain, and Italy.

Expansion in the British Isles. Luther's movement created a special situation in the British Isles. The Reformation was at first of little interest to the average British subject, but, subsequently, it found adherents both in Scotland and in England. It was not, however, the religious question but, instead, the personal problems of King Henry VIII which caused England's reforms to assume worldwide importance during the 1530's. Henry was a despotic, perfidious, and utterly selfish, though not incompetent, ruler who achieved little in international relations but much of importance in internal affairs. He prevented a resurgence of the power of the nobility, preserved order, strengthened royal absolutism, and chose to cooperate with Parliament (and even enlarged its powers) rather than to subdue it. He incorporated Wales into England. It was he who carried out the break with Rome. He had originally attacked Luther, but, when the pope refused to give him a dispensation so that he could discard his wife (Catherine of Aragon, a relative of Charles V) and marry his mistress, Anne Boleyn, who he hoped would bear him a son, he decided to make use of the predicament in which the pope found himself owing to the Protestant movement. Step by step, with the help of successive advisers (some of whom he executed after they had served his purpose)—Cardinal Wolsey, Sir Thomas More, Thomas Boleyn, John Fisher, Archbishop Cranmer, Thomas Cromwell—he separated England from Rome. He had himself recognized as head of the English Church, dissolved the monasteries (whose wealth he confiscated), discontinued the payment of taxes to Rome, and, in 1539, arranged for Parliament to confirm a statement of faith, the "Six Articles," which, while preserving essential Catholic doctrines, in essence refused to acknowledge papal authority. Thus, a true moral and doctrinal reformation

was not consummated in Henry VIII's England; but the position
of the papacy was undermined, and after Henry's death in 1547 the
real reformatory work began.

OUTBREAK OF RELIGIOUS WARS
AND THE RISE OF CALVINISM

The changes under Henry VIII obscured the religious issues
everywhere in Europe and emphasized the political aspects of the
Reform movement. In vain did Luther hope for a re-establishment
of Christian unity upon the basis of a Church adhering to the idea
of justification by faith and using a simplified service. Until his
death in 1546 he remained extremely active, interpreting the Bible,
instituting schools and seminaries, installing superintendents, writing
numerous works, and giving advice to secular authorities. But the
political and economic implications and their unavoidable practical
effect were beyond his understanding. Two distinct parties, a Catholic and a Protestant League (the latter under the name of
"Schmalkaldic League"), had already been formed in Germany.
Once Luther's authority was removed by death, war broke out
between them.

Schmalkaldic War. This war was the first in a long series of
internal struggles between Catholics and Protestants in many
countries. It indicated that the situation had developed beyond the
possibility of compromise. By 1546, this impasse was realized not
only by the Protestants but also by Charles V. He, too, had worked
for a reunion of the faiths—trying to reach it through the convening of a general Church Council. But the popes had opposed a
general Council. Even after the death of Clement VII, popes willing
to effect moral reform in the Church consistently withheld their
co-operation. In their refusals they were supported by France, which
engaged in one war after another against the Hapsburgs and which
profited from the split within Germany. Charles had no alternative
but to seek to re-establish unity by force of arms. He declared war
on the Protestants, and a first battle, fought at Mühlberg (1547),
brought him startling success: his forces routed the Schmalkaldic
League and captured its two chief leaders. But the emperor's triumph
served only to further frighten the pope and various foreign
princes. Although Charles, showing his customary moderation, had
imposed only a truce, the so-called "Interim" (1548), and had re-

doubled his efforts to find a permanent solution through a general Council, no reconciliation was effected. Hence, a few years later, when his chief ally deserted him and his armies were defeated, he finally gave up all hope for the re-establishment of unity.

Peace of Augsburg (1555). In 1555, a peace of fundamental importance was signed at Augsburg. It granted each German prince the right to establish for all his subjects that religion which he himself professed. Thereby, Lutheran princes, and with them Lutheran states, gained equal rights and status with Catholic ones— even though the peace forbade any future converting of Catholic bishoprics into secular Protestant states.

Abdication of Charles V. Charles suffered two other disappointments. His troops failed to recover territories in Lorraine which the Catholic French, co-operating with Protestant German princes, had annexed; and the marriage of his son Philip to the English Queen Mary, daughter of Henry VIII, did not bring the hoped-for union of Spain and England—for the marriage remained without a child who could inherit both thrones. Exhausted after forty years of endeavoring to guide the fate of the world, Charles finally decided to divest himself of his various crowns. In a series of moving ceremonies—especially that of Brussels in 1556—he installed his son Philip as his successor in Spain, Italy, and the Netherlands, and his brother Ferdinand in the German Empire and in Hungary. The Hapsburg possessions were thus divided, and he himself retired to a monastery in Spain where he died three years later.

Rise of Calvinism. By the time the Peace of Augsburg had been concluded and Charles had abdicated, the split in the Christian Church had in any case become irreparable; the Protestant forces had been augmented by another reformatory group—the Calvinists.

John Calvin (1509–64), a French law student, was early influenced by Luther's thought. He had turned to theology and had fled France as a result of one of Francis I's sporadic, politically inspired persecutions of heretics. In 1536, he published his fundamental work, the *Institutes of the Christian Religion.* He found asylum in Switzerland, and at Geneva he eventually established his political and religious leadership. Like Luther, Calvin based his teachings on the Bible, not on Church authority, and like Luther, he preached justification by faith; but he accepted Zwingli's interpretation of the sacraments. He insisted that no man can achieve the good ex-

cept by the will of God, who has predestined our actions. Therefore, man should abandon himself entirely to God, who, to a certain
extent, reveals his will to man and who allows man to lead a
virtuous, and possibly prosperous, life on earth and to do good
works. In the sphere of public affairs Calvin demanded that the
Church be given a leading role in the community. Pastors, teachers,
deacons, and elders, constituting a supervisory consistory, were to
direct all action and watch over education, morals, and orthodoxy.
Such a church government was actually established in Geneva; it
saw to the abolition of all remnants of Catholic worship, censored
books, prohibited all luxuries and most amusements, and emphasized prayer and work. It went so far as to drag the famous scientist
Servetus, who had already been accused of heresy by the Catholic
Church, but who also opposed Calvinist ideas of the Trinity, before
its tribunal and to have him burned at the stake (1553).

EFFECT OF CALVINISM. Calvinism spread even more rapidly than
Lutheranism. It was more international in character, was based
more on rationalism and less on mystic beliefs, and was more in
line with the economic trends of the age. It more easily reconciled
Christian ethics with business points of view. It described thrift as
a virtue, and prestige as a sign of moral strength, and it allowed
reasonable interest-taking—a fundamental requirement for the development of modern capitalism. It spread rapidly to the Netherlands, France, England, Scotland, and Poland. In many countries it
became a powerful political, as well as economic, tool. In Scotland,
where French Catholic influence within the royal family was resented, the fervent preacher John Knox spread its tenets.

THE COUNTER REFORMATION

Pressed from many sides, the Catholic Church finally initiated
reforms—though too late to save Western Christian unity. Again
and again, the Church had hesitated, deliberately avoiding recourse
to the customary means of settling disputes, namely, through the
convening of a general Council. The popes feared not only the
power of the emperor in a Council but also a renewal of the struggle
between pope and Council for supremacy within the Church and,
in addition, the opposition of the clergy to the papacy. They were
wary of the nationalist tendencies all over Europe and anxious to
avoid possible losses of funds and of prestige.

The Beginnings of the Catholic Reformation. Nevertheless, for some time the Reform movement had shown considerable strength. A number of reforming orders, such as the Theatines and Capuchins, had been founded and several reform popes had been elected. Most prominent among them was Hadrian VI (teacher and friend of Charles V), a Netherlander and the last pope who was not Italian. But his reign had been short and he had been succeeded by Clement VII, a luxury-loving Medici and typical Renaissance prelate. Only after Clement's death did the Reform movement find new official support. Yet, when in 1545, at the insistence of Charles V, a general Council had assembled in Trent, the popes had still obstructed its work. Only after Charles V had abdicated and the Hapsburg power had been divided, did the moment seem propitious to the popes for promoting the reform work of the Council.

The Founding of the Jesuit Order. By the time the Council convened again, the popes had received unquestioning obedience and aid from an unexpected source, the newly founded Society of Jesus—the Jesuits. A wounded soldier, the Spaniard Ignatius of Loyola (1491-1556), had turned from his former profession to become a soldier of Christ. He had written a book of *Exercises* which taught the need for prayer, meditation, self-control, practical moderation, and training of the will to obtain salvation. He gathered disciples and organized an order, for which he won recognition from the pope and which he placed like an army at the pope's absolute disposal. The purposes of the order were to combat heresy, spread Catholic education, and carry on missionary work. For the sake of effective results, the Jesuits did not hesitate to ally themselves in their work with the powerful of this earth, to make questionable political compromises, and to employ all practical means—force as well as persuasion, Inquisition as well as prayer—to regain heretical lands. They devoted special attention to the colonies.

Conclusion of Council of Trent (1563). Thus strengthened, the popes reconvened the Council, which had held only intermittent sessions, and in 1563 brought it to a conclusion. They achieved what they had set out to do. Since the Protestants did not recognize the authority of the popes, or the decisions of any council unless based entirely on the Scriptures, a compromise with them was excluded from the outset. Instead, the Council reasserted the Catholic point of view. It affirmed the doctrines that scriptures and traditions are equally binding for the faithful and that the supremacy of the pope is incontestable; it promulgated an "Index" of books which Catholics were forbidden to read without special dispensation. It refuted heresies and reaffirmed old dogmas. It prescribed measures to improve Church discipline and the morals and training of the clergy, it prohibited malpractices in regard to indulgences and adoration of saints, and it abolished certain administrative abuses. The Council of Trent thus concluded a reform of the Church from within and rejuvenated the Catholic-Christian spirit.

CONTRIBUTIONS OF THE REFORMATION

Reformation and Counter Reformation left a deep imprint upon the Western world. They affected its intellectual trends, its economics, its national developments. They stimulated education, changed social relationships, and led to new legal concepts and new laws. As two or more different faiths were to live subsequently side by side, a measure of tolerance became necessary, and the possibility emerged for the individual to make a choice in religious matters. Indeed, the cause of individualism, which the Renaissance, humanism, and capitalistic enterprise had fostered, was also advanced by the Reformation.

CHAPTER VI

THE AFTERMATH OF RENAISSANCE
AND REFORMATION (1555-1603)

YOUTHFULNESS, confidence, enthusiasm, thirst for beauty and man-
liness (*virtù*) had marked the early sixteenth century and made
possible the achievements of the High Renaissance; they no longer
characterized the second half of the century. In only two corners of
Europe, i.e., Spain and England (both of which had previously
made few contributions to the glory of the age), do we find a sudden flowering of culture; but in these countries the Renaissance
took on a more mature, more intellectual, aspect and found its
major expression in literature and science. Many of the great artists
were by then either dead or, like Michelangelo and Titian, in their
old age. The great humanists (Erasmus, Reuchlin, More), the religious leaders (Luther, Zwingli, Calvin, Loyola), the mighty Renaissance princes and patrons of culture (from the Medici, Sforza,
Este, and other families) had passed from the scene, as had
Copernicus and Machiavelli. On the political stage, in addition to
literature and natural sciences, did the second half of the sixteenth
century still bring forth a considerable number of personalities
and events inspired by the great age that was coming to a close.

THE POLITICAL SCENE

After the abdication of Charles V in 1556, the idea of European
Christian unity, as it had been conceived during the Middle Ages—
ever since the crowning of Charlemagne in 800 or of Otto the Great
in 962—was not revived. Spain, France, and Germany were to make

successive attempts at establishing some form of unity by imposing their own hegemony on the rest of the Continent, but in each case it was national ambition rather than a general European concept that directed their efforts. Indeed, more than ever before does the history of Western civilization become, after Charles V's abdication, the story of individual countries, and often it is the character of a prince which leaves its sharp imprint upon the civilization of an age. Thus, William the Silent of the Netherlands, Ivan the Terrible of Russia, Philip II of Spain, Elizabeth of England, and Eric XIV of Sweden lent color and distinction to their times. Among the dramatic events which they witnessed and to which they contributed were the War of Independence of the Netherlands, the struggle over the Baltic question, the Battle of Lepanto, the Night of St. Bartholomew, and the destruction of the Spanish Armada.

Italy. On the European stage during this period, Italy played the role of an object of action by other nations rather than being itself an actor. This country witnessed the decline or disappearance of its vigorous city-states and the weakening of the political position of the papal territories. Almost entirely under Hapsburg domination, it served as a bridge between Spain and Germany. The commerce of the Italian cities steadily lost its world significance; the wealth of other countries overshadowed theirs.

Germany. Located in the heart of Europe, Germany similarly declined in political importance. The Hapsburgs produced no new ruler of the stature of Charles V, and their resources were exhausted in wars to maintain the Empire and the Catholic faith. Such common institutions as the diets no longer functioned satisfactorily, the independence of the states comprising the Empire increased, and borderlands were lost. Thus, the Netherlands was joined to Spain, and subsequently its northern parts achieved independence; Livonia fell prey, first, to Russian, then to Swedish and Polish, invaders; western borderlands in Lorraine were annexed by the French; and the bishopric of Basel joined the free Swiss cantons. The eastern frontiers of the Empire continued to be exposed to inroads by the Turks, who remained in possession of Hungary with her silver mines; most of the eastern trade routes via the sea to the rich grain resources of the Slavic and Baltic countries fell into the hands of enterprising Dutch traders. However, individual German states (notably Brandenburg, Saxony, and Bavaria), succeeded in achieving their own aggrandizement and gained international prestige. Such states, rather than the Empire as a whole, became increasingly the centers of German might and German culture.

Spain. The role of leadership in Hapsburg affairs shifted accordingly to the Spanish branch of the house. Philip II (d. 1598) proved to be an outstanding ruler. Though lacking the balance and wisdom of his father, personally cruel, and jealous of his own best generals, advisers, and servants, he was a man devoted to the fulfillment of his duties as king. He worked tirelessly, persistent in all his undertakings; in a sense, he was the first Western ruler to understand, and build, a modern bureaucracy.

INTERNAL POLICIES. Under Philip II, Spain's great military tradition was maintained. Arts and literature flourished; numerous universities were established; Catholic scholars were attracted; geographical studies were advanced; and Spanish architecture found its grandiose expression in the mighty, somber palace of the Escorial built by Philip. Manners, fashions, and court etiquette and ceremonials were evolved that served as models for all Europe. Yet, the administration of the enormous Empire set tasks for which Spain was not equipped. The wealth coming from the colonies was largely wasted; it stimulated, not industry, but pride, sloth, and luxury. Since the Spanish nobleman considered business activities unworthy of his attention, and since the merchant class was small, foreigners were allowed to exploit the country's natural resources. Taxation remained high; debasement of the currency became unavoidable; and the government lost its credit standing through repeated bankruptcy of the treasury. Simultaneously, agriculture declined, and large estates, given away by the Crown as rewards to noblemen, were used only for pasture. The population, impoverished, gradually decreased. This process of economic decline was speeded by the expulsion of Jews and Moors who, through their trade and agriculture, had contributed much to the country's prosperity.

RELIGIOUS POLICIES. Philip maintained strict absolutism. Though a devout Catholic, he did not permit political influence by the Church, but kept the clergy dependent, used the Jesuits for the advancement of Spanish aims in Europe and America, and, on one occasion, even made war on the pope and besieged Rome.

COLONIAL POLICIES. Just as Philip dominated in the affairs of the Spanish clergy, so he personally supervised, despite the obstacle of distance, the administration of government in the New World. He followed the established policy of appointing viceroys, but, in matters of policy, he kept them subservient to the "Council of the Indies." The *encomienda* system (landholding by the feudal nobility and forced labor by natives) was retained, and large estates were granted to Spanish noblemen in the colonies. After the intervention of the friar Bartolomé de las Casas with Philip's father Charles, the Indians were no longer subjected to slavery. Trade with the New World remained a royal monopoly; large fleets were sent there annually, under the protection of convoys which fought off the English and French pirates and smugglers.

FOREIGN POLICIES. In foreign policy, Philip pursued the sole aim of defending the Spanish Empire. He was only partially successful. Closely co-operating with the German Hapsburgs, he fought and decisively defeated France. Allied with Venice and the pope, he engaged in war against the Turks and, in 1571, was victorious at Lepanto, one of the greatest naval battles of all times, which upset Turkish domination in the western Mediterranean. He invaded Portugal in 1580, when the royal family there had died out, annexed the country, and thus gained its rich dependencies in Africa and Asia. But in vain did he seek to retain control of the Spanish and Portuguese links with the empires. Throughout his reign, he had to fight the English on the seas, and after years of struggle his ambitious plan to destroy the English navy and to end English competition with the help of a great "Armada" miscarried. In 1588 the Armada, after being defeated by the English, was destroyed by storms. In all his foreign policies, Philip used and supported Catholicism, out of conviction as well as expediency, so that it ultimately appeared as if the defense of the old faith was the main objective of his policies.

The Netherlands. Despite Philip's high ability and industriousness, his reign ultimately turned out to be disastrous for Spain. His failure is attributable not so much to repeated bankruptcies, or to loss of an Armada or to a revival of French power, as to the crucial mistake which he made in the Spanish Netherlands.

OPPRESSION; DUKE OF ALBA. The Netherlands constituted the greatest asset within Philip's realms. He had inherited them from his father who, being a native, had understood (even though he did institute many harsh measures) how to retain their loyalty. Philip was dependent upon their wealth. But, instead of promoting Dutch and Flemish trade and winning good will, he tried to rectify a catastrophic financial situation in Spain by imposing a crippling sales tax upon the Low Countries and thereby threatened the merchants with ruin. Moreover, through his arbitrariness and arrogance he exasperated the Netherlanders, who were accustomed to a large measure of freedom; and finally, through the protection of the Catholic faith, the enforcement of the decisions of the Council of Trent, and the Inquisition, he sharpened the antagonism of the largely Calvinist Dutch toward their Spanish overlords. When the Netherlanders petitioned for reforms, Philip sent a large army under the able Duke of Alba to enforce Spanish rule and taxation. As a result, the Netherlands rebelled. Alba crushed the revolt and executed two of the leaders, Egmont and Horn; a third, William the Silent of Orange, who escaped, became the hero of liberty in the great struggle which ensued.

WAR OF INDEPENDENCE; WILLIAM OF ORANGE. The War of Independence of the Low Countries against Spain has remained an inspiration and model throughout the ages. William was a true Machiavellian; *The Prince* was his constant companion. He was called "the Silent" because he knew how to hide his thoughts behind a garrulous flow of words pertaining to nonessentials. He was successively Catholic, Lutheran, Calvinist; he married four times—for purposes of expediency; he was French (Orange), German (Nassau), and Dutch. An inefficient general, he was regularly defeated by Alba. He knew as little of economics as of military science. But he had an inflexible will, he was a political genius who knew how to command the loyalty of others, he showed tolerance whenever his political strategy called for it, he was modern in his point of view, and he was interested in realities rather than in appearances. Under his leadership, the Dutch and the Flemish recovered from their defeats; they equipped a small navy of so-called "Sea Beggars" to harass Spanish shipping; and, after the recall of Alba in 1573, they forced the Spanish army to relinquish most of the country. In 1581, the independence of the Netherlands was declared. But the war was not yet won. When Philip II sent Prince Alessandro Farnese of Parma to Flanders, Farnese, a man fully the equal of William in political acumen, succeeded in regaining the southern areas of the Low Countries. In the midst of the struggle, in 1584, William was murdered; but the Netherlanders fought on, stubbornly and courageously. They did not succeed in freeing the entire country, but they did retain independence for part of it; for the country was divided. Its southern portions remained Spanish and

Catholic; the north established itself as an independent republic in which Protestantism was predominant, the Orange family provided political leadership, and soon (under merchant or "bourgeois" control) the economy became again the most flourishing of Europe.

France. The internal policy of France centered around the religious problem and the struggle for maintenance of royal authority. Her foreign policy was guided by opposition to the Hapsburgs and, particularly, to Spain. But France was in no position to establish good government at home or enforce her will abroad. Not only was she decisively defeated by Spain in 1559, but religious wars ravaged the country and undermined law and order.

RISE OF THE HUGUENOTS. The dominant issue in France during the second half of the sixteenth century was the issue of national unity. The Reformation had split the country. Two parties had been formed: the Catholic, directed by the Guise family; and the Protestant, or "Huguenot," led by the Calvinist princes of Condé and of Navarre and by Admiral Coligny. Periods of persecution of the Huguenots alternated with periods of toleration. France might have emulated Germany (where, ultimately, both religions were recognized and existed side by side) or Spain (where Catholicism existed exclusively) but she followed neither example. Indeed, the historical importance of the French situation lies in the facts that the religious questions did not long remain the chief problem and that, as so often happens, the conflict between the two groups turned into a triangular struggle. A third party, the "Politiques," was formed. This party, which was not greatly concerned about religion, put nationalistic aims and centralization of government above all other considerations. Without delay, the queen mother, Catherine de Medici, who had an ambitious, intriguing character, embraced its tenets, for they coincided with her own absolutist aims. She played the other two parties against each other. Thus, the country was torn by internal strife, and disorders unmatched elsewhere occurred. The climax came when Catherine, faced by the possibility of a Protestant triumph, turned openly against the Protestants and instigated the outrage of the Night of St. Bartholomew. Under the pretext of a reconciliation she lured the Protestant leaders to Paris, whereupon these men and some twenty thousand of their adherents throughout France were massacred (1572).

CIVIL WARS AND RELIGIOUS SETTLEMENT. The events of the Night of St. Bartholomew led, after the shock of the stunning blow had passed, to a prolongation of the internal wars, for the Politiques now sought to destroy the Catholic party. Politiques, Catholics, and Protestants—each party led by a Henry—therefore continued to fight the other two in ever shifting alliances (War of the Three Henrys). After utter exhaustion had been reached, the country impoverished, the farms destroyed, international prestige lost, and two of the Henrys murdered, the surviving Henry of Navarre, of the house of Bourbon, leader of the Protestants, succeeded in ending the struggle. Putting the political issue before all others, he made terms with his opponents, he obtained recognition as king, and he himself turned Catholic. But he also pleased the Protestants by issuing the famous Edict of Nantes in 1598. This edict granted the Protestants freedom of conscience (the right to public worship) and the right to hold office. He guaranteed the latter right to the Protestant minority by permitting them to possess, and to fortify, a number of towns of their own in France.

England. While the ambitions of individuals, disruption in domestic affairs, and foreign wars were bringing ruin to France, a comparatively peaceful era and concentration on her national aims made it possible for England to enjoy a period of prosperity which coincided with the English Renaissance. The term "Renaissance" is possibly somewhat misleading, since achievements in various areas, such as sculpture and painting, were scant and mediocre. Nevertheless, in music—with the development of the madrigal—and in literature—with the masterpieces of the great Tudor poets and drama-tists (especially Shakespeare)—as well as in the splendor of court life, we find typical Renaissance traits.

ECONOMIC EXPANSION. In England during the second half of the sixteenth century, the enterprising Renaissance spirit also asserted itself in commercial affairs and in geographical explorations. The shipbuilding industry expanded rapidly; sea captains and pirates made England the foremost maritime power. Hawkins, Raleigh, and Drake sought trade routes westward; Chancellor established an eastward route to Russia via the northern tip of Europe; and Jenkinson initiated English trade with the tsar and indirectly, through the tsar's realms, with Persia. Overseas expansion led to industrial expansion, the establishment of joint-stock companies, and the growth of a credit system. As in Spain, so, too, in England the results were a decline in independent farming and the wider introduction of enclosures, which, in turn, increased sheep grazing and thus stimulated the textile industry. The burgher and the merchant improved their economic position, and the national standard of living reached a higher level.

RELIGIOUS SETTLEMENT. Unlike many of the Continental powers, sixteenth-century England was spared religious wars. Under Edward VI (d. 1553), who succeeded Henry VIII, the politico-religious changes made by the latter began to be extended to the realm of religious doctrine. Through two successive "Acts of Uniformity," a *Book of Common Prayer* was introduced and Protestant views regarding the authority of the Bible, justification by faith, and the nature of the sacraments were accepted. But Edward's successor, Mary Tudor (d. 1558), favored Catholicism, and her reign brought harsh persecutions of Protestants, hundreds of whom perished. Her own life was tragic and her rule short. Married to Philip II of Spain, she embraced not only the Catholic faith, but also the Spanish cause, which was contrary to English commercial interests. Moreover, England in 1558 lost her last stronghold on the Continent, the port of Calais. In turn, Mary's successor, Elizabeth (1558–1603), reverting to the policy of Edward VI, reintroduced a Protestant form of worship. Elizabeth accepted the innovations which had been introduced by the Acts of Uniformity, but she modified somewhat their anti-Catholic emphasis. "Thirty-nine Articles" set forth the Anglican confession of faith. A party of so-called "Puritans" desired more far-reaching changes, but, in order to preserve an all-national Church which the ruler could control, they were suppressed. For the same reason, Roman Catholics were now persecuted, perhaps no less than the Protestants had been during Mary's regime.

EXTERNAL AFFAIRS. England's foreign policies under Elizabeth were dominated by rivalry for commercial expansion and by fear of the power of Spain, France, and Scotland. This fact drove the country into sharp opposition to Catholic nations. It led to a bitter, repressive policy in Ireland (which Spain tried at times to use as a stepping-stone for an invasion of England). It disturbed the relations with Scotland and its Catholic ruling house of Stuart. Indeed, it brought death to Mary Stuart, the queen, a fugitive from her own country and a refugee in England, who, accused of participating in Jesuit conspiracies against the life of Elizabeth, was executed in 1587. It led to incessant, though undeclared, war with Spain and constant attacks on Spanish shipping. This situation reached its climax in 1588, when, finally, open war broke out and the Spanish

Armada was defeated. Opposition to Catholicism—and to Spain—brought, on the other hand, cooperation with the rebelling Netherlands. As to France, no consistent policy could be pursued, inasmuch as Franco-English relations depended upon ever-changing French relations with Scotland and Spain.

ELIZABETHAN ACHIEVEMENTS. By the time Elizabeth died, the English treasury was exhausted, and Parliament had become restive. Nevertheless, and despite the personal shortcomings of the queen, the Elizabethan Age stands out as a glorious era. Through the influence of literature and science, a gentler spirit had come to pervade England, a country which the Italians and French had long regarded as barbarian. Elizabeth's regime had built the foundations of political power, economic prosperity, and a vigorous, self-reliant body of citizens. Parliament and the bourgeois class, which were to hold the key to the future, emerged strengthened, and a "church" existed which combined traditionalism with Lutheran and Calvinist reforms and supported national unity under the monarch.

Scandinavia and Poland. The great issues of the day—the religious struggles, the capitalistic enterprises, and political centralization under a strong ruler—also continued to affect the small nations of northern and eastern Europe where they led to a further redistribution of power, mainly at the expense of Denmark. This change affected the situation in the entire Baltic area; for more than a century after the discovery of America, Baltic trade remained much more important than the transatlantic traffic.

DENMARK-NORWAY AND SWEDEN. Denmark-Norway, having lost control over Sweden in 1523, sought to adapt herself to the changed conditions. She succeeded in reestablishing order at home and brought religious strife to an end, with consequences favorable to the Lutheran cause. She also built up her economy with the help of the huge income derived from tolls which she levied upon ships passing from the North Sea into the Baltic Sea through the "Sound," the only navigable lane available—a narrow passageway controlled by Denmark. But she continued to squander her resources in futile wars against Sweden. The Swedes, on the contrary, made better progress. Having won their independence under the able, cautious, parsimonious Gustavus Vasa, they developed their rich mines, increased their production, channeled traffic through their own ports, and built up a large treasury. This policy enabled them (under Gustavus' sons and successors) to survive bitter wars against Denmark, Poland, and Russia. With the conquest of Estonia in 1561, they became the foremost Baltic power. Yet, Sweden, too, lacked the economic resources, the population, and the modern commercial spirit which would have enabled her to compete successfully with the Western trading nations.

POLAND-LITHUANIA. Like the Swedes, the Poles cherished dreams of a large empire and of dominion over the Baltic sea lanes. In 1525, they had already established their overlordship of Prussia; in 1562, their Lithuanian partners incorporated southern Livonia; in 1569 Poland had compelled Lithuania to accept complete integration; she had forced Danzig into submission; and in 1582, after a series of wars against Russia, she had annexed large Russian territories. Such diversified holdings demanded an efficient and tolerant central authority. But while arts, crafts, and literature flourished and the upper nobility enjoyed a life of luxury, the country as a whole did not develop the necessary progressive spirit and internal cohesion. The generally weak monarchy, motivated since the end of the Council of Trent by the aim of proselytizing in behalf of Catholicism, failed to control the unruly, chauvinistic nobility, which was backward in economic concepts and antagonistic to the development of a merchant class. Nowhere else was the social gulf among classes, nationalities, and religions so great as in Poland. Thus, conquests of territory contributed, not to the growth of the commonwealth, but to its destruction.

Russia. In the meantime, Russia was being governed by one of her most eminent rulers, Ivan IV (Ivan the Terrible). Ivan IV continued the work of consolidating the Russian realms begun by his grandfather Ivan the Great. He succeeded in incorporating the vast territory along the entire course of the Volga; he attempted to conquer Livonia in order to gain ports giving Russia access to the sea and, failing in this, he established permanent connections with the West by welcoming English merchants who had opened the northern route around the North Cape. He brutally suppressed all potential opponents, kept princes (boyars) and Church under his absolute rule, personally monopolized many economic activities, and surrounded himself with a powerful bureaucracy which was at his complete command. He catered to other English and Dutch traders who supplemented the Hanseatic merchants on the Baltic sea lanes. He strengthened the new links with the West by inviting craftsmen, introducing Western techniques, and expanding diplomatic relations. It was under Ivan the Terrible that Russia started her eastward march across the Urals. A band of intrepid Cossacks, led by Yermak, invaded Siberia in 1580 and began Russia's mighty eastward movement. As a whole, Ivan IV's reign meant rapid progress for Russia politically and economically and expansion eastward; but it also led to territorial losses in the West, to moral debasement, and to all the vicious consequences of autocracy which endangered internal stability.

THE CULTURAL SCENE

With the fading of the great age of the Renaissance in the second half of the sixteenth century, there began a period which in art history is known as "Mannerism." This era constituted the link between the High Renaissance and the coming baroque period. Despite the name, this age of transition was not devoid of sincerity and originality; although works of genius, such as had been produced in the two preceding centuries, were rare, there was still left a love for the beautiful and for *virtù* which made possible the creation of works of art that fulfilled the Renaissance ideal.

Art. Among the great painters, the Venetian school, which had begun late to flourish, preserved longest the tradition of the earlier masters. Elsewhere, craftsmanship rather than genius marked the work of the leading artists. A younger generation of artists showed less youthful exuberance, less passion. They displayed a primary interest in form; and, in developing further the later, disintegrating trends of the Renaissance, they arrived at an emphasis upon conventionality and ornamentation. One lonely towering figure stands out: El Greco (d. 1575), who lived in Spain. His sense of the tragic is expressed in his beautiful, somber, deeply emotional canvases.

Music. In music, too, a different spirit became noticeable. The fresh and vigorous, though often vulgar and popularizing, trends of the early century gave way to greater delicacy and refinement. Under pressure from the Council of Trent (which had set aside a special session for the discussion of music) the influence of pagan morals, the imitation of classical models, and the emphasis on worldly, sensual, bodily features were, as in other arts, condemned. The Tridentine fathers demanded, instead, a purification of music along the lines of Christian tradition, accentuating severity and restraint. Soon there emerged one of the most outstanding composers, the Italian Palestrina (d. 1594), who had studied under Renaissance Netherland masters. He fulfilled the demands of the Council, yet preserved and furthered the stylistic innovations of his predecessors, their polyphonic style and counterpoint. The earnestness, clarity, and tonal purity of his motets and masses were cherished by popes and art patrons alike. Palestrina, his contemporary Orlando di Lasso, and a school of their followers have ever since been regarded as pre-eminent forces in the development of early modern music.

Simultaneously, secular music was cultivated both in Protestant and in Catholic countries. The Netherlands and Germany, with their continued emphasis on harmony, lost the lead they had held previously, and Italy, "perfecting instrumental melody," came to the fore and inspired musicians in other countries. Even England, which had excelled in this art (and which, with masters like William Byrd, continued to create independent works of remarkable beauty), was influenced increasingly by Italian music. New or improved instruments, such as the harpsichord and the violin, appeared, and many compositions were written for instruments instead of for voice alone. Furthermore, music was written for theatrical performances, and toward the end of the sixteenth century, through a combination of music and drama, the modern opera was born.

Literature. Intellectualism, which penetrated musical compositions, became still more apparent in literature. Printed books increased in number and influence. Excellent histories were written, such as that of Philip II by Cabrera and a Universal History by De Thou. (Other histories—for example, the Ecclesiastical History of the Magdeburg Centuries and a history of the times of Charles V by Sleidanus—served propagandistic purposes in favor of religious causes.) In Spain, the novel made its appearance. Everywhere, descriptions of travel, such as the accounts collected by the Englishman Hakluyt, became popular. A growing public enjoyed poetry and drama: authors, such as the Italian Tasso (d. 1595) and the Englishmen Spenser (d. 1599) and Marlowe (d. 1593), gained merited fame in their own lifetimes. France produced two writers of lasting significance: Rabelais (d. 1553), who, with the aim of entertaining, created in his *Gargantua* a lasting mirror of human weaknesses, full of fantasy and humor; and Montaigne (d. 1592), a sensitive, philosophical man of genius, who was strongly affected by the skepticism of his age and who, in a spirit of unaccustomed detachment, wrote the *Essays*, in which he analyzed human nature so well that this work has served ever since as a guide to everyday living. But the two most notable writers of this period were the Spaniard Cervantes (d. 1616), who wrote *Don Quixote*, and the English dramatist and poet Shakespeare (d. 1616). They probed the depths of human nature and aspirations, and they left in their works of lasting beauty an ever-meaningful heritage for posterity.

Science. In science, a basis for rapid advances had been laid by the Renaissance masters through their exact and imaginative approach, their sober observations, and their numerous careful descriptions of nature. In the latter part of the century, the Dane Tycho Brahe (d. 1601) was "mapping the sky," and the fundamental work of Copernicus was carried further by Galileo (d. 1642), who (after perfecting the telescope and making scrupulous observations which led to numerous discoveries) confirmed Copernicus' findings. Galileo realized the importance of insight and imagination, so long as they did not lead to "postulating in advance." He did not hesitate to propose hypotheses, but he based them on mathematical thought and then checked results experimentally. He thus found and described the law of falling bodies and the motion of the pendulum, and he enunciated the principle of inertia. Equally stimulating was the work of the English statesman Francis Bacon (d. 1626). Although, in his search for a scientific method, he overemphasized experimentation and observation, and although he lacked necessary mathematical knowledge, he prepared the way for future scientific endeavors by advocating an "inductive method of reasoning" and by insisting, like Galileo, on the necessity of doubting traditional concepts and values. Advances paralleling those in astronomy and physics were made in other subjects. Gilbert of Colchester (d. 1603) made important discoveries in magnetism. In botany and zoology, detailed new and advanced descriptions of plants and animals were published—even though much fanciful information still marked such scientific literature.

Geography. Progress in geography was aided particularly by the achievements of the preceding half-century. Maps drawn in the second half of the sixteenth century (for example, those of the German map maker Mercator) showed—after more than a thousand years of comparative stagnation in this craft—remarkable perfection. They profited from the theoretical advance in science which made possible mathematical projection, and from the practical experience gained through explorations and discoveries, replacing the numerous superstitions inherited from ancient and medieval times. The new maps facilitated and thus further stimulated explorations. Although no important new seaways were discovered, distant lands were explored; large areas in America, Russia, and even Japan were made known to the Western world. Products such as coffee, which Venice began to import on a large scale, or the potato, which was first planted in 1584, became popular among Europeans. Much of the work of discovery was undertaken by merchants. The traditionally conservative groups—the Hanseatic and Venetian traders—were pushed more and more into the background by enterprising Portuguese, Dutch, English, and Scotch merchants, whose daring undertakings were backed by well-organized, powerful, and rich joint-stock companies; and the travelers came home not only with profits, but also with intriguing accounts of the foreign lands they had visited.

Religion. As man turned his attention increasingly to exploration of the world around him, he lost some of his interest in questions of dogma. No theological works appeared in the second half of the sixteenth century that could compare in importance with those of the first half. Religious passions, however, remained strong, with bitter consequences upon the lives of nations. The Inquisition lost much of its terror, especially after the outbreak of the War of Independence of the Netherlands, but the number of civil wars increased. Catholicism recovered and regained strength in many lands. By 1600 in Poland, Austria, parts of southern and western Germany, the southern Netherlands, and France, the large Protestant minorities had been reduced; in Spain, Portugal, and Italy, Protestant groups had been crushed; in Protestant northern Germany, in England, and in Scandinavia, Catholicism had made inroads; and, despite political changes in England, Ireland had remained faithful to Rome. Moreover, Catholic refugees from England and other Protestant countries founded colleges abroad as rallying points for their persecuted compatriot coreligionists. Much of this religious situation was due to the more rapid adjustment of the Catholics to the rational trends of the age, whereas the Protestants, often cherishing a mystical faith, adhered to the letter of the Scriptures.

CHAPTER VII

THE EMERGENCE OF THE MODERN STATE SYSTEM (1603–1648)

THE SEVENTEENTH CENTURY saw the development of trends which were to culminate during the eighteenth century in the so-called "Age of Reason." The passions and religious fervor of the preceding century were overshadowed by increasingly rational attitudes toward life. Even the seventeenth-century "religious" wars, which witnessed strange alliances between opposing creeds, reflect new political concepts rather than a concern about dogma and faith. New power relationships emerged; new aims, differing from those of the Renaissance and evincing heightened national feelings, were pursued; and a new type of diplomacy, one that was to endure until the twentieth century, was developed.

THE INTERNATIONAL SCENE

Two factors stand out in the political history of the seventeenth century: the rise of France in Europe, and the rise of England in overseas territories. The chief loser was the House of Hapsburg, both in Spain and in the Empire. The position of superior power which Spain had held in the period following the discovery of America had actually rested on shaky foundations, for the maintenance of that position had overtaxed the material and spiritual resources of the country. Similarly, in the Empire the Hapsburgs lacked both the military and the economic bases for the preservation of imperial authority, whereas France and England could build or structures adapted to the modern world that was emerging from the Renaissance. Furthermore, there was a third area of wide political importance—its role indistinct, to be sure, during the seventeenth century but already marked by signs of future greatness. This area comprised the colonial territories in America, to which European civilization was transplanted.

EXPANSION OF EUROPE

The drive of the Modern Age of Western civilization, expressed in Europe's world-wide undertakings, is without parallel in any other civilization. One of the most significant phenomena in the history of modern times is this process of "Europeanization" of the globe. The principal elements of European culture (religions, law concepts, political thought, languages, industrial techniques, customs and manners—the entire classical and medieval heritage) gradually spread everywhere. To be sure, European colonies and Eastern civilizations also made substantial contributions to the life of Europe; but very much greater were the contributions Europe made to them.

Settlement of America. Settlement of the American continent was the most important phase of European expansion. The settlers came principally from three centers: Spain, France, and England. During the seventeenth century, Spain tried both to consolidate and to extend its holdings, while France and England, joined by Holland, Sweden, and Denmark, not only established themselves in the northern parts of the continent, but also began to seize some of the Spanish possessions.

SPANISH AMERICA. Under Charles and Philip II, Spain had worked out an administrative system for her colonies, and she did little to change it. Her policy was conservative. Government in America remained in the hands of viceroys who were responsible to the home government. The *encomienda* system was also preserved. With the gradual exhaustion of the easily accessible mining resources, increasing attention was paid to the agricultural wealth and opportunities of the New World. Spanish colonization was greatly aided by the Catholic Church, which enlarged its missionary activities and helped to expand Spanish rule to the American hinterland. In Mexico and Peru, in the La Plata region and in Portuguese Brazil, and in Colombia and Paraguay, Dominicans, Franciscans, and, especially, Jesuits dominated in cultural and, sometimes, in political affairs. They adapted themselves to new surroundings, allied themselves with native ruling groups, and undertook programs of education which gave them influence over the children and thereby opened the gates to the influx of European institutions and customs. They interested themselves in the economic welfare of the natives; they tried to protect the weak against exploitation; in Paraguay they went so far as to encourage communistic institutions. Of course, the civilization which they introduced was indirectly beneficial to the home countries, which gained a large labor force and with its help could exploit the natural resources of the colonies.

FRENCH AMERICA. In American territory claimed by France, European culture was less pervasive than it was in the Spanish areas. French colonizing centered in Canada, where it began around 1611, a region sparsely populated and lacking readily available natural resources (except furs and timber). Consequently, compared with Spain, France showed much less interest in America. Emigration from France to the New World was negligible, nor did the French organize any nationally important trading companies in their colonies. As a result, political and social conditions developed that differed markedly from those in Spanish America. The home government did not set up any elaborate administration, and it did not maintain close relations with the colonists and natives. Both groups were equally subject to the laws. In Canada, the precepts and influences of Catholic Orders were dominant.

ENGLISH AMERICA. England proved to be more active than either Spain or France. Her colonies in North America, which for a time had to compete with Swedish and Dutch settlements, were largely occupied by Protestants; and at an early date the English colonies set a pattern that differed sharply from the ones set by the French and the Spanish. The English settled in Virginia, beginning with the Jamestown colony in 1607. Eventually, despite severe hardships and early political difficulties, they succeeded in establishing prosperous agricultural enterprises. Virginian wealth came to be based largely upon the production of tobacco, for which the English, following the Spanish example, found it advantageous to make use of Negro slaves. A trading company in England, the Virginia Company, was granted proprietary rights, but the actual administration of affairs was quickly taken over by a local representative assembly of the settlers. In 1620, another colony, still more independent of the home country (owing to dissenting religious beliefs), was founded

in Massachusetts by Puritan émigrés. In accordance with the Mayflower Compact—an agreement entered into by passengers during
the journey to America—in this colony, too, a representative assembly of all freemen held the reins of government. In New England,
during the early period of settlement, the problem of survival was
even more difficult than it had been in Virginia, for the settlers had
to face similar disadvantages of climate and soil and, in addition,
continuous internal dissension and the hostility of the native Indians.
The success of the colonists must be attributed to their habits of
hard work, their united defense (often brutal) against the natives,
and their conviction as to the righteousness and eventual victory of
their cause. During the 1630's immigration to the New England
colonies assumed substantial dimensions, and, in 1634, an English
colony was founded in Maryland.

   Expansion into Asia. The seventeenth-century establishment of
European dominance in America was not at all matched by comparable expansion into Asia. The Europeans established themselves
in numerous ports and some inland trading places and entered into
lucrative commercial relations. But no territories could be occupied
as in America, no populations could be subjugated and their resources exploited. Nor could the Europeans permanently introduce
Western religious beliefs and social patterns, nor settle in the already
populous regions of southeastern and eastern Asia. To be sure, in
the sixteenth century, Loyola's colleague, the Jesuit Francis Xavier,
had spread the Catholic faith in southeast Asia. Early in the seventeenth century, Catholics in Japan may have numbered half a
million, and even in China converts had been made. But, in the
East, owing to the vigor of the old indigenous civilizations and to
the strength of their economic, social, and religious institutions, the
process of Europeanization (already rendered difficult by strife
among the Europeans themselves) was retarded. Of little effect
were the contributions of missionaries, traders, and soldiers, and
even this limited influence was restricted chiefly to southern Asia
and failed to leave important traces in China and Japan.

EUROPE'S POLITICAL SCENE

   It was during the seventeenth century that European expansion,
especially in lands across the Atlantic, produced those changes in
the political power constellation of Europe which had been fore-

shadowed in the age of discovery. The nations which had been the first to explore and settle the New World—Spain and Portugal— were, however, not the ones to benefit permanently from their achievements. Whether for reasons of geographical location and climate or for reasons of individual ability and spirit of enterprise, it was not the Latin countries in the south of Europe but the seafaring nations in the Germanic North which reaped the fruits of colonization. Germany herself did not share in this development, nor did the Slavic East of Europe which, far removed from the Atlantic sea lanes, continued along its own independent cultural path.

Decline of Spain and Portugal. The death of Philip II in 1598 marked a decisive turn in Spain's role. To be sure, literature, music, and the arts continued to flourish, and the country entered what has become known as its "Golden Age." But economic conditions deteriorated. The administration of the colonies became increasingly costly and the wealth of the colonies was squandered for luxuries and for prestige. Ever more desperate efforts had to be made, especially in the struggle with England, to keep the sea lanes open. Prices continued to rise; initiative was lacking; and emigration and wars checked population growth. In fearful persecutions, the remnants of the Moorish and Jewish populations were eliminated. The army decayed, and under incapable kings the bureaucracy failed to function satisfactorily. In 1640, Portugal again made herself independent of Spain, but by then she herself was engulfed in the general economic and political decline. And when, by the middle of the century, the income from the East and from the New World began to dwindle (partly because of the exhaustion of the great silver mines worked since 1545) the shift in power from the Iberian domains of the Hapsburgs to the lands of rival dynasties in the North became evident.

The German Empire. The possessions of the Austrian Hapsburgs, and with them the whole German Empire, underwent a similar decline, but for different reasons. Germany suffered from political fragmentation and lack of central authority; from a decrease of trade in the Mediterranean area and therewith of the commerce across the Alps which fed the great South German centers; from lack of harbors needed in order to develop transatlantic trade; and from conservatism, both of the South German bankers and of the North German merchants of the once powerful Hanse.

Men of genius became a rarity in the intellectual as well as the political, religious, and business spheres. Moreover, the Peace of Augsburg was often violated; the balance of strength continued to shift with the growth of Lutheranism in some regions, the strength of the Counter Reformation in others; and foreign powers—England, Spain, and France—saw opportunities to further their political objectives by interfering in German affairs and helping now one side and now the other.

THIRTY YEARS' WAR (1618–1648). As a result, a terrible civil war broke out in 1618. It began as a religious war between Catholics and Protestants when, during negotiations, Emperor Ferdinand II's ambassadors to Bohemia were hurled out of a window in Prague ("defenestration"). This affair quickly involved foreign nations, for the Bohemians promptly deposed Ferdinand as their king and replaced him with a Protestant, the Elector Frederick of the Palatinate, who was a relative of the English king. Frederick suffered a major defeat in 1620. Shortly thereafter, although Protestant Denmark came to his aid, the imperial and Catholic forces again proved their superiority. Under the leadership of the great generals Wallenstein and Tilly, the imperial armies forced the Danes and their Protestant allies to retreat, and (in 1629) the first two (Bohemian and Danish) phases of the war ended. Ferdinand regained the crown of Bohemia and in the same year promulgated an Edict of Restitution which cost the Protestants all the church lands secularized by them since 1555. In fact, it appeared that the war would end with the triumph of the Catholics until, fearful of this eventuality, the foes of the Hapsburgs combined their efforts. They found a capable standard-bearer in Gustavus Adolphus, king of Sweden, devout Protestant, wise and generous statesman, and a leader shrewdly aware of Sweden's interests. Soon after his accession to the throne, he had entered the long struggle for Baltic hegemony and had proved his generalship by conquering the Polish possessions in Livonia. He now saw a chance to help Lutheran brethren and simultaneously complete his domination of Baltic shipping by conquering Germany's Baltic coast. As these aims implied war on the Hapsburgs, he obtained subsidies from Catholic France, whereupon a third (the Swedish) phase of the war began. At the head of a splendid army—well equipped with artillery—he pushed deep into the heart of the Empire. In his plight, the emperor had to recall Wallenstein, whom he had ungratefully dismissed. In

1632, a decisive battle was fought at Lützen in Saxony. Wallenstein was defeated, and Protestantism was saved. But Gustavus Adolphus was killed. Without him, the Swedes were reluctant to continue the war, and Wallenstein's star commenced to rise again. But when he began secret preparations for making himself ruler of a centralized German national state, he was murdered (in 1634)—a turn of events which the emperor did not regret. In 1635 Ferdinand consented to a compromise peace, which was concluded in Prague. But, since Hapsburg power was not yet broken, the French stirred up the Swedes anew; moreover, they persuaded the Dutch to attack the Spanish Netherlands, induced the state of Savoy to seize the Hapsburg possessions in Italy, and themselves put troops of their own into the field. Thus, the devastating war continued during a fourth period, which lasted another thirteen years.

PEACE OF WESTPHALIA (1648). Peace was concluded in 1648 at Münster and Osnabrück, two towns in Westphalia. The Empire survived and Hapsburg influence remained an important factor in European affairs. But imperial authority was greatly reduced, the central administration of the German Empire was further weakened, and its more than three hundred component states were accorded almost complete independence. Some of the individual states, such as Brandenburg and Saxony, gained territory and achieved status as European powers. The independence of Switzerland and of Holland was recognized. Calvinists gained equal rights with Catholics and Lutherans. The claim of France to the western territories of the Empire in Lorraine, which she had annexed, was confirmed, and so, too, was the claim of Sweden to the northern provinces along the Baltic Sea and the mouths of Germany's rivers. The real winners of the war were France (who reached the peak of her power in Europe) and Sweden. Germany was devastated—even if not so fearfully as has often been asserted. Still, in some regions the population had declined by a third or more. Towns and villages had to be rebuilt, agriculture had to be re-established, and the intellectual centers had to be revived.[1]

Despite long negotiations and its numerous provisions, the Peace of Westphalia did not bring many changes. Yet, it marks one of the most significant moments in the history of Western civilization

---

[1] The Peace of Westphalia was supplemented by two additional treaties: one between France and Spain (the Peace of the Pyrenees, 1659), and another among Sweden, Poland, and Brandenburg (the Peace of Oliva, 1660).

because it confirmed, and in a sense codified, the changes that had taken place in the political system of Europe. The aspirations toward international organization represented by the "Holy Roman Empire" were not revived; the "national state," exemplified by France, triumphed, and future interrelationships in Europe had to be based on the fact that in the diplomacy of the several countries religious considerations would be subordinated to those of national self-interest. During the Westphalian peace negotiations, new procedures and methods of diplomacy were actually worked out which were to persist for almost two centuries.

Russia. While Hapsburg power and the role of central Europe were on the decline, the countries on the flanks of the Continent were gaining strength and prestige. Russia emerged from a struggle with Poland to become the leading power in the East. At the beginning of the century, she had gone through a disastrous period of social revolution, political disintegration, dynastic rivalry, and external war (the "Times of Trouble," 1605-13). Out of it emerged a new autocratic regime and a new dynasty, the Romanovs, and only with their election in 1613 was internal peace restored. The Romanovs ruled with the help of a new "service nobility" which, through their holdings of land and serfs, controlled the wealth of the country and which, simultaneously, formed the backbone of the administration. The reorganization was achieved at the expense of the old, independent nobility, which was rendered powerless; of the peasantry, which was reduced to complete serfdom; and, eventually, of the Church, which was brought under tsarist control. A new law code was published in 1649. Of greatest importance was the fact that the Ukraine, largely inhabited by Cossacks, was conquered. Thus Russia expanded westward; closer contacts with Western nations were established; and the balance of power between Russia and Poland was permanently changed in favor of Russia. Immigration, especially that of the Germans, English, and Dutch, was encouraged; and European techniques, knowledge, artisanship, and luxury goods increasingly infiltrated the country.

The Netherlands. The increase of power of the large nation on the eastern flank of Europe was matched by a corresponding, if not greater, rise of western Europe. In the West, economic rather than military power formed the basis for growth and preponderance. Hence, a small country, such as Holland, was enabled to become a great power. When, during the wars for independence, Antwerp had been ruined, Amsterdam had become the financial center of the Western nations. The advantages gained by the Dutch owing to this shift were augmented by a policy of tolerance. Refugees from various lands—including Jews, and especially those from Spanish dominions—were readily accepted and they helped to establish many-sided trading connections. Owing to their industry and skills, the immigrants contributed to Holland's economic prosperity. The government was run by the wealthy burghers, who kept taxation low; agriculture, fishing, the textile industries, shipbuilding, and transportation flourished. There was a high level of cultural activity. Thus, Holland became a center of the expanding book trade; new universities were founded; scholars and artists could do their work in an atmosphere of comparative freedom and tolerance.

England. In the Netherlands, despite continued opposition of various groups to the landholding nobility, the assumption of political power by the wealthy bourgeoisie and the subordination of military to economic objectives took place without grave internal crises. But the necessary adjustments in the other great maritime nation of the North, in England, encountered much greater difficulties.

THE STUARTS. After the loss of her Continental possessions, England had become an insular power, and this brought unexpected security. Nationalistic expansion was no longer directed toward European lands, but toward overseas colonies. But internal tensions developed. Elizabeth, who had refused to marry, was succeeded in 1603 by James I of the House of Stuart. Under this ruler and his successor Charles I, the controversial issues about the condition and control of the Church and the immunities and rights of Parliament, all of which had been deferred during the reign of Elizabeth, were reopened. These issues were complicated by various factors: inflation, the increased costs of government, the heavy expenditures incurred by English diplomacy as carried on since Elizabeth, and the wasteful factions of the Stuart court. To meet this critical situation, the kings were compelled to increase taxes and customs duties, sell administrative offices, and pursue financial policies repugnant to a Parliament which desired, above all else, to maintain economic stability and prosperity. As parliamentary opposition grew, the kings became more and more arbitrary, further increasing the general dissatisfaction. Soon, every powerful group in the country was antagonized—including even some of the landholding nobility, for whom the Stuarts seemed to have special sympathy. Eventually, the opposition, though divided as to ultimate aims, was united in its desire to limit the power of the Crown and to participate in policy-making. The ensuing deadlock was reinforced by the friendly attitude of the Stuarts toward Catholicism and by their pro-Spanish point of view which impeded the realization of English nationalistic and mercantile aims.

REVOLUTION. The widespread discontent, which was intensified by the unpopularity of the advisers appointed by Charles I and by his failure in foreign affairs, induced Parliament to draw up a "Petition of Right" in 1628. This petition demanded an end to taxation without act of Parliament, to arbitrary imprisonment, to billeting of soldiers in private houses, and to martial law in time of peace. The king, though he insisted upon his "divine right," signed the petition, but in the following year he dissolved Parliament and ruled without it for eleven years during which the country prospered. However, opposition to royal absolutism again developed when the king, who was in dire need of new funds in order to combat piracy in the Channel, tried to levy additional taxes. His right to do so was challenged by John Hampden, but was sustained by subservient judges. Popular passions were further aroused by the king's conciliatory policies toward Catholics and by the harsh treatment which he and his Archbishop Laud directed against nonconformist Puritans. This religious issue, added to the numerous other grievances, brought matters to a head. When Charles insisted on forcing the sects to accept the Anglican service, they took up arms in rebellion. Then the king had to summon Parliament (in 1640) in order to recruit troops. Once reassembled, Parliament presented certain demands, namely, that the king must not be allowed to dissolve it at will, that meetings must be held regularly, and that all special jurisdiction claimed by the kings since Tudor times must be relinquished. Parliament insisted that it must control all income and eventually ordered the arrest and execution of some of the king's closest advisers, including Archbishop Laud.

CIVIL WAR. These demands and actions failed to solve the problem, for Parliament itself was divided. One party was sympathetic to royal absolutism; another favored the interests of the rich entrepreneurs; another supported a more popular point of view; and there were still other groups, including the so-called "Levelers," who espoused communistic principles. In addition, Parliament was split by the religious issue; Anglicans, Calvinists, and Catholics disagreed about religious tolerance and state control over the Church. The various economic and religious groups kept shifting their positions and loyalties in accordance with swiftly changing political circumstances. Thus, no clear alignment of sides had been established when, in 1641, a revolution broke out in Ireland over the question of settling Protestants in northern Ireland (Ulster); and in 1642, the king himself, believing that the time to re-establish his own authority had arrived, took up arms against Parliament. Civil war began. Twice beaten in battle, Charles I fled to Scotland, but was extradited and handed over to Parliament. Even at this point, taking advantage of the divisions within Parliament, he was able to defy the opposition until a determined Puritan minority under Oliver Cromwell organized a stanch and fanatical army which defeated the royal forces. The Puritans then reassembled the legislature as a "Rump" Parliament (purged of all members unsympathetic to their cause) which brought the king to trial. In 1649, having been adjudged guilty of treason, Charles was executed. Under Cromwell's leadership, the Rump Parliament set up a new government.

France. While civil war prevented the establishment of royal absolutism in England, in France absolutism reached its peak of development. Intelligent rulers, such as Henry IV (assassinated in 1610) and a long succession of unusually able ministers, who supported royal power, contributed to its success.

Sully. The first of the great ministers was Sully (fl. 1600–1610), an intelligent, honest, and efficient Calvinist in the service of Henry IV. Under his guidance, a great deal was accomplished to repair the damage sustained from a half-century of civil war. Brigandage was suppressed, most of the dissolute army units were disbanded, and peace was maintained both within the country and in foreign affairs. The privileges of the nobility were severely restricted, and officials from among the bourgeoisie were appointed. The treasury was restored to a healthy condition by measures such as the farming out of tax collections.[2] The new system of tax collection, providing the treasury with a low but certain income, was used mainly to collect the *taille* (a property tax levied upon all landowners outside the ranks of the nobility). Sully put a stop to tax abuses, especially the

---

[2] "Farming out" meant that the right to collect certain taxes was sold to the highest bidder, who paid an agreed sum into the treasury and kept for himself what he was able to collect in taxes.

imposition of illegal taxes, and he made certain that the royal domain was managed on a profitable basis.

ABSOLUTISM AND MERCANTILISM. As there was widespread satisfaction with a system that had re-established security and order, there was no need for action by the Estates-General, representing the people. The king and his first minister made all decisions. In economic affairs they adopted mercantilist policies with a principal aim of increasing production. They facilitated trade by building roads, canals, and bridges, clearing land, and draining marshes. By means of subsidies and granting of monopolies, they aided old-established industries (e.g., paper and textiles) as well as new industries (e.g., silk manufacturing). They sent explorers out to lay claim to new colonies, especially in Canada, and enacted new navigation laws to prevent ships owned by foreigners from transporting goods to French possessions. In foreign affairs, they adhered to a traditional anti-Hapsburg policy, but avoided war.

RICHELIEU. The same policies which had been formulated by the dour Calvinist Sully were pursued by the luxury-loving Catholic, Cardinal Richelieu, who in 1624 became chief minister under Louis XIII, the son of Henry IV. Richelieu, who was a learned man with wide cultural interests, possessed an iron will, vast ambition, and a realistic understanding of politics. He put an end to the political irresponsibility and wasteful practices which had marked the period following the death of Henry IV and sought to strengthen the rights of the Crown. He refused to convene the Estates-General, which had feebly attempted to regain its authority; he deprived the nobility of most of its remaining powers, ordered the royal forces to seize its strongholds and execute some of its leaders, and, by means of hard-fought military campaigns, forced the Huguenots to sur render their fortified towns which had been stipulated as inviolate by the Edict of Nantes. The cardinal did not, however, destroy their religious freedom, for he was interested only in political matters. In fact, Protestant forces were Richelieu's chief allies against the Haps-burgs during the Thirty Years' War. Reforms were introduced in the army and the navy, enabling them to provide adequate protection for the colonies. As in Sully's time, most of the government officials were recruited from the middle class. Provincial administrators (intendants), judges, and other high officials constituted a new social group, the *noblesse de la robe,* which remained the politically most influential segment of the population until the Revolution of 1789. All of Richelieu's measures were designed to maintain French prestige abroad and Bourbon absolutism at home. When Richelieu died (1642), France was, indeed, on the road to supreme power in Europe. His very able successor, Cardinal Mazarin (d. 1661), who resembled Richelieu in being vain, greedy, ambitious, and shrewd, was just the man to preserve what Richelieu had built and to add to it. Mazarin's career ushered in the "Age of Louis XIV."

PHILOSOPHY AND ARTS

The Peace of Westphalia, terminating the intense religious and political conflicts engendered by the Reformation, laid the legal basis for the modern European state system. At about the same time, the works of the great thinkers on the Continent determined the future direction of Western intellectual endeavors. More and more, Europeans were devoting themselves to scientific investigations of nature, and this had a profound impact on their philosophy. Thus both in the political and in the intellectual sphere, the mid-seventeenth century is correctly regarded as a dividing line between two major periods in the history of Western civilization.

Science and Philosophy. Among the scientists and philosophers representing the new spirit of inquiry which was to modify Western culture for centuries, three men stand out: Kepler (d. 1630) who, even though he devoted much attention to problems of medieval scholarship and to astrology and other pseudo sciences, made one of the greatest contributions to an understanding of nature in formulating his famous three laws ("Kepler's laws") which accurately described the motion of the planets; Galileo (d. 1642), who continued the work in physics and astronomy which he had started in the previous century; and Descartes (d. 1650), the mathematician and philosopher who became the foremost progenitor of the "Age of Reason." Descartes occupied himself with an investigation of man's ability "to know." He postulated the "self-evident" fact: *Cogito, ergo sum* (I think, therefore I am) and from this fact proceeded rationally and logically to draw conclusions. To him God appeared as the "First Cause," and mechanistic laws ruled in nature. This view of a cause-and-effect relationship in the universe led him to postulate a dualistic reality—a dualism of mind and matter. It is noteworthy that Descartes also developed the principles of analytical geometry and contributed to other sciences, such as optics.

The work of seventeenth-century cosmologists and philosophers was greatly aided by new developments in mathematics, anatomy, and physiology, and even social sciences such as law. Contributions to mathematics included the invention of logarithms by the Scotsman Napier in 1614. In anatomy, a notable contributor was the Englishman William Harvey (d. 1657), who correctly described the system of blood circulation and thus paved the way for the development of modern physiology. In law, the scientific trend inspired the Dutchman Hugo Grotius (d. 1645) to formulate proposals for a body of international law relating particularly to war and peace.

Education. Progress in science was closely connected with improved standards in education. New universities were founded in both Catholic and Protestant countries—e.g., in Catholic South America and in the Protestant Netherlands. A first college (Harvard, 1636) was established in North America. Among the leaders in the advancement of education during the sixteenth and seventeenth centuries were the Jesuit colleges which had originally been designed to expound the decisions of the Council of Trent, to further the Counter Reformation, and to purge the schools of secular Renaissance influences and of immoral authors. Soon the influence of the Jesuit colleges spread widely, as they helped to improve the training of the clergy so that the priests would not only deliver better sermons but also more conscientiously fulfill their other religious tasks. They promoted humanitarian activities within their own institutions and throughout the community. Francis de Sales and, especially, Vincent de Paul were among those influenced by their work who earned lasting fame caring for the sick and the aged and building charitable institutions. The Jesuit colleges became important centers of all types of learning, successfully applying new pedagogical principles and particularly encouraging the accumulation of facts in many fields of knowledge.

Literature. In literature, the towering figure of Shakespeare still dominated in the first decade of the seventeenth century. He was followed by important, though less universally influential, poets such as John Donne (d. 1631) and Ben Jonson (d. 1637). While Donne's lyrics show great originality and warmth of feeling, Jonson's comedies evince less of the passion which marked the age of the High Renaissance and display more of the moderate, rational, and reflective style of the baroque period. The latter is also true about the works of the famous writers in Spain's "Golden Age"—

the dramatists Lope de Vega (d. 1635) and Calderon (d. 1681). While their works reflect a certain spiritual fervor such as the preceding century had shown, they, too, evince rational tendencies, stylistic restraint, and a strong emphasis on form.

Art. In painting, sculpture, and architecture, the first half of the seventeenth century saw the baroque style come into full bloom. As in the case of other major movements in art history, the baroque movement (1600–1750) passed through several stages of development. Many of the qualities associated with the term "baroque"— in particular, the general conception about its theatricality, over-ornamentation, sentimentality, and bombast—are derived from its later evolution. Yet, these characteristics with their appeal to the senses do not constitute the only, or even the most important, element of the baroque style. Like all art of the seventeenth century it was also marked by dynamism, by orderliness despite exuberance, by an assertion of life and faith, and by a mastery of form which has given it permanent value. A certain balance and harmony prevailed which, while providing a needed reaction to the extreme individualism of the High Renaissance, emphasized intellectual strength and connected the art of the seventeenth century with the rational tendencies of the age. Spain produced perhaps the greatest master of the baroque, the painter Velasquez (d. 1660). The baroque style was introduced in the North by the Flemish painter Rubens (d. 1640) and his school, who, even though they adhered to some traditional attitudes, opposed the Puritan trends of Calvinism and post-Trent Catholicism. Rubens was followed, though, by a new, more serene school of painting, including his pupil, the famous portrait painter Vandyke (d. 1641).

Music. The baroque style developed in the art became equally evident in the music of the seventeenth century. To some extent the free inventiveness of the preceding period was diminished, with less emphasis on content and more on form; the structure of music had to correspond to an elaborate system and possess a balance such as the taste of the time demanded. Even "ornamentation became stylized." The polyphonic style receded; in what was termed "The New Music" (after an Italian composition published in 1602) "monody," i.e., monophonic music, prevailed. Instrumental music, owing much of its inspiration to the songs of the sixteenth century, became popular. The sonata form was created. Italian opera made further progress and spread to the northern countries of Europe. In Germany, Protestant Church music flourished, with its beautiful choral preludes and other compositions, especially those written for the organ. The two outstanding masters of the period were Monteverdi (d. 1643) in Italy and Heinrich Schütz (d. 1672) in Germany. Thus, the period which saw the terrors of the Thirty Years' War and of the civil war in England, of the Times of Trouble in Russia, and of mass expulsions in Spain was by no means devoid of beautiful and inspiring achievements.

CHAPTER VIII

THE AGE OF LOUIS XIV (1643–1715)

THE SECOND HALF of the seventeenth century was not so much a period of new dynamic events as one of consolidation and gradual evolution. In political affairs, it witnessed the continuation of absolutism in France and of an opposite trend toward a parliamentary regime in England. It brought the rise of Brandenburg and continued progress in the Westernization of Russia. It also witnessed the growth of European civilization in the centers established earlier on other continents—especially in North America. But its truly great and lasting contributions were made in philosophy, science, and art. Not for Louis XIV's political exploits nor for the economic developments of his time is the age named after him so renowned; it is famous for the achievements of great philosophers, writers, and scientists. Their rational approach to life and to nature brought to maturity the ideological trends which had been growing in Europe ever since the views of the Nominalists had prevailed over those of the Realists during the late Middle Ages. The characteristics of the baroque, particularly its intellectuality and harmony, pervaded the cultural sphere; and since these characteristics developed most fully in France and spread from the example France set, they provided justification for naming the period the Age of Louis XIV.

THE POLITICAL SCENE

The Peace of Westphalia had signified open acknowledgment by European powers of what had long been a fact, namely, that the supreme position of emperor of the "Holy Roman Empire of the

German Nation" no longer commanded wide respect and had become essentially a shadowy honor devoid of practical significance. Even the etiquette of diplomacy was revised in accordance with the actual distribution of power; special consideration was accorded not only to France but also to newly emergent nations such as Sweden and England.

France. When he came to the throne one year after Richelieu's death, Louis XIV was but five years old. He was ten at the conclusion of the Peace of Westphalia, twenty-three when he took the reins of government into his own hands, and almost seventy-seven when he died. Even if it had not been for the strength of his personality, such a long term as a ruler—the longest of any monarch in European history—could not have failed to leave a deep imprint, especially since he ruled during an age of "absolutism."

MAZARIN. During the first eighteen years of Louis XIV's reign, the direction of French affairs was entrusted to Cardinal Mazarin. It was Mazarin who concluded the Peace of Westphalia (1648) whereby France was raised to the first place in Europe. It was also he who sealed the fate of the nobility. Seeking to profit from the financial straits in which the young king found himself, the nobility staged, in 1648, a rebellion, the so-called "Fronde." This revolt was abetted by the highest law court, the Parlement of Paris, which was subservient to the nobility's interests. The Parlement demanded for itself the rights to control taxation, to appoint *intendants* (provincial governors), and to supervise legislation. This last right it could exercise by refusing to "register" any laws which it considered contrary to custom or infringing upon existing privileges. Had it succeeded, a development toward parliamentary government would have been unavoidable, although—owing to the composition and the policies of the Parlement—the traditional privileged classes would have gained more than the commercial interests. But Mazarin energetically opposed the Parlement and bloodily suppressed the Fronde. Simultaneously, he lent his hand, for the sake of unity, to the reduction of a puritanical movement within the Catholic Church, known as "Jansenism." This movement had had considerable influence on education, had tended, though Catholic, in the direction of Calvinism, and was bitterly opposed by the Jesuits. When Mazarin died in 1661 and Louis XIV took personal control, the concentration of power in the hands of the king was such that a challenge had become impossible.

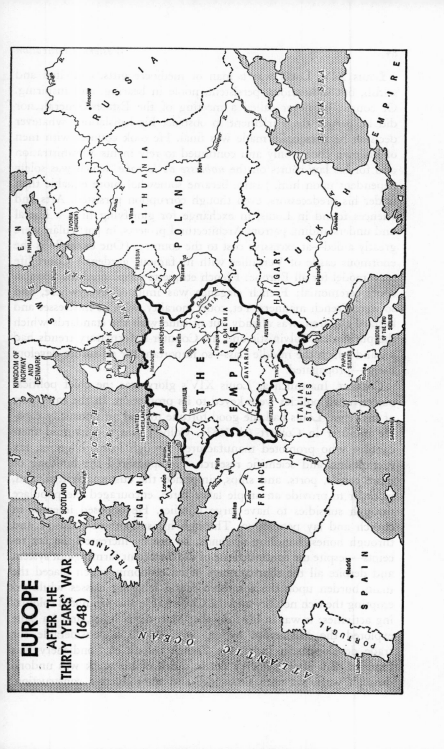

EUROPE
AFTER THE
THIRTY YEARS' WAR
(1648)

Louis XIV. Louis was a man of mediocre gifts, conceited and selfish, but industrious, persistent, noble in bearing, and inspiring. Of course, he never called a meeting of the Estates-General, nor did he permit the Parlement to obstruct his legislation; whatever decision he personally made was final. He took counsel with men of his own choice only and continued to rely in his administration and for his law courts on the *noblesse de la robe,* which was solely dependent upon him. Justice became somewhat more equable than under his predecessors, even though corruption persisted. Arts and sciences found in Louis, in exchange for glorifying him, a liberal and understanding patron. Architectural projects, in particular, were greatly aided—at excessive cost to the country. (One example is the enormous castle of Versailles with its famous gardens.) Court life set a model for all Europe: French etiquette supplanted the Spanish court ceremonial; French elegance was imitated everywhere, and so were French manners. Yet, court morality, with its mistresses and bastard children, was already out of tune with the standards which the puritanical Calvinistic and the Counter-Reformatory trends had set and which the middle class—so important for all future developments—propagated.

COLBERT. Inasmuch as Louis XIV's glory was the chief political objective, all policies were keyed to its promotion. In the early part of his reign, Louis had the good fortune to find an unusually capable minister in Colbert (d. 1683). Colbert was a convinced mercantilist who promoted manufactures through loans, bounties, tax exemptions, and scientific research. He sponsored the building of more canals, ports, and ships, simplified the customs system, and, in order to provide an ample labor force, encouraged the populace through subsidies to have large families. He opposed idleness in church and lay population. Through his support of industry and through honest handling of funds, he greatly increased the tax receipts—despite the continued use of the inefficient farming-out system and despite all the shortcomings of an economy which placed the main burden upon the commercial and laboring classes while exempting the rich nobility and the Church. He also promoted colonizing activities: it was in his time that Marquette, Joliet, and La Salle explored the Mississippi region, with which a considerable fur trade developed. In India, the French colony of Pondichéry was founded. But after Colbert's death, much of his work was undone through wars, wasteful financing, and unproductive construction.

Taxes became stifling to industry; excessive government controls discouraged merchants and industrialists; schools had to be closed; and the population began to decrease. Worst of all, motivated by his desire to eliminate any dissenting and possibly rebellious group (and thus guarantee stability under the king) and also by his religious bigotry, Louis XIV revoked the Edict of Nantes in 1685. Persuasion had long been employed in efforts to convert Huguenots to the faith of king and majority; when its success turned out to be limited, a policy of persecution was instigated. Hundreds of thousands of Huguenots were forced to emigrate—to the loss of France and the gain of the German states, Holland, England, and other countries which welcomed them.

FRENCH EXTERNAL POLICIES. Equally ruinous were Louis' foreign policies. Numerous wars were provoked merely for his personal "glory." The economic interests of the country were primary factors only in the first war (the purpose of which was to further the mercantilist policies of Colbert) and in the last war (the purpose of which was to establish overseas hegemony). All the other wars were contrary to the economic interests of France. Enormous sums were expended to build an army superior to that of Spain—an undertaking achieved owing to the outstanding ability of men such as Louvois, Vauban, and Turenne. More money went into subsidizing allies, who were also lured with promises of territory that would be seized from the Hapsburgs. The myth that the natural borders of France were the Rhine, Alps, and Pyrenees served as an excuse for a policy of ruthless French expansion into Holland, Germany, Italy, and Spain. Finally, these wars of expansion proved to be exceedingly costly. The first, the "War of Devolution," was fought for the possession of the Netherlands against a Triple Alliance of Holland, England, and Sweden. When peace was made at Aix-la-Chapelle (1668), it brought an extension of France's frontiers northward. A second war, undertaken against the Dutch, failed to bring further gains. Initial victories were followed by defeats, and the Peace of Nijmwegen (1678) constituted a draw. In the following years, subsequent to certain sham legal procedures by so-called "Chambres de Réunion," the German territory and city of Strasbourg and several Italian towns were annexed. These annexations became long-term gains; but at the time they merely served to arouse so much apprehension that in 1686 another defensive coalition against France, including nearly all the European powers, was formed. A third war, the highly destructive "War of the League of Augsburg," lasted until 1697. Then, in the Peace of Ryswick, Louis was forced to surrender some of his earlier conquests and to grant commercial advantages to the maritime nations. Shortly thereafter, the Spanish line of the Hapsburgs died out, and in an effort to prevent any future Austrian-Spanish family link and co-operation, Louis put forward the candidacy of his grandson to the throne. As a result, in 1701 a fourth war, that of the Spanish Succession, broke out. Again a "Grand Alliance" of most European powers was formed; able generals such as the Austrian Prince Eugene of Savoy and Marlborough of England defeated the French armies. Only the death of the allied (Hapsburg) candidate for the Spanish throne and French diplomatic victories at the very end of the war saved Louis from utter ruin.

PEACE OF UTRECHT (1713). Finally, in the years 1713 to 1715, peace treaties were concluded at Utrecht, Rastatt, and Baden. Austria thereby gained territories in the southern Netherlands and Italy; England secured vast colonial and commercial advantages, including rights to the lucrative slave trade (the *asiento*) in the Spanish colonies; Prussia increased her domain; and the Dutch obtained land, fortified positions, and commercial rights in areas along their southern frontier. As for France, she maintained her role as a great power, and a French prince was allowed to keep the Spanish throne—though subject to restrictions. Thus, when Louis XIV died in 1715, cursed by the population, the glory of France—even in the political arena—was still not seriously impaired.

England. French policies in the second half of the seventeenth century redounded to the nation's prestige and left a lasting impression throughout the Continent; England's attention, on the other hand, was focused on her own insular affairs. By concentrating on immediate practical tasks, the English succeeded not only in overcoming the dangers of revolution and civil war, but also in laying a firm basis for their future as a world power.

CROMWELL. Four years after the execution of Charles I, Cromwell made himself "Lord Protector." During his administration, considerable political and economic progress was made, even though Parliament had since 1648 played a role subordinate to Cromwell and the army, and new elections had not been held because Cromwell, whose backers were in the minority, could not risk them. Revolts were organized by royalists who were eager to put the decapitated king's son on the throne but were held down; by the Scotch, whom Cromwell sought to reconcile; and by the Irish who were brutally oppressed. No basis for a new, legal form of authority was developed. Yet, Cromwell proved to be a capable ruler. Merchants benefited when the enforcement of navigation acts, aimed especially at Dutch competition, stimulated British shipping. Prosperous trade, in turn, encouraged industries. Cromwell successfully defended the colonial possessions, organized new colonies, and defeated Holland and Spain—all of which helped to expand British trade. In the religious sphere, despite his strict Calvinist leanings, the Lord Protector tried to avoid trouble by means of a moderately tolerant policy.

RESTORATION. Notwithstanding its manifold successes, the Cromwell government was hated for its revolutionary origins, its absolutist trends, its Calvinistic moral standards, and its program of burdensome taxes favoring the military caste and the overseas merchants. Powerful conservative forces were especially resentful. Consequently, within two years of Cromwell's death (which occurred in 1658), Stuart royalty was re-established. Charles II was recalled from exile. But before his "restoration" he had to agree to parliamentary elections. The new Parliament restored the dominant position of the Anglican Church, proclaimed an amnesty for political opponents, and assumed supervision of the king's activities—his foreign policy, choice of advisers, purse, and military forces.

CHARLES II. The reign of Charles II was colorful. Despite disasters, such as the plague and a terrible fire that consumed large areas of London, it was marked by gaiety and artistic and literary achievements, as well as by extravagance and immorality in which king and court, imitating France, set an example. During this regime, wealthy individuals obtained more national influence. Some of the old-established feudal rights were abolished. Political parties began to take shape: the Whig, which favored representative government and middle-class commercial interests; and the Tory, which supported royal rights, the Anglican Church, and the interests of the landed nobility. Yet, both parties, despite dissensions and corruption, followed policies designed to strengthen the country as a whole.

GLORIOUS REVOLUTION (1688). The division into parties gave the king, during his last years, an opportunity to increase his influence in the government and to secure the succession of his brother, James

II. Under James, who was a Catholic, greater tolerance was shown to Catholics—even though they had been barred from public office by the Test Act of 1673 and even though intolerance toward them remained undiminished in Parliament and in the community at large. James encouraged the return of absolutist trends, and he also entered into close, economically undesirable co-operation and political alliances with Spain, France, and other Catholic nations. The English consoled themselves with the hope that, since the old king had no sons, on his demise these trends would constitute no more than a brief setback. However, the king ultimately did beget a son, giving rise to new fears about Catholic influence. In 1688, a revolt, known as the "Glorious Revolution," began; but, before blood was shed, James fled, and Mary, his Protestant daughter, and her husband William of Orange, governor of the Netherlands, were invited by Parliament to take over the reins of government. Parliament reasoned that thereby not only the Protestant cause, but also English international interests, would be served, for thus Holland would be brought into a firm alliance and could provide a bulwark against France. Yet, Parliament was careful to impose certain conditions, specified in the "Bill of Rights," to which the new rulers and their successors would have to submit. Parliament was to decide all matters of taxation, to control the army, and to supervise legislation. Free elections were to be held regularly, and a right of petition was to be guaranteed to all subjects. No excessive bail or excessive fines were to be required. No Catholic was to be king of England. Moreover, through a Toleration Act passed in 1689, Protestant dissenters gained the right to free exercise of their religion, although, like Catholics, they were still deprived of political rights and were excluded from public service.

RESULTS OF THE REVOLUTION. Absolutism was thus defeated in England, and Parliament emerged supreme. It was not a democracy that was created. Parliament suffered from traditional weaknesses, from untrained representatives, and from perpetual corruption; furthermore, only men of wealth were eligible for membership, and the government continued to be controlled by the landholding aristocracy. These men were wise enough to take the interests of the commercial classes into account so that business enterprises prospered. Neither William (d. 1702) and Mary (d. 1694), nor their successor, Queen Anne (d. 1714), attempted to interfere with the functions of Parliament as set forth in the Bill of Rights. A long-desired union with Scotland was consummated in 1707; from then on, Scottish representatives sat in the same Parliament with Englishmen.

ENGLISH FOREIGN POLICY. The direction of England's external affairs during the entire period from Cromwell until Queen Anne depended upon the maneuvers of Louis XIV; accordingly, England was forced alternately into alliances with Holland, France, or Spain. The constant instability in foreign policy was intensified by divergent interests within England. On one occasion Charles II (d. 1685) himself accepted bribes from Louis XIV. But underlying all shifts of policy, there were three steadfast aims: elimination of competition in colonization; opposition to Catholicism; and support of the weaker powers on the Continent to counterbalance the predominant powers. These aims were largely achieved. With the help of a navy greatly strengthened in Cromwell's time, the English eliminated the Dutch as serious colonial rivals and annexed their American colonies; they displaced Spain in control of the seas and seized Spanish overseas territories. England encouraged opposition to any Catholic rulers who tried to spread their religion abroad, and welcomed refugees from Catholic countries. Alliances with small nations made it possible for them to join in the resistance to Louis XIV until France had been defeated and her bid for European hegemony had been thwarted.

Holland and Spain. The rise of England paralleled the decline of the two other great maritime powers, namely, Holland and Spain. After three wars waged against them by England between 1652 and 1674, the Dutch lost their leading position in world affairs; and their merchant marine, formerly several times the size of England's, had been severely contracted. Perhaps the three factors contributing most to this decline were the continuous wars, the conservatism of the wealthy ruling merchants, and the weakness of the central government owing to political strife. In opposition to the party led by the House of Orange, and favoring unification, there was another party led by men like De Witt and favoring provincial independence. Nevertheless, Holland remained among the leaders in finance, transportation, agriculture—especially vegetable gardening and floriculture—and fishing; and she maintained her prestige in scholarship, science, and the arts. Spain, too, still excelled in literature and art, but her political and economic decline was more rapid. Poverty remained widespread, the population of the third estate increased very slowly, and the masses had no influence in the royal absolutist regime which was backed by a wasteful, ambitious landed aristocracy. Wars, both in the colonial areas and on the Continent, continued to drain the treasury and resulted only in loss of territory in the New World (especially in the Caribbean area) as well as in Europe (along the Pyrenees).

Austria. The other Hapsburg power, Austria, understood better than Spain how to adjust to changing conditions. In fact, the Austrian Hapsburgs recovered rather quickly from the consequences of the Thirty Years' War; and what they lost through the lack of German unity they made up for through an increase of their *Hausmacht*. Despite the westward shift of economic and commercial centers, they recovered a key position in European international affairs and could resume expansionist policies. When, in 1683, their most dangerous enemy, the Turks, who had regained their strength under the able leadership of the Vizier Ahmed Kuprili, once more penetrated to the gates of Vienna, the Austrians, with the help of the Polish King John III Sobieski, won a decisive victory. Subsequently, the Austrian armies under the command of Prince Eugene pushed deep into the Balkans. In the Peace of Karlowitz (1699) Austria regained long-occupied Hungary from the Turks. At home, the arts of the baroque flourished; Vienna became a foremost cultural center, excelling in music, architecture, philosophy, and court poetry. There was a great religious revival. The Austrian population increased substantially.

Brandenburg. Among the other German states, the most significant developments occurred in Brandenburg. This state, which had Berlin as its capital, was soon to become Austria's rival in a contest for leadership in Germany. Several factors contributed to its rise: its territory was greatly expanded after the Treaty of Westphalia; it was centrally located; it had an industrious population; and, in that age of absolutism, it was fortunate enough to be governed by a succession of able rulers. The most famous was Frederick William of the House of Hohenzollern, the so-called "Great Elector" (d. 1688), whose measures during his long regime made it possible for the country to recover from the devastations of war. Mercantilist policies were pursued. Subsidies, tariffs, and monopolies were arranged in order to promote industries, such as glass and textiles; land was reclaimed; new agricultural products were sponsored; and even some attempts at colonization were made. A decline in population was counteracted by the welcoming of immigrants; in particular, exiled French Huguenots were encouraged to immigrate by the Edict of Potsdam (1685) and were generously endowed with land, houses, schools, churches, and means to establish themselves successfully in agriculture and industry. Simultaneously, a strong army was organized, in which the nobility, deprived as elsewhere of its old feudal privileges and prestige, found a new special field of activity within the framework of a centralized state. The bureaucracy was inspired with concepts of duty and honesty. Wars were avoided so far as possible; the unavoidable ones (waged sometimes with the help of French subsidies) against Swedes, Poles, and Austrians were essentially victorious. The success of the Great Elector's policies was evinced, after his death, by the fact that his successor (who inherited, in addition to Brandenburg, the Hohenzollern possessions on the Rhine and in Prussia) acquired the status of king.

Colonies. During the second half of the seventeenth century, European overseas colonies underwent changes reflecting the shift of power among the mother countries. Spain found herself exposed to continued grave hardships, especially in the Caribbean area, owing to incessant attacks by English, Dutch, and French squadrons, pirates, and smugglers. In 1655, Jamaica, which was regarded— because of its sugar production—as one of the most valuable assets of the Spanish Empire, passed into the hands of England; moreover, with all its wealth now added to the English economy, this island, like other conquered areas, became another outpost for English commercial and cultural penetration. Similarly, Portuguese domination in the East fell to pieces as the Dutch and other antagonists seized one territory after another. It was only in America, in Brazil, that Portugal, albeit with difficulty, succeeded in maintaining her position. The resources of Brazil helped to compensate Portugal for many of the losses suffered in the East; the newly discovered diamond mines, together with Brazilian gold and agricultural products, became sources of a steady income. The Dutch, in turn, though gaining colonies in Asia and Africa, lost their holdings in America (on the Hudson and on the Delaware). Lastly, in the Far East, all Europeans lost their rights and privileges in Japan, which expelled the foreign traders and permitted only a small, narrowly confined, and closely supervised group of Dutchmen to retain a tenuous foothold.

Wherever changes in ownership occurred, corresponding changes in colonial life developed. These were especially pronounced in English North America. An ever-increasing stream of immigrants came to American shores. By 1700, all the original thirteen colonies of North America had been established. One of these was the highly prosperous Quaker colony of Pennsylvania, which devised a new pattern of colonization. The French in America could not match the development of colonies by the English, notwithstanding the fact that their mercantilistic-minded officials such as Colbert sought to promote exploration and settlement. The average Frenchman was very reluctant to leave his beautiful and prosperous homeland; despite their wealth in furs, spices, fish, and sugar, his colonies had little attraction for him.

The three large colonizing powers developed three different systems of colonial organization. The French set up few institutions and left it up to the traders to win the co-operation of the natives and secure profits for the homeland. The Spanish settlers remained under close supervision by their mother country. The English colonists were given a large measure of self-government. During the Cromwellian revolution, they took advantage of the troubles at home to strengthen their position, and during the Restoration and the revolution of 1688 they further increased their liberties. Even though the mother country regained much of her lost authority when the revolutionary period was over, the attitude of the English colonist remained strongly independent and self-reliant. With his primary attachment to the land on which he lived, he felt himself far removed from the scene of the wars against Louis XIV, into which he was drawn, and he referred to them as "King William's" or "Queen Anne's" wars, as if they were private undertakings of his rulers.

THE CULTURAL SCENE

The large space which the political events of the later seventeenth century take up in the history of the time bears witness to the growing influence which political institutions, political thinking, social relationships, and national aspirations were to exercise in the life of modern man. In the Age of Louis XIV the modern European state system was completed and modern diplomacy was developed; simultaneously, the tenets of the age found expression in many theoretical political writings.

Political Thought. The protagonists of absolutism included the Frenchman Bossuet (d. 1704) and the Englishman Hobbes (d. 1679). These thinkers defended the prevailing concepts of the divine right of kings, though they did not identify absolutism with arbitrary rule: Bossuet insisted that the royal will must be permeated with Christian doctrine, and Hobbes thought that it must be administered in accordance with the principles of a "natural" right to self-preservation. As Grotius had done, both demanded morality in international relations. Their views were soon challenged by John Locke (d. 1704), who in his *Treatises on Government* and *Letter on Toleration* defended the idea that the relationship of ruler and subject is based, not upon divine right but upon a social order which binds both parties. In this view, every subject has a right to liberty and property and may justly revolt if his rights are violated.

Philosophy. Locke, who was a man of affairs as well as a philosopher, derived his views from logic and observation as his *Essay concerning Human Understanding* shows. Though he accepted the existence of God, he was an empiricist. Empiricist trends underlay the work of most other philosophers of the age—notwithstanding Hobbes's criticism of Descartes's "mechanistic" approach and notwithstanding Pascal's attempts to harmonize Christian thought with that of his own age. Besides Locke, other leading philosophers were the Dutchman Spinoza and the German Leibnitz. Spinoza (d. 1677), who, like Locke, defended the individual's right to political liberty, is most famous for his "pantheism," which implied that everything is a part, an evidence, of the divine and that "God" works as a mathematical law permeating the universe. Leibnitz (d. 1716), one of the most famous "polyhistors"—i.e., men of universal interests and many-sided achievements—emphasized mathematically ascertainable laws of nature and relegated God to the place of an initial cause. He saw the world filled with innumerable individual units of differing complexity, all independent of one another, following their own laws, yet in harmony with the world, the "best of all possible worlds," as made by God.

Science. An age so devoted to logical thinking, mathematics, and experimentation necessarily produced remarkable scientific results. Numerous instruments (e.g., the telescope, microscope, air pump, and pendulum clock) were invented or improved; statistical systems were devised and technical methods in industry and mining were improved. The Frenchman Pascal (d. 1662), inventor of the barometer, developed a mathematical theory of probability; the Englishman Boyle (d. 1691) laid the foundations for modern chemistry by investigating the pressure properties of gases; another Englishman, Halley (d. 1742), observed and described the comets; the Dutchman Huygens (d. 1695) investigated theories of light, and his countrymen Swammerdam (d. 1680) and Leeuwenhoek (d. 1723) studied microscopic organisms. Botanical works appeared in great numbers. In 1684, Leibnitz completed his system of the calculus, a monumental achievement. But the greatest scientist of the age, and one of the greatest of all times, was the Englishman Newton (d. 1727). This many-sided genius, who was active in politics and eventually became a master of the mint, devised independently a system of the calculus (1687) and carried on so many studies in physics, optics, and astronomy that he laid the basis for many areas of modern science. He disclosed his greatest single discovery, the law of gravitation, in 1687. In all his work, Newton rejected transcendental speculation or hypothetical reasoning; he insisted that the prime aim of the scientist should be to describe accurately natural occurrences and their ascertainable causes.

A special place in the history of this age belongs to the Academies of Sciences, the first of which was founded in London in 1662, to be followed (in 1666) by one in Paris and, later, by others in Prussia, Austria, Russia, and elsewhere on the Continent. Their activities included philosophical discussions about nature and its laws as well as the presentation of scientific papers on mathematical, biological, and physical problems. Many of the greatest minds of the age participated in their work and found in them the best forum for new ideas, testing them, and publicizing conclusions. Men such as Leibnitz considered them so vital for the development of the intellectual forces of a nation that he recommended the founding of an academy of science to the Russian emperor as his foremost task.

Literature. In the perspective of today, the advances of the sciences overshadow the late seventeenth-century accomplishments in literature and art; yet, these were by no means negligible. In France, creative writers included the celebrated dramatists Corneille (*Le Cid*) and Racine (*Britannicus, Athalie*), and the sharp, satirical critic of society, Molière (*Bourgeois Gentilhomme, Tartuffe*). La Fontaine became famous for his *Fables*. At this time the trend toward classical literary tradition, which demanded adherence to normalized rules and conventions, as well as precepts of "good taste," and, in a sense, duplication of the rational patterns of the day, reached its height. But this trend also imparted a certain sterility to some literature of the Age of Louis XIV, which not only deterred later generations, but as early as 1680 brought about a "Battle of the Ancients and the Moderns." Against the formal demands of the Ancients, there arose a cry for freedom of expression by the Moderns. Nevertheless, throughout Europe the classical French literature of the seventeenth century as represented by the Ancients had a decisive influence. Everywhere it was imitated and praised as the perfection of taste and the model for values. Only in England did men of genius build or preserve a different tradition. There, Milton (d. 1674; *Paradise Lost*), Bunyan (d. 1688; *Pilgrim's Progress*), Dryden (d. 1700; poems, satires) stand out. Germany produced little; Grimmelshausen's *Simplicissimus* represents a lasting and potent literary contribution, but only the beginnings of a national literature emancipated from French models can be traced.

History. In still another field, France made an important contribution. In Mabillon (d. 1707) she had a man whose legal studies, impelling him to undertake a methodological investigation of medieval documents, laid a foundation for systematic procedures and standards in history. This discipline thereby became a science which has served as a source of basic information concerning social conditions and human behavior.

Architecture. In the arts, the baroque style dominated. It was superbly expressed by means of numerous palaces for which Versailles, grandiose in concept and clear in line, served as model. The buildings, fountains, statues, and specially designed shrubberies and flower beds, all geometrically arranged to satisfy the taste of the age, were everywhere imitated. The baroque style with its grace and lightfulness was well adapted to church construction, and some of its finest examples are found in southern Germany, Switzerland, and Austria. In England, on the other hand, eminent architects continued resolutely in the classical, medieval, and Renaissance traditions. Christopher Wren designed St. Paul's Cathedral in London. Although the international influence of such architecture was slight, another side of the architectural arts in England came to constitute a real contribution to the stylistic concepts of all Western countries. This was the English garden, which, in contrast to the art of France, emphasized naturalness; lovely groups of trees or shrubbery, carefully and yet naturally arranged on wide lawns, appealed deeply to those who remained unsatisfied with the formal ornamental style of the Age of Louis XIV.

Painting. In painting, the French could pride themselves on the landscapes of Poussin (d. 1665) and Lorrain (d. 1682). A more lasting impression was, however, left by other nations. Catholic Spain contributed one great painter, Murillo (d. 1682), but it was the Protestant, secularly oriented Dutch painters—masters such as Franz Hals (d. 1666), Vermeer (d. 1675), and the landscape painter Ruisdael (d. 1682)—who excelled. Yet, though their achievements may have been outstanding in any age, these artists were overshadowed by the genius of Rembrandt (d. 1669), whose luminous portraits and moving biblical scenes have a power, depth, veracity, and human significance equaling the best ever created.

CHAPTER IX

THE AGE OF ENLIGHTENMENT
(1715–1774)

THE EIGHTEENTH CENTURY is known as the "Age of Enlightenment." To a degree, the Age of Enlightenment constituted a
conscious reaction to the artificiality of the times of Louis XIV, but
in essence it carried on the trends of that period. It propagated and
spread the light of reason among wider groups and called for action
on the basis of rational thought. It emphasized science over religion,
thought over faith, doubt over traditional authority. It believed that
if scientific investigation were applied not only to inanimate nature,
but to all aspects of human life, natural laws could then be discovered which, like Newton's law of gravitation, would explain
human action, and that human action could then be so directed as
to bring continuous progress to mankind. Thus, attention was
focused upon investigations of phenomena in the natural sciences
as well as upon investigations of social conditions, politics, and
ethics.

POLITICAL ENLIGHTENMENT

The practical application of enlightened theories in the political
and economic life of Europe was promoted by the appearance of
"enlightened monarchs" or "despots." As the term "despot" indi-
cates, the concept of the "divine right of kings" or of "absolute
monarchy" was retained. Enlightened monarchs were, indeed, far
from accepting ideas such as those of Locke concerning the natural
rights of the governed in relation to their rulers. But they showed

their affinity with the enlightened thought of their age insofar as they did not claim that identity of themselves and their states which Louis XIV had expressed in the arrogant statement, *L'Etat, c'est moi,* implying the sacrifice of the welfare of the individual to the glory of the king. Instead, they accepted ideals of tolerance, humanitarianism, equal justice, and other ideals which the Age of Reason proposed. Frederick the Great's enlightened dictum, "I am the first servant of the state," reflected the new views about the proper character and function of a ruler.

THE NATIONAL SCENE

With the exception of England (whose parliamentary system, despite its many weaknesses, did not necessitate paternalistic guidance by a monarch), of Poland (which was in the throes of anarchy), and of France (which remained too much under the spell of Louis XIV), almost all European countries had their "enlightened" rulers: Prussia, Frederick the Great; Austria, Joseph II; Spain, Charles III; Sweden, Gustavus III; Russia, Catherine the Great; and Denmark, Portugal, and Spain, ministers such as Struensee, Pombal, and Aranda, respectively. Frederick the Great of Prussia was the most representative example of enlightened despotism.

Prussia. Prussia had developed rapidly in the eighteenth century. In the time of Frederick's father, the efficiency of the government and of the army had been greatly improved; and under a deeply religious, despotic, and extremely parsimonious ruler, an honesty rare in eighteenth-century administrations had prevailed. Serfdom had been reduced, the judicial system improved, and Prussia's rank in Europe firmly established. When Frederick II, "the Great" (d. 1786), came to the throne in 1740, he therefore inherited a most efficient governmental machinery. Making prompt use of his excellent army, he succeeded by three Silesian Wars in doubling his realms and economic resources and in raising Prussia to the status of a first-class power. His fame, however, rests not only on his generalship in war, but especially on his enlightened rule during thirty-six years of peace. Himself an irreligious man, he was a model of religious tolerance: Jesuits, Jews, and Protestants alike found refuge in his lands. Justice was dealt out speedily, humanely, and with great efforts at impartiality; often, the poor were favored. Promotion for ability was common, even though Frederick reserved the top posts in the army for the nobility and retained many class distinctions. Agriculture was the king's chief concern; immigrants were welcomed, wastelands recovered, modern technical improvements introduced; serfdom was practiced in its mildest form only; housing for workers was provided; the raising of new crops, including the potato, was encouraged. The king supervised things personally. He resettled the veterans, to whom he distributed land, seed, and horses. In his policy toward industry, he was essentially a mercantilist. He passed measures to stimulate production and trade, subsidized the silk industry and the new porcelain industry, founded a state bank, stabilized prices through state purchases or sales, developed mines in newly conquered Silesia, and prohibited the importation of luxury goods (e.g., tobacco and coffee) because payments for them would diminish his bullion. His long and varied career encompassed a miserable childhood and youth under the strict hand of his despotic father, an industrious period in the service of the state, and an arduous old age. This pathetic, lonely person, who preferred to wear shabby clothes, had given up all his former love of luxury, comfort, the arts, music (he was devoted to the flute), and communion with philosophers (e.g., Voltaire, who had spent many years at his court); but when he died, his name was a legend everywhere in Europe.

Austria. In Austria, Joseph II (d. 1790) was Frederick's great admirer and imitator. Austria had started on a steep decline. With Prussia challenging her leading position in Germany and with Hapsburg princes incapable of modernizing their multinational state and bent mainly on the preservation of their *Hausmacht,* she could no longer maintain her standing. Joseph's mother, Empress Maria Theresa—though a kind, conscientious ruler—had pursued an overly conservative policy. New, enlightened policies were introduced by Joseph who, however, pushed his reforms forward at such a pace that he caused as much disturbance, revolt, and setback as progress. Yet, he did improve administration and education; he introduced civil marriage, abolished serfdom, and furthered toleration and equality for all, including Jews.

Russia. The remarkable improvements which enlightened despotism brought to numerous nations should not deceive us as to its inherent weakness. As its very nature required the continued use of arbitrary absolute rule, its advantages depended upon whether or not the government was in the hands of a conscientious and progressive monarch. It proved injurious if such a monarch was followed by a less progressive successor. This aspect of enlightened despotism was demonstrated by events in Russia. Enlightenment came to Russia in the early eighteenth century largely owing to the personal influence of Peter I, "the Great" (d. 1725). He was a man of inexhaustible energy, who personally and conscientiously attended to innumerable duties and supervised an almost incredible amount of detail. He reformed the administration, removed clerical influences from state affairs, built a civil service based on ability, and reduced class discrimination in law courts. Following mercantilistic principles, like other enlightened despots he improved the economy of his state; in his time, the iron production of Russia surpassed that of England. He reformed the army and through successful wars expanded the national domain. He accorded special attention to the Westernization of his country—a trend which had begun under his father. He sought to improve educational standards and to introduce the teaching of foreign languages. He founded an academy of sciences; he obtained teachers from foreign lands, especially Germany, technicians from Holland, and traders from England; he sponsored explorations in Siberia and in the Pacific and Bering Sea regions; he tried to transform the manners, appearance, and clothing of his countrymen in imitation of Western models; and he founded St. Petersburg to provide a permanent link with the West (1703). But his impatience, arbitrariness, brutality, and vulgarity were gravely damaging to the nation, and indolent successors, some of whom sought to eliminate the existing political and intellectual guidance of foreigners, almost ruined his work. Only when Catherine II, "the Great" (d. 1796), came to the throne, were enlightened policies renewed. This German princess, though she lived dissolutely, excelled in intelligence, devotion to duty, administrative ability, and artistic and literary taste. Under her direction, French instead of German influences were strengthened; plans for enlightened legislation were developed; hospitals were improved, and vaccination was introduced. However, the two fundamental weaknesses in the Russian system, autocracy and serfdom, prevented the development of a healthy peasant class, of progressive industry, and of a strong middle class. Many revolts of the peasants occurred (including the fearful rebellion of Pugachev); toward the end of the century, the nation, notwithstanding its territorial extension, improved education, and increased production, faced greater social problems than at the beginning.

Poland. The rapid progress of Russia brought an end to the political prestige enjoyed by her smaller neighbors. In particular, it brought the collapse of Poland. This collapse was hastened by the deplorable situation within the country—anarchical conditions, the arrogance and luxury of a small upper class, and the miserable status of the masses. Disunity among the upper and lower nobility made it impossible for any individual or group to run the government efficiently; this invited foreign interference and soon proved detrimental to Polish interests. Moreover, an arbitrary policy in favor of Catholicism alienated Orthodox and Protestant sectors and was doubly dangerous inasmuch as the majority of Poland's inhabitants were not Polish but Lithuanian, German, or Russian. In 1772 these conditions led to a division of the country among Russia, Prussia, and Austria, the so-called "First Partition," which restored most of the non-Polish territories to the neighbors from whom they had been alienated.

Sweden. Sweden narrowly escaped the same fate. Her time of greatness under Gustavus Adolphus had been short. Not long after his death, Brandenburg had begun to regain some of the annexed German lands; and by 1721 Sweden's Livonian possessions had all been lost to Russia, and the rest of her German territories had been relinquished to the German states. With their territory reduced to its former dimensions, the Swedes prudently took the necessary steps of adjustment. Absolutism (which, in contrast to the oligarchic regime in Poland, succeeded in eliminating the menacing power of an anarchical nobility) was followed by enlightened despotism. Industry and trade prospered; the condition of the peasants (serfdom had never been widely practiced) improved substantially with the end of military adventures; and a measure of popular representation (by means of a national diet) helped to stabilize the government on a sound basis.

Spain and Portugal. Enlightened despotism brought revival even to Spain and Portugal. Although she lost much territory in the Pyrenees region and in the colonies and much of her population in numerous wars, Spain gradually regained her strength, beginning her recovery in 1713 when the succession to the throne was definitely settled. To be sure, England had gained a stake in Spain's valuable slave trade but Spain adjusted herself to the new conditions. Trade restrictions were relaxed, new industries were established, the schools and the army were modernized, and the downward trend of population was reversed. Under Charles III (d. 1788) and his minister Aranda, the government functioned honestly and efficiently, reduced taxes to encourage private enterprise, and, in line with the trend toward a more centralized administration, abolished internal customs barriers which had obstructed trade. In the colonies, the regime gave up the system of *encomienda,* appointed able *intendants,* and redivided the gradually expanding territory into appropriate administrative units. The pervasive influence of the Jesuits in state affairs was eliminated. Simultaneously, neighboring Portugal carried out similar reforms, both in Portugal and in Brazil.

France. Unlike other European countries, France, the home of enlightened philosophy, did not adopt progressive ideas in her own political system. Whether under the dissolute but capable and intelligent regent, the Duke of Orleans (d. 1723), or under lazy, luxury-loving Louis XV (d. 1774), France after the death of Louis XIV retained the outmoded institutions of the previous century. Only in religious affairs was a more liberal policy instituted. The nobility retained its economic advantages, the administrative service and tax system were left unaltered, colonization was but halfheartedly supported, and the wasteful court continued to drain the treasury. About 1720, the Scottish financier John Law attempted to reestablish French credit. He organized a state bank, stabilized the currency, took over tax collection, and founded the Mississippi Company, a large colonial enterprise. But his fundamentally sound efforts to expand production and trade were misdirected owing to his personal ambitions, leading only to mad speculation and economic collapse; and French credit fell to a new low. Under the circumstances, neither the peaceful policies of two able ministers, Dubois and Fleury, nor the essential prosperity of individual merchants and peasants, aided by the natural wealth of this (at the time) most populous and productive country in Europe, could forestall the rapid political deterioration of the French administrative apparatus.

England. The evolution of the English government in the eighteenth century followed neither the pattern of French absolutism nor that of enlightened despotism. Nor did England's past political experiences, her social conditions, her technological and industrial advances, and her overseas commitments favor either such path. Instead, Parliament extended the scope of its political leadership. During the early eighteenth century, the Stuarts failed in attempts to regain the throne, which, after the death of Queen Anne, was handed over to Germans from Hanover. The first two Hanoverian kings, being chiefly concerned with their Continental possessions, paid scant attention to English affairs; in consequence, Parliament was able to exercise its powers without hindrance. A financial storm arose from the speculations and collapse of the South Sea Company (an enterprise similar to that of John Law in France); but it was weathered without undermining the credit of the country. With flourishing commerce and with successes in international diplomacy, the authority of parliamentary government increased. A strong national bank, sound money, and an adequate and broadly based system of taxation—which, unlike the French system, did not exempt the nobility—supported a healthy treasury. Under the cautious and efficient administration of Sir Robert Walpole (d. 1745), peace was maintained, and, owing to his influence, enduring precedents for the conduct of government were established. As a "prime minister" (the first in English history) he surrounded himself with advisers who could count upon the support of their parties—Whig or Tory—in Parliament. He thus secured the backing of Parliament (especially of the House of Commons), to which, in a sense, he thereby became responsible. The advisers themselves became the king's ministers, and the group as a whole, the "cabinet," became the executive organ of the state. Despite widespread bribery, dishonesty, and a policy of catering to interests of minorities and favored individuals, and despite the fact that the nation at large was not represented in Parliament (which was composed of representatives of only a small fraction of the population—comprising mainly the privileged, wealthy landowning group), the basic interests of the whole nation were safeguarded.

This system was endangered when the third Hanoverian, George III (d. 1820), came to the throne in 1760. Opposed to the Whigs who had been in power for decades, he chose his ministers, not according to party affiliation, but according to his personal preference, and he held them responsible to himself alone. However, his policies—often opposed by men like the elder Pitt (d. 1778)—were not crowned with success. During his reign, England lost her thirteen colonies in North America, and internal affairs took a course different from that envisaged by him. For notwithstanding his attempts to increase his royal prerogatives, the parliamentary system developed further; and in the economic sphere, mercantilist views were increasingly replaced by laissez-faire theories. With the progressive introduction of steam power, industrialism and modern capitalism set the pattern for future production methods and relations between government and business.

THE INTERNATIONAL SCENE

The direction which the internal developments in the individual national states had taken in the second half of the seventeenth century and the path on which they proceeded during the following fifty years entailed new international relationships. By 1700, there had gradually and automatically developed a system, which then became the conscious property—indeed, became a theory of international relations—of the European diplomats. It appealed to the rational attitude of the age and to its sense of order. It is known as the "balance of power" on the Continent. Such a balance was not really new; it constituted a normal aim within the European community, as it had within many an earlier state system. But at the beginning of the eighteenth century, it gained importance because the danger of French hegemony under Louis XIV had again focused attention upon the problem. The "balance of power" meant that no single power or group of powers should be permitted to develop enough strength to dominate all the others. The policy of upholding it served England well, since it prevented the emergence of any overwhelmingly strong European competitor. Whenever the balance was upset, England would throw her weight on the weaker side and, assuming the role of protector of the weak, try to re-establish the balance. The advantage of the system was that the independence of the various states (especially the smaller ones) could thereby be safeguarded; the disadvantage was that it hindered European co-operation and led to incessant wars. For changes in the balance of power were unavoidable owing to the pressure of economic developments or to the emergence of strong-minded personalities in positions of authority.

International Objectives. Within the framework of the balance of power, of course, many of the old and long-standing trends in European policies persisted: France's objectives to expand to the

Rhine and to prevent a renewed collaboration of Empire and Spain such as had existed when both were under Hapsburg rule; England's policy of keeping European attention focused on European problems rather than on overseas acquisitions, and of preventing the conquest of the entire Channel coast by any strong power; Hapsburg Austria's aspirations to increase the *Hausmacht* and retain ascendancy over the Turks; Spain's ambitions to preserve her Italian possessions and to keep her overseas trade routes open; Prussia's endeavors to reduce Hapsburg influence in the German Empire and to secure the territories separating her outlying possessions on the Rhine and in East Prussia from the center, Brandenburg; and, finally, Russia's expansionist zeal and urge to gain access to the Baltic and Black seas.

Balance of Power and the European States. Such aims and aspirations led to numerous entanglements which, within the system of "balance of power," could generally not be resolved except by resorting to war. Diplomacy, despite the assumed reasonableness of men, failed. However, the wars were largely "cabinet wars," fought with small armies in restricted areas, arousing little passion, and affecting the general populations of the countries much less than either the religious wars earlier or the great national wars later. The destructive power of the weapons was limited, national and religious hatreds were absent, and, as if by convention, mutual respect and consideration among the warring yet interdependent princes prevented excesses in the conduct of war as well as the annihilation of states in the making of peace.

THE GREAT NORTHERN WAR (1700–1721). Before Louis XIV's last war (the War of the Spanish Succession) had begun, another war—the Great Northern War between Russia and Sweden—had broken out. After brilliant initial victories, the Swedish King Charles XII, considered one of history's great military geniuses, was decisively beaten at Poltava (1709). But it took the Russians another twelve years to evict the Swedes from all Livonia and to secure in the Peace of Nystad (1721) long-coveted harbors on the Baltic Sea. This achievement so increased the prestige of Russia that henceforth, in their diplomacy, all the European nations had to take her views into consideration.

WAR OF THE POLISH SUCCESSION (1733–1735). A new war broke out in 1733. Despite the efforts of Dubois and of Fleury to keep France from being involved while she was still trying to recover

from the wars of Louis XIV, the minor question of the succession to
the Polish throne brought her into this new entanglement; for
Hapsburg and Bourbon vied with each other for control of the
succession. The war ended with the failure of the Bourbons to
secure the crown for their candidate.

WAR OF THE AUSTRIAN SUCCESSION (1740–1748). The Hapsburg
success was short-lived, for soon Austria found herself threatened
from another side. Upon the accession to the imperial throne by
Maria Theresa (for whose right of succession her father had sacrificed manifold Hapsburg interests), a series of other wars broke
out. On the one hand, Prussia attacked Austria. Ignoring Prussia's
promise to respect a "Pragmatic Sanction," by which most European
powers had consented to Maria Theresa's succession, Frederick II
of Prussia invaded and conquered Silesia (1741). On the other hand,
France, which also sided against Austria, became involved in a new
war with England. This seemed to be an opportune time for Maria
Theresa to try to recover Silesia; but in 1745 her armies were again
defeated by Frederick. France, her other enemy, was beaten by
England, however, and not until 1748 was peace restored (peace of
Aix-la-Chapelle). This prepared the ground for a revolution in the
balance-of-power system. For both France and Austria, traditional
rivals, were so weakened that neither had to fear the hegemony of
the other. They therefore composed their age-old differences, came
to an understanding, and allied themselves against the victors,
Prussia and England.

SEVEN YEARS' WAR (1756–1763). As a result, in 1756, a new war,
the Seven Years' War, broke out, which took on global dimensions.
For Russia joined the Franco-Austrian alliance, while Spain entered the conflict against England. The war was fought on three
continents—Europe, Asia, and America. In Europe, it centered again
around Prussia's struggle for the possession of Silesia. Despite a
series of brilliant victories, Frederick soon found himself in grave
straights. Only the death of Russia's empress, Elizabeth, solved his
predicament; for Elizabeth's successor, Peter III, an admirer of
Frederick, withdrew the Russian armies. France and Austria were
compelled to make peace on the basis of the *status quo*, and Frederick kept Silesia. In Asia and in America (where the war became
known as the French and Indian War) England, which contributed little but money to the European phase, gained the upper

THE "REVERSAL OF ALLIANCES" BEFORE THE OUTBREAK OF THE SEVEN YEARS' WAR

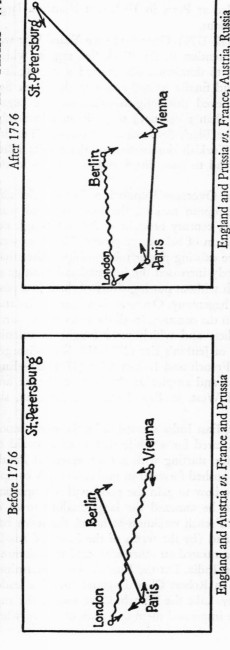

Before 1756

St. Petersburg

Berlin

Vienna

London

Paris

England and Austria *vs.* France and Prussia

After 1756

St. Petersburg

Berlin

London

Paris

Vienna

England and Prussia *vs.* France, Austria, Russia

IN ORDER to understand shifting European alliance systems, it is useful to keep in mind that there existed three basic rivalries:

(a) between France and England (1) over the possession of English territories on the continent, in France. (This began in the High Middle Ages and was solved by 1558 when England lost Calais, her last stronghold on the continent.) (2) over domination of the Channel coast. (This began in the High Middle Ages and was solved when in 1831 Belgium was founded as an independent and neutral state.) (3) over colonial possessions. (This began around 1600 and was solved by 1898, by the incident of Fashoda when France yielded to England and the "Entente cordiale" was established.

(b) between France (Valois, later Bourbon) and Austria (Hapsburg) over hegemony in Europe. (This began in the Late Middle Ages and was solved in 1756 when England and Prussia had challenged them successfully (see chart above). The realignment led later to the marriage of the Austrian princess Marie Antoinette and the French king Louis XVI.)

(c) between Austria and Prussia over hegemony in Germany. (This began with the rise of Brandenburg under the Great Elector, 1640–1688, and was solved by 1866 when Prussia defeated Austria and, five years later, established the new German empire.)

THREE POWERS came close to establishing hegemony in Europe: Spain (1492–1598); France (1648–1815); Germany (1870–1945).

hand. The peace, concluded at Paris in 1763, cost France a large part of her overseas possessions.

Russo-Turkish War (1772–1774). Once the Seven Years' War was over, Russia turned her attention to the Black Sea region, which Peter the Great had tried to dominate. She started a war against Turkey, was victorious, and finally gained access to the Black Sea (1774). Having once achieved this long-coveted aim, she began (and continued for more than a century) to push on relentlessly, seeking to secure all of the Black Sea coast, to eliminate Turkish influence in Europe and Turkish domination of the Straits (Bosporus and Dardanelles), and to gain direct and free access to the Mediterranean.

Balance of Power and Overseas Expansion. Despite alternating alignments of the European nations, the long series of wars which mark the eighteenth century brought shifts in (though not the destruction of) the system of balance of power. The wars were fought in order to preserve existing power relationships rather than upset them, and they merely increased the international prestige of Prussia and Russia, though without putting either of them in a position to attain continental hegemony. Overseas, however, no balance of power was preserved; on the contrary, in all the wars which paralleled the European conflicts and which were fought in colonial areas—especially the War of Jenkin's Ear (1739–41), King George's War (1743–48), and the French and Indian War (1754–63)—England expanded her power and empire at the cost of France and Spain. Both in East and West, in East India and America, she gained predominance.

East India. At the time, East India seemed to be the most important colonial prize. It appeared for a while that France would be able to secure this prize, for, starting with her settlement at Pondichery, she had vigorously pushed forward in mid-century. A competent agent, Dupleix, knew how to gain the good will of important local princes, and in 1746 he annexed the large trading town of Madras. When, owing to French weakness at home, the town had to be ceded back to England (by the terms of the Peace of Aix-la-Chapelle in 1748), he concentrated on other areas and won domination over most of southern India. But the English were determined to drive the French out. In Robert Clive England found a leader equal to Dupleix in ability. Like the French, Clive sought the support of native princes. He impressed them as a man of action when he revenged the capture of Calcutta by a native prince, and he wooed their services through generous gifts. Then he turned against the French. Unfortunately for France, Dupleix, accused of dishonesty, had been recalled in 1754, and his able successor, Lally Tollendal, obtained no help from the home government. Consequently, the British, who dominated the sea lanes and invested the necessary funds, defeated the French in the decisive Battle of Wandiwash (1760). Tollendal was recalled and put to death by an ungrateful government. Peace was concluded in Paris in 1763. Notwithstanding all the efforts and sacrifices of the French agents, and notwithstanding the economic importance of the colony, France had to surrender most of her holdings in India to the British. Promptly, the British set about reorganizing the administration of their colony. After recalling Clive, without reward for his services in the struggle against France, they deprived the East India Company of its control over the country and subjected the government to strict supervision from London. Warren Hastings was sent to India as governor in 1773, and with his regime a new chapter in England's—and India's—history began.

NORTH AMERICA. At the Peace of Paris in 1763 France lost not only India, but also most of her North American holdings. In the course of the eighteenth century, the French had tried to turn the colonial empire, which mercantilist theory and thirst for glory had driven them to acquire, into a possession that would yield practical returns. Their colonies in Canada, the Mississippi Valley, and the Caribbean Islands showed considerable promise. Trading in commodities (sugar, timber, fish, and furs) and in slaves to and from the homeland and among the colonies increased. However, not only competition with England but also the pressure of English colonists in North America upon the thinly settled French dominions hindered peaceful progress. As in India, the English home government backed the commercial interests, the flag following the trade, and in 1745 the colonists in America attacked and conquered the French fortress of Louisbourg. The terms of the Peace of Aix-la-Chapelle required the English to return the fort to France, but ill-feeling between the English colonists and their French neighbors led to continuous localized encounters especially in Acadia (Nova Scotia) and in the Ohio Valley. By 1754, these localized conflicts had developed into a general war. England sent expeditionary forces to America, but they, as well as the American colonists themselves, were defeated. The resulting danger to the colonies brought more concentrated efforts, especially when the energetic and able William Pitt assumed the direction of affairs in England. Naval forces sent to America destroyed the French fleet, and on land English troops in 1759 and 1760 conquered Quebec and Montreal. Disaster now threatened the French. Belated Spanish intervention on the French side failed to re-establish a balance of power against England. Unable to continue the war, France and Spain had to submit to British demands. In the Peace of Paris, Spain gave up Florida; and the French, choosing to retain the commercially profitable islands in the West Indies, ceded Canada and the Mississippi region.

The Thirteen Colonies. At the time of the Peace of Paris, the English people hardly foresaw that the most valuable part of their American possessions would be lost—at least politically—within scarcely more than a dozen years. During the Seven Years' War (the French and Indian War), the colonists had co-operated but reluctantly with the mother country. Whether the colonists had originally come from England, Scotland, and Ireland or from Switzerland, Germany, and Holland, and whether they had emigrated for political, economic, or religious reasons, they were generally animated by a thirst for liberty. They had moved to a new land not only for material gain, but also for independence and for freedom from compulsion. They objected to all exploitation of their land by the mother country and therewith they objected to English mercantilist tactics. Moreover, they pressed steadily westward from the seaboard and were angered at the interference of European issues and diplomacy with their expansionist objectives. Having already secured a large measure of self-government, a prosperous economic status, and (as men like Franklin demonstrated) a considerable amount of intellectual stature, they were unwilling to take upon themselves burdens which the British, having incurred large expenditures in the wars against France, tried to impose upon them without their consent. They denounced a Stamp Act (1765), which Parliament devised as a source of revenue from the colonies; and they forced its repeal in the following year. But Parliament, insisting upon its right to tax the colonies for revenue, imposed other burdens: The Declaratory Act, Townshend Act, Quebec Act, and so-called "Intolerable" Acts succeeded each other quickly, providing either for new taxes or for customs duties or fines. The situation was aggravated further because these impositions coincided with the absolutist tendencies of George III. Violent propaganda started, supported by men brought up in the spirit of enlightenment—for example, Thomas Paine, who demanded a radical break with England. The dissatisfied colonists finally assembled a "Continental Congress," which first prescribed a boycott of British goods and later, in 1775, raised an army. This was followed, in July, 1776, by the assembling of representatives from the various colonies, who took the decisive step and declared the independence of the American colonies.

CULTURAL ENLIGHTENMENT

No matter how important the changes were which occurred in the political scene of England and of the enlightened countries on the Continent, the social and intellectual pattern of the West was still more deeply affected by the economic evolution of the eighteenth century. Mercantilist practices had to be modified as the modern capitalistic system based on new production methods got under way. Agriculture and industry had to be adapted to the new technical knowledge and scientific spirit. Everywhere, the coal and iron industries expanded. Serfdom, which had restricted the labor supply for industries, became constantly milder in form or disappeared entirely; or forced-labor obligations were transformed into money obligations which allowed greater mobility for the peasant and a broader labor market for the entrepreneur. An educated bourgeoisie aspiring at higher material living standards increased in importance. These changes were less noticeable in Central and Eastern Europe where lack of colonial possessions prevented direct access to raw materials and limited the markets. But they were evident in the Western countries, where private enterprise benefited from colonial supplies, from technical interests, and—especially in England—from political emancipation. The Western countries, rapidly increased their trade with America, the Near East, and India, and, in order to maintain this prospering trade, they promoted domestic industries and quickly introduced technological improvements. Spinning and weaving machines (invented by Hargreaves, Arkwright, and Whitney) were used, and large organizations with well-planned methods of production and distribution were built. Of course, the costs had to be borne by the former free artisans and the workers who, as Hogarth's pictures show, lived in hopeless misery.

Economic and Legal Thought: Humanitarianism. It was in line with these changing economic conditions and with the philosophical views emphasizing nature and natural laws that economic thinking changed. Mercantilism with its manifold regulations appeared to interfere with the free play of "natural" forces. Freedom was advocated as the basis of prosperity. Some held that not money or bullion but the total product, which resulted from labor exploiting especially the resources of the soil and subsoil, constituted wealth; these were the "physiocrats," headed by Quesnay (d. 1774) in France. Others applied the theory of freedom to a broader area, especially to trade and industry. They exhorted the governments to adopt the doctrine of laissez faire (the doctrine that noninterference in the free and natural play of economic forces would work to the benefit of mankind). The most famous advocate of this view was Adam Smith (d. 1790; *Wealth of Nations*). Underlying the thought of these economists was the twofold goal of finding natural laws and of contributing to progress, to the "happiness" of men. With this aim in view, the economists exercised a profound influence on law. Quesnay, for instance, advocated that governments confine themselves to restraining the evildoer and not interfere with the citizen's legitimate activities; for man (in the view of Quesnay and his fellow economists) has a right to work as he pleases as long as he does not hurt others. Adam Smith similarly favored the unimpeded right to work; for wealth (he argued) is the result of labor.

In the same spirit of promoting freedom and humanitarian aims, various reformers denounced restrictive laws. Beccaria, about 1764, inveighed against the use of torture. Prison for debtors was assailed as useless and inhumane, serfdom was condemned, and superstitions, such as those responsible for the persecution of "witches," were ridiculed.

Science. With the practical economic effect of rational thought and scientific orientation clearly visible to the intelligentsia of the eighteenth century, there is little wonder that further efforts were made to expand scientific knowledge. Academies of science, like those of England and France and of the new powers Prussia and Russia, played a leading part in this trend. Expeditions for geographical discovery were sponsored, and descriptions of foreign lands—of their fauna, flora, rivers, and mountains—were published. A Dane in Russian service, Bering, found the straits separating Asia and America. The Germans Gmelin, Steller, and Pallas, also in

Russian service, explored Siberia from the Urals to China and the Pacific. Other explorations were undertaken by English and Frenchmen in the New World. Automatically, European ideas were thus spread to many parts of the globe; and conversely, considerable influence was exerted by newly discovered areas upon the economics, politics, manners, and thought of the Old World. The discoveries abroad contributed much to the imposing work of Buffon (d. 1788), who described the animal world, and of the great Swede Linnaeus (d. 1778), who undertook the fundamental task of classifying plants on the basis of their reproductive organs. In physiology, Haller investigated respiration and the development of the embryo; Spallanzani (d. 1799) proved that spontaneous generation does not occur in nature. To the already flourishing fields of mathematics and astronomy, men such as the Swiss mathematician Euler (d. 1783) and the philosopher Kant (d. 1804) made notable contributions. In chemistry and physics many discoveries were made. Boerhaave (d. 1739) and especially Priestley (whose work on oxygen, published in 1774, was fundamental) paved the way for scientific chemistry, which was soon developed by Lavoisier. Benjamin Franklin (d. 1790) occupied part of his time with scientific problems; to him, his contemporaries owed a broad understanding of electrical forces, of the significance of positive and negative electrical charges, and of the conservation of electrical energy. In medicine, immunization against smallpox was achieved.

Technology. Theoretical knowledge was soon applied to practical problems. Reaumur's work on the analysis of steel was published in 1722; reliable measurements for longitude and latitude aided navigation; a steam engine was invented in 1705 by Newcomen and later modernized by Polzunov (1764) and Watt (1768). Even in the world of art, technology had an effect, as shown by the improvement of musical instruments.

Social Sciences. Developments in social science were as significant as those in the natural sciences. The three Frenchmen, Montesquieu (d. 1755), Voltaire (d. 1778), and Rousseau (d. 1778), added little to the insights already gained by the English social thinkers, such as Locke and his successor Hume (d. 1776). But their practical influence as propagandists for the new social ideas far surpassed that of their English predecessors. Montesquieu in his *Persian Letters* derided contemporary conditions in France, and in his *Spirit of the Laws* (1748) he emphasized the importance of the material basis of all social institutions and the influence of climate on the laws

and character of a nation. He advocated a type of government limited by checks and balances. Voltaire, poet and historian, directed
his wit against prejudice, tradition, intolerance, and injustice. He
firmly believed in the perfectibility of mankind. Rousseau, the most
sensitive of the three great Frenchmen and the only political radical,
defended (in his *Nouvelle Héloïse* and his educational treatise
Émile) a new, utopian way of life which, he thought, could result
from man's turning away from civilization—back to nature. Thereby,
he hoped, man would be led to virtue and happiness. In his *Social
Contract* Rousseau set forth his thoughts on the inalienable rights of
man and on popular government. His ideas were spread further by
the so-called "Encyclopedists"—such men as Diderot (d. 1784) and
d'Alembert (d. 1783), who, like Voltaire and Rousseau, faced censorship, exile, and imprisonment, yet pursued their work of propa-
gating "enlightened" thought. They published a comprehensive
alphabetical dictionary in which they used the entries of political,
religious, and other terms for a discussion of enlightened ideas. In
a similar vein, discussions were launched in the numerous *salons*
where intellectuals met, in the pamphlets which flooded England
and France, and in the newspapers which, with the increase in
literacy, found an ever-widening public.

Religion. Though the entire movement of the Enlightenment
appealed to man's conscience and humanitarian feelings, its overconfidence in progress, its neglect of man's metaphysical urges, and
its materialism were bound to lead to criticism and reaction.

ATHEISM AND DEISM. To be sure, only a few of the enlightened
thinkers altogether rejected the thought of a God and religion.
(Hume, who saw in religion an outmoded state of man's evolution,
and d'Holbach [d. 1789], a determined atheist, were among them.)
But there was a strong trend in the direction of atheism, attributable,
on the one hand, to conventionalism and rigidity within traditional
churches, and, on the other, to the failure to find a faith that would
reconcile traditional religious beliefs with new scientific insights. A
vague middle position was provided by "deism." The deist rejected
traditional revelation and with it the dogma of the existing Christian churches. While accepting a God as a first cause and as a
source for the good, he built his view of the universe on the basis
of rationalistic thought and mathematical laws.

PIETISM AND METHODISM. Deism lacked deep emotional appeal and
was soon surpassed in importance by a countermovement, antagonis-

tic to rationalism, which had set in during the seventeenth century. It had originated with the German pastors Spener and Francke; their initiative had developed the pietist trend, and this "pietism" now brought to Christian communities a new devotion, spirituality, and charity, as well as a revived mysticism and missionary fervor. Emphasis was placed not on reason but on the attributes of the heart. The movement satisfied the longings of many seeking a truly Christian life; but with its individualistic tendencies, it also led to conflicts with state authority. Pietist groups, such as the Moravians under the leadership of Count Zinzendorf, were forced to emigrate, and many went to the New World, where they eventually exercised a certain distinct cultural influence. Likewise, many adherents of Wesley (d. 1791), who had sponsored in England a similar revolt against "natural religion" emptied of Christian content, came to America. Everywhere, the Age of Enlightenment thus saw two conflicting trends: the one toward rejection, the other toward re-affirmation, of the Christian doctrine.

Literature. The interests of the age and its preoccupations with societal structure and with laws of nature and progress left a definite mark on literature. In France, the outstanding writers were, of course, Voltaire and Rousseau; but two works of special interest, the Abbé Prevost's *Manon Lescaut* and Bernardin de Saint-Pierre's *Paul et Virginie,* stirred even more deeply the hearts of eighteenth-century readers and deserve mention as permanent treasures of world literature. The French language held first place in educated circles in all countries. England contributed notable works such as *Robinson Crusoe* by Defoe (d. 1731) and *Gulliver's Travels* by Swift (d. 1745); and an imposing number of authors of wide renown appeared, including Pope (d. 1744; *Essays on Thais*), Fielding (d. 1754; *Tom Jones*), Sterne (d. 1768; *Tristam Shandy*), Oliver Goldsmith (d. 1774; *Vicar of Wakefield*), as well as Samuel Johnson and his biographer Boswell (d. 1795). Germany witnessed with Klopstock (d. 1803) and Lessing (d. 1781) the beginnings of one of her greatest, and one of the world's most important, periods in literature. It was Lessing in particular who freed the eighteenth century from the artistic chains imposed by the classical French tradition and who recalled the great and free heritage of Shakespeare to a public which in its desire to imitate the baroque and the French classical style had been inclined to forget or belittle the great English poet. Russia, too, began to produce significant literature; a polyhistor, Lomonosov, laid foundations for the literary as well as scientific evolution of his country. A number of historians of lasting importance appeared in the mid-eighteenth century. Besides those who, in the tradition of Mabillon, investigated and edited sources, there were two, Voltaire and Gibbon (*Decline and Fall of the Roman Empire*), who combined artistic style with sound scholarship. Historical interest was thereafter steadily heightened; classical studies increased rapidly; excavations in Pompeii and in Greece by the German archaeologist Winckelmann revealed to the world the beauty and meaning of the classical heritage.

Art. With the growth of a reading public, the visual arts—painting, sculpture, and architecture—once chief conveyers of ideas, declined in significance. Except for the English painter Gainsborough (d. 1788) and the engraver Hogarth (d. 1764), both interested in social conditions, the one representing the nobility, the other depicting the vices and misery of the poor, we find hardly an artist of accomplishment. The baroque style deteriorated into "rococo." Rococo still possessed a certain charm and intimacy, but it increased the trend toward sentimentality, affectation, and overornamentation.

Music. Simultaneously, however, with shallowness in the rococo arts, we witness in music some of the greatest, most meaningful works ever created. During the second half of the seventeenth century, the innovations of the preceding period had already borne manifold fruits. The violin and the violoncello had been brought to perfection; and composers of the stature of Corelli (d. 1713) and Alessandro Scarlatti (d. 1725) in Italy, and Purcell (d. 1695) in England had promoted the art of the contrapuntal style and created instrumental music of rare beauty. Reflecting both a rational trend and sincere emotion, they added purity, simplicity, and strictness of form to a content rich in thought and feeling. They prepared the way for the greatest masters—and these were to adorn the first half of the eighteenth century. It was then that Bach (d. 1750) and Handel (d. 1759) composed their works, which are unequaled in the history of music. Handel, besides writing numerous other works of the highest achievement, also excelled in the opera. Bach did not publish any opera; it was in his compositions for orchestra, organ, and harpsichord, in his chorales and sonatas, in his *St. John* and *St. Matthew Passion,* and in his *Art of the Fugue* that he embodied the profoundest Christian inspiration and human sense of beauty, grace, and compassion, which retain everlasting meaning.

CHAPTER X

AGE OF REVOLUTION (1775–1795)

THE FERMENT CREATED by the ideas of the Enlightenment spread rapidly among thinking people in all Western countries. Progress made possible by new methods of production added to the unrest, and impatience grew despite reforms introduced by enlightened governments. With a firm belief in the perfectibility of mankind, individuals belonging to the most diverse social strata demanded far-reaching changes in the organization of society. In the face of this trend toward social evolution, many who held economic and political power stood firm. Instead of seeking ways to adapt themselves to the new situation, they rejected any idea of a retreat from their privileged positions—hoping, in the spirit of Louis XV's "*Après moi le déluge,*" to be able at least to postpone the day of judgment. Nevertheless, the ideology of freedom and equality, and the fervor engendered by it, undermined irrevocably the faith in the old order even of those who had a material interest in it. Thus, without a serious economic crisis, the soil was prepared for a quick, violent transformation of social and political institutions.

REVOLUTIONARY MOVEMENTS IN THE COLONIES

The first great assault upon the traditional social system occurred in England's thirteen American colonies, which were comparatively free and prosperous and subject to rather generous, progressive government. It was led not by the oppressed, but by those who had little to gain except the fulfillment of certain ideals rooted in the spirit of the Enlightenment.

Birth of the United States. After the thirteen English colonies had declared their independence in 1776, they faced the task of making their program a reality. The struggle encompassed two phases: first, liberation from foreign domination; and second, establishment of a working government in line with the most progressive ideology of the age. Notwithstanding vigorous opposition by conservative forces, both tasks were successfully accomplished.

AMERICAN WAR OF LIBERATION. In order to achieve their goal of self-determination the colonists undertook armed resistance against the most formidable power of the time. The war lasted seven years, but it was won (despite many setbacks and internal dissensions) by the American troops under the inspired leadership of Washington (d. 1799). The English had the advantage of overwhelming naval superiority but they conducted the war halfheartedly, and troops and generals sent to America were ill-equipped. The Americans, on the other hand, had concluded alliances with France and Spain in 1778 and had received decisive support from them; American leaders, Washington in particular, performed their duties with great devotion and perseverance. In 1783 the English general Cornwallis and his troops were forced to surrender at Yorktown, whereupon the British home government acknowledged American independence. The peace treaty concluded in the same year at Paris sealed England's loss of her thirteen colonies and, moreover, forced her to surrender Florida and the Mediterranean island of Minorca to Spain. France gained nothing except acknowledgment of her claims to French settlements in America.

THE CONSTITUTION OF THE UNITED STATES. Even before the end of the war, the colonists had provided for postwar co-operation among themselves. They drew up the "Articles of the Confederation," which vested most legislative and executive powers in the representative houses of the individual states and limited the powers of the central government. This first attempt provided so weak a link among the various states that the formation of a healthy nation became a dubious prospect. Moreover, economic conditions after the war were unsatisfactory; a number of revolts occurred; bitterness between factions persisted; efficient tax collection for the commonweal was impossible for lack of a central enforcing agency; and issues such as westward expansion and the problem of slavery divided the states. Although, during this period, the eastern seaboard states voluntarily surrendered their claims to western lands which they could have acquired, and although this willingness also indicated some possibility of future co-operation, the leading figures in the colonies—Franklin, Washington, Adams, Jefferson, Hamilton— were concerned about dissensions. In 1787 several of them met with like-minded leaders in a new Constitutional Convention which eventually agreed upon a "Constitution" providing for a firmer union and a potentially effective, yet carefully balanced, central government. With acceptance of the Constitution by the legislatures of all thirteen colonies (ratification by nine was required), the "United States" came into being. George Washington was elected first president (in 1789), and the new state began to function as a republic, very different from European models, and one which, through its progressive Constitution, was to exercise considerable influence on political and social thought and organization in Europe; yet, the new nation was also a true child of Europe—of the French enlightenment and the Anglo-Saxon legal tradition.

Unrest in South America. The example set by the United States could not be followed in other colonial areas. In Spanish and Portuguese South America, training in self-government was lacking. A gulf existed between the Europeans, who included many wealthy and well-educated people, and the Indians, Negroes, and mixed races who were in the majority. Should they lose home support, the European settlers feared that the lower classes would rise in revolt and overwhelm them. Moreover, the economic situation did not favor independence. Despite the abolition of the *encomienda* system, agriculture was still backward, mining depended on the markets in the home countries, and business organization was weak. Uprisings against Spain and Portugal took place between 1780 and 1784; but, since allegiance was stronger than the spirit of revolt, the winning of independence was long deferred.

Activity in Asia and Africa. No revolutionary outbreaks occurred in other continents, where independence movements would have had to originate with native (non-European) populations. The latter, notwithstanding their great numbers, never developed military power to equal that of the Europeans, who could therefore not only maintain their position but also extend their territorial holdings. Consequently, Europeans seized additional colonies in Africa and India. During Hastings' administration, India came almost completely under English rule. Furthermore, a whole new continent was opened for colonization when, in 1787, a penal settlement was established in Australia, which eventually developed into a prosperous commonwealth.

REVOLUTION IN EUROPE

Shortly after Europe witnessed the startling innovation of a republic in America, it was shocked by a terrible revolution against the "Old Regime" in France. This appeared to be another result of the philosophy of enlightenment. Revolts also occurred in other countries—in Belgium, Italy, and Poland—and in still others the threat of rebellion brought reforms. But none of the other revolutions compared with that of France in dramatic and lasting impact upon all Western society.

Conditions before the Revolution. The fact that the revolution in France became a major event of Western history in the eighteenth century should not lead to the conclusion that French institutions were altogether backward. French rulers had not been entirely lacking in political enlightenment. After the death of Louis XV in 1774, under kind, modest, but weak-spirited Louis XVI and his capable minister Turgot (d. 1781), attempts had been made to improve agriculture, to provide greater freedom for trade (by abolishing the numerous internal customs barriers and improving the roads), to dissolve the remnants of serfdom, and especially to end the abuses of an inequitable tax system. Also, the highest law court, the Parlement, had been given increased authority. But the Parlement had been inclined to abuse its position in favor of the privileged classes, and the reactionary forces everywhere were still strong. Turgot was dismissed in 1776 and the divisions among the French people in regard to law, customs barriers, tax systems, and weights and measures, all of which favored the traditional distribution of power, were essentially preserved. Class distinctions were upheld in favor of the first two estates (the clergy and the nobility) while the third estate (the middle class and the peasantry—the latter alone accounting for four-fifths of the population) remained politically without rights and were discriminated against when seeking high positions and economic advancement. Overland traffic was unsafe, vagabondage commonplace. Moreover, each social stratum was divided within itself; each of the three estates had its wealthy and its poor constituents; often the wealthy individuals belonging to one estate co-operated with those in another rather than with members of their own estate.

Path to Revolution. Under such conditions, the incentives to revolt were manifold. (1) There were the ideologies of the age, the philosophy of enlightenment, of freedom, of equality, and of political rights for the bourgeoisie; the idea of free enterprise, of free development of trade, and of free access to all positions in state and army according to ability instead of birth; the rejection of the corrupted morals of court and nobility; and the opposition to existing types of censorship. Actually, many members of the nobility, bored with a sterile life, had themselves accepted these ideas; they gathered in fashionable *salons* frequented also by the intellectuals (the *philosophes*) of the time, and these *salons* became centers for the dissemination of the new concepts. (2) There were political incentives, the example of the American colonies, and the dissatisfaction with foreign policies and with the military defeats of France at a time when a nationalistic spirit was spreading everywhere. Furthermore, feelings ran high against the ignominy of a bureaucracy built upon the basis of favoritism, against the corrupt law courts, and against the still-existing though seldom-employed *lettres de cachet,* which meant arbitrary arrest at the king's pleasure. And there was growing resentment against the entire system, which was out of tune with contemporary conditions under enlightened monarchies or parliamentary regimes. (3) There were personal grievances; the weakness and vacillation of an otherwise well-meaning king; the haughty demeanor and extravagance of the queen, Marie Antoinette, an Austrian princess; and the influence of favorites who were little concerned with the welfare of the country and whose abilities contrasted sadly with those of the leaders of dissatisfied groups. (4) Most important however, were the economic motives for dissatisfaction. To be sure, it would be incorrect to surmise that poverty was exceptionally widespread in France. Actually, in France conditions among the lower classes compared rather favorably with those in England and other countries; and under an efficient government, reforms could have overcome existing difficulties. But confidence in the government's ability was lacking, and the people had to contend with a steady rise in prices, intermittent food shortages, and recurrent periods of unemployment. Moreover, many among the powerful privileged classes were determined to preserve the inequalities of the tax system. The land tax, or *taille,* continued to be levied only upon the property of the third estate in accordance with assessments made by those who, under the system of farming out taxes, had purchased the right to collect the *taille.* The nobles, on the other hand, paid an amount that they themselves regarded as appropriate; and the clergy confined itself to a voluntary "gift." The salt tax, or *gabelle,* was imposed upon everyone, but, since salt was an indispensable commodity, the tax was burdensome primarily to the poorer segments of the population. The *corvée,* a tax in the form of compulsory work for the lords by those peasants who had not yet become free, was levied exclusively on the lower classes; moreover, in addition to the *corvée,* the landed nobility enjoyed privileges, such as special milling and hunting rights. Then, there were tithes, and extra tithes (*vingtième*), a wine tax (*trop bû*), and other levies. Finally, stringent laws made it difficult for the peasants to escape the tax burdens; nor could they lighten them through purchase of additional land, for this was prohibited.

Outbreak of the Revolution. The foregoing difficulties might have been overcome, despite the weak and class-biased government, had not the public treasury been depleted and had not the Parlement opposed legislation which would have made necessary funds available through taxation of the privileged groups. The credit of the government was soon exhausted, whereupon the king was persuaded to call a meeting of the long-abandoned Estates-General. Accordingly, elections were held throughout France, the people gave their representatives written instructions in so-called "cahiers" enumerating their grievances, and, in May, 1789, the Estates-General assembled. It broke up in June over the question of voting, for tradition did not allow each representative an individual vote—instead, it allotted one collective vote to the representatives of each estate; and the third estate composed of the middle classes and peasants feared that they would always be outvoted by the combined clergy and nobles. The representatives of the third estate therefore convened on a near-by tennis court, where, under the inspired leadership of the noted orator Mirabeau, an oath was taken not to disband until voting by head was introduced and a constitution for all France was drafted. The king capitulated, but this political victory of the lower classes did not solve their economic difficulties, for it brought further increases in unemployment and, finally, produced the first violent uprisings. On July 14, "the Bastille," in which innocent political victims of absolutism were assumed to be confined, was stormed by a mob. Although the Bastille held only seven inmates, the storming of the prison was a signal of the approaching storm. Unrest spread throughout France; some of the nobility hastily fled the country; ordinary citizens armed themselves; and the populace adopted a new, revolutionary flag.

The Constitution. Under the impact of these events, a memorable night session of the reassembled Estates-General was held on August 4, 1789, at which the privileged classes divested themselves of most of their prerogatives: serfdom was abolished; equality of taxation was introduced; eligibility for governmental jobs was extended to every qualified citizen irrespective of his class or wealth; and all internal customs barriers were abolished. It was a momentous step. This was followed by a Declaration of the Rights of Man (August 26, 1789) proclaiming equality, liberty, and justice, and guaranteeing property rights to all. In the face of such drastic changes, the king proved himself unequal to his task; when a mob marched to his palace in Versailles, he weakly submitted to its demands and moved his court back to Paris—"closer to his people." In the meantime, revolutionaries formed "clubs" (Jacobins, Cordeliers, Feuillants, and others) and enthusiastic leaders (e.g., Marat, Danton, and Robespierre) took over their direction.

These events and changes did not, however, alleviate immediate material difficulties, and therefore the Estates General took another momentous step. In order to avoid imminent state bankruptcy, it decreed the confiscation of all church lands; and a new currency (the *assignats*), based on land, was issued. In the next year (1790) a constitution was drafted (the abbot Siéyès played a leading role as constitution-maker) establishing a limited monarchy. The country was redivided into eighty-three "departments," each administered by elective officers; religious freedom was proclaimed; a jury system was introduced; and voting rights were granted to the taxpaying—i.e., the wealthier—segment of the population. A representative assembly was given legislative powers and control of finances. Furthermore, a "civil organization of the clergy" was introduced; monasteries were abolished; clerical offices were to be filled by electoral vote of the communities; and papal power was confined to the right of consecration. The clergy, having lost their lands, were to have their salaries paid by the state and, in exchange, were to take an oath to uphold the constitution.

Repercussions Abroad. The new institutions meant a move toward radicalism, and this, combined with the agitation of French *émigrés,* led to repercussions abroad. Foreign monarchs began to fear for their own safety and for the political system on which their authority rested. The situation worsened when Louis XVI was persuaded in 1791 to seek refuge abroad but, together with his entire family, was intercepted at the Belgian border. Strikes were called and bloody new riots occurred. Thereupon, the Austrian emperor decided to come to the aid of his French sister; and other monarchs joined him in organizing an army to invade France. The Russian empress, Catherine—once a friend of enlightened ideas, but now old, conservative, and thoroughly afraid of any revolutionary movement—used the opportunity to act upon a scheme of her own. Fearing similar disturbances in anarchical Poland, she proposed and, together with the Prussian king, carried out a second partition of Poland. Too late had the Poles begun to undertake overdue internal reforms; too late had patriots, such as Kosciusko, begun to direct their efforts toward modernization of Polish institutions. Even a reformed Poland, in which, it was feared, the revolutionary virus might be active, was no longer acceptable to her neighbors. The second partition was followed in 1795 by a third one, whereby Russia, Austria, and Prussia abolished the Polish state.

War. Meanwhile, in 1792, revolutionary France had answered the threats of the European powers with a declaration of war. A leftist party, the "Girondists," had taken over the government and had begun to confiscate the property of the *émigrés* and to deport any priest who refused to take the prescribed oath in support of the constitution. When Louis opposed these measures, another move toward radicalism—typical of all revolutions in progress—occurred, and his palace, the Tuileries, was invaded. The king and his family were subjected to numerous indignities. Just then, an arrogant and ill-timed manifesto by the commander of the allies leading a victorious army into France contributed to the furor of the revolutionaries. Again they invaded the palace, massacred the guards, and forced the royal family to seek refuge in the hall of the assembly. The assembly decided to jail the king and order new elections on the basis of an equal, general franchise. The vote ushered in the new assembly, the "Convention," which was more radical than any of its predecessors. Under the pressure of the Jacobins, who formed a more extreme left wing than the Girondists, a republic was proclaimed. Just then, at Valmy the French troops gained their first decisive victory over the foreign invaders, and this helped to strengthen the position of the Convention.

Terror. The Convention proceeded promptly to depose the king, declare a republic, introduce a new calendar—dating from the Revolution instead of the birth of Christ—and abolish all remaining tax burdens on the peasants. It also brought the king to trial, condemned him, and (in January, 1793) had him executed. Thereafter the guillotine worked constantly in a "Reign of Terror" which led to a series of revolts in western and southern France against the revolutionary government and to an even more dangerous consequence—an all-European war. Spain, England, and Holland joined Austria and Prussia in an alliance against France. But revolutionary France met the danger with resolute action. Contrary to all military tradition, a general draft was ordered. A large army was promptly organized and a Committee of Public Safety was appointed. Composed largely of Jacobins, this Committee soon dominated both in the Convention and in the Girondist government; the latter was forced to resign. Centralizing all power in its own hands, the Committee then pushed through legislation which actually abolished, as revolutions tend to do, the very freedoms which it advocated. In vain did an opponent murder one of the most radical leaders, Marat; Danton and Robespierre continued the revolutionary program. A new constitution was drafted; laws were passed against speculators in land or foodstuffs and against anyone suspected of disloyalty. Social legislation was broadened, though property rights were still respected. Religion was attacked and a "Cult of Reason" introduced, which, however, soon made room for a "Cult of the Supreme Being" reflecting vague deistic concepts and belief in the immortality of the soul. In 1794, Robespierre seized complete control and had Danton himself arrested and guillotined. Robespierre was a man of fanatical devotion to Rousseau's utopian teachings, untiring and incorruptible. But suspicious of everyone else, he promoted the "Great Terror" whereby he intended to cleanse the nation and introduce the new age—that of the brotherhood of men.

Reaction. But now, after five years of stirring events, of insecurity, of disruption of traditional ties, a point was reached when the re-establishment of security and order seemed to many more desirable than liberty and utopia. A reactionary party emerged which succeeded, in July, 1794 (9th of Thermidor) in overthrowing Robespierre's regime and sending him to the guillotine. The powers of the Committee of Public Safety were abolished, restrictive laws revoked, revolutionary clubs closed, and some priests allowed to return. In 1795 a new constitution was promulgated which provided for a "Directory" of five men and for two representative houses elected by people of property. Thus ended the Revolution. It had had no socialistic content; indeed, throughout the upheaval, property rights were regarded as inalienable, and the small and weak working class, whose belated separate uprising under Babeuf was readily suppressed, gained nothing. Nor did the Revolution bring the hoped-for political liberty, equality, and brotherhood of man or solve France's financial problems. But it did end absolutism, feudal privileges, arbitrary arrest, the mercantilist economy, and church predominance. It brought France glory by formulating the Rights of Man, by fighting for them, and by setting, as in Louis XIV's times, an example for other nations. It gained for the peasants full possession of their lands and freedom from feudal burdens, and it brought success to the middle class, which through its wealth became the dominating factor in the state.

CHAPTER XI

THE NAPOLEONIC ERA (1795–1815)

A S IS OFTEN THE CASE with revolutions, after running through a phase of reform, followed by a period of tranquillity, then of further reform, of violence, terror, and further terror, and then back through reaction to despotism, the French Revolution ended in dictatorship. A "gilded youth," which sought to "enjoy" life again after the great issues demanding unselfish devotion had been settled, engaged in numerous follies in dress, manners, and behavior, and neglected the tasks which newly gained liberty necessitated. But the man to direct France's destiny for the next two decades was already on hand: Napoleon Bonaparte (1769–1821). It was he who gave his name to the period from 1795 to 1815, from the end of the revolution until the end of the great international wars produced in its aftermath. To be sure, the name which reflects the predominantly political preoccupations of past historians does not do justice to a period which belonged, culturally, to the greatest in Western civilization. And while it was France that excelled in the sciences, it was another country, Germany (which, of all the great powers, played the least important and least successful political role), that contributed most to the greatness of the age in other cultural areas. Three names suffice to indicate achievements in that country: Kant, Goethe, and Beethoven.

POLITICAL STRUGGLES IN EUROPE

The counterrevolutionaries of 1795, together with large groups in France and in other European nations, were disappointed in their hopes, which the end of the revolution had aroused. Terror was ended, internal order was restored, a measure of security was again provided for the average citizen, and the fears of France's neighbors were alleviated. But the revolutionary and nationalistic elements in France were not satisfied with the results; they helped to pave the way for the rise of Napoleon who, obsessed with dictatorial ambitions, gave Europe two decades of even more dangerous and destructive upheavals.

Rise of Napoleon. Napoleon was a Corsican by birth, who had studied military science in France and had been a member of Robespierre's party. He had excelled as a general of artillery in the war against the English. His exceptional ability, friendly relations with one of the members of the Directory, and advantageous marriage with an influential widow, Josephine Beauharnais, brought this capable young general the command of an army which, at his own suggestion, was sent into Italy to terminate the war by attacking the Austrian possessions there. Although Prussia and Spain had signed a peace treaty at Basel in 1795, renouncing the entire left bank of the Rhine in favor of France, and although Holland had been defeated and had become a "Batavian Republic" under a French protectorate, Austria and England had continued the war. The Italian campaign, conducted brilliantly by Napoleon, brought a string of victories and therewith glory to France; it made plunder available to fill France's empty treasury; it spread revolutionary ideas abroad; and it ended not only with Austria's withdrawal from the war, but also with the acquisition of extensive territory gained in the Peace of Campoformio (1797). Having defeated Austria, Napoleon prepared to attack England. He contemplated an assault across the Channel, but gave up this plan in favor of an attempt to break England's "life line" to India through the conquest of Egypt. Napoleon conducted another brilliant campaign, winning a great victory at the pyramids, but, after a British sea victory at Aboukir, he was unable to reach his objective because the French lost control of the Mediterranean supply lines. He was fortunate to escape with his life; he fled to Paris, leaving his army to perish in Egypt.

The Consulate (1799–1804). In the meantime, the Directory had squandered the spoils of the Italian campaign and had forfeited the confidence of the nation. Its foreign policy, at first successful, had by 1799 provoked a new anti-French coalition, this time joined by Russia; and Russian and Austrian troops, under the command of Suvorov, had driven the French out of most of the Po Valley. At home, inflation raged, and new revolts threatened. This was the moment which Napoleon regarded as opportune to carry out his own ambitious plans. In October, 1799, he overthrew the government and dictated a new constitution, which provided for a consulate in which he himself took first place as the executive power. He saw to it that his action was confirmed by a plebiscite.

Napoleon's next step was to reconquer Austrian Italy. After another brilliant campaign, including a great victory at Marengo (which consolidated his position against republican opponents at home), and after defeating the Austrians again at Hohenlinden, he induced the latter to make peace at Lunéville (1801). With one opponent thus eliminated, he turned his attention to England and successfully pressed the British to sign a peace treaty (at Amiens, 1802), which restored to France all colonies seized by England since the beginning of the war.

Napoleon then set to work on internal reforms, initiating a despotic, but highly beneficent regime. The revolutionary era was declared at an end; the normal calendar was reinstated. A concordat was concluded with the pope, which—although it did not return church lands—restored the prestige of Catholicism so that dissatisfied priests, peasants, and burghers were pacified. Religious tolerance was extended even to Jews. Government finances were systematized, a central bank was founded, and a new currency (the franc, backed by a sound tax system) was introduced. Agriculture was promoted; the raising of new crops (e.g., beet sugar) was encouraged in order to make Europe independent of imports from English colonies. Roads, tunnels, harbors, and canals were built. The school system was expanded, higher education aided, and the French Academy reorganized. Highly beneficial legal reforms were effected by means of the *Code Napoléon*. Based on Roman law, it embodied many of the liberal, equalitarian, and humanitarian concepts for which the revolution had been fought, and it became a model for the entire Western world.

Napoleon's European Conquests. Intense, personal ambitions and the very nature of his regime impelled Napoleon, however, to initiate enterprises less peaceful than domestic reforms. Aspiring to become a "new Charlemagne," he had himself crowned emperor in 1804, and he then precipitated further wars. In 1805, he defeated

Austria and Russia in his most famous battle, at Austerlitz; in 1806, he destroyed the Prussian army and conquered nearly all of Prussia. Numerous smaller German states were abolished; many were transferred to French jurisdiction. The Holy Roman Empire, which had endured nearly a millennium, declared itself dissolved; the Hapsburgs kept only the emperorship of Austria and their *Hausmacht*. An attack on England was contemplated, but invasion plans were abandoned after the French naval forces had been destroyed (in 1805) by Nelson's fleet at the Battle of Trafalgar. Nevertheless, Napoleon set up a barrier against England by prohibiting importation of British goods on the Continent, thus establishing the "Continental system." Moreover, his troops invaded and occupied most of Spain and Portugal, and even ventured to attack the papal states. Russia was forced to make peace and conclude an alliance with France (Tilsit, 1807).

Decline of Napoleon's Empire. Napoleon's conquests created a problem of overexpansion, for he lacked the resources needed in order to protect and administer his acquisitions. The halfhearted, mutually distrustful alliance with Russia, providing for a division of European hegemony between the two partners, gave little assurance of safety. Furthermore, Napoleon had to contend with serious new difficulties. His treatment of the papacy, culminating in the annexation of the papal states (1808) and the arrest of the pope, had alienated the Catholics and their sympathizers; censorship and arbitrary restrictions had infuriated the liberals; the military campaigns had exhausted French man power and had intensified the popular discontent within France. The revolutionary ideal of liberty seemed lost, for a new nobility had supplanted the old. The people were weary of war, but peace did not come. Moreover, Napoleon was aging rapidly; his intellectual power and military genius seemed to be declining at the same time that his enemies were learning to overcome his strategy. His megalomania—reinforcing his habitual distrust of others and his steadfast loyalty to his family—had caused him to place his brothers and sisters on various European thrones, but their lack of capacity soon showed this move to have been ill-advised. Nationalistic fervor—a most significant asset, which had repeatedly inspired the French—now aided the cause of his opponents. In Spain guerrilla warfare, vigorously supported by the English, brought a constant drain of French strength; yet England gave no indications of wanting to make peace. Revolts occurred in Holland, Switzerland, Italy, and the Tyrol. Since the Continental system could not be enforced along all the coasts of Europe (enforcement would have been contrary to the interests of the various nations), it actually worked to the advantage of England rather than of France; smuggling increased, bringing with it more discontent and greater disregard of law and order. Austria risked a new war against France in 1809. Though defeated again (and forced to allow the emperor's daughter to marry Napoleon, who had therefore divorced Josephine), the Hapsburgs demonstrated the possibility of continued resistance. Finally, of greatest importance was the rising anti-Bonapartist tide in Prussia, where, owing to the labors of men such as vom Stein, Hardenberg, and General Scharnhorst, thoroughgoing reforms were undertaken. Planning a war of liberation, the Prussians adopted many practices utilized during the French Revolution. They modernized and centralized the administrative system, abolished old-fashioned guilds, and eradicated serfdom. They extended the scope of religious freedom, and they founded new schools and universities. While the government adopted many of the liberal concepts of the Napoleonic law code (and granted new political rights to the people), poets and educators stirred up a widespread feeling of national pride.

Russian Campaign: 1812. To meet the danger, Napoleon should have strengthened his alliance with Russia. Instead, he antagonized her by insisting on the enforcement of the Continental system, and he insulted the tsar in petty ways. Finally, he decided to break up the alliance. Aware of his aggressive intentions, Russia brought an end to two wars in which she was engaged: one with Sweden over the possession of Finland, and another with Turkey over territory along the Black Sea coast. But Napoleon tried to forestall her. In June, 1812, he ordered a French invasion and the dramatic war, described in Tolstoy's *War and Peace,* began. The Russians were forced to retreat; and after a terrible but indecisive battle near Borodino, Napoleon entered Moscow. But by then, Russia had collected her strength, whereas Napoleon had lost half his army and now found himself beleaguered in the capital city, where shortly after his entry a terrible fire broke out that deprived his troops of supplies and shelter. With winter approaching, the tsar turning a deaf ear to French peace offers, and a Russian army under Kutuzov threatening from the east (cutting off escape to South Russia where Napoleon had planned to spend the cold season), the invaders were forced to retreat. This retreat became, owing to the severe weather, French disorganization, and Russian attacks, one of the worst military disasters in history.

Wars of Liberation. Under Prussian leadership, a widespread revolt against the French began almost as soon as the remnants of Napoleon's army reached German soil. Many of the conscripted troops deserted the French cause, and a great wave of enthusiasm spread throughout the Continent; at last, after numerous defeats and victories, an alliance of Prussian, Austrian, Russian, and Swedish troops defeated Napoleon decisively in the Battle of Leipzig (October, 1813). The French troops were forced to flee beyond the Rhine and back into France. In the meantime, the combined forces of England, Holland, and Spain had attacked from north and south; and in March, 1814, an allied army marched triumphantly into Paris. Napoleon abdicated; and upon the advice of the wily minister Talleyrand—a man who had already served the Catholic Church, then the Revolutionary regime, then the Directorate, and then Napoleon—the victors reinstated the Bourbons. Thus, Louis XVI's brother, Louis XVIII, called back from exile in England, began to rule as a constitutional monarch under a "Charter." A "Peace of Paris" re-established France's borders as they had existed in 1792.

Waterloo (1815). A necessary reorganization of the European political framework was undertaken in a Congress, convened in Vienna by the victors. Prince Metternich, first minister of Austria, presided; Alexander I of Russia, the Duke of Wellington from England, and Hardenberg of Prussia were the chief figures. Almost all the nations of Europe participated in the grandiose meetings; eventually, even Talleyrand, representing the new Bourbon France, was admitted. Relations among the allies were tense, since Austria and England wanted to reduce Russia's commanding power and prestige, whereas Prussia sought the backing of Russia for her numerous territorial wishes, and France attempted to divide the victors by promoting the demands of various small nations. Advised of these dissensions, Napoleon returned to France from exile on the island of Elba, but, despite enthusiastic receptions in many places, his arrival was premature. Faced with this renewed threat, the allies composed their differences. At Waterloo (1815), Anglo-Prussian forces under Wellington and Blücher decisively defeated the hastily raised army of Napoleon. Again compelled to abdicate, he was now sent to the lonely, arid island of St. Helena, where he died in 1821.

Congress of Vienna (1815). In the meantime, at the end of June, 1815, the Congress of Vienna concluded its proceedings. With statesmanlike wisdom, the peacemakers did not crush defeated France, but re-established her authority in all areas within the borders she had possessed in 1790. Extra-European issues were left untouched, for the two peace treaties in Paris (in 1814 and 1815) had already dealt with them; they had given England all she had demanded by way of colonies, including the island of Malta, and had made her heir to the profitable French slave trade. Germany as a whole was reconstituted as a loose federation of about thirty-eight states with an Austrian as president. Austria herself regained and extended her Italian holdings, and Prussia annexed large areas in central Germany. Russia seized most of Poland (which was made a kingdom under the tsar) and obtained recognition of her domination over Finland. Sweden, in exchange for Finland, took over Norway, which Denmark, Napoleon's long-time ally, had to relinquish. Holland and Belgium were united into one new state. In general, the Congress aimed to restore their old domains to the legitimate rulers of the period before the wars or to give them due compensation. A belt of sufficiently powerful nations was drawn around France to deter her from future aggression. National aspirations, which had been strengthened by the revolutionary spirit, were ignored in favor of an effective balance of power in Europe. At the insistence of Alexander I, the treaties were supplemented by a "Holy Alliance," an international organization intended to guarantee brotherly co-operation among the rulers and paternal treatment of their subjects. This alliance was designed to safeguard both the international arrangements made at Vienna and the existing internal status of the various countries.

POLITICAL DEVELOPMENTS IN THE AMERICAS

Significantly, before the Napoleonic era had ended, America had begun to play an important part in Western affairs. Although the wars of the French dictator had not embraced the Western hemisphere in the same way as the Seven Years' War fifty years earlier, the French revolutionary spirit and Napoleon's conquests had a radical effect on the New World. They affected South and Central

America, for the conquest of Spain and Portugal by Napoleon removed the ruling dynasties and forced the American colonies to search for a new source of governmental authority. The Napoleonic wars had some effect in the United States, too, although there the republican idea, the spirit of freedom, and the principles embodied in the Rights of Man needed no propagation. The Napoleonic period, primarily because it forced the British to concentrate their attention upon Europe, gave the United States an opportunity to build the nation without interference from England.

North America. At the time the French Revolution broke out, Washington had just become president of the United States. During his administrations, steps were undertaken to perfect the system devised by the Constitution—steps which were of considerable import for all of Western civilization because they dealt with the issue of federalism versus a highly centralized union, state, or empire. This problem of sovereignty was to become for many other areas an acute, vital, yet never fully solved question. In the United States, a Bill of Rights was introduced into the Constitution by amendment, and a Supreme Court and a national bank were created; these developments involved intense controversies over the desirability of interpreting the Constitution broadly or of adhering to it strictly. The division of opinion divided the country, resulting in the formation of political parties. Despite bitterness and strife under Washington's successors, Adams (elected 1796) and Jefferson (elected 1800), political parties proved eventually advantageous; for, while the issue of the interpretation of the Constitution was decided in favor of those who advocated the broader view, the tradition of a legal opposition was established and continued criticism led to progressive improvements. In her external policy, the United States followed the advice of Washington to avoid European entanglements, but she could not escape them entirely. In 1803, she accepted Napoleon's offer to sell French Louisiana and thereby not only protected herself against Spain, but also enlarged her territory enormously. She defended her right to unimpeded overseas trade, and, when forced to it by English blockades and embargo acts, reasserted her position by even entering into a new war against Britain. After victories and defeats (the English burned the newly built capital of Washington), a treaty was signed at Ghent in 1814. The peace treaty gave little to either side, but it reaffirmed America's independent statehood. Henceforth, the United States had an opportunity to develop her own resources further, to continue her westward march across the continent, to attract vast numbers of new immigrants of all countries in search of economic advancement, and to enter a period of "good feeling."

South America. In South America, the delayed independence movement had received a new impetus when Napoleon's occupation of Spain and Portugal had interrupted the exercise of legal authority of these nations over their American colonies. Revolts under inspiring leaders, such as Bolívar, Miranda, Morelos, and San Martín, occurred, and by 1811 Venezuela and Paraguay had achieved independence. Mexico followed in 1814, the La Plata region in 1816, Chile in 1818, and Peru in 1821. Attempts of the Spanish and Portuguese kings after their restoration to regain their authority failed, but so did all efforts of the South American nations to form a federation. Individually, however, they were organized as nations which were soon able to influence, first, the economic life and, later, the cultural and political life, of the Western world. Brazil, which likewise separated from the motherland, played a special role; she alone did not become a republic, but in 1822 made Pedro, the son of the last Portuguese regent, an emperor.

CULTURAL TRENDS

Notwithstanding the fact that Napoleon's wars left hatred, destruction, and death in their wake, in some other respects they had a permanent and beneficial influence on the progress of civilization. Not only had they engendered, especially among France's adversaries, enthusiasm, devotion, and idealism; they had also, despite the conqueror's dictatorial ambitions, propagated many of the ideas of the French *philosophes* and had instilled abroad the thirst for liberty and equality. The introduction of the Napoleonic Law Code in many parts of the Western world is but one example of this fact. The impact of the entire movement of revolution and war was much deeper because it came at a time when, with the economic victory of the bourgeoisie, and its progressive attitudes, opposed to the reactionary order of the Old Regime, the cultural development was in flux. Men were ready to test (and, possibly, to integrate into their institutions) the new sentiments; their minds were open to unorthodox ideas concerning politics, society, art, and science.

Advancements in Pure Science. Indeed, during the forty years from 1775 to 1815, owing to an acceleration in the impetus which the seventeenth and early eighteenth centuries had given to logical thought and to investigation of nature, many additional, fundamental scientific insights were gained. They were embodied in a wealth of scholarly treatises of revolutionary character. (1) In chemistry, the pioneer work of Priestley and Cavendish (d. 1810; studies of hydrogen, ca. 1766) was continued by these same men and by others—by Gay-Lussac and Avogadro and most notably by Lavoisier (guillotined 1794). Lavoisier carried on the investigation of oxygen and hydrogen, established the fact that matter may alter its "state" but not its "quantity," studied the connection between oxidation and respiration, and placed chemical nomenclature on a scientific basis. He enunciated the principle of the conservation of mass. (2) In biology, the works of the Swiss von Haller and the Frenchman Lamarck (d. 1829) were outstanding. (3) In astronomy, there was the work of Kant and Herschel (fl. 1787) and the great Laplace (d. 1827), whose conception of the origin of the planets opened new vistas for the study of the universe. (4) In geology, men such as Saussure excelled, investigating rivers, mountains, and glaciers. (5) In mathematics, besides Laplace—famous for his development of the calculus—Lagrange (d. 1813) was the leading figure; his special contribution lay in his investigation of geometrical problems. (6) In medicine, therapeutic studies were greatly advanced; tissue physiology was investigated; vaccination was improved by Jenner (1796); and the danger of scurvy was reduced after experience with fresh fruits and vegetables had been gained during Captain Cook's trip around the world. (7) In electricity, Galvani's discovery of animal electricity led to Volta's work (1799) on electrical currents and on the storing of electricity in batteries. (8) In archaeology and history, a new stage was entered with Winckelmann's discoveries and Herder's philosophy of the history of mankind. As for philology, Napoleon's Egyptian campaign had brought the discovery of the so-called "Rosetta stone" which made possible the deciphering of hieroglyphs.

Advancements in Technology. Along with the advance of theoretical knowledge came progress in technology. In 1807 a successful steamship was operated in America, and in 1814 Stephenson's locomotive was constructed in England. Balloons to carry human beings aloft were designed and used. Numerous improvements were introduced in two basic industries: mining and textiles. The use of interchangeable machine parts spread and made possible cheaper, more efficient production. Division of labor increased. Agriculture yields rose with growing understanding of nature and with the use of machinery. Iron and steel gained undreamed-of importance.

Britain took the leadership in technological advancement; for her colonial empire, greatly expanded during the Napoleonic Wars through the acquisition of territories in South Africa and India, not only made industries possible, but also necessitated their expansion and modernization. This growth of her industrial capacity led in turn to the importation of her goods into numerous independent states as well as into colonial possessions. Both European and American nations came to depend upon British machinery. To be sure, the English working population endured numerous adverse consequences of technical advances, suffering grievously through unemployment and low wages; and the government was slow in extending protection to the workers. For the "classical" economists of the age, in line with Adam Smith's laissez-faire policies, believed that, through free play of economic forces, adjustments would come by themselves; and they hoped with Jeremy Bentham (ab. 1789) that the "greatest good for the greatest number" would eventually result.

Religious Liberalism and Mysticism. The utilitarian spirit expressed by the economists and promoted by the mathematical, mechanistic trends of the scientists engendered, like the "enlightenment" of the preceding half-century, a reaction which was strengthened by the miseries accompanying revolution, war, and industrialization, and which expressed itself in a religious revival. This took two different directions. On the one hand, it led to a liberal interpretation of Christian doctrine, with emphasis on love for all and on undogmatic tolerance. (Schleiermacher [d. 1834] in Berlin was to lead this movement toward religious liberalism.) On the other hand, a revival of mysticism took place, an inner rejection of the evils of the world, of its self-assured knowledge, its techniques, and its struggles; and with this revival came a search for direct communion with God. Such feelings were expressed by numerous groups; typical was the example of the Russian Baroness Krüdener, who sponsored a revivalist movement and whose influence played a part in bringing about the formation of the Holy Alliance by

Alexander I. Simultaneously, there was also a renaissance within the traditional churches; in their search for guidance away from the materialistic path on which scientific knowledge seemed to lead, many people turned especially to Catholicism.

Philosophy. Philosophy was another field upon which the growing scientific and utilitarian spirit continued to leave a deep impression. Toward the end of the eighteenth century, belief in the unlimited possibilities of human understanding was badly shaken; so also was belief in the perfectibility of man. Philosophers could not avoid the conclusion that there are limits to human knowledge and that scientific laws are inadequate to explain man's ethical and spiritual nature. It was the achievement of Kant (d. 1804; *Critique of Pure Reason*), the greatest of philosophers after Descartes, to propose a philosophical system that embraced both an understanding of physical science and a recognition of the human moral instinct. Kant held that physical science gives man a dependable knowledge of the world about him, but that a moral law—an inner voice of duty—gives man a unique role in the material universe. This moral law, like that of nature, touches our rational nature, leads us to a sense of brotherhood with all men. "Freedom," he insisted, is a condition necessary for the full development of man's rationality and of his ethical behavior. Kant did not stand alone, for at least three great compatriots of his built on similar foundations: Fichte (d. 1814), Schelling (d. 1854), and Hegel (d. 1831). All three were, like Kant, heirs of enlightenment and all emphasized the need for freedom; Hegel postulated freedom as the ultimate aim of history, in the pursuit of which God's will expresses itself.

Music. The powerful forces of rational investigation which contributed so much to the advancements in science and philosophy did not, significantly, dim the love of beauty and the spirit of imagination, fantasy, and vision which mark so many of the greatest achievements in art. In music, in particular, some of the most beautiful works in world history were created. Germany continued, after the death of Bach, as the center of musical life, her great musicians overcoming the conventionality, galantries, mere elegance and shallow love of ornamentation which dominated in France and Italy (except in the works of a few masters like Rameau). Virtuosity, so highly cultivated in the Romance countries, was regarded by the German artists with distrust. Though abandoning to a certain extent the contrapuntal style of Bach, they continued his work and created piano sonatas, symphonies, and string quartets which addressed themselves to the deepest emotions of man. They also wrote operas of lasting import. Thus, the musical world entered its own "Classical Age." Verbal descriptions cannot convey an impression of the inspired works of Gluck (d. 1787), Haydn (d. 1809), Mozart (d. 1791), and Beethoven (d. 1827), or even of the many lesser composers. To be understood, they must be experienced in the medium in which they were conceived. With Beethoven, the youngest of the group, the Classical Age came to an end; and in his later years he himself introduced a new period—that of Romanticism.

Painting, Architecture, and Sculpture. Far less meaningful for future generations than the great works in science, philosophy, and music were the works in the fine arts created during the Revolutionary and Napoleonic periods. Perhaps because of the absence of artists of true genius or perhaps because painting, architecture, and sculpture were not so well suited to express the spirit of the age as they had been in Renaissance times, they did not bring forth high achievements. The Frenchman David (d. 1825) is practically the only painter worth mentioning—aside from the strange and very modern genius of the Spaniard Goya (d. 1828), whose scenes of the Spanish war against France endure as a most realistic and gripping monument of the horrors of a time which prided itself on its idealism. Nor was greatness shown in architecture and sculpture; these arts were rather influenced by neoclassicism, i.e., an imitation of classical models. With its simple, restrained lines, its clarity and dignity of style, neoclassicism was received as a welcome relief from baroque and rococo, even if it lacked original creative thought.

Literature. In contrast to the fine arts, literature possessed the traits which made it an adequate and influential means of expression of the age. It came to its highest development in Germany. Politically and industrially backward and incapacitated though she was, Germany in the late eighteenth and early nineteenth centuries produced perhaps the greatest men of genius in literature, as well as in music and philosophy. The period from 1760 to 1800 is regarded as Germany's "Classical Age of literature," which then was followed by Germany's "Romantic Age."

CLASSICISM. The two great figures in Germany's Classical Age, following Lessing, were Goethe (1749–1832) and Schiller (1759–1805). Animated by high idealism they expressed in classical form the eternal aspirations of man in his longing for freedom and self-expression. Their works (Goethe's lyrics, *Sorrows of Werther, Goetz, Wilhelm Meister,* and *Faust;* Schiller's ballads, *Robbers, Wallenstein,* and *Wilhelm Tell*) have been translated in all civilized languages and have remained a source of inspiration ever since.

ROMANTICISM. The two men were followed by a long line of Romantic poets. "Romanticism," which represents one aspect of the reaction against the artificiality of earlier ages and the exclusive pretensions of rationalists and mathematicians, is a much abused term for one of the most meaningful developments in Western culture. Although its sentimentality, vagueness, and overenthusiasms were to antagonize later generations, its love of nature and of man in his noble aspirations, its search for inwardness, its sensitivity to beauty, and its youthful ardor and imagination were to remain ever inspiring. It placed the accent on the worth of the individual.

German Romanticism inherited artistic restraint and clarity of expression from the preceding Classical Age. It avoided much of the sentimentality and morbidity evinced elsewhere. Among its most famous representatives were Novalis, Kleist, Eichendorff, Mörike, who wrote beautiful lyrics and short stories, and E. T. A. Hoffmann, famous for his tales. At about the same time, the English Romantic movement was highlighted by the poems of Wordsworth, Coleridge, Byron, Shelley, and Keats. Italy, France, and Russia, too, had their periods of Romanticism, the Frenchman Chateaubriand being regarded as one of the founders of the Romantic movement. Everywhere, the ideal of freedom was extolled; imagination and sentiment, sometimes pervaded by mystic beliefs, fired poetic fantasy. The Romantic writers found a special source to draw upon, little considered in the past, yet inexhaustible in its depth, in the stories and folk tales which had lived on in the oral traditions of the various nations and to which Herder, in particular, had drawn attention— calling to mind the long-buried treasures of the Slavic world. Folklore thus became one of the chief fountains of inspiration, not only for poets, but also for philologists, historians, social critics, and educators. Similarly, the Roman Catholic world of the Middle Ages captivated the emotions of many and in turn affected the religious trends of the age.

CULTURAL CROSSROADS: GOETHE'S *FAUST*

At this crucial point in the history of modern times—a point when Western civilization appeared to be developed to its fullest, but when, in reality a gradual change toward new horizons was beginning—stands Goethe's majestic two-part dramatic poem *Faust*. Just as Dante's *Divina Commedia* came at the highest point of the Middle Ages and on the eve of the Renaissance, so *Faust* was written at a time of cultural transition. Goethe himself may be called "the last of the polyhistors," a man of action as well as of thought, a scientist and philosopher, a statesman and prime minister, an artist and a poet. In *Faust* he both sums up the spirit of the Modern Age and expresses its aspirations. His hero Faust is an adherent of no formulated human or divine creed but is an eternal seeker after truth. Disappointed by years of study, which have included the black art of magic, Faust makes a compact with Mephistopheles which stipulates that he must surrender his soul if ever he becomes satisfied—if ever he becomes ready to confess that he has achieved what he has been striving after. Mephistopheles tries Faust with pleasures of dissipation and carnal love, of wealth, of classical perfection, and of worldly power. But not until Faust is old and blind does he discern his goal: creative work, the winning of new life for a new and free people. This goal, of course, will never really be attained; it remains an ideal to strive for. Thus in Faust is summarized modern man—eternally dissatisfied, eternally seeking, eternally striving, and through creative endeavor eternally aspiring toward new horizons.

CHAPTER XII

NATIONALISM, LIBERALISM, INDUSTRIALISM (1815–1830)

WARS, IT HAS BEEN SAID, do not alter the course of events but may retard or accelerate changes already in process. Despite the reactionary tenor of the Congress of Vienna, the Napoleonic Wars seem to have accelerated certain Western trends. For centuries, steady progress had been made toward the formation of national states. With the rise and fall of Napoleon, the process was speeded up. The "Age of Nationalism" was at hand, and with it an age of of "Liberalism" and "Industrialism."

Nationalism had been gradually developing within Western civilization since the end of the Middle Ages. From that period on, an otherworldly orientation and the concept of an all-controlling church had been giving way to wider worldly interests; gradually the ideal of a united Christendom had become subordinated to the particular needs and ambitions of individual nations. Nationalism was based on a conviction that peoples with a common language, having a common history and tradition, and possessing a common attitude toward life should be united into single independent states. To such a state each member should show his supreme loyalty.

Liberalism, as a rule, was coupled with nationalism in the nineteenth century. At that time, liberalism was not only an attitude toward life but also a political and economic program. It aspired to achieve the freedom of the individual. It envisaged equal justice for all, a constitutional government, and the free development of every member of society according to his natural gifts and his education regardless of birth. Its main creed had been embodied in the "Rights of Man" of the French Revolution.

Industrialism was a correlative of liberal thought. The right to private property was one of liberalism's chief tenets. Therefore, liberalism favored the growth of capitalism. Capitalism, in turn, provided for the economic exploitation of the scientific discoveries of the past and made possible the new production methods which eventually came to characterize all Western civilization. The machine replaced the work of the craftsman, and an "Age of Industrialism" led to fundamental sociological changes, encompassing moral as well as material, and possibly even biological, aspects of Western civilization.

Nationalism, liberalism, and industrialism were opposed, naturally, by the conservative groups of the populations—by the royalty and by many among the clergy and landed aristocracy who were rooted in the way of life before the French Revolution. National aspirations, liberal views, and industrial production methods were, however, promoted by a young generation—heirs of the Enlightenment, who believed in "progress." These "progressives" comprised idealists from many camps, especially professors and students, professional men, and businessmen, who had steadily gained in economic weight and intellectual leadership without gaining proportionately in political rights.

PERIOD OF CONGRESSES (1818–1823)

The leading statesmen of 1815 were mainly conservatives. Having rearranged the political world at Vienna (with the vanquished nation treated wisely—i.e., generously), they now sought the preservation of their product. Afraid of further change, they had devised at Vienna a system of international consultation, which was to be used whenever a challenge arose.

Congress of Aachen (1818). The first occasion to apply this system came when France asked to be relieved of various burdens put upon her after her defeat. This issue was successfully met because some of the victorious nations desired an early restitution of French power to balance that of Russia. The statesmen met in a Congress at Aachen (Aix-la-Chapelle) and agreed to end the occupation of France and to reduce her war indemnity. They refused, however, to settle other issues ardently advocated by the liberal bourgeoisie, such as the abolition of the slave trade and the widening of international co-operation. Incidentally, this Congress was notable for the fact that it was under the influence of "bourgeois" international finance in which the Rothschild banking family was prominent. This influence affected the political decisions of Austrian, English, and other representatives.

Congress of Carlsbad (1819). The following year, 1819, witnessed a second occasion for international consultation. Liberal agitation had increased; disturbances had been caused, especially in Germany, by enthusiastic university students who demanded constitutional government and longed for a united nation. In order to prevent the spreading of such ideas, which would have undermined the hegemony of Austria, Metternich called a Congress at Carlsbad. Suppressive measures were decided upon; censorship of newspapers and books was established in Germany, and restrictions were imposed upon universities.

Congress of Troppau-Laibach (1820–1821). Repression could not stop the growth of national and liberal sentiments. They showed themselves everywhere—in Italy, Spain, Portugal, Greece, and Latin America. Particularly threatening to the existing system were rebellious outbreaks in Austria's Italian provinces. Consequently, the international machinery of Vienna was once more set in motion. A new Congress was held in Troppau, Austria, and later continued in Laibach. Metternich succeeded in winning Tsar Alexander's support, and under the banner of the "sacredness and inviolability of treaties," the two insisted on strict maintenance of the *status quo*. But, in the meantime, divergencies of opinion and interests, both among nations and within each nation, had increased; and England in particular saw her advantage in a relaxation of the Viennese system. She refused to co-operate in the military action which was decided upon and which in consequence had to be undertaken by Austria alone. Nor did a second issue jeopardizing the peace settlements, namely, the Greek struggle for independence from the Moslem Turk, lead to better co-operation. (Condemned in principle, Grecian independence yet found support from both Russia and England, who were eager to reduce Turkish power.) Similarly, accord was not reached in matters touching overseas revolts in Latin America.

Congress of Verona, 1822. The next, and last, Congress was held at Verona and concerned the national movements in Greece,

Spain, and Latin America. The Greek issue led to the same dissensions as those of the previous year, and no international action was taken. As to Spain, the old monarchy, which had been re-established after the war, had been overthrown in a bitter rebellion and the liberal constitution of 1812 had been reintroduced. Fearful for her own political system, France, which had been readmitted to the council of nations, protested and demanded armed intervention. Again, England refused to participate in a military venture and France was left to act alone. She proceeded to subdue the Spanish forces and to restore the reactionary government of the king. With regard to Latin America, Britain showed herself at still greater odds with the Continental powers. She saw in autonomous Latin American republics an important prospective market and wished to prevent the interference of other European powers. She therefore addressed herself to the United States, which in turn issued independently, in 1823, the "Monroe Doctrine." Thereby all attempts by the Congress of Verona to arrange matters in Spain's former colonies and to forestall the extension of the liberal-national revolt there were frustrated, and European collaboration came to an end.

Results. The Holy Alliance and the Congresses constituted an attempt at international organization and co-operation in line with objectives generally engendered by all-encompassing wars. As with later experiments, the attempts of 1815 to 1823 came to naught, because some of the victors used the new organization for nothing else than to prevent change. Perhaps it is correct to state that the Congresses were "an offense to the moral conscience of Europe" (Robert Palmer). However, England's foreign minister Canning had already rejected the concepts of morality as an unfit guide for national policies, even if, as he cynically added, "they justly immortalize the hero." National self-interest was extolled everywhere, and the different political climate of the preceding age could not be re-established. A measure of international anarchy came to prevail such as had been unknown to past centuries when common dynastic principles, interests, and connections had dictated common policies.

REACTION VERSUS LIBERALISM (1815–1830)

Once the unrest of the postwar period had been calmed, reaction (or at least conservatism) triumphed in most parts of Europe. Not

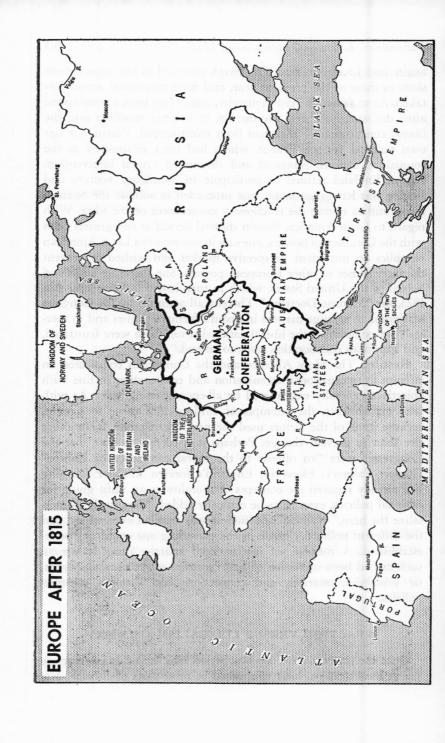

EUROPE AFTER 1815

only in Russia, but also in Austria, Prussia, England, and Spain, the governments generally suppressed movements for an extension of civil rights and freedoms. France, for a time, followed a more moderate path, but eventually also reverted to reactionary views. The United States alone among the Western countries built further on the foundation of liberal principles. Yet, liberalism, being far from its climax, gained additional ground among the educated classes and created new disturbances. These affected the international situation (which was now under firm control by the conservative statesmen) less than the internal situation in the various European countries. Within little more than a decade, liberal aspirations led once more to revolution.

France. In France, King Louis XVIII ruled from 1815 to 1824. While holding extremists in check, he followed a conservative path, in line with the Charter (or constitution) which the victors had imposed on France. This Charter provided for monarchical rule limited by certain legislative powers which were vested in an assembly. The assembly was elected by the landowners and upper middle class, constituting about 4 per cent of the population and thus representing the small well-to-do sector of the French people. But the very introduction of a Charter indicated a break with Bourbon absolutism and Napoleonic dictatorship and permitted a beginning of popular participation in government. The Charter protected civil rights; and the Napoleonic Law Code was retained along with other reforms. The principles for which Charter and Code stood were, however, abandoned when Louis XVIII died and his brother, Charles X, succeeded him. Charles attempted to secure for his friends, the old *émigrés* of the Revolution, an enormous sum to compensate them for the loss of lands; he sought to restore former Church privileges and offended the spirit of his time by exacting the death penalty for thefts of sacred objects; he suppressed public opinion and imposed a stamp tax and other restrictive measures upon newspapers; and in personal conduct, he displayed pre-Revolutionary royal splendor. Simultaneously, he tried to divert the attention of his people from his internal policies by catering to their frustrated thirst for glory and by engaging in a new military venture—an expedition for the conquest of Algiers. His ill-conceived policies brought about the breakdown of his own regime.

Central Europe. In Italy and the Germanies, Metternich's conservatism dominated. Except in three German states—one of them the small principality of Saxe-Weimar where Goethe was prime minister—no constitution was developed. The *Code Napoléon* with its liberal spirit was not retained; in essence, government was administered in accordance with principles of enlightened despotism. This conservative trend brought conflict with the liberals. In Italy, a number of secret societies were founded, like the *Carbonari*, which supported the liberal cause. In Germany, a comparable liberal movement led to unrest among students and to the formation of *Burschenschaften* (fraternities) and other liberal societies. The Italian movement attracted some outstanding men, among whom were the writers Manzoni and Gioberti and the famous politician Mazzini. In Germany, idealistic thinkers—the great scientist Humboldt, the philosopher Fichte, the statesman vom Stein, the poet Arndt, the brothers Grimm, and many others—joined the cause. However, liberal hopes in Italy came to naught when attempts at revolution failed in 1820 and 1821. Thereafter, justice favored the old privileged class again, clericalism was supported anew, scientific education was hindered, and censorship controlled public opinion. Foreign domination remained. In Germany, also, the liberal forces proved too weak. In 1817, students organized a festival on the Wartburg, where revolutionary speeches were made; and in 1819, a liberal murdered a poet, von Kotzebue, who was accused of spying for reactionary Russia. This event spurred Metternich to call the Congress of Carlsbad, mentioned above; its decrees and repressive police measures put a stop to the agitation and initiated a period of calm and firm conservative rule.

England. Similar conservatism marked English policies. The court was old-fashioned and dissolute. The office of prime minister from 1815 to 1830 was in the hands of the Tory party, which dominated in Parliament and passed little progressive legislation. Suffrage was restricted even more than in France. Modernization of agriculture was neglected; the common fields were almost entirely enclosed; freeholders constantly diminished in number; and corn laws were passed which provided for protective tariffs on grain imports and benefited only the few rich landlords. Little was done for the impoverished. A severe business crisis, following the war period, brought unemployment; desperate outbreaks of the workers were answered with suspension of the *habeas corpus* in 1817 and in one instance, in 1819, were bloodily suppressed. A stamp tax and censorship were introduced and public mass meetings were forbidden. Little understanding was shown for the fact that while England grew rich—while London inherited the position of financial center of the world formerly held by Amsterdam and while the Midlands became "the workshop of the world"—the workers and the lower bourgeoisie reaped meager benefits. Only slowly, with improvement in business in the early 1820's, did a countermovement appear within the Tory party itself. So-called "liberal Tories," like Peel and Canning, gained influence. Owing to their endeavors, penalties for political offenses were eased and the police system made more lenient; tariffs were reduced, trade policies were liberalized, the currency was stabilized through the introduction of the gold standard, and some attempts to pass labor legislation were initiated. In 1828 and 1829, laws were passed which accorded long-withheld political emancipation to dissenters and Catholics in England. But other far-reaching liberal legislation had to await, in England as elsewhere, the shock and impetus of the French "July Revolution" of 1830.

Russia. Despite the reputation for liberalism which the Russian tsar Alexander I had acquired in his youth, reaction proved to be strongest in Russia. Liberal tendencies, which could threaten existing autocratic institutions, were crushed, and nationalistic aspirations, which caused unrest among subjugated nationalities like the Poles, were ruthlessly combated. Early in Alexander's rule, his confidant, the minister Speransky, had proposed a reform program: consultative assemblies on the national level, a measure of local self-government, gradual reduction of serfdom, and lessening of class distinctions; and after the Napoleonic Wars, plans were made for modernization of agriculture and industry. But the lack of qualified administrators and the concomitant corruption, as well as the growing conservatism of Alexander, checked progress. Few improvements were undertaken in the educational system, the law courts, or the provincial administration. Serfs remained in bondage except on the estates of the German Balts, who foresaw the economic advantage of emancipation. The constitution and autonomy granted to the Poles were often violated. Universities were founded, but their work was subjected to police supervision. Obscurantism flourished. Additional bondage was introduced through the establishment of military colonies. The unhappy inhabitants of areas set aside for these colonies became permanent soldiers and were, together with their families, subjected even in peacetime agricultural work to the absolute command of the military authorities. They received material care during their entire lifetime, but they lost all individual rights. As a result, when Alexander died in December (Russian *Dekabr*), 1825, a revolt broke out. This "Dekabrist" revolt, initiated to bring freedom and constitutional government to Russian lands and led by idealistic young officers (most of them from the nobility) who were imbued with the liberal spirit of Europe, was put down with extreme brutality. From then on, the new tsar, Nicholas I, combated all liberal leanings. Again, Russia was insulated from Western influences, and the old autocracy imposed its despotism anew.

The United States. While political and economic liberalism was losing ground among the governments of Europe and all but disappearing in Russia, it was gaining in the United States. Democratic institutions grew; voting privileges were consistently extended; educational opportunities were broadened, and humanitarian issues were given wide attention. After Jackson became president in 1829, democratic processes were speeded up.

However, a number of problems emerged which were unknown to other countries in the Western world. Some of these problems arose from the fact that in the United States (as in Russia) farmers had the opportunity to cultivate wide areas of unsettled territory, an opportunity altogether impossible in the narrowly confined British and Continental nations, faced with the necessity of intensive cultivation. Some problems had to do with industrial policies quite different from those of other Western countries. (The American idea of a protective tariff, for instance, was out of keeping with liberal European economic theory.) Other problems derived from the fact that the Union was young and developed a political system of its own. Among the problems was that of foreign immigration which led to heated debates. Others were connected with the westward movement, a prolific source of controversy; with the question of Negro slavery, which brought bitter strife and was settled only temporarily in 1820 by the Missouri Compromise; and with the "nullification" of a federal act by one of the member states owing to the tariff legislation of 1832. Thus, internal problems of the United States combined with factors peculiar to its geography and political origin forced the country on a course in many respects different from that of Western Europe.

REVOLUTION

In 1830, whatever feeling of security the conservative groups of society may have been able to preserve in the face of concessions which, especially in England, had been forced upon them, was shattered when a new revolution broke out in France. It was at first feared that this would lead to an upheaval comparable to that of 1789; and perhaps this fear contributed to the quick surrender of the French king. But in its course, the Revolutionary movement did not again overturn society; instead, it was stopped in its early stages. Actually, the instigators had never envisaged more than the restitution of those liberal principles on which the post-Napoleonic settlement had been based. New social ideas were not at stake.

July Revolution (1830). The July Revolution was brought about by the shortsightedness of Charles X, who violated the Charter and ignored petitions asking him to respect it. Finally, he issued "four ordinances," whereby the electoral law was arbitrarily changed to the exclusive advantage of the landowners, new elections were decreed, and the freedom of the press was further curtailed. On July 27, 1830, when the printers went on strike and barricades were put up in the streets of Paris, King Charles X quickly fled. Then the moderate royalist forces under the veteran leadership of Talleyrand and Lafayette succeeded in preventing bloodshed. They deposed Charles and accepted his cousin Louis Philippe, prince of Orléans, as a suitable successor to the throne. Louis Philippe had always boasted of his liberalism; he was proud of his "bourgeois" ways; and he could be expected to respect the Charter. The "four ordinances" were revoked; censorship was abolished. By the lowering of voting qualifications, the electorate was approximately doubled, and the citizens' National Guard, formed to counterbalance the regular armed forces controlled by the king, was reorganized to insure the gains of the revolution. The reforms satisfied the upper bourgeoisie; sporadic further revolts by the industrial proletariat (still poor and weak) were ruthlessly suppressed, and by 1833 quiet reigned under the guidance of Louis Philippe's "July Monarchy."

Repercussions in Western Europe. The July outbreaks in Paris set off revolts throughout Europe. The neighboring Belgians, ever dissatisfied with the Vienna arrangement which had forced them into a union with Holland, rebelled—clamoring for constitutional government and national independence; and within a decade Belgium was established as an independent state. Disturbances occurred in Switzerland and Italy. In Germany, a number of princes hurried to grant their peoples long-promised constitutions; the unification movement, advocated by liberal and national groups, made some progress, at least in the economic sphere. Under Prussian leadership, a *Zollverein* or customs union, created earlier, was extended to include almost all the states of northern Germany. In England, after fifty years of Tory rule, a Whig cabinet took over in 1830; and, under Grey, energetic work was started to reform the electoral law. In 1832, though not without meeting violent resistance, a first "Reform Bill" was passed. It abolished "rotten boroughs" (electoral districts which, though depopulated, had still enjoyed the traditional right of representation in Parliament) and created new electoral districts in urban areas. It thus broke the monopoly of the land-owning nobility, with its medieval privileges, just as the Catholic Emancipation Act had broken that of the Anglican Church, and made room for broader representation of the bourgeoisie. To be sure, the industrial proletariat gained nothing; nor was the composition of Parliament promptly changed. But the First Reform Bill paved the way for future reforms.

Repercussions in Eastern Europe. The July Revolution indirectly helped the Greeks. Since 1819, they had struggled against the sultan. England and Russia had given them aid and in 1827 had destroyed the Turkish fleet at Navarino, and Russia had continued the war until she could impose the Peace of Adrianople. With Turkey beaten and the liberal national movement invigorated by the July Revolution, Greece's claim to independent statehood was recognized; and in 1832, the new nation was established. Actually, it was only in isolated Russia that the July Revolution failed to have a tangible effect. For there the bourgeois class was too weak, the universities were too small and too firmly controlled, and ever since the Dekabrist rising the autocratic government had been alert to any revolutionary action. The July Revolution did spread, however, to Poland; there a terrible uprising ended with the brutal suppression of the rebels and the abolition of Poland's constitution. It accelerated the Russification of Poland and brought increasingly strict censorship to stifle all independent thought.

CHAPTER XIII

SOCIETY, ARTS, AND SCIENCES
(1815–1848)

THE STIRRING EVENTS of the great French Revolution and the Napoleonic Age, despite the widespread suffering and sense of failure that ensued, did not destroy the idealism which had marked the preceding Age of Enlightenment. A strong element of unrest remained. Intellectual vigor was remarkable, and social questions and scientific problems were attacked with unequaled fervor and discernment. But, despite its efforts and enthusiasms, the generation which lived in the years following the Congress of Vienna experienced bitter disappointments.

SOCIETY: PRACTICE AND THEORY

In a sense, the Revolution of 1830 accomplished what, owing to its excesses and subsequent dictatorship, the great Revolution of 1789 had failed to achieve. Professional men and those who controlled finance, trade, and the growing industrial apparatus gained almost everywhere a full share in the exercise of political power. "Bourgeois" views penetrated all facets of Western civilization.

New Social Stratification. In line with the trends of the times, social stratification was modified. The old nobility retained much of its landed wealth and of its role at the royal courts and in the administrations of many countries, but it no longer set the pattern in manners, taste, and social attitudes. The proportion of peasants in the population (they had been freed from serfdom everywhere except in eastern Europe) declined, even though they still comprised the overwhelming majority; they achieved no active political role. Industrial workers increased their numbers, but, owing to their economic weakness, they were unable to influence either national or economic policies. It was thus the middle class, the bourgeoisie, which impressed its stamp upon the age; and within this group, the "captain of industry," as the historian Carlyle called him, or simply the successful self-made man shaped the ways of modern society. His specialized knowledge, ambition, and (in some cases) erudition and culture enabled him to challenge the old upper classes. He gained his influence by means of hard work. He adopted or imitated many of the views and prejudices of the old society, but he was also receptive to modern ideologies. As a whole, the middle class cherished liberal thought, to which it owed its rise; it generally advocated equality of opportunity, favored the founding of schools and universities, and was interested in the progress of science. Although many supported the religious institutions of the past, they showed less religious fervor. They were tolerant in their treatment of minority groups, such as the Jews; the latter were emancipated politically, and many of them attained leading positions in science and trade. Bourgeois society was devoted—though often more in theory than in practice—to "propriety," stability, and honesty; and it served as a new patron of arts and learning.

Mechanization of Industry. The "rise of the bourgeoisie" owed most of its impetus to the mechanization of production methods. Mechanization brought changes so profound that later the expression "Industrial Revolution" was coined to describe the era—a misleading term, for no revolution took place, but rather "a series of economic changes" which were drawn out over a long period of time. These changes came first, and proceeded most rapidly, in England. Her insular position, fast-growing population, insufficiency of foodstuffs but control of raw materials at home and in her colonies, and —most of all—enterprising commercial spirit favored early adoption of new production methods. Mechanization of the textile industry started the spiral of general industrialization, for it led to the growth of machine industry, which, in turn, stimulated coal and iron mining, shipbuilding, and, after 1825, railroad construction. Trade increased, prices rose, a boom resulted, and new industries came into being. Other European countries followed, albeit at a slower pace. In France, where coal and iron were scarce and agriculture was flourishing, and where cheap labor was neither abundant nor concentrated in urban areas, industrialization was delayed. Spain, Italy, Germany, the Netherlands, and the Scandinavian countries lagged still farther behind.

Social Theory. The mass poverty resulting from industrialization was most sharply felt in England; she became not only the industrial, but also the social, workshop of the world. It was there that theorists occupied themselves most intensely with the new economic and social problems. Medieval thinkers had condemned covetousness, ambition, competition, and economic exploitation. Though not overly concerned with poverty, which was considered inevitable in human society, they had demanded Christian charity. They had insisted on a "just" price and had opposed interest-taking. They had approved regulation of trade and enforcement of quality standards through guilds and monopolies. Most of these fundamental views had been reversed by the classical economic theory of eighteenth- and early nineteenth-century England. Ambition was no longer considered a vice; price determination by the laws of supply and demand, without reference to ethical principles, was regarded as natural and proper; interest-taking was accepted as a normal function of the money market; monopolies were condemned, and regulation of trade and production as to quality and quantity was left to "natural" forces. In line with liberal trends, and inspired by Adam Smith's laissez-faire views, economists defended modern capitalism and private property, extolled the division of labor, and investigated the economics of money, rent, labor, and value. Most of them held to the liberal proposition that the free play of economic activities would bring the most favorable general conditions, that each person is the best judge of his own interests, and that the individual serves society best when he promotes his own interests. But an increasingly pessimistic strain can be noticed even among these economists. David Ricardo felt that social interests could never be harmonized. Sismondi doubted that new production possibilities could improve the situation of the masses and prophesied a succession of crises which would forever disturb social relationships. Malthus, following in this liberal path, insisted that population will always tend to outrun the means of subsistence; he therefore considered economic planning and artificial relief measures to be senseless.

Social Reality. Evidence furnished by the actual social situation seemed, indeed, to support such pessimistic views. Industrialization brought unforeseen results. The personal relationship formerly existing between employer and employee was lost in the conduct of the new large-scale enterprises; individual workers became mere units in a chain of production. Their employment and wages came to depend less upon personal achievement than upon impersonal trends and business cycles. They no longer took pride in, or gained satisfaction and a comfortable living from, craftsmanship and skill; low-paid unskilled workers (often women and children) sufficed to attend to machinery; and family incomes declined. Many farm laborers were cruelly uprooted and separated from the soil from which they had drawn strength and a measure of security. They had to perform monotonous tasks as a result of the widespread division of labor, and they were exhausted by excessive working hours and long trips to and from their work. Living in dismal slums, they no longer had the solace of the quiet and beauty of the countryside. To be sure, scientific progress opened new vistas; it was now possible to prolong the average life span, to introduce some new comforts of life, and to reduce manual labor through machinery that performed miracles of strength, speed, and precision. But, at first these benefits were only for the few and were paid for by both worker and peasant, whose lives were spent in toil. Man's ambitious and ruthless competitive instincts were stimulated; wealth was increasingly being concentrated in the hands of entrepreneurs, and the gulf between rich and poor continued to widen. Even on the land, the newly gained freedom from serfdom was of little benefit to the peasant; the need for scientific farming methods, for fertilizer, for the planting of new mass crops, such as potatoes and sugar beets, and, consequently, for financial means forced many to quit their homes. A smaller number of farmers could feed the increasing populations. There was a change in the population ratio of town and country.

Challenging Economic Thought. In view of such conditions, many leading thinkers in the second quarter of the nineteenth century began to occupy themselves with a revision of economic theories.

MODIFIED LAISSEZ-FAIRE. Jean Say abandoned much of the position of the classical economist and taught that utility is the measure of value and that labor must be judged by utilitarian standards. Friedrich List advocated a certain amount of state direction and a protective tariff; and John Stuart Mill, somewhat later, insisted, like List, on a measure of regulation and on social reforms directed by the state.

UTOPIANISM AND ANARCHISM. A more radical departure from the laissez-faire theory can be traced to various idealistic groups of the first half of the nineteenth century. Of special importance were the "utopians" who, believing in the goodness of man if wisely led, expected a better future from the full development of his rational and moral qualities. Their views and aims were best represented by Robert Owen, an English textile worker who had become owner of a mill. Starting with social improvements in his own factory, where he limited the working hours of children, paid wages during periods of unemployment, and instituted schools for workers and looked after their health, he then turned his attention to British national problems. He moved temporarily to America and, in 1825, founded in New Harmony, Indiana, a colony for people who would renounce private property. Those who lived there adopted uniform housing, clothing, and education; they worked as a community and received credit for their labor in accordance with the extent of their participation in the activities of the community. The project collapsed, however, because the participants lacked the devotion and individual initiative Owen had expected. A more scientific approach than Owen's can be ascribed to Saint-Simon. This noted Frenchman, a wealthy count and convinced Christian who sacrificed all his possessions for his ideals, taught that society must be scientifically planned, that true freedom consists in serving the community, and that spiritual values depend upon the economic situation. He held that property corrupts man. In this, his compatriots, Fourier and Proudhon, agreed with him. But not from society, church, or state— agents of law, protectors of property, and therefore vicious—did the latter two expect salvation; they expected it from individual man's rationality. Reason, they thought, would induce men to enter freely into contracts with fellow men; and on such a basis a healthy, moral, and stateless (anarchical) society could be built. In opposition, Louis Blanc extended Saint-Simon's views, insisting that, at least for the time being, the state alone could guarantee a fair distribution of wealth. He therefore demanded that governments attend to the task of organizing work. In many respects, Blanc represented the view of the modern socialist camp.

SOCIALISM. Socialism—in its early stages indistinguishable from

communism—was not a nineteenth-century invention. It had ante-
cedents in some of Plato's teachings, in the Gospels, in Thomas
More's writings, and in certain Egyptian and Aztec institutions.
Nineteenth-century socialism differed, however, from earlier parallel
movements essentially in that it addressed itself mainly to the new
industrial worker and only indirectly to the peasant. It concerned
itself largely with the relationship of entrepreneur and laborer and
with questions of profit. It embraced a great variety of views, with
some socialists basing their precepts on moral grounds, others on
materialistic concepts. But all had in common the fundamental
principle that private property is evil and that the means of production, and possibly even those of distribution, should be in the
hands of the community. They demanded an equal distribution of
the national wealth, with remuneration for everyone according to
his work or according to his needs. Traditional concepts, including
inherited religious views, were rejected by most of them; socialists
tried to be "scientific."

Social Legislation. Under the impact of utopianism, anarchism,
and scientific socialism, both workers and governments acted to
cope with the problems of the new industrial age. Workers gave up
the destruction of machinery and other desperate measures, to which
they had resorted in their ignorance at the beginning of mechanization. Instead, they began to form associations and unions, which
were to give strength to their cause. (They organized the first trade-
union, an illegal enterprise, in 1824.) They also began to organize
producers' and consumers' co-operatives in agriculture, industry, and
trade, in order to bring a sector of the national economy under their
own control and to share in the profits made possible by the new
production methods. Governments reacted by passing reformatory
factory legislation, beginning with provisions for sanitation and for
the whitewashing of buildings, and continuing with regulations
against the exploitation of children. In 1819, England forbade the
employment of children under nine years of age for work in cotton
mills; factory codes (1833) and other laws for the protection of
women and children followed, even though enforcement was slack.
By 1847, a maximum working day of ten hours had been established
for women and minors in certain trades. But all European governments held out against recognition of the workers' right to form
associations or to resort to strikes. Nor did they propose unemploy-
ment-relief measures; they attributed poverty and hardships to the

assumed laziness of the individual; in fact, especially in England, attempts were made to meet the problem of poverty by making governmental "poor relief" worse than poverty itself.

LITERATURE, SCIENCE, AND ARTS

Preoccupation of thinkers with societal changes did not hinder a vigorous literary and artistic life after the Napoleonic Wars were over.

Literature. Goethe died in 1832, one year after finishing *Faust*. Germany continued to create—for example, with a poet like Heine—beautiful lyrical poetry and, with the great romantic writer E. T. A. Hoffmann, some of the most enchanting tales of fantasy. Moreover, in a period when the drama was neglected and "became divorced from popular stage production," Germany contributed two eminent playwrights: Grillparzer and Hebbel. With penetrating psychological insight into the problems arising from man's life situation, the latter paved the way for the modern drama. In France, the age of the novelist (*romancier*) dawned. Stendhal, Balzac, and Flaubert wrote their great novels, and the elder Dumas composed his famous historical stories. Perhaps the most important was Victor Hugo, whose historical novels have continued to enjoy wide popularity. In England, as in Germany, the "Romantic movement" continued. Keats, Shelley, and Byron died young (in the 1820's), but Wordsworth lived until 1850. Wordsworth had won fame before 1800 with his poetry and essays, marked by rejection of classicist trends and by emphasis on a direct and warm relationship to nature; he continued to create similar works which served as a model for many of his contemporaries. Romanticism lived on also in the famous historical novels of Walter Scott and in the writings of Thackeray, and, to a certain extent, even in the social novels of Dickens. Literature in the English language was enriched (perhaps for the first time) by American writers, among whom Poe, Cooper, and Hawthorne gained international renown. Like America, Russia entered the world's literary stage as a newcomer; her writers displayed unique artistic gifts. Pushkin with his exquisite lyrics, powerful dramas, and enchanting stories stands at the beginning of a long list of Russian artists of notable genius; and the novels of Gogol (*Dead Souls*) and Goncharov (*Oblomov*), depicting the strange atmosphere of the Russian landscape, humanity, and way of life, captured, owing to the unique mastery of the art of presentation, the imagination of readers everywhere. Writers of accomplishment also included Mickiewicz in Poland and Manzoni in Italy.

Philosophy and History. Except in Germany, the first half of the nineteenth century was not fruitful of lasting philosophical works. In England, a shallow utilitarianism was expounded. Even Jeremy Bentham, with his sober studies of human nature and his love of liberty and desire for progress, showed in his search for the "greatest happiness for the greatest number" little insight into the human condition. But in Germany, Hegel, Fichte, and Schelling kept alive the traditions of the great thinkers: in man's search for freedom they saw the goal of history and the workings of Providence. Their idealism was opposed by a fourth eminent philosopher, Schopenhauer, who posited a deep pessimism: not in moral attitudes but in man's will to live, he saw the driving force of human action, and ideas were to him but reflections of that will and of man's selfishness. Philosophical thought came to be increasingly interwoven with historical studies, for, out of combined progress in these fields, came a new understanding of man's attitudes, aspirations, and environmental conditions. A great collection of historical sources was started in Germany, the *Monumenta Germaniae Historica*; Niebuhr wrote his fundamental work on Roman law; and the most famous of modern historians, Ranke, began his long and fruitful career. Ranke's aim at scrupulous, scientific, and sober investigation "of what actually happened" was soon adopted by all European scholars.

Science. The influence of the physical sciences upon nineteenth-century thinking was very effective. The fundamental work of the investigators of the eighteenth century was broadened and applied. Faraday discovered electromagnetic induction. Gauss, Helmholtz, Maxwell, and many others undertook studies of light and electricity and of heat and energy, and investigated electromagnetic waves and electrochemistry. Fraunhofer discovered the method of spectrum analysis; thermodynamics was studied; and on the basis of such fundamental work, new machinery, appliances, and lighting systems were invented. The most varied kinds of power-driven apparatus (for steamships, locomotives, and motors in factories) were created. Coal and steel became the most important industries, setting standards whereby the material progress of a country could be measured. Likewise, the fields of geography and geology were scientificallv developed (e.g., by Alexander von Humboldt and Sir Charles Lyell).

Art. While literature and science flourished, the fine arts produced little of lasting merit. Two painters of note appeared in England: Turner and Constable, the one famous for his paintings of Venice, the other for his landscapes. France took pride in Delacroix and Ingres. But other countries had no painters or sculptors of more than mediocre stature. The same is true of achievements in architecture. The neoclassical style of the early nineteenth century, represented by men such as the Danish sculptor Thorwaldsen, gave way to another imitative art form, the neo-Gothic; but little of lasting beauty was created. Cities, which grew rapidly, showed an increasingly dismal picture: ugly and pretentious dwellings and often graceless villas and public buildings began to mar town and countryside—especially in newly industrialized regions.

Music. "Romanticism," which, as does every great trend, embraced not only one but many areas of human endeavor (painting, literature, religion, history) became dominant in the field of music during the early nineteenth century. In opposition to the formal rules established in the Classical Age of music, the Romantic composers sought freedom of self-expression, delved into the mysteries of human life, and, above all, tried to depict emotion. Inspired by folk traditions as well as by patriotic movements of the Napoleonic era, they created some of the most beautiful works ever written. The most famous "Romantic" was Schubert (d. 1828). In addition to chamber music and symphonies, he composed *Lieder* which have become a permanent treasure of the musical world. His tradition was carried on by men like Schumann and Mendelssohn. Outside of Germany, Berlioz and the Polish exile Chopin in France excelled, the latter equally great as pianist and as composer of nocturnes, dance tunes, and preludes. In opera, the chief Romantic work was *Der Freischütz* by the German Weber, while in the Romance countries Donizetti and Rossini (*Barber of Seville*) stand out. The Italian composers adhered rather firmly to traditional forms and, lacking some of the depth of feeling evinced by the Romantics, often catered to the demands of a public which wanted to be merely entertained and amused, and was fascinated by virtuosity.

CHAPTER XIV

BOURGEOIS ERA AND REVOLUTION
(1830–1848)

IN INTERNATIONAL AFFAIRS, the period from 1830 to 1848 was one of the quietest in European history. This fact proved the wisdom of Europe's most prominent statesman of the age, Prince Metternich; for, despite his conservatism, he had succeeded in establishing a power balance that maintained a lasting peace for Europe. But internal affairs in the various European nations did not bear the same peaceful stamp; the conservatism of the statesmen acted as a brake on normal progress and as a stimulus to radicalism.

NEW CONSERVATISM VERSUS NEW LIBERALISM

As soon as the upper middle classes had attained (through the revolutions of 1830) positions of leadership in most of western Europe, they themselves became a conservative force. The cause of liberalism was, however, not buried. It was carried on by individuals from many camps, who evinced little evidence of "class" divisions but who were motivated by idealism and conviction.

England. Owing to changes resulting from the growth of industries, England found herself in a precarious situation. Shifting social stratification, transformation of the English countryside, and new objectives in economic as well as in international affairs raised a variety of problems for which satisfactory answers could be found only slowly.

GENERAL PROBLEMS. During the early thirties, the British continued to be harassed by tensions between the industrial workers and the new entrepreneurial groups and between the latter and the land-owning nobility. Thus, discontent persisted. To be sure, social reform legislation, in addition to the political Reform Bill of 1832, was passed. Parliament promulgated factory codes, improved health and sanitation systems, carried through church and municipal reforms, and made long-overdue arrangements for the abolition of slavery in the empire. But all this was insufficient. There remained the problems resulting from urbanization, the problem of poor relief, and the issues of free trade or protective legislation and of centralized or decentralized government; numerous humanitarian questions remained unsolved. Riots occurred, and the threat of general revolution persisted.

POLITICAL PARTIES. As a result, the political leaders could no longer defer more resolute steps toward modernization. The accession of a young queen, Victoria, in 1837, marked the turning point. Court life, which had been dissolute and extravagant under her predecessors, was reformed, and the governing parties were reorganized. The old Tories split, and a "Conservative party" emerged. This party—opposed as it was to the increasingly strong bourgeoisie, to the rich industrialists in the Midlands, and to the ambitious merchants—promoted as a rule the interests of the large landowners. (Occasionally it sought, as advocated by one of its members, Shaftesbury, an alliance with the working class.) The Whigs also reformed. They came to be known as the "Liberal party," but, in line with the nature of liberalism, they found themselves divided into numerous factions. There were those like the best-known members—Grey, Palmerston, and Melbourne—who were close to the more progressive Conservatives; others who were radicals and insisted on speedy reforms; and again others, like the Irish leader O'Connell, who espoused special interests. Essentially, the Liberals stood for laissez-faire, trusting that the greatest progress would result if substantial freedom of action were allowed to the individual. Backed by a majority of the voting public, they formed a succession of cabinets. But as neither they nor the Conservatives represented the industrial workers, there arose still other groups and movements, most of them opposed to extreme liberalism as well as conservatism and some of them anticapitalistic. Among them was the Anti-Corn Law League, founded by Cobden. It aimed at the abolition of the tariffs on grain which protected the landed gentry but adversely affected the industrial workers and the industrial entrepreneurs alike. Another was the

Chartist group, which included factory workers, miners, and many intellectuals devoting themselves to the cause of humanitarianism and democracy. The Chartists demanded economic improvement for the workers, social equality for all, and radical changes (such as universal male suffrage) in the electoral system. But the Chartists were disunited with regard to the choice of means—peaceful or revolutionary—by which to achieve their aims. They lacked sufficient funds to build an organization which would enable them to gain control of the government. Yet, they succeeded in keeping alive the issue of social reform. Millions of petitions were sent to the House of Commons to advocate their cause; well-known public figures (including the reformer and poor-law commissioner Edwin Chadwick) and leaders of the Anti-Corn Law League supported their program. But almost a century was to pass before their major proposals were to be carried out.

INTERNAL REFORMS. The internal realignments, the formation of new leagues and parties, and the vigorous political propaganda accompanying the changes could not help but increase general unrest, and this convinced the ruling forces by the middle of the 1840's of the necessity to make further concessions. Therefore, factory codes were improved; laws providing more adequately for the protection of workers were passed; and, most importantly—in 1846, when Peel was prime minister—the Conservative party, though split, had the Corn Laws repealed. Therewith, a chief grievance of the businessmen and industrial workers was eliminated. But repeal had many untoward consequences, for it caused distress among the farmers, especially in nonindustrialized Ireland, where potato blight and subsequent famine had caused widespread distress even before repeal. It also led England eventually to adopt a more aggressive colonial policy in order to safeguard its imports of foodstuffs and its markets for industrial goods—tempting her to engage in wars which were both costly and damaging to her reputation. Once the repeal of the Corn Laws had been achieved, hopeful Chartists continued their demands for further reforms. But when another revolution broke out in France (the February Revolution of 1848) and danger of violence threatened England also, the reform movement was interrupted. The government preferred to use repressive measures, a policy which caused widespread resentment and impelled many to leave their country and seek a better life in the New World or in Australia.

Guizot — arch conservative forces during July Monarchy

Thiers — led liberals

FOREIGN AFFAIRS. The specifically English problems caused by the rapid growth of industry, of finance, and of trade led to a specifically English foreign policy. The country now isolated itself more and more from Continental affairs, satisfied that the existing balance of power was a guarantee of safety. It concentrated on overseas policies and the protection of the sea lanes to its various colonies. Its Asiatic possessions were expanded by penetration into Burma; and in the 1840's, an attack was launched on China, prompted by a Chinese law prohibiting the importation of opium from India and by the destruction of some English-owned opium stores in China. This attack, which was widely condemned because it implicitly coerced the Chinese to allow, for the sake of British economic interests, the sale of the dangerous drug (banned elsewhere), came to be known as the "Opium War." China, defeated, was forced to pay damages, to revoke the prohibition of opium, to open a number of ports to British traders, and to grant them numerous privileges on Chinese soil.

France. In France, a conservative course was followed during the reign of Louis Philippe. Wisely enough, this king turned his back on the doubtful glory of the battlefield, and his government, led in the 1830's by the historian Thiers, worked for internal prosperity. During Louis Philippe's reign, French population growth, stopped in Napoleonic times, was resumed. Public works were sponsored, schools were founded, and relations with the Catholic Church were normalized. The arts flourished, and France once more took her place as an outstanding cultural center of the Western world. However, dissatisfaction grew. Reactionary royalists who supported the claims of the deposed Bourbons, nationalists who dreamed of Napoleonic glory, liberals who demanded wider constitutional rights than the Charter provided, and socialists who wanted political power for the workers never reconciled themselves to Louis Philippe's rule. Within a few years, newspapers began to ridicule the king for his "bourgeois" ways and views, and Louis Philippe found no better means of dealing with the situation than the re-enactment of repressive legislation. This only increased resistance. Thiers resigned and another historian, Guizot, became prime minister. Through unpopular measures, through his opposition to the Church, his refusal to enlarge the franchise, and his dishonesty in dealing with the parliament, he in turn contributed in the course of the years to a further decline of Louis Philippe's prestige. By the end of 1847, the

France

Thiers liberal

Dissatisfaction

Royalists
Nationalists
Liberals
Socialists

Louis reacts with repressive legislation

Guizot becomes prime minister

middle class — lip service to representative govt — no faith in democracy opposition began to organize large public banquets which offered occasions for revolutionary speeches. When on February 22, 1848, one such banquet was to be held, the government forbade it. This became the signal for open revolt, and a third French revolution, the "February Revolution" of 1848, got under way.

Germany. As in France, so in Germany the period from 1830 to 1848 was one of external calm and internal seething. The influence of Metternich prevailed throughout, and, notwithstanding minor modifications, his system remained in essence as he had planned it.

INTERNAL CONDITIONS. Most of the German states were governed efficiently, though in the tradition of enlightened despotism rather than according to liberal standards. Inasmuch as industrialization, with its initial dislocations, had not yet been experienced in Germany, economic conditions were comparatively favorable. German philosophers, poets, and musicians were admired everywhere; German universities, with their eminent men of science and scholars in the humanities, drew students from all other parts of the world. But underneath the placid surface much dissatisfaction smoldered, for little account was taken of national aspirations or of liberal social demands. The cause of representative government made little progress; for example, newspapers and books remained subject to censorship. In most places, the nobility with its agrarian interests retained the highest administrative, military, and diplomatic positions, while the bourgeoisie played a subordinate role.

NATIONALITY PROBLEM. Economic and social questions were complicated by problems of nationality. In the Hapsburg areas of the German federation, the numerous non-German nationality groups—Italians, Czechs, Hungarians, and others—began to clamor for self-government. But the Germans in all areas agitated for a closer union, for one great Germany. Fearful that the latter demand would endanger their multinational empire, the Hapsburgs opposed all unification moves, while Prussia, vying for leadership within a German federation, identified herself to a certain extent with the aspirations for one united nation. This conflict in basic objectives, dividing the Hapsburgs and Prussians into hostile camps, was sharpened by their divergent attitude in social and political matters. Austria with her "Metternichism" appealed to the conservative forces and to the vanity of the small princes, while Prussia aligned herself with the forces demanding change. Prussia established the *Zollverein* (customs union) and introduced trial by jury and free dom of the press which pleased the liberals. When general unrest mounted in 1847, the king of Prussia even called a diet or parliament composed of representatives of the people. But this measure was half-hearted, and no legislative powers were vested in the diet, nor was a constitution promulgated. Thus, nowhere was real progress made toward the solution of critical problems, and when the February Revolution broke out in France, unrest in Prussia was as great as it was in Austria; the call to revolution found a wide and enthusiastic echo everywhere in German lands.

Italy. Like Germany, Italy was disunited as a nation; but in addition, most of her territory was subject to foreign rule—Sicily and Naples to the Spanish Bourbons; the Central Provinces (Parma, Modena, Tuscany, etc.) to various Austrian princes; and Lombardy as well as Venetia to the Hapsburg empire. Only Piedmont and the Papal States had Italian rulers—the one the House of Savoy, the other the pope. Misrule prevailed in all parts of the nation, progressive forces were suppressed economically as well as politically, and the population was divided over political and religious questions. Neither industries and agriculture nor political institutions prospered; and poverty was widespread. Intellectual activities were a major concern only among the small upper crust of the populations; the anti-Catholicism of many people in this upper crust prevented much contact between them and the masses. Nor did unity exist among the leaders. Some were republicans, some royalists; others played with the idea of a unified Italy ruled by the pope, and still others were without any plan. A movement called "Young Italy" and envisaging a *risorgimento,* a rebirth of the nation, was initiated, but it remained weak; and rebellions, which occurred at regular intervals, achieved little. Thus, a revolt undertaken in Genoa in 1834 by a young enthusiast, Garibaldi, resulted in failure and the exile of its leader. In 1846, new hopes for a change were aroused by the election of a rather young pope, Pius IX, who was credited with liberal leanings and administrative ability. The worldly-wise Metternich was little disturbed, remarking cynically that "a liberal pope is inconceivable"; and actually, the expectations of the patriots were not realized. Nothing was left to them but to look for leadership from Piedmont, the only other independent Italian state. Lured by the opportunity for its own aggrandizement, the House of Savoy accepted the challenge and began, like the Prussian royal house in Germany, to move ahead on the road of liberal reform. It even granted a constitution; and although its sincerity about reforms remained as doubtful as that of Prussia, it could, because of the nationalistic issue, assume the desired role of leadership in Italy when the February Revolution occurred in France.

Russie [margin note]

Russia. During the period from 1830 to 1848, while economic conditions and political trends were working slow changes in Europe and accumulating enough pressure to cause revolutionary outbreaks, conditions in Russia remained stagnant.

autoracy/ orthodoxy/ + nationality [margin note]

INTERNAL POLICIES. After suppression of the Dekabrist revolt, Russia had restored tsarist power, keeping intact the rule of the landlord class and the institution of serfdom. Adopting the slogan, "autocracy, orthodoxy, nationality," the government made few progressive moves. It did promulgate a new law code along lines proposed by the old statesman Speransky; it did improve public finance, modernize the administrative organization, extend some civil rights to the wealthier classes, and accept more of the principles of private capitalism. But it suppressed all demands for constitutional government, social changes, and religious freedom; and it did little to check corruption. Serfdom, the most critical problem, and a hindrance to Russia's modernization and economic growth, was left untouched, and so was the question of nationalities within the empire. In vain did some of the greatest Russian writers raise their voices in criticism; they were silenced and exiled, their works suppressed. Circles concerned with political problems were banned; groups and movements, such as the Slavophils and Westernizers— the former seeking progress through imitation of an imaginary Russian spirit evincing co-operativeness and true Christianity, the latter advocating social changes paralleling western European scientific and liberal trends—were condemned. Universities were kept small, their students closely supervised, and any courses (for example, science courses) considered dangerous to traditional views were sharply restricted.

EXTERNAL POLICIES. Nationalistic external policies were vigorously, though not successfully, pushed. An expansionist drive was launched southeastward into the Transcaspian regions and central Asia, but the expeditionary force perished in the steppes. Another advance was attempted in the direction of the Turkish Straits, stimulated by the fundamental aim of Russian policy to rule the coasts of the Black Sea and eventually gain domination of the Straits of Bosporus and Dardanelles. Under Nicholas I, the Russians came close to their aim when, in 1827, the Peace of Adrianople and, subsequently, the Treaty of Unkiar Skelessy (1833) gave them not only territorial concessions, but also special rights in the Straits and a voice in internal Turkish affairs. But in 1841, an end was put to this southward penetration. When new troubles in Turkey occurred, England, Prussia, and Austria insisted on joint international, instead of unilateral Russian, action; thus a turning point was reached in the development of Russia's foreign policies.

United States. Unencumbered by old-established aristocratic traditions, the United States, a republic in a world elsewhere dominated by monarchs and vested landed interests, continued during the period 1830 to 1848 to escape most of the complex social problems confronting other Western nations.

INTERNAL CONDITIONS. The United States' population enjoyed civil rights. Hereditary privileged classes did not exist; the franchise, accorded in England or France to no more than a tenth or a twentieth of the population, was almost universal; the government and law courts were democratically organized. The settlement of western lands continued to act as a powerful force for democratization. Although life (except for the upper middle class of the eastern states and the plantation owners of the South) was comparatively hard and competition was sharp, America held out promise for all and, with her geographic advantages, offered opportunities for material progress unequaled in the Old World. Yet, numerous social issues persisted, even though they were of a kind differing from those in other parts of the Western world. Among them were the race problem and slavery, the question of unity between the agricultural South and the increasingly industrial North, and the issues of protective tariffs, centralized government, enforcement of law, westward expansion, and immigration.

FOREIGN POLICIES. Despite her safe geographical location, the United States early had shown strong nationalistic tendencies. Fearful of European colonialism, she had proclaimed the Monroe Doctrine (in 1823), which aimed at preventing foreign powers from gaining additional footholds in the New World. The successful development of the nation stimulated nationalistic feelings and a measure of imperialism. This was evinced by the fact that the westward movement was often accompanied by the eviction or extermination of Indians; by economic imperialism, reflected in the tremendous growth of the lumber industry and in the swift development of mining for copper, silver, and gold; by foreign wars and the annexation of territory—for example, Texas in 1845, and other large Mexican areas in 1848; and by treaties, such as the compact with England regarding the Canadian border. Thus, while domestic unrest and international calm marked the European scene, in North America the situation was reversed. Internally, the country progressed without revolutionary outbreaks; but externally, expansion and wars marked the period from 1830 to 1848.

REVOLUTIONS OF 1848

The Revolutions of 1848 were not so dramatic as the great Revolution of 1789. Their effect, however, was hardly less incisive. Whereas the French Revolution of 1789 came at the end of a period, of the *ancien régime* with its feudal heritage, the Revolutions of 1848 occurred at the beginning of a new age. They introduced the socialistic element into the political arena of the bourgeois world. The same industries that gave the middle class its strength had deplorable working conditions and thus brought a quick challenge to middle-class predominance. Magnanimous and idealistic as the liberal creed which animated the bourgeoisie seemingly was, it proved to be in many ways illusory. For, instead of furthering "the greatest happiness of the greatest number," its unregulated functioning created unexpected misery and necessitated an early modification.

Revolution in France. On February 22, 1848, a banquet forbidden by the government was held in defiance of the regime. Cries of "Vive la republique" were heard; in the night, street fighting began; and within a few days, the king, who wanted no shedding of blood on his account, abdicated and fled to England—as Charles X had done eighteen years earlier. A republic was declared; Lamartine, the historian, Louis Blanc, the socialist, and several other liberals formed a provisional government.

PROVISIONAL GOVERNMENT. The new government was handicapped from the beginning. It had inherited an almost bankrupt treasury and could do nothing about the crop failures and business stagnation which had preceded its assumption of power. Dissensions among its members became quickly evident. Socialists like Blanc and Ledru Rollin demanded immediate changes in the economic structure of the country. They insisted on the establishment of na-

tional workshops which would provide work—no matter how unproductive—for the unemployed. They demanded high taxes from *Socialists*
the well-to-do, the nationalization of the means of production, and *US*
equal civil rights for all. They raised the red flag of revolution and *Republicans*
formed radical clubs along patterns set in 1789. The moderates
agreed to the establishment of the national workshops, concentrated
on political reform, civil rights, universal suffrage, and democratiza- *Rep. win*
tion of the National Guards. They remained faithful to the tricolor. *elections +*
In April, elections were held in which they scored an overwhelming *work ag.*
victory over the as yet small industrial working class. Now in con- *Socialists*
trol of the government, they excluded the socialist representatives *in gov't*
and rejected antiliberal and anticapitalistic proposals. This policy
led to another rebellion. In May, a mob invaded the new assembly. √

JUNE DAYS. The uprising was followed by further disturbances *June Days*
and a wave of arrests; the workshops were now closed, and the
jobless were sent to the provinces or drafted into the army. Thereupon agitation mounted, hunger riots broke out, and the leftist *Cavaignac*
opposition joined forces with the reactionary right, equally bent— *unites +*
though for different reasons—upon the overthrow of the provisional *republicans*
government. Toward the end of June, an organized rebellion oc- *to victory*
curred which the government proved unable to subdue except by
granting dictatorial powers to an army general, Cavaignac. Under *const*
his iron regime, the revolutionaries were defeated, civil liberties *made—*
were suppressed anew, and a constitution acceptable to the right *acceptable*
and the center parties was drafted. Then, new elections were held *center +*
to choose a president for the republic. The people in the provinces, *right*
eager to restore national unity and prestige, and the bourgeoisie *Elections*
in the cities, who wanted a government strong enough to deal with *& 1848*
labor revolts, voted against the provisional government. On Decem- *Louis*
ber 10, 1848, Louis Napoleon was elected head of the Second *Napoleon*
Republic.

Revolution in Germany. As soon as news of the February
Revolution reached Germany, rebellions started. The long-suppressed
opponents of the government believed the time for introducing
liberal institutions had come at last.

END OF METTERNICHISM. In Vienna, liberals petitioned for constitutional government and civil rights. They were joined by members of the numerous nationalities forming the Hapsburg domains,
who demanded autonomy. Barricades went up in the streets. In
March, there was violence in Berlin and in the Rhineland. Outbreaks

in Dresden, Munich, and other capitals followed. In Budapest, liberals and Magyar nationalists, under the leadership of Louis Kossuth, rebelled. The whole Metternich structure toppled, and the aged minister was forced to resign and flee. With him, the symbol of the old order was gone. Everywhere, the German princes granted constitutions to their peoples. Even the emperor of Austria signed a constitution and acknowledged an autonomous status for Hungary and Bohemia. Such actions failed, however, to satisfy the liberals, who demanded, as a right of free citizens, constitutions of their own design. New revolts occurred in Vienna, Budapest, Prague, and Milan; the Slavs in Bohemia organized a first Pan-Slav Congress, and the Italians, under Piedmontese leadership, declared war on Austria. The emperor fled; in December, 1848, he was forced to abdicate. But his Prussian colleague, Frederick William IV, proved to be more fortunate. More pliable, and unencumbered by nationality problems, the Prussian king had survived two days of violence and humiliation in March. He had promptly permitted a diet to meet and had watched it waste its time on a number of radical but unimportant acts, such as the abolition of titles and orders. By autumn, he had recovered control. He granted a constitution which, with its liberal stipulations, surpassed the expectations of even the more radical groups. Having taken the wind out of the sails of the liberal movement, he began to rebuild his own power. In a similar way, other German princes retained their thrones and regained authority.

FRANKFURT PARLIAMENT. Naturally, the revolutions in Germany were influenced not only by the liberal forces, but also by the problem of nationalism. The hopes of all patriots were aroused and in May, 1848, the diet of the federation was replaced by a new, nationally elected parliament. Liberals, who predominated in the assembly, promptly attacked the problem of the unification of the country. They prepared a constitution which was to extend civil rights, suffrage, and personal liberties to all German peoples, and they discussed various plans for a united Germany: whether it should be a firm union or a loose federation, a monarchy or a republic, and whether Hapsburg Austrian territories and their numerous foreign dominions should be included to form a "Greater Germany" or excluded to leave a "Little Germany" under Prussian leadership. But, since parliament lacked executive power, the dualism of Austria and Prussia proved to be an insurmountable obstacle. Too late did the advocates of the *klein-deutsche* (The "Little Germany") solution prevail; in April, 1849, they offered the imperial crown to the king of Prussia, but he refused to take it from the hands of the representatives of the people instead of the princes. Nor did participation in a war against Denmark in support of the North German province of Schleswig further the cause of unification. Thus, the energies of the parliament were wasted, and soon it was reduced again to insignificance.

Revolution in Italy. Liberal and nationalistic aspirations succeeded in Italy no better than in Germany. Revolution in Vienna promptly stimulated uprisings of nationalists and liberals in Italy. In January, revolts had occurred in Sicily, and the ruling Bourbons had granted a constitution. In the beginning of March, many of the larger towns were ablaze: in Naples, Rome, Florence, Venice, and Milan, the banners of the insurgents were raised. Pressed hard by events, Piedmont declared war on Austria, and simultaneously patriots under the leadership of Mazzini and Garibaldi attacked the Papal States. However, their poorly organized forces gained only temporary successes. In the north, after a brief retreat of the Austrians from Milan, the rebels were routed by Austrian Field Marshal Radetzky in two battles, at Custozza and Novara, and Piedmont had to sue for peace. Resistance collapsed in Venice, too. In the central region, Mazzini and Garibaldi had taken Rome, the pope had fled, and a Roman republic was established. But the two leaders proved incapable of organizing an effective government, and their republic came to an early end when French and Austrian troops came to the aid of the pope. In 1850, Pius IX returned. In the south and in Sicily, the revolt was suppressed by the former rulers. Everywhere, the old institutions were revived and nationalistic and liberal aspirations had to be deferred.

Revolution in the Smaller European Countries. Revolutionary fever spread to many of the smaller nations of Europe. In Switzerland, a new constitution was drafted which at last firmly established the unique multinational and multilingual republic, based on democratic principles and committed to a permanent neutrality that Switzerland still adheres to. In the Scandinavian countries and in Holland and Belgium, too, institutions were brought into conformity with the demands of the age. Repercussions of the February Revolution were felt among the Slavic nations subjected to Turkish rule, and in Spain and Portugal. Thus, with the exception of Russia, where autocracy and police force cut the roots of every liberal movement, and of the United States, where citizens already possessed what European liberals were fighting for, the areas of revolution encompassed most of Western civilization.

Effects of the February Revolution. Historians have considered the Revolutions of 1848 largely a failure, pointing out that the order existing since 1830 or earlier was not shattered; that the upper bourgeoisie remained in control in western Europe, and that the middle class failed to win control of central Europe; that liberalism and nationalism continued as the dominant trends of the age; and that the political map of Europe was not altered. Yet, a significant change had occurred. The working class had emerged as a claimant to power. Equalitarian trends thereafter increased, and liberal constitutions were promulgated in most European countries. Serfdom disappeared in all areas except Russia and Turkey. A more realistic climate of opinion now prevailed, checking the overoptimism of the liberals. Nationalism, though still unsuccessful in both Germany and Italy, had shown its strength and was intensified among the peoples of these countries and among many additional national groups. Finally, the revolutions, ending in failure, drove thousands to the shores of the New World, where their enthusiasm, skills, and labor helped to build firm foundations for a society which conformed to their principles.

CHAPTER XV

POLITICAL REORGANIZATION
(1848–1870)

THE DYNAMISM of the quarter century following 1848 contrasts
sharply with the quiet prevailing during the preceding quarter
century. In 1852 Louis Napoleon made himself emperor of France;
in the same year Cavour became prime minister of Piedmont; in
1855 the "tsar-liberator" Alexander II came to the throne of Russia;
in 1860 Lincoln was elected president of the United States; and in
1862 Bismarck became prime minister of Prussia. All of them
worked not to preserve the existing institutions but to effect their
transformation. In the pursuit of their aims, all—except the Russian
emperor—resorted to force. Wars, though not of continental or
global scope, mark the period between 1848 and 1870; and by 1870
the balance of power established by Metternich had changed, the
previously existing societal structures on Europe's flanks (in Russia
and the United States) were altered in the wake of emancipation
movements, and a new aggressive spirit expressed itself in a renewed expansionist drive of Western civilization to other continents.

EUROPE BETWEEN 1848 AND 1870

The first few years after 1848 seemed to bring a renewal of
reactionary political policies. However, this mood soon vanished.
Progressive trends made themselves increasingly felt in most European countries. Not only liberal but also socialist strength increased
and concessions had to be made to the very forces which had been
defeated in the Revolutions of 1848. Constitutions were liberalized,

the franchise was everywhere extended, social legislation was broadened, and nationalistic ambitions were furthered.

France. The republican dream of the French enthusiasts of 1848 was short-lived. Within three years the president of the Second Republic, Louis Napoleon, making free use of bribery and violating the constitution through arbitrary changes in the electoral law, had himself elected to another ten-year term as president; a year later, in December, 1852, he proclaimed himself emperor "Napoleon III."

NAPOLEON III (1852–1870). Realizing the growing importance of public opinion, Napoleon set to work shaping it to suit his ambitions. He won the well-to-do middle class by pledging the restoration of order; the working class by publicizing the socialistic leanings of his youth; monarchists, Napoleonists, and army officers by promising them glory; the bureaucracy by granting higher salaries; and the clergy by supporting the papacy against Italian nationalists and republicans. To all, he promised peace. Once in power, this "sphinx-like" man muzzled the press, harassed the universities, exiled opponents, and permitted the schools to revert to Church supervision. He tried to control judicial decisions. He traveled about making speeches, catering to the vanity of his people and propagandizing his own role. He beguiled the masses by reintroducing universal suffrage, but allowed their representative assembly no more than a shadow existence. He married a haughty, conservative Spanish woman, Eugenie, and with his contradictory actions and suave speeches succeeded in deceiving not only the people of France, but also many outside her borders. Statesmen gave him the support withheld from his amiable predecessor and thus enhanced his prestige. Some historians feel that in many respects he set an example for later totalitarian rulers.

HEIGHT OF NAPOLEONIC SYSTEM. During the first ten years of his rule France prospered, so that the opposition of many intellectuals and liberals seemed unfounded. Banks and credit institutes were organized, industries encouraged, railways and telegraph facilities built, new methods in agriculture sponsored, and the hard conditions of laborers—at least in certain areas—mitigated. The fashion industry was promoted by Eugenie. Mutually advantageous low tariffs were negotiated with neighbors; the Chevalier-Cobden Treaty of 1860 provided for free trade with England. Broad new boulevards were constructed which beautified Paris and simultaneously served as a precaution against possible insurgents. A great international exposition and festivals to encourage trade made France the focus of world attention. Ominous signs appeared, however, with Napoleon's ambitious foreign policies, which, contrary to his promises, brought war after war. Within two years of his accession, Russia was invaded by France in alliance with England; and after victory was won, a pompous peace congress was held in Paris, from which the French gained little but vain prestige. Senegal in Africa was annexed. An extremely bloody war, waged in Italy against Austria in 1859, brought the acquisition of the Italian territories of Savoy and Nice.

Crimean War 1854

DECLINE OF NAPOLEONIC SYSTEM. Owing to experiences during the Italian war, or to the ill-health of the emperor, or to fear of mounting discontent resulting from the changing temper in France, the Napoleonic system was relaxed after 1860. Attempts were made to liberalize the government; press and parliament were given greater freedom and influence; and more attention was paid to the grievances of the working class, whose right to strike was formally recognized in 1864. But new foreign adventures wrecked the empire: wars were started in Morocco and Syria; Annam was conquered in 1862; large funds were invested in the construction of the Suez Canal; and when the United States became involved in civil war, an expedition was sent to conquer Mexico. The disastrous expedition to Mexico, which began with the conquest of Mexico City and ended with defeat and the execution of Napoleon's puppet emperor Maximilian, introduced the last chapter of Napoleon's rule. Another blow was dealt to his prestige in 1866 when Prussia defeated Austria and by means of generous peace terms put an end to the internal German rivalry which had always benefited France. Napoleon tried in vain to strengthen his position by offering further concessions within France and by attempting to obtain compensation from Prussia for French neutrality during the Prusso-Austrian war. In 1870, a new issue, the succession to the Spanish throne, impelled him to take the decisive step of risking another war—this time against Germany. Within little more than a month, he was himself captured. While a prisoner in Germany, he was deposed; and, for the third time, France became a republic.

1860 – system relaxes

Austro-Prussian War 1866

1870 – war of SA succession ↓ Franco-Prussian War 1870

Germany. The Revolution of 1848 had meant a setback for German nationalistic aims as well as for liberal aspirations of the people. It had demonstrated the weakness of both middle class and proletariat—a weakness resulting from the slow development of industry and business, and the lack of great social leaders who might have inspired the middle class. The year 1849 had brought new uprisings in Vienna, new conflicts in Italy, and a resumption of the revolution in Hungary. All were in vain; reaction followed.

REACTION. In Austria the new minister, Schwarzenberg, understood well how to carry on the traditions of Metternich and made but minimum concessions to the new spirit. Rather, he helped to re-establish the authority of the emperor and the prestige of the Hapsburgs within the German federation and thereby to revive the conservative spirit of prerevolutionary days. Prussia likewise failed to promote either liberal or national institutions. Although she perceived that the unification of the German states might make her the leader of a new Germany, she was forced after a conference with Austria at Olmütz in 1850 to give up such aspirations; and hopes disappeared both for a liberal Germany and for a united Germany under a constitutional monarchy. The southern German states followed the political example of Austria, and nothing more than the existing loose federation with its ineffectual Frankfurt parliament survived. The next decade was one of quiet and conservatism in political affairs and of progress in the economic sphere. Particularly in western Germany, industrialization was speeded; coal mining and steel production greatly increased. As in France, banks were founded, railways built, and foreign trade expanded. The sciences flourished; and the high standards of the German universities continued to make the country the West's center of scholarship. Not until a crisis occurred in Prussia over an army budget, did grave political issues again stir the country. Then, however, a succession of rapid changes took place.

BISMARCK. In 1861, Prussia's parliament had refused to appropriate funds demanded by the king in order to carry out a new army program; the liberals tried to use this occasion as a means of gaining political concessions in exchange for support. The army, however, was of decisive importance in the struggle between Prussia and Austria for hegemony in Germany, and as a last resort the king appointed as prime minister a man who had been a representative at Frankfurt and more recently ambassador to Russia and then to France. This man was Bismarck—son of a small-scale landowner, a nobleman and a conservative. Bismarck solved the budget problem by unconstitutional means, collecting the necessary taxes without parliamentary authorization. He strengthened Prussia's position by helping Russia to put down a Polish rebellion in 1863. Then he induced Austria to join Prussia in settling another problem. The German provinces of Schleswig and Holstein had long been united dynastically with Denmark and had maintained that relationship even after the German states, under the sponsorship of the Frankfurt diet, had supported a Schleswig revolt in 1848. But when in 1863 the Danish ruling family died out, the Danes decided to annex Schleswig altogether. Bismarck took advantage of this situation to whip up national enthusiasm for action to prevent annexation; war was declared, and, despite a valiant defence by the Danes, the provinces were conquered. The administration of the territory was then divided between Austria and Prussia. But soon dissensions arose between the two states which Bismarck welcomed (he may even have helped to create them), for they gave him an opportunity to settle the issue of Prussian or Austrian leadership in Germany.

SOLUTION OF AUSTRO-PRUSSIAN DUALISM. War broke out in 1866. To the surprise of all Europe, Prussia beat the Austrians and their South German allies within seven weeks. The excellence of the Prussian army, its use of the newly invented needle gun, and the brilliant strategy of General Moltke were responsibile for the victory in the one decisive battle at Sadowa. Peace followed promptly. Acting with prudence, Bismarck made no demands on Austria except that she should not oppose a rearrangement of German affairs contemplated by Prussia. The only territorial loss incurred by Austria was in favor of Italy, who had been induced to attack Austria from the south and to whom Venice had to be surrendered. As a result of the new situation, the Hapsburgs withdrew from involvements in internal German affairs and devoted their attention to reconstituting their empire. A dual monarchy was established—that of Austria-Hungary. The two areas were governed by the same ruler and pursued a common policy in public finance and foreign relations, but each managed its internal affairs independently. Owing to the influence of the conservative, wealthy landowners, especially in Hungary, the Hapsburgs failed to extend similar local autonomy to the Slavs and thus carried their reorganization only halfway. In the meantime, Bismarck set to work on the reconstruction of Germany. North German states which had supported Austria were incorporated into Prussia; South German states were

*North
German
Confederation
formed*

left independent, but concluded secret military alliances with Prussia and, in 1867, joined the Prussian Customs Union. The North German Bund, a new federation under Prussia's presidency, was formed, and a common parliament was established.

FOUNDING OF THE GERMAN EMPIRE. It was then that, alarmed by the emergence of a greatly strengthened Prussia, Napoleon III incautiously asked for territorial compensations in Germany. His several suggestions were rejected. The position of France was further weakened when there appeared on the horizon the specter of a new dynastic combination between her eastern and southern neighbors, Prussia and Spain, menacing her from two sides. Having had their own revolution, the Spaniards offered their vacant throne to a Hohenzollern prince distantly related to the Prussian king. The French protested and in July, 1870, ordered their envoy to ask the Prussian king, who happened to be vacationing at Ems, for a declaration to the effect that he would withhold his consent. The king telegraphed his prime minister about the incident, and the telegram—the famous *Ems depêche,* innocuous enough in itself— was edited and published by Bismarck in such a way as to inflame national feelings in Berlin as well as in Paris. During the subsequent commotion Empress Eugenie, excitable, arrogant, and overly ambitious, contributed statements which helped to create a mass hysteria in Paris. In confusion, the French declared war and hostilities (the Franco-Prussian War) began. World opinion was mainly on Prussia's side, and Prussian troops, joined by those of all other German states, overwhelmed the French forces. Two entire French army corps were taken prisoner—one, in which Napoleon III was captured, at Sedan, the other at Metz. When the German armies were at the gates of Paris, Bismarck arranged for the crowning achievement of his policies; in the French palace of Versailles, a united "German Empire" was proclaimed, and the Prussian king was designated as its emperor. The nation was established as a constitutional monarchy—a union of some twenty states which embraced all German peoples except those living in the Hapsburg empire. Shortly thereafter, Paris was taken. The Prussians exacted from defeated France a high indemnity and the return of Alsace and Lorraine to Germany. The latter provision was demanded less for national than for strategic considerations as well as for the sake of the rich iron ore mines of the region.

Italy. Italy's path to unification was much more devious than that of Germany. Among the most serious obstacles were subjection to foreign rule, retarded economic development, a lack of capable leaders, and the existence of the Papal States. The success of efforts at unification hinged upon the role of Piedmont; yet, in 1849, Piedmont herself was defeated in war and torn by inner struggles.

CAVOUR. It was Count Cavour who changed the situation and prepared Piedmont for Italian leadership. Beginning his career as prime minister in 1852, he proved to be one of the most astute statesmen of his time. He realized that only liberal policies and economic strength could give Piedmont the necessary prestige and influence. Hence, he reduced tariffs, entered into favorable commercial treaties with neighboring countries, encouraged railway building, improved Franco-Italian relations by the tunneling of the Alps at Mont Cenis, and modernized the army. To the liberals he made concessions, such as legalizing civil marriage and suppressing mendicant orders, but he protected Church life where it did not interfere with politics.

STEPS TO UNIFICATION. Cavour next applied his energies to external policies, and his first objective was to "put Italy on the map." For this purpose, he joined England and France in the Crimean War, which demanded many sacrifices but served Italian interests insofar as it gave the king of Piedmont a chance, after the victory, of showing himself triumphantly in Paris and London and of having Piedmont participate in the Peace Congress of Paris in 1856. There, Cavour brought up the Italian problem, extolled Piedmont's future role, and laid the groundwork for an alliance with France, an alliance which was consummated two years later. Once this was achieved, he provoked war with Austria and, supported by Napoleon III, defeated the Austrians in two extremely bloody battles, at Magenta and Solferino. The latter has remained memorable because it was there that a young Swiss banker, Dunant, who happened to be present on business with Napoleon, conceived the idea of organizing a relief institution for the wounded and prisoners. Subsequently, Dunant founded the Red Cross. Lest war be prolonged and new risks be incurred, the French emperor, shortly after Solferino, deserted the Italian cause. Fearing that Italy might become too powerful or that Prussia might intervene, he concluded a peace treaty with Austria at Villafranca. This treaty secured for Piedmont the province of Lombardy, but it did not bring unity to the whole of Italy. Disheartened, Cavour resigned. Yet, the process of unification had been set in motion. Within a year, after Cavour had returned to his premiership, the Central Provinces revolted against their various Austrian rulers and, by plebiscite, also joined Piedmont. Napoleon's recognition of this second step in Italian unification was gained at the expense of ceding Savoy and Nice to France. But almost simultaneously, a third step was taken. With the connivance of Cavour, Garibaldi led a band of a "thousand" volunteers into Sicily and succeeded in quickly driving out the Spanish Bourbon rulers. Crossing back to the mainland, he marched upon Naples, which was occupied while Piedmontese troops simultaneously coming from the north seized part of the Papal States. In 1861 the king of Piedmont was proclaimed king of Italy, Florence became the capital, and a constitution was drafted. Only Venetia and Rome were still lacking to complete Italian unity when, in the same year, Cavour died.

FULFILLMENT. In 1866, after Prussia's victory, Italy seized Venice. The capture of Napoleon III in 1870 enabled her to take Rome; as soon as the French emperor could no longer hold his protecting hand over the papacy, the Italians invaded Rome and put an end to the temporal power of the popes. A history of more than a thousand years was thus concluded. Denouncing the "evil" spirit of the time, Pius IX retreated into the Vatican and refused ever to set foot again on the soil outside, thus making the popes voluntary prisoners for more than half a century. Rome became the capital of Italy. To be sure, many problems remained: Italy had achieved unity only with foreign help, and her national strength remained at a low level; she had not solved the burning question of peace with the papacy; her economy offered no firm foundation for a prosperous commonwealth; her jurisdiction did not include Italian populations in the southern parts of South Tirol, in Dalmatia, Savoy, Nice, Corsica, and Malta. Yet, she had become an independent united country, with a constitutional monarchy, and she could take her place among the modern nations of Europe.

England. If the period from 1848 to 1870 witnessed great innovations in France, Germany, and Italy, it brought few changes in England. Enjoying her "splendid isolation," her industrial wealth, and her bourgeois, "Victorian" way of life, she continued on the path of gradual democratization and of colonial expansion. Owing to the backing of the industrialists in the manufacturing cities of the Midlands, in Manchester, Birmingham, and Sheffield, the Liberal party stayed in power; and prime ministers of considerable ability—Russell, Derby, Palmerston, and, later, Gladstone—directed the government. Consistent support was given to business, and various regulations helped to improve conditions for the working class. In 1867, when for a short time the Conservatives under Prime Minister Disraeli were in power, a second Reform Bill was passed which extended the franchise to large additional segments of the middle class. Emigration to all parts of the empire was encouraged so that ties with the mother country would be strengthened and markets for British goods would be developed. In foreign affairs, a vigorous colonial policy was pursued. In Africa, British holdings were extended through missionaries and merchants, who were followed by occupation troops—"the flag following trade." New concessions were demanded from China. In India, an uprising of the natives in the British army, the so-called "Mutiny," was fiercely suppressed, whereupon the administration of the country was put entirely under the direction of the British government. In Canada, reforms were undertaken; during the 1850's, the country gained control of its internal affairs, and, in 1867, the British North American Act recognized the fact and Canada became a "Dominion." Special attention was paid to the safeguarding of communication lines between the mother country and her colonies. Russia was prevented by the Crimean War from gaining free access to approaches to the Mediterranean and, by wars and treaties with Persia and Afghanistan, from reaching the land route to India.

RUSSIA, AMERICA, AND ASIA

The years from 1848 to 1870 were also of decisive importance to Russia and the United States, and likewise to Asia, where the impact of European science and industry, and the climate of opinion conditioned by them, was sharply felt. Decisive events were the abolition of serfdom in Russia and of slavery in America and the opening of the Far Eastern countries to Western trade.

Russia. For Russia, the decisive moment came with the Crimean War. It revealed the backwardness, inefficiency, and corruption of Russian institutions and forced the government to undertake long-overdue reforms.

CRIMEAN WAR AND EXPANSION IN ASIA. Provoked by Napoleon III's meddling in Turkish affairs, but essentially reflecting English-

Russian rivalry, the Crimean War (1854–56) brought little glory to any participant. Russian soldiers fought valiantly, and their defence of the fortress of Sebastopol has become famous. But their leaders and their equipment were lamentable; and motley French, English, Italian, and Turkish troops, though just as badly led, were enabled to defeat the Russian colossus and impose stifling peace conditions. Russia was deprived of all special rights enjoyed on Turkish soil and forbidden to maintain fortifications along her Black Sea border or to keep warships there. Various earlier conquests were restored to Turkey. With her drive southward stalled, nothing was left for Russia but to renounce further advances in Europe and to turn her attention eastward. There she met with better success. Penetrating Central Asiatic regions, she occupied Tashkent, Bokhara, Samarkand, and Khiva; she also sent troops and settlers under Muraviëv into the Amur region, forcing China to relinquish the territory. In 1860, she built the harbor of Vladivostok on the Sea of Japan. She penetrated Manchuria; and she occupied Sakhalin. But these successes in the East, conpensating somewhat for the failures in the West, did not make the government overlook the need for correction of the country's internal weaknesses. Nicholas I had died during the Crimean War; his son Alexander II faced the difficult task of converting Russian institutions to meet the demands of modern times.

EMANCIPATION. The defects of the Russian system were rooted in the institution of serfdom, which made it impossible to modernize and industrialize the country. Serfdom was universally condemned by economists, sociologists, and idealists. It was the chief target of the "intelligentsia," as the important group of the population was called which, composed largely of members of the free professions, students, and merchants, had been driven more and more into opposition to all aspects of the existing political system Many of them came from ranks of the high nobility, but they too preferred exile and disgrace to living under iniquitous conditions, no matter how much, personally, they could have profited by them. The literary critic Belinsky, the politician Herzen, the social philosopher Samarin, the anarchist Bakunin—these intellectuals and innumerable others unceasingly protested in their writings (much of which had to be published abroad) against the evil of autocracy and its counterpart, serfdom. Alexander may not have listened; but the lesson of the Crimean War could not be overlooked. In 1856, he appointed a commission to prepare the needed reform work. He insisted that any plan include provisions to give the peasants (1) freedom, (2) an economic basis for their lives—namely, land, and (3) due compensation to the former owners whose land was to be transferred to peasants. Owing to the steadfast co-operation of the progressive landowners themselves, the gigantic task of liberation was accomplished within five years. Neither fear of its possible revolutionary consequences nor opposition from reactionary quarters could stop the work—nor could lack of financial means, bureaucratic impediments, or difficulties resulting from the diversity of conditions in the various parts of the empire. On February 19, 1861, twenty-three million serfs and their families were declared free and land allotments were made to them. A transitional period, however, was provided, during which the peasant did not gain actual ownership of the land but remained a member of a village community (*mir*), in which ownership was vested, and which provided for communal cultivation of the fields. The *mir* received certain rights of jurisdiction over its members and was responsible for the special "redemption tax," which was in the course of some forty years to reimburse the state for its compensation payments to the landowners.

FINANCIAL AND JUDICIAL REFORMS. Once the government had ended serfdom, it proceeded rapidly with additional reforms. State finances and the tax system were reorganized, a state bank was created, and a regular budget was set up. State monopolies were abolished and numerous personnel changes were made. Educational reforms followed. Universities were given more freedom, women were admitted to secondary education, public education was extended, and censorship regulations were modified. In the political and judicial sphere, district assemblies ("zemstvos") were established to decide local issues. Equality before the law was formally acknowledged, secret interrogation and flogging were prohibited, a jury system was introduced, and judges were freed of governmental control. Municipalities received charters for self-government; and, finally, through universal conscription, the arbitrary levying of troops was ended. Reform measures were slowed down by a revolt of the Poles in 1863 and an attempt on the life of the tsar in 1866; but by 1870 Russia had, without civil war and revolution, achieved a reorganization which enabled her to enter upon the Modern Age. **United States of America.** In America, foremost in the practice of liberal democracy, it was, paradoxically, the same issue of involuntary human servitude and its economic consequences which constituted the most retarding factor and incendiary problem of the period from 1848 to 1870. The issue concerned a smaller sector of the population than it did in Russia, but in America the practice of full "slavery," as opposed to "serfdom," was more revolting to modern man's conscience. It was also more complicated, and had an effect on the political scene inasmuch as it involved racial antagonisms and aroused regional jealousies.

EMANCIPATION. During the 1850's, the United States experienced a rapid development of her productive forces; the output in industry and mining increased, the national wealth grew, and liberal institutions continued to foster an enterprising and inventive spirit. But the problem of Negro slavery divided the country into geographic, ideological, and economic segments. In 1854, the Missouri Compromise of 1820 (prohibiting the extension of slavery) was repealed. and, at the very time that the European nations were maintaining relatively stable governments, America was being subjected to widespread controversies threatening the peace of the land. Within a few months after Lincoln's election in 1860, the Southern states seceded from the Union and war started. Owing to poor organization on both sides and to the ruthless use of modern deadly weapons, the war caused extremely heavy casualties on both sides and fearful devastation in the defeated South. Victory for the industrially stronger North did not come until 1865. However, in 1863, about two years after Russia's freeing of the serfs, Lincoln had issued his Emancipation Proclamation. This measure included no provision for giving land to the freedmen, provided no basis for their economic life, and did not, in fact, even gain for them the equal rights set forth in amendments to the Constitution. Yet, the war achieved much. It abolished personal slavery, settled the political problem of unity, shifted the balance of power definitely in favor of the North, and paved the way for greater modernization and national economic prosperity.

EXPANSION. The vigorous nation pushed on to new tasks. In 1867 the United States purchased Alaska from Russia, and in 1869 completed the first transcontinental railway. The government made available new territories for agriculture and encouraged business enterprise by passing more effective protective tariffs; a consequent boom helped even the defeated South to regain economic health and contributed immensely to the political strength of the nation.

Colonial Areas. Events during the period from 1848 to 1870 changed the political and social structure both of the European continent and of North America; they also transformed the relationships between Western civilization and the rest of the globe. For a new era of expansion in Western countries began and spread their scientific methods and techniques to all other lands. This process took place not only in regions completely or partially under Western domination, but even in independent nations which adopted Western ways on their own initiative.

ASIA. The course of Westernization in Asia was different from that in Africa because Asiatic countries had developed a relatively unchanging culture on a high level, whereas numerous civilizations in Africa remained primitive. Of the Asiatic countries, one—Japan —succeeded in introducing Western ways without becoming colonized. During the regime of Emperor Meiji, Japan, having been forced to open her ports to Western traders in 1854, averted the dangers of domestic revolution and foreign subjugation by adopting reforms along European models. Other peoples of Asia had to accept Western ways involuntarily, being forced to do so by Western economic and, sometimes, military penetration. Sumatra and other parts of Indonesia, rich in sugar and coffee, were occupied by the Dutch, who arbitrarily imposed Dutch customs and institutions. Weak, impoverished China, rent by internal disorders and rivalry between conservative and reform factions, had to establish diplomatic relations with the West, accord extraterritorial rights and cede ports to Western governments, and even renounce many old ties with other Eastern nations. Only constant bickering among the Europeans themselves saved China from losing her independence; as it was, Britain, which had begun the Opium War against her, attacked her once more, and British troops, together with French contingents, looted Peking in 1860. In India, after the Mutiny of 1857, the British imposed their jurisdiction and customs. Their policy of "salutary neglect," which meant indifference to the domestic needs of the country, was combined with a gradual enforcement of Western political and legal concepts, so that part of the upper class was slowly Anglicized. Many Indian students received an education in England, and Indian markets and resources were integrated into the British economy. In Persia and Afghanistan, both England and Russia exerted a dominant economic and political influence.

AFRICA AND THE AMERICAS. In Africa, the northern coast became the chief object of European penetration. Construction of the Suez Canal began in 1859; it was opened for traffic in 1869; and French, English, and Spanish interests were built up among the Moslem peoples of North Africa—then largely under Turkish overlordship. The Western nations also expanded their activities and influence in North and South America. Immigration, the settlement of vast areas, the building of railways, and the integration of the whole region into the Western economy acted as powerful forces, spreading in all parts of the Western Hemisphere the concepts, social customs, and industrial techniques of the West.

IMPERIALISM. In the late nineteenth century imperialism meant the building of European empires embracing weaker, mainly "underdeveloped," "colonial" nations and constituted a violent form of nationalism. Like all colonizers, the imperialist nations often brought a modicum of order, law, certain ethical and religious precepts, as well as a measure of education to their colonial areas. But in their search for raw materials, industrial markets, fiscal revenues, and national prestige they were also led to an often ruthless exploitation of the inhabitants of these areas. For the sake of maintaining control over them, many wars were fought, many injustices committed, and independence movements were suppressed.

CHAPTER XVI

REVALUATION OF VALUES
(1848–1870)

THE RAPID TRANSFORMATION of the *political* stage of the West by the thought, fervor, and endeavors of men like Cavour, Bismarck, Napoleon III, and others, and by events like the emancipation of serfs and slaves in Russia and America, was duplicated in the contemporary *cultural* scene by equally rapid changes. In the sciences, Darwin's evolutionary theory changed previously held concepts far beyond the field of biology for which it was conceived. In the arts, the traditionalism of a century was overturned by the revolt of the impressionists. In literature, the novels of Dostoevsky and Tolstoy with their search into man's subconscious strata revealed hitherto unknown perspectives. In the religious field, scholarly research and historical criticism of the Scriptures attacked complacent inherited views, and a bitter conflict took shape between a society trusting in science and progress and individuals vigorously reaffirming Christian tenets and creeds. Finally, the whole social pattern of Western civilization was called into question and repudiated by the work of Karl Marx.

History. A particularly important new role, in line with scientific views, was assumed in the middle of the nineteenth century by the study of history; for a growing consciousness of the past's significance for man's present condition could be witnessed. Avoiding the often utopian, idealistic, and imaginative approach marking the Age of Enlightenment, historians used sober scientific methods and engaged in conscientious source studies, on which they based their writings. In this regard, they followed in general the principle stated by Ranke—to describe "what actually happened"—and their method came to be applied in various fields outside that of history proper. But they combined their aim of pure scholarship with that of the *philosophes* of the eighteenth century who were ready to interpret, to educate, to propagandize. Historical writings therefore became a force of national significance promoting national traditions and national consciousness. Especially influential were Carlyle and Macaulay in England and Bancroft and Parkman in the United States. On the Continent, Mommsen's masterful work on Roman history, written with detachment, was supplemented by historians like Sybel and Droysen, who extolled the Prussian state, and outside of Germany by Thiers and Michelet in France, who presented to their compatriots the glories of the French Revolution and Napoleon.

Literature. European literature, in the main, followed along paths that had been established earlier in the century. Germany offered little that could compare with her past accomplishments. France continued to maintain a high level of prose fiction through the works of Zola, Maupassant, and others. England had a number of skilled essayists, critics, and some excellent novelists, and a poet, Browning, who achieved wide distinction. The United States contributed the poems of Whitman and the novels of Melville. But if one speaks of the achievements of individual nations, it was Russia which produced the outstanding masterpieces. In Russia, dissatisfaction with prevailing conditions led to a grave spiritual crisis, and out of the crisis emerged the searching, penetrating social and psychological novels of Turgenev (*Fathers and Sons*), Dostoevsky (*Crime and Punishment*), and Tolstoy (*War and Peace*). On the whole, it was the novel which appealed to the largest literate public, the upper middle class.

Music. In the field of music, post-1848 Europe maintained remarkably high standards. Brilliant performers such as Paganini and Chopin, who had gained their fame in the period before 1848, were followed by the great virtuoso Liszt, who through his new harmonic conceptions contributed much also to the art of composition. Still more significant were the achievements in the opera. The nineteenth century found operatic creation at its apex. Towering over the excellent French composers, such as Gounod (*Faust*) and Bizet (*Carmen*), were the two mighty figures of Wagner and Verdi. While Verdi devoted himself to Italian opera, with its emphasis on voice and melody, and brought it through the greatness of his art to new heights, Wagner traveled an independent path based on his view of opera as a musical drama which demanded serious texts of poetic worth. Wagner wrote his own librettos and he allocated to the orchestra a more essential role than previous composers had done. His work, based on sagas and folklore, may show many romantic traits, yet it constitutes one of the most beautiful and enduring expressions of the age. The symphonic and concert music of the mid-nineteenth century did not attain such excellence, notwithstanding notable works by Brahms (the foremost symphonic composer of his time) and significant contributions by Berlioz and other composers.

Arts. Painting, too, received a new and lasting impetus. Denouncing the neoclassic as well as the neo-Gothic, pre-Raphaelite, and other contemporaneous art movements, the names of which reflect their emphasis on imitation instead of original creativeness, some of the greatest painters staged a revolt against the traditional approach. Artists in Paris took the lead. Paris had grown steadily as an art center, where masters such as Corot, Millet, and the caricaturist and critic of contemporary society, Daumier, had produced and exhibited their works. Now, a new school of art, "Impressionism," was developed by Manet, Monet, Degas, and other brilliant artists who sought an artistic expression that departed sharply from the fashions, habits, and techniques of the past. Developing new concepts in the use of color and reproducing the "luminous" quality of the air, they depicted man and nature in so fresh and inspiring a manner that they stimulated many disciples to carry forward the task of artistic reinterpretation.

Philosophy. In the field of philosophy, nominalist tendencies, which had steadily grown since the late Middle Ages, attained a final triumph. Despite the acceptance of numerous traditional concepts in metaphysics, rational analysis had in the seventeenth century characterized the work of Descartes, Spinoza, and Leibnitz. Eighteenth-century philosophers of the Enlightenment had similarly put their trust in reason rather than faith, and following them— despite idealistic and ethical judgments—Kant, Hegel, and Fichte had also emphasized the function of reason. This trend came to a climax in the mid-nineteenth century, with the philosophy of Comte, who rejected all views based upon metaphysical speculation. In his "positivist" system he depicted metaphysics and religion as evidences of primitive stages of mankind's development. To him, the future was to be shaped by science, based on logic and observable facts. Only by science would man reach his highest plane. A scientific approach underlay the empiricism of John Stuart Mill, who directed his attention to man's social organization and became an advocate of democratic and liberal concepts—even though he distrusted their effect on man's spirit. The same confidence in reason as the best guide to truth inspired David Friedrich Strauss, who applied the scientific method to the Scriptures, which he subjected to a searching criticism. This investigation led him to challenge the historical accuracy of many parts of the Bible; together with Renan, who saw in the record of Christ's life the story of an extraordinary human being and the exposition of the highest ethical code, he added strength to a movement which rejected traditional, and especially transcendental, beliefs and which looked toward science, logic, and reason for man's guidance.

Science. Western civilization, having developed a steadfast confidence in reason and science, pressed forward in its investigations of nature, searching for laws governing natural phenomena, and seeking to apply scientific knowledge to practical problems.

PHYSICAL SCIENCES. In chemistry, Mendeleev, one of the first great Russian scientists, simultaneously with the German Meyer, drafted the atomic table of the elements; there were many basic discoveries in both inorganic and organic chemistry; Liebig laid foundations for a broad application of chemical knowledge to agriculture. A petroleum industry was founded. In physics (especially thermodynamics and electricity) fundamental principles were discovered, and large industries applying the new knowledge evolved, including industries developing new inventions (e.g., telegraphy and photography).

MEDICAL SCIENCES. Of the most immediate benefit for man were the scientific advances in medical sciences. Physiology, especially man's cellular structure and nervous system, was carefully studied; problems of nutrition were investigated. In bacteriology (to which Pasteur and Koch made fundamental contributions) important knowledge was gained and the germ theory of diseases was widely disseminated; long-established theories of spontaneous generation were discarded. As the causes of dread disease were traced to bacteria, antitoxins and other means of preventive and curative treatment were developed. Antisepsis became generally employed, and anaesthesia prevented untold suffering. Similarly in embryology, insights of lasting benefit were achieved.

BIOLOGICAL SCIENCES. But the most notable advance, leading to new insights of basic significance, was made in biology. Many scientists, studying the life histories of plants, of lower animals, and of human beings had concluded that an evolutionary process was taking place. A scientist like Erasmus Darwin or Lamarck, a poet like Goethe, a philosopher like Hegel, a social thinker like Malthus, had foreshadowed such views. The decisive step, however, was taken when Erasmus Darwin's grandson, Charles, explained life in terms of a struggle for existence, in which the weak members among plants, lower animals, and men are constantly being eliminated and only the "fittest" survive. Thus, it was shown, a natural selection takes place; and through heredity, the natural qualities of those surviving are passed on from generation to generation until new species fit to survive are evolved. This theory of evolution was propagated with almost religious fervor by a number of Darwin's disciples, and as it brought a deeper understanding of nature's evolutionary processes, it also led to a rethinking of traditional beliefs outside the field of natural sciences.

Religion. No area of human endeavor was more deeply affected by evolutionary views specifically (but also by the whole of science, scientific methodology, historical criticism, and the climate of opinion of the Age of Liberalism and Nationalism) than was that of the Christian churches. To be sure, the Catholic Church had had experience in adapting herself to the demands and views of many successive ages. The Protestant churches, not open to authoritative reinterpretation and many of them more rigid in their literal beliefs in the Scriptures, possessed less of such experience. Both were now forced to face a world where scientific explanations were accepted for the evolution of the universe, the creation of man, and the relationship of man and nature, and for connections between man and human society, between the psychology of man and his natural heritage.

CATHOLIC ATTITUDE. In the presence of such issues, the Roman Catholic Church, under the firm hand of Pope Pius IX, took a resolute stand. Since the Age of Enlightenment, she had fought a new wave of irreligion and atheism. In the first half of the nineteenth century, she had succeeded, despite the progress of science, in making numerous conversions, including the famous case of

John Henry Newman in England. She had the satisfaction of seeing in England the emancipation of the Catholics in 1829 and the re-establishment of the Catholic hierarchy in 1850; she had normalized her relations with France; she had survived the onslaughts of the Italian nationalists and their occupation of Rome in 1848; and even among some of the foremost religious thinkers of Orthodox Russia she met with a friendlier spirit. She therefore felt equal to dealing with evolutionary and other scientific views. Unconcerned with conflicting scientific interpretations, she propagated in 1854 the dogma of the "Immaculate Conception" of Mary. In 1864, Pius IX issued his "Syllabus of Errors." Without hesitation, he stated in eighty short statements that science and reason are unable to explain all natural forces; that salvation cannot be gained outside the Roman Catholic Church; that the Church cannot dispense with temporal power; that marriage cannot be a Christian marriage without Church rites; and, in a last most important paragraph, that progress, liberalism, and modern civilization are altogether at variance with the teachings of the Church. This strong statement, rejecting any thought of compromise, was followed in 1870 by the declaration of the "infallibility" of the pope in ex-cathedra pronouncements on matters of faith and morals.

PROTESTANT ATTITUDE. Papal indictments of and warnings against the unrestricted belief in science, in human progress, and in contemporary civilization shocked many Catholics; still less approval did they find among many Protestants. But divided as Protestants were into a multitude of groups—liberals with vague pantheistic ideas, fundamentalists with belief in the literal truth of the Scriptures, and a majority holding various middle roads—they could take no united stand. As a whole they found themselves less at odds than were the Catholics with the climate of the time, with capitalism, industrialism, liberalism, and nationalism. But science raised difficulties for Protestants, too. In particular, Strauss' higher criticism and Charles Darwin's evolutionary theories could not be reconciled with their traditional teachings. Indeed, scholarly investigation, unconcerned with Christian ethics, and Darwin's implication that organisms evolve in response to natural conditions led to a stronger reaction among Protestants than among Catholics.

Social Theory. Science and evolution necessarily had an impact also upon social theory and were used by some of the radical thinkers to support their condemnation of existing social conditions.

Socialists, in particular—who often found themselves in conflict with nationalism and liberalism, with religion, and with all traditions—gladly propagated the scientific creed.

ANARCHISM. The most extreme socialist wing, the anarchists, rejected everything man had held in esteem, except modern science. Following Proudhon, the anarchists saw in the state the "root of all evil" because, by coercion, it corrupted man, and because its laws served only a small propertied ruling group. Utopians at heart—including men like the Russian aristocrats Bakunin and Kropotkin—the anarchists expected progress and morality only from a scientific age when all peoples would enjoy complete political and economic freedom. By persuasion, or preferably by a cleansing revolution, they wished to create a new society in which law would be replaced by voluntary contracts. Only a fully free society, where neither state, family, marriage bonds, nor property and law would exist and where science and rationality would reign —only such a society, they thought, could be expected to bring perfection to humanity.

MARXISM. In contrast to the utopianism of the anarchists, another socialist trend was based on the scientifically conceived ideas of Karl Marx. A German by birth, Marx collaborated with his friend Friedrich Engels in writing a *Communist Manifesto* published in France in 1848; and in 1867, while he was living in England, the first volume of his famous work, *Das Kapital,* appeared. Marx's teachings are complex and open to various interpretations. With their emphasis on economic forces, they reflect the climate of his age and have become of fundamental importance in later times. Marx insisted that "history is the history of class conflicts," that the means of production and changing economic processes determine the law, politics, and morals of each succeeding society. He believed that with capitalism the world had entered a stage which would bring forth the last and greatest class conflict. He asserted that capitalism, being interested in profits and not in the satisfaction of human needs, deprived the worker of an adequate share in the profits from his production by reserving for the capitalist all "surplus value" resulting from the laborer's toil. It would lead increasingly to the concentration of wealth in a few hands and to greater misery for the masses. Labor had become a mere commodity utilized for the benefit of the capitalist. Dangerous business cycles would continue to haunt the world until the *proletariat,* the workers of all countries, had united, revolted, and brought about the collapse of the entire system. Thus, through a dialectical process, according to which everything produces the seeds of its own destruction, capitalism would destroy itself. The state would wither away and all men would be compensated for their labor according to their work and their needs.

Socialism in Action. If other socialist or communist theories had, through the ages, inspired many revolutionary outbreaks, Marxism with its more scientific investigation of the relationship of economics and history laid foundations for a far more relentless and thoroughgoing movement. Its practical effects were correspondingly far-reaching.

FORMATION OF SOCIALIST PARTIES. By the time the full impact of Marxism was felt, the social situation, compared with the early stages of industrial development, had greatly changed. Socialists had gained strength through union. Toward the middle of the century, they had forced state authorities to recognize the right of collective bargaining. Then, realizing that political control was necessary for the emancipation of the workers, socialists began to form their first political parties. They sought representation in parliaments, where they opposed liberal as well as conservative aims, rejected military appropriations, and denounced the churches and nationalism. While thus rejecting the major creeds and loyalties of the age, they undertook to build a new loyalty—that to the international working class; for this purpose they founded, in 1864, the "First International" of labor unions.

LA COMMUNE. A new opportunity to strengthen the socialist cause, which by then had been profoundly influenced by Marx's teachings, came in 1870. Promptly upon the defeat of the French at Sedan and Metz and the collapse of the French Empire, revolutionary outbreaks were sponsored in Paris. Clubs on the order of the Jacobins were formed, and subsequent elections brought a great increase of socialist strength in the National Assembly. In March, 1871, when many social and political ties were broken and a victorious foreign army stood at the gates of Paris, organized revolution began. The government was forced to flee to Versailles, and a city council (the *Commune*), composed of radical and international socialists, was established as the executive agency. This revolution was of unique importance: whereas the revolutions of 1789 and 1830 had been sponsored by the bourgeoisie against the

"old regime," and that of 1848 by an alliance of the bourgeoisie
and the proletariat, the Revolution of 1871 was undertaken by the
proletariat against the newly dominant bourgeoisie. Bakunin and
many other socialists and anarchists took an active part in it, while
Karl Marx, though considering it premature, applauded the aims
of the revolutionaries. The course of the uprising was, however,
tragic. Both sides committed incredible atrocities; and when the
bourgeois government of France under the old Thiers finally put
down the Commune, a legacy of hatred remained that was to
poison all class relationships, not only in France but throughout
the Western world.

CHAPTER XVII

THE ERA OF BISMARCK
(1870–1890)

A DEFINITE CONFIGURATION in Western civilization is traceable for the period from 1870 to 1890. Politically, nationalism was strong everywhere; democracy was the stronger the farther West one looked, autocracy the farther East. Economically, industrialism, based on scientific attitudes and technical inventions, was the chief mark of the age. It advanced quickly in the northern and Protestant countries, more slowly in the south and where Catholicism dominated. Culturally, the trend was toward wider participation of all groups of the population in national affairs, toward expansion of literacy, toward science, and away from traditional metaphysical beliefs. The arts flourished, but strong utilitarian tendencies were felt in many areas. As a result, there developed numerous new tensions—internally between workers and entrepreneurs, externally between nations. But no major revolution occurred, nor did an all-embracing war break out. With the help of uncommonly able and responsible statesmen in the key countries, progressive legislation brought improvements in internal affairs (especially for the less privileged classes), and adroit diplomacy helped to settle international disputes.

THE EUROPEAN STATES AND THEIR ALLIANCES

The era after 1870 is frequently named for Bismarck, who in 1871 became Germany's first chancellor and who remained until 1890 the dominant figure on the international political stage. Having achieved the unification of Germany by means of three wars, he devoted himself for almost two decades to the preservation of a European peace which was to permit the consolidation of the newly founded German Empire. "Seldom," the liberal *Manchester Guardian* once wrote, "has power so vast been employed so well." The "Era of Bismarck" is marked by the growth and rooting of constitutional government in many countries, by world-wide industrialization and social progress, and by struggles between states and the Catholic Church as well as between capitalistic governments and socialist parties. Diplomatically, it witnessed a broad international system of alliances which replaced the old balance of power (an undependable ideal) that had been Metternich's aim.

Germany. The German Empire brought into being in 1871 consisted of some twenty states, most of them ruled by local princes. Owing to the enterprising spirit of its merchant class, the strength of its military establishment, and the efficiency and honesty of its administrative apparatus, it quickly attained a position as one of the great world powers.

INTERNAL AFFAIRS. In Germany the period from 1870 to 1890 was marked by economic growth and by the flourishing of intellectual, and especially scientific, studies in the universities. On the other hand, events of these two decades reflected exaggerated nationalistic trends; they demonstrated the weakness of the constitutional order, as conceived by Bismarck; and they brought to the fore the specific problems of Catholicism and socialism.

Constitutional Arrangements. The German emperor, who was simultaneously king of Prussia, acted within the limits of a constitution which gave him authority to direct military and foreign affairs and to appoint ministers. Legislative power, however, was vested in the *Bundesrat* and the *Reichstag*. The former constituted a conservative factor. The great political struggles were fought out in the *Reichstag,* the popular representation of the German people. The Reichstag was made up of conservative, liberal, Catholic, and socialist parties, and its members were elected by the entire male population.

Problem of National Unity. Bismarck's task of welding Germany into a powerful unit was not unlike that facing the United States with her sectional interests. The problems confronting the chancellor were rooted in differences of economic conditions between an agricultural east and an industrial west; in dissimilarities of religion, customs, and political traditions between southern and northern German states; in nationality issues involving the Poles and Danes living in eastern and northern border regions and the French inhabitants of Alsace-Lorraine. (The latter area did not become a separate state of the union and was, for some time, administered poorly.) Yet, the populace in all the states took pride in Germany's prestige, her economic progress, her army, and her educational system; a shared interest in German culture facilitated the task of unification.

Economic Conditions. Unification made possible the vast expansion of Germany's industrial capacity. In steel production Germany climbed rapidly and soon challenged and then surpassed England. Owing to her growing population and to excellent scientific research, her chemical, electrical, and machine industries flourished. The organization of cartels and the modernization of techniques made production more economical and efficient. Trade connections with all parts of the world were established, the merchant marine grew, a nationalized railway system proved successful, and during the 1880's colonies were acquired. Despite a number of financial crises—including one crisis engendered by the sudden influx of gold from payments of France's war indemnity—German banks and holding companies proved sound and gained world-wide importance. Yet, agriculture suffered reverses, as in many other newly industrialized countries. Much concerned, Bismarck vacillated between a policy of protective–tariff legislation to further agriculture and a policy of low tariffs to further the new industries.

Confessional and Socialistic Issues. During Bismarck's administration two great issues disturbed Germany's internal peace: (1) the issue of the proper relationship between the state and the Catholic Church, and (2) the issue of socialism. The "infallibility doctrine" of the Church had raised grave misgivings throughout the Western world because it seemed to demand a double allegiance from Catholic citizens. Bismarck in particular, was disturbed, inasmuch as separate Catholic interests in predominantly Protestant Germany could endanger the unity of the country; and his misgivings increased when a Catholic political party, the "Center," was founded. A struggle between Bismarck's government and the Catholics, a *Kulturkampf,* ensued. It centered around educational facilities; Bismarck wanted to see Catholic institutions under strict state supervision. He had stringent laws enacted against sectarian schools, and he sought to bar or control Catholic religious orders. Everywhere, the liberties of the Catholics were infringed upon. But since Bismarck's repressive policy, though backed by liberals, did not succeed, he took advantage of the first opportunity (upon the death of Pius IX) to make a compromise, revoke the restraining laws, and seek the support of the Center party in order to fight a potentially more dangerous enemy: socialism. For after 1875, the various socialist groups had gained vastly in power by merging into a "Social Democratic party." This party had won a number of seats in the Reichstag, where it opposed much of the imperial legislation and all military bills. The chancellor met this threat by means of two seemingly contradictory policies. On the one hand, he used force to impede freedom of speech and press and to exile or imprison socialist leaders. On the other hand, he wisely tried to deflate the program of the socialist party by satisfying as many of its demands as seemed justified. This latter policy led him to institute a bold program of social legislation which was to become a model for all nations. In 1883, he introduced compulsory health insurance for workers; in 1884, accident insurance; in 1889, old-age insurance. Employers and employees had to share with the government the costs of such insurance.

FOREIGN AFFAIRS. In foreign affairs, Bismarck hoped to achieve European peace and German security by isolating France and building German alliances with other nations. He sought friendly relations with England through a policy of restraint in regard to German demands for colonies and through co-operation in practical issues. In 1873 he drew Austria-Hungary into a close alliance, for which he had prepared the ground by using moderation in the war settlement of 1866. He induced Russia to join this alliance, thus forming, despite Pan-Slav agitation and Russo-Austrian rivalry, a "Three Emperors' League." In 1882, he negotiated a second alliance system, which included Germany, Austria, and Italy, later known as the "Triple Alliance." He made treaties with Rumania and other small nations. All in all, friendly ties connected Berlin with London, Vienna, St. Petersburg, Rome, Bucharest, and other capitals. Yet, Bismarck did not succeed in maintaining intact all such ties. Relations with England cooled during the 1880's. Those with Russia likewise weakened. The Three Emperors' League was threatened in 1875 because of personal jealousies; it was suspended in 1878 when, following a victorious Russian war against Turkey,

Bismarck failed to support Russia's demands for spoils; and because of the incompatibility of Russian and Austrian aims, it was allowed to expire in 1887. Although Bismarck considered Russia the "pivot" of German security, he succeeded in replacing the League only by a shaky secret German-Russian "Reinsurance Treaty," which survived no more than three years. In 1890 the seventy-five-year-old chancellor was dismissed from office by the young Emperor William II, who had succeeded to the throne in 1888 and who refused to renew the Reinsurance Treaty. Thus ended Bismarck's international system.

France. Germany's vigorous economic and political growth from 1870 to 1890 was not paralleled in France. The required initiative was lacking; the population remained stationary and the nation continued to devote itself primarily to agricultural pursuits, whereas industries developed but slowly. The war of 1870–71 had left France without a legitimate government; it was the National Assembly which was obliged to conclude the Peace of Frankfurt with Germany. Not until 1875 was a regular government organized; and not until 1879, after many attempts by royalists to reintroduce a monarchy, was the "Third Republic" definitely established. A parliamentary regime, with two legislative chambers, was set up, the members being elected by general manhood suffrage on an equalitarian basis. The legislature included many divergent forces—monarchists, liberals, republicans, and socialists. The president of the republic became a mere figurehead.

INTERNAL AFFAIRS. A number of years elapsed before the new government earned respect and confidence at home and abroad. Corruption marked its first two decades; scandals occurred over the sale of Legion of Merit awards and over the building of the Panama Canal; and in 1887, General Boulanger, a new "man on the white horse" (reminiscent of Napoleon), aided by nationalists, threatened to set himself up as a dictator. Moreover, disunity was created by widespread materialism and religious skepticism among liberal bourgeoisie and the workers, which clashed with the Catholic traditions of the conservatives and the peasantry and led to much anticlerical agitation. Disunity was increased by repressive acts against socialists. Yet, beneath the surface, France did make progress in numerous respects: her army was reorganized; her economy recovered from the disasters of war and revolution; living conditions for workers improved; civil rights were no longer violated, as they had been in Napoleonic times; artistic life continued to flourish and to attract foreign visitors; and there were substantial advances in education.

EXTERNAL AFFAIRS. In external affairs, France was held down in Europe both by her own dreams of a *revanche* (revenge) for 1870, which disoriented plans for readjustment to the new international situation, and by the strength of Germany on the Continent and of England on the seas. Moreover, by seizing Tunisia, which Italy coveted, and by establishing a French protectorate there, she incurred the hostility of the Italians. For two decades, France remained isolated. Yet her Tunisian conquest compensated in a measure for the failure of some of her nationalistic plans; and it was followed by an act incorporating Algiers into the empire. There, as in Tunisia, French law was introduced, and many settlers from France spread French customs, language, and culture.

England and the British Empire. The British Isles had remained untouched by the wars of France, Italy, Germany, Austria, and Denmark. In "splendid isolation," though carefully watching events on the Continent, England continued to devote herself to the affairs of her own empire.

INTERNAL AFFAIRS. After 1870, conservative and liberal governments alternated more rapidly than in preceding years. Both parties had outstanding leaders: the Conservatives Disraeli, the Liberals Gladstone. Though wholly opposed in their attitude toward life, both leaders worked capably and with great success, each in his own way, for the aggrandizement of their country. The economy made rapid progress; measures for the protection of business interests and laissez-faire policies were now increasingly accepted by Conservatives; and the workers gained by the legalization of labor unions. Progress was made also toward broader democracy through the introduction of the secret ballot and, in 1884, through a Third Reform Bill, which still did not make the right to vote general but which conferred it on about three-quarters of the male population. Thereafter, radicalism became less extreme in its demands and, instead, a mild evolutionary socialism was propagated by a "Fabian Society" founded in 1883. The Irish problem remained unsolved. Against much opposition in England, Gladstone sought to settle it by concessions; land laws were passed, and religious peace was sought on the basis of an act, passed in 1869 and providing for the disestablishment of the Church of Ireland. But as an essentially agricultural land, with an almost medieval system of British land-lords and Irish peasants, Ireland was bound to suffer from English policies, which were keyed to the trading and exporting of manu-factured goods. Starvation conditions had existed ever since the "potato famine" of 1845; and Irish hostility, derived from alien rule and kept alive by economic difficulties, smoldered.

EXTERNAL AFFAIRS. In external affairs, England pursued a vigorous imperialistic policy. Reciprocally, she became increasingly dependent upon her empire. The British consolidated their holdings in the Far East and built up their trade with China and Japan. They maintained their position in India by strengthening their commu-nication lines and by acquiring, in 1875, sufficient shares of stock in the Suez Canal Company to give them control. They purchased the shares from the Egyptian king, who had received them in exchange for his permission to allow the construction of the canal through his territory, but whose love of luxury depleted his finances and forced him to sell the securities. Next, they styled Queen Vic-toria "Empress of India," and extended their sphere of influence into Afghanistan and Persia, thereby preventing a Russian approach to India; and they vigorously increased their colonizing activities in Africa. (Scientists and missionaries often formed an advance guard. For example, the famous Livingstone was impelled by his geographical interests and Christian zeal to explore central Africa. Commercial, and then political, entrepreneurs followed.) Acquisi-tions were also made on Africa's west coast, concerning which the English effected an agreement with the Portuguese. This in turn was followed by an agreement with all major powers of Europe, concluded in Berlin, where principles for the colonization of Africa were laid down. Soon the map of Africa showed no unclaimed space. Moreover, in 1882, at a time of riots in Egypt, the British navy, taking advantage of the situation, suddenly shelled Alexandria, causing much loss of life among the populace and inflicting great damage to property, and followed up this action by seizing the entire country. It is true that English rule in Egypt was not oppres-sive, that law and justice were improved, and that English purchases of tobacco and cotton benefited at least some sectors of the popula-tion. But Egyptian national sentiment was deeply hurt; a revolt led by the so-called "Mahdi," the leader of a Moslem sect, lasted a decade before it was suppressed.

Italy. Between 1870 and 1890, Italy experienced unique difficulties which affected adversely her political, as well as her economic and cultural, life.

INTERNAL AFFAIRS. Inexperienced in self-government, Italy struggled long for an efficient administration. Unwise expenditures harassed her; capable leaders and a sound bureaucracy were lacking; corruption prevailed, and illiteracy was so widespread that it took a long time to build a working parliamentary system. National pride demanded the maintenance of a powerful army and navy, involving huge costs and excessive taxation; yet, the effort was hardly warranted. More fundamental were other handicaps. The population increased; and, as scarcity of raw materials prevented industrial development, poverty, too, increased. Many enterprising citizens chose to emigrate to America; others joined radical parties which encouraged riots and peasant revolts, and the anarchist movement grew. Finally, although the Italian government through a unilateral "Law of Guarantees" accorded sovereignty in the Vatican to the papacy, paid an indemnity, and allowed religious institutions to function, the popes remained unreconciled. In a predominantly Catholic country, this split inevitably created difficulties.

EXTERNAL AFFAIRS. An Italian foreign policy could be evolved only slowly, inasmuch as none had existed before Italy became a nation. Friendship with England and an alliance with Germany eventually formed the basis of a definite policy. The British had been favorable to Italian national ambitions; their good will continued to be important for, dominating the Mediterranean Sea and Malta, they could have become a threat along the extended Italian coast line. Germany had proved equally sympathetic; despite Italian-Austrian rivalry over territories claimed by "irredentist" Italian nationalists, the Triple Alliance was concluded with Italy and Austria in 1882. A treaty of friendship was also negotiated between Italy and Russia. Only with neighboring France did relations remain precarious. The attitude of the French had been equivocal during Italy's reunification struggle; they had seized Italian territories and had competed with Italy in colonial areas, and in 1881 they took Tunisia.

Russia. The evolution of Russia from 1870 to 1890 followed a path which differed from that of Europe more sharply than at any other time since the reforms of Peter the Great—with the exception of the age of Nicholas I. Intellectual movements asserted themselves which claimed for Russia a unique role in world his-

tory. Revolutionary and conservative groups shared these pretensions, though for divergent reasons. They expected their country
to defeat the materialism of the West and to spread everywhere
the philosophy of a Russia that alone possessed the spirit of Christian, or of communistic, neighborly love and co-operation. Significantly, such beliefs were held in the face of the deep national
and social rifts which existed within the country, in the face of
strong economic pressures toward greater Westernization, and in
the face of Pan-Slav expansionist ambitions.

INTERNAL AFFAIRS. Few institutions of Russia existing in 1870
qualified the nation to take the place it dreamed of either among
the Slavic countries or among the world powers. To be sure, after
emancipation and reform, the way was opened for economic readjustment. But since autocracy was preserved, political modernization was slow.

1. Economic Conditions. Foreign capital, foreign entrepreneurs,
and foreign technicians helped to develop Russia's natural resources.
Numerous industries were founded; coal, steel, and oil production
rose and copper and gold mining increased. Soon after 1870 a vast
railroad-building program was undertaken, serving, as elsewhere,
both economic and military aims. The network was expanded southward in order to facilitate the export of grain and oil via the Black
Sea and simultaneously to prevent a repetition of the military
disasters experienced in the Crimean War.

2. Social Conditioning. As a result, new social problems developed.
Increasingly affected by Western trends, the now growing and
ambitious bourgeoisie found itself ideologically more and more in
conflict with the autocratic government. A like conflict existed between the government and the factory workers, who suffered as
elsewhere from the hardships of early industrialization and who
aspired to obtain political rights and economic improvement. Still
more dangerous was the dissatisfaction of the peasants. Legal restrictions and burdens weighed heavily upon them, for their
individual holdings were generally too small for adequate subsistence; the redemption tax was high and made it difficult for
most peasants or village communes to acquire sufficient additional
land and to introduce modern techniques. The institution of the *mir*
with its collectivism hindered initiative, reduced profits, and led to
much strife. Moreover, certain enterprising peasants (the "kulaks")
understood how to exploit the situation and to accumulate large

acreage purchased from others who were unable to make an independent living. This kulak class became an important psychological factor in arousing resentment among the masses. The government tried to meet the emergency by applying progressive, as well as repressive, measures. It continued the reform work, passed social legislation, reduced the redemption tax, gave more independence to the *mir,* and improved the zemstvo system. On the other hand, it maintained the autocracy of the tsar, refused extension of civil rights, and did nothing to eradicate the corruption which permeated the entire bureaucracy. It intensified police methods, built up its espionage network in town and country, and continued the fearful system of exiling opponents to Siberia while leaving their families destitute at home.

3. *Political Conditions.* Under such circumstances, a threatening mood of resistance grew among all social classes. Idealists among the nobility, middle-class people desiring political rights, workingmen in need of further social legislation, peasants burdened by taxes and poverty, religious groups dissenting from the official orthodoxy, Jews agitating for equality, Poles and Finns and other aliens resenting Russian domination—all were united in assailing the existing institutions. The intelligentsia became the leader of the discontented masses; artists and writers, who played a more prominent role than ever before, often devoted their works to social criticism. To most of the reformers, a constitutional system in line with Western customs seemed hardly sufficient; many felt that social rejuvenation would be possible only through revolution. In the 1870's, anarchists, whose primary desire was to destroy the state completely, gained an importance equaled nowhere else in Europe. Nihilists, who rejected all traditional values, and terrorists, who insisted that the times called for practical revolutionary deeds instead of mere theories, arranged for assassinations of leading officials, which culminated in 1881 with the murder of Tsar Alexander II. Marxists carried the teachings of Marx and Engels to the industrial workers; and "populists" (*narodniki*) sought to gain salvation for Russia by winning over the peasants. The radicals instituted the *v narod* ("to the people") movement, which had two purposes: (1) young intellectuals were to live with peasants and become familiar with their ideas and needs; and (2) they were to propagate revolutionary ideas among the peasants. After the murder of Alexander II, nihilism, terrorism, and populism abated somewhat; but,

despite stern measures of his successor, Alexander III, who fostered his grandfather Nicholas' aim of "autocracy, orthodoxy, nationality," Marxist socialism continued to grow. In 1883, an all-Russian socialist organization, forbidden at home, was founded abroad by Plekhanov. The socialists directed their associates in Russia in the work of spreading Marxist ideas among the Russian workers, agitating for shorter working hours and higher wages, and sponsoring strikes.

EXTERNAL AFFAIRS. In foreign affairs, Russia sought co-operation with Germany. She used the Franco-German War as a pretext to abrogate the Black Sea Clause imposed on her at the Peace of Paris, and, after Germany's victory, formed with her and with Austria the Three Emperors' League. By concluding this alliance and by subsequently making separate arrangements with Austria, she prepared to pursue her major aim: the resumption of her drive southward toward Constantinople.

The old aim of gaining control of Constantinople and the Straits had become a major objective for newly influential nationalistic forces in Russia—the Pan-Slavs, who, ever since the first Pan-Slav Congress in Prague in 1848, had looked forward to a mighty Slavic empire under Russian leadership. When, during the 1870's, southern Slavic nations rebelled against Turkey and "Young Turks" sponsored a movement to modernize their country (which would have interfered with Russian intentions regarding Constantinople), the Pan-Slavs seized the opportunity to agitate for war, which soon materialized (Russo-Turkish War of 1877–78). Backward technically and weakened by the maladministration of corrupt and inefficient sultans, Turkey was quickly defeated and forced to sign a peace treaty at San Stefano whereby she had to surrender most of her European possessions, to grant independence or autonomy to her Slavic groups, to agree to the formation of a Greater Bulgaria as a substantial power, to give the Russians special rights in the Straits, and to relinquish part of the Southern Caucasus. This treaty aroused fears in England and Austria, who wanted to preserve Turkey as a buffer, and the British insisted on its cancellation. They forced Turkey to cede Cyprus to them and then undertook to defend the freedom of the Straits Thus threatened, Russia agreed to an international Congress, which Bismarck was persuaded to convene in Berlin. The Peace of San Stefano was set aside, the formation of Greater Bulgaria (which would have had an outlet to the Mediterranean Sea via the Aegean) was prevented, and international, rather than Russian, control of the Straits was arranged. Russia gained only some territory in the Caucasus and in Bessarabia and the recognition of the independence of Serbia and Rumania. The outcome of the Congress, which seemed to have rendered most of the war sacrifices futile, embittered Russia not only against England and Austria, but also against Germany (which, in order to prevent a general European conflict, had supported England). Not until 1881 was the Three Emperors' League renewed—and then only because of Russia's dependence upon German markets and German supplies for her industrialization.

Frustrated in Europe, Russia resumed her Asiatic ventures; by 1884 Russian troops stood at Merv, not far from the Indian border. This advance led to further conflict with England, which brought another renewal of the Three Emperors' League and (after the expiration of the League) the conclusion of the Reinsurance Treaty, which lasted until 1890.

THE UNITED STATES

In the period 1870 to 1890, developments in the United States became more and more like those in Europe. With the world-wide progress of democratization, including measures in behalf of civil rights, political differences diminished. In the economic sphere, the two decades witnessed in America, as in Europe, a rapid expansion of business and industry. Population growth was, however, more rapid in the United States, whose low death rate and high birth rate, combined with steadily rising immigration, resulted in an annual increase far above the rate in other Western countries. These demographic and economic factors enabled the United States to play an increasingly important role in world politics.

Internal Affairs. Notwithstanding cyclical difficulties, material progress in the two decades after 1870 was enormous. Manufacturing and mining flourished, trade expanded, more railways were built, new banks were founded, and urbanization was accelerated. This situation led naturally also to the emergence of many problems, some of which the United States shared with the countries of Europe. Thus she, too, was beset by labor problems involving wage conflicts, working conditions, and strikes. She, too, had to build a large bureaucracy for the federal administration, and in 1883 enacted laws governing the civil service. She, too, had to meet the challenge of extreme economic liberalism; thus, in 1887, important restrictive legislation (the Interstate Commerce Act) was passed to regulate the railroads.

On the other hand, there were still a number of developments and problems peculiar to America. They concerned primarily (1) the expansion of agriculture (and the settling of western areas), (2) the question of immigration, and (3) the attainment of financial stability. (1) Despite industrialization, farming remained the chief occupational pursuit. In contrast with European limitations, however, the agricultural area could still be increased; between the Mississippi and the Rocky Mountains were vast regions, formerly used for cattle grazing, which were being converted to agriculture. As these areas became populated, new states had to be admitted to the Union. (2) New problems of immigration had to be solved, for the bulk of the newcomers no longer came from Germanic countries, but from southern and eastern Europe and possessed a racial and social background different from that of most earlier immigrants. More of them settled in urban than in rural districts, and the process of integrating them into the traditional American ways of life appeared to take longer. (3) Economic and financial developments gave rise to serious problems. Prior to World War I the United States was consistently a debtor nation; this created financial issues—e.g., there was agitation for the use of silver as currency, instead of strict adherence to the single, gold standard, as in most European countries.

External Affairs. In general, European problems in international relations held little interest for Americans. Nevertheless, although the United States entered into no alliances, remained disinterested in the distribution of power overseas, and stayed out of the race for territory, she became involved in a number of foreign issues. Population shifts to the West Coast and the acquisition of Alaska forced upon the nation a more active role in the Pacific area, where American interests impinged upon those of Japan, England, Russia, and Germany and necessitated commitments and international conventions. Economic strength brought greater interest in Latin-American countries and led to the First Pan-American Congress in 1889. The westward expansion within the United States and controversies with England dating back to the Civil War period made new agreements with England necessary; these were eventually achieved through arbitration by the German emperor and through the so-called "Halifax award," which settled the questions of the Oregon boundary and of the Newfoundland fisheries, respectively.

THE SMALLER NATIONS

The trends and problems of the great powers were duplicated among the smaller nations, although few of these countries played any influential role on the international stage. Only among the Balkan nations did problems arise which led to wars; and only Portugal, Holland, and Belgium were active in colonial affairs. In all cases, a regulating influence was exercised by the great powers; thus, in the Balkans, peace arrangements were dictated by the large nations; and in the colonies, when the ruthless exploitation of the Congo by the Belgian king became known, an international conference was called and a settlement imposed. As a rule, the smaller countries devoted their attention to internal improvements. Switzerland and Denmark set an example with their advanced educational systems; these and other small countries succeeded in creating living conditions for their peoples more satisfactory than those of larger countries. Democracy was strong in the small western and northern countries, although patriarchal and absolutist forms of government continued to prevail among Russia's and Turkey's neighbors in eastern Europe. Unique roles were played by Switzerland, which had the most nearly perfect democracy in Western civilization; by Spain, which failed to rid herself of obsolete feudal institutions and which missed modernization in economic affairs as well; and by Latin-American countries, where geographical disadvantages, underdeveloped economic resources, and political inexperience created favorable conditions for the rise of dictatorships. Even in Mexico, where a vigorous reform movement was led by Juarez, and after him by Diaz, progress in the direction of modern liberal institutions was slow.

CHAPTER XVIII

ECONOMIC AND CULTURAL TRENDS
FROM 1870 TO 1914

THE PERIOD FROM 1870 to 1890 and from then on to 1914 has been frequently criticized as an era of "bourgeois complacency." Actually, a measure of complacency did prevail among the bourgeoisie—and perhaps justifiedly. Having gained dominating influence in the state, its well-to-do members looked with pride upon the expansion of material wealth and comfort, upon the economic growth and the prestige of their various nations, and upon the standards of "solidity and propriety" which had for long constituted their ideals. Moreover, they witnessed the spreading of literacy from which they expected general progress in political and moral behavior. They rejoiced at the important scientific discoveries, at the insight gained into the workings of nature, and at the taste and artistic achievements of contemporary writers and painters— even though these, in the judgment of later generations, did not measure up to the standards of previous eras. But even while flattering themselves with their humanitarianism, satisfied citizens shut their eyes to many disturbing conditions. Underneath, currents existed which indicated growing dissatisfaction. These currents could be felt not only among the economically less favored classes, but also among the privileged. Indeed, many of the leading thinkers questioned the possibility of a continuous "progress," which liberals, believing in the innate morality and good sense of man, sought with the help of education, and which socialists, convinced of an inevitable evolutionary process, expected from the climax of capitalism and the resulting revolution and emancipation of all men.

Philosophers of the late nineteenth century reflected a deep pessimism, and many social thinkers were attracted by nihilistic views.

ECONOMIC CHANGES

In the five decades before 1914, sharp competition both between private enterprises and between nations led to an enormous expansion of industry in most Western countries. Population growth speeded up the process. Agriculture absorbed an ever-decreasing share of the available labor force and capital. Materially, the results of industrialization were beneficial, even if the benefits did not reach the less favored classes until mass production became possible. Socially and politically, the effects seemed less promising. Class antagonisms increased, and often socialist propaganda accused the industrialist (notwithstanding his essential conservatism in business and his rejection of undue risks) not only of exploiting the worker, but also of gaining undue influence in political affairs, of promoting colonialism and instigating wars. Business affairs claimed the energies of many outstanding figures: for example, Carnegie, who built a steel empire; Nobel, who invented dynamite and erected large munitions plants; Krupp, who presided over huge armament and machine industries; Rockefeller, who founded the Standard Oil Company; and Alfred Mond, who organized vast chemical enterprises. Competition constantly eliminated some of the self-made businessmen and brought others to the fore; unlike the former nobility, the captains of industry depended upon individual inventiveness and personal ability for maintenance of their positions, rather than upon class, birth, or even inherited wealth.

Population. Of particular importance in the economic scene was the rapid increase of productivity made possible by the swift growth of populations. Despite losses through emigration, the population in countries such as Germany, England, and Russia gained some 65 per cent during the years from 1870 to 1914. By then, about 425 million people lived in Europe, and another 135 million Europeans resided in overseas territory, making up a record total of a third of the population of the entire globe. Many capitals with millions of inhabitants had arisen in the West—among them London, Paris, St. Petersburg, Berlin, Vienna, and Rome. No matter what advantages city life offered by way of excitement, opportunities, educational facilities, and independence, or what disadvan tages by way of hurried, competitive, unhealthy, and insecure conditions, the migration from country to town continued unabated.

Industry. Urbanization not only facilitated industrialism and economic growth, but also made them inevitable. Innumerable technical inventions were devised. Heavy industries increased manifold. Chemical industries began the large-scale output of medical preparations and the production of many synthetic materials for manufacturing. Especial importance was gained by the rubber and oil industries, which benefited mainly the United States and England as well as enterprising small countries, such as Holland. Steam power was to some extent replaced by electric power. In 1914, Germany produced one-third of the entire world output in electricity, the United States ran a close second, and even small countries like Sweden and Switzerland, owing to natural resources, gained world-wide importance as producers of electricity and electrical machinery. New industries developed in the field of communication—e.g., the telephone, wireless, and motion-picture industries. Trains and ships were improved in speed and comfort; the first electrical streetcars appeared in Berlin in 1879; bicycles became a popular means of transportation; the first modern automobiles were constructed in the 1890's; and, eventually, airplanes were developed. (The Wright brothers undertook the first flight in the United States in 1903; the Frenchman Blériot crossed the channel to England in 1909.) Progress in transportation necessitated numerous auxiliary industries, the construction of highways, the extension of railway nets, and the building of canals, such as the Panama Canal and the various inland waterways. The pace of life was accelerated; speed became a primary factor in the life of Western man.

Finance. As industries grew rapidly, inventors and producers often did not possess the funds to finance their business ventures. By borrowing they became dependent upon banks, trusts, and holding companies, so that power came to be concentrated in the hands of financiers and promoters. Financial institutions began to determine business policies; they put their representatives on boards of directors and exerted pressure on their clients to conclude mergers and market-sharing agreements, or to form cartels. Small independent businesses diminished in number and influence. Large corporations, with limited liability, predominated; and a comparatively small minority of stockholders exercised control despite a wide distribution of shares. Fluctuations of the market and business cycles speeded up the process of consolidation into large units.

Agriculture. Industry constituted the most dynamic part of the Western economy; however, agriculture still comprised the largest sector of the economy. Only in England, where urbanization had progressed furthest and where one-half of the entire arable land of the country was owned by a fraction of 1 per cent of the population, was the small landowner almost entirely eliminated. In Germany a large percentage of the population still owned landed property or worked on the land; in France and the United States more than one-half of the population continued to derive a livelihood from agriculture, and in Russia almost three-quarters were peasants. But, so far as increased productivity is concerned, agriculture lagged far behind industry. Age-old farming methods were widely retained, and the system of agricultural holdings—whether those of large almost feudal estates in eastern Europe or those of small individual peasant estates in western Europe—was not adequately modified to meet the new conditions. Technical knowledge was not widely disseminated; conservatism prevailed; and agricultural banks, credit institutes, and co-operatives, which sought to provide capital and efficient marketing organizations, achieved only limited success.

Economic Effects on the International Situation. The shifts in the national economies could not help affecting the international scene and destroying the existing power balance of the nations. Industrialization made "younger" nations come to the fore and older ones decline. England's position was particularly affected. She still had certain advantages: her colonial empire, London's financial prestige, and substantial profits from her carrying trade, her foreign investments, and her world-wide insurance. But as her share in world exports was sharply reduced, her political influence was diminished. The distribution of British manufactures (steel products, cutlery, machinery, and even textiles) encountered difficulties, and, because of her dependence upon foreign markets and upon her imports, England could not easily protect herself by means of protective tariffs. Her most successful competitors, Germany and the United States, had begun to industrialize late and thus had benefited from British experience. They proved less conservative than the English, acquired more modern machinery and more readily adopted new inventions and new techniques of production and distribution. They protected domestic manufactures by erecting tariff walls; the United States, like Russia, had never accepted free trade, and Germany, though vacillating, imposed higher duties than those in effect before 1870. Both countries used their newly gained economic dominance to further their political aims. As for France, her wealthier classes proved overcautious; instead of investing in speculative industries, they preferred high and "safe" rents and thereby prevented the country from gaining the position which brisk economic activity could have given her even after the political debacle. France, too, increased tariffs steadily during the period 1870 to 1892. As for Russia, her share in world production rose quickly, though she gained little prestige in world affairs because the size and needs of her domestic market made it impossible for her to become a leading exporter of any products except grain and textiles.

Economic Effects on Social Conditions. Changes in their economies affected the power and prestige of nations; they also affected the life of the individual. The social distance between upper and lower classes was further widened. More money was made available to the former; and money could buy a variety of goods and services undreamed of in previous centuries. People in the lower classes, on the other hand, could scarcely earn their subsistence. During depressions, such as those of the middle 1870's and the early 1890's, many of them lost their only capital—the opportunity to work gainfully; during the boom periods which prevailed in the years before the First World War, the same people suffered from the swift inflation. Moreover, early in the twentieth century, the use of assembly-line methods of production reduced the need for skilled labor, speeded up manufacturing operations, making work monotonous and exhausting, and created additional unemployment. Using a variety of means (such as propaganda, political parties, unions, and strikes) the workers, who were often led by idealistic members of the well-to-do classes, intensified their struggle for redress.

EFFECTS ON SOCIAL LEGISLATION. The most important social consequence of the economic situation was the increasing introduction of social-security legislation. As mentioned, the German government had been first to realize the value of satisfactory labor conditions to the state itself and, concomitantly, the responsibility of the state toward its less fortunate members. In a series of persuasive speeches, distributed over a period of years, Bismarck had convinced the members of the *Reichstag* that fear of introducing a "socialistic element" into legislation should not check laws promoting the welfare of all citizens. He therefore had advocated, and Germany had introduced, staggered income taxes which put the main tax burden on those who possessed capital; and in the years from 1881 to 1889, laws had been passed for state-guaranteed accident, old-age, and health insurance, covering low-income industrial workers. This insurance plan was broadened and improved in subsequent years, and was imitated in most Western countries. In France, which had recognized labor unions since 1884, a series of factory codes was promulgated in 1892; and in 1898 laws providing for workmen's compensation appeared. Old-age pensions were introduced between 1893 and 1910. In Russia, during the same period, government decrees brought the improvement of labor conditions and the utilization of various types of social insurance. England moved ahead more slowly; yet, by 1911 she had not only passed social-welfare laws dealing with old-age pensions, workmen's compensation, and national insurance, but had also introduced unemployment benefits, staggered income taxes, and land and inheritance taxes. Of the great powers, only the United States failed to follow the trend toward social legislation. The imposition of a federal income tax required a constitutional amendment which was not passed until 1913; federal inheritance taxes were not levied until after the First World War; and social insurance legislation was not enacted until the great depression in the 1930's.

EFFECTS ON ATTITUDE OF THE CHURCHES. The spirit behind social legislation was consistent with the demands of the principal religious denominations. Among the Russian Orthodox and some Protestant sects, it was mainly a few individuals and reform groups who associated themselves with political forces demanding social improvement and social security; but the voice of the Catholic Church was strong and positive. Pope Pius IX had (in his Syllabus of Errors) denounced the uninhibited liberal view. In 1891 his successor, Leo XIII, published an encyclical (*Rerum novarum*), in which he repeated Pius' condemnation of socialism, communism, and unchecked liberalism; but he simultaneously pointed out the moral obligations of the wealthier classes, and he approved the solicitude which governments evinced in their efforts to improve the living conditions of the masses and to restrict business practices harmful to the working class.

EFFECTS ON SOCIALIST PARTIES. The endeavors of governments and churches to improve social conditions did not stop the growth of socialism. On the contrary, that movement was accelerated—especially in prosperous times when workers, by withholding their labor, had a weapon in their hands, albeit one which misfired in times of depression. Moreover, socialism gained from the growing consciousness in all circles that industrialism had raised problems which needed the attention of society. Everywhere, socialist parties secured wide influence. In Germany, the Social-Democratic party, founded by Lasalle in 1863, sent two representatives to the first imperial diet in 1871. When Bismarck's repressive laws were abolished in the 1890's, this party sent more than forty representatives to the diet, and more than a hundred (or almost 30 per cent of the total) in 1914. In France, despite equally vigorous suppression in the 1870's, the development was similar. Around 1900, a socialist was chosen as a cabinet minister. The same trends could be witnessed in the smaller countries of northern and western Europe. In Russia, moderate and radical socialists were elected to the Russian parliament (shortly after a representative system had been established in 1907) in which they had considerable influence. In England and America, however, the socialists failed to secure representation. Socialist Labor parties, to be sure, were founded in both countries before the turn of the century; but especially in America, Marxist ideology lacked appeal to the factory worker, and in both countries the tradition of a two-party system prevented socialists from making much headway in elections. Yet, in England as well as in the United States, the socialists achieved some of their aims—the English party by contributing indirectly, in 1906, to victory for the Liberal party, bringing Asquith and Lloyd George into power; and the American Socialists by supporting Populists and other third parties in their efforts to accelerate reform legislation.

EFFECTS ON SOCIALIST PROGRAMS. All socialist parties steadfastly advocated the abolition of private property; they also continued to oppose colonialism and militarism and to work for international co-operation of the laboring classes. In 1889, they organized a "Second International" of Labor, which identified itself with Karl Marx's teachings. But as time went on, it became increasingly difficult for them to preserve a united front. To many, Marx's theory that the class struggle is unavoidable and revolution inevitable seemed more and more doubtful. The skeptics organized a "revisionist" movement in Germany, a Fabian Society in England, and a moderate "Menshevik" wing of the Socialist party in Russia. The anarchists lost whatever strength they had gained; in fact, not the radicals, but the moderate socialist groups—advocating a transformation of society by legal and democratic means—seemed on the way to triumph within the labor movement.

CULTURAL CHANGES

In the period from 1870 to 1914, some of the most fundamental theoretical work in science was accomplished in Europe. At that time the investigation of radiation and atomic structure brought its first important fruits and Einstein formulated his relativity theory. Not only in Europe, but particularly in America, special attention was being given to ways of applying the newly acquired theoretical knowledge to the solution of practical problems. Many technological inventions were made which affected every aspect of Western man's daily life. But insight into the social and spiritual condition of man did not advance correspondingly. Nihilistic tendencies appeared in various humanistic fields; and often the generation maturing around 1900 (the generation of the *fin de siècle*) has been described as wanting in spirit and enthusiasm and as evincing decadence. In the field of art, hardly any gifted artist appeared who could compare with the finest masters of other times, although shortly before World War I, when the social world that had been created in the eighteenth and nineteenth centuries was crumbling, some meaningful original work was being done.

Science. The last quarter of the nineteenth century and the years before World War I brought a revolution in science comparable to that caused by Newton's discoveries in the seventeenth century. Consistently, the scientific method had been perfected; and with the help of new instruments (themselves the result of the advances in science) observations were made, especially in atomic physics, which traditional Newtonian concepts could not explain. Solutions and a new understanding of nature were achieved through the work of Planck and Einstein. A comparable situation developed in the biological sciences, as the limitations of Darwinism, despite vigorous propaganda of enthusiastic disciples, were recognized and new hypotheses were formulated to explain facts obtained by means of new observations.

BIOLOGY AND MEDICINE. In biology, the theories of Darwin were spread by Huxley and other disciples. They influenced the various subdivisions of biology as well as other branches of science, such as anthropology, physiology, and sociology. Doubtful conclusions, however, were reached when scientific data concerning plants or animals were applied to man, or when data about a whole species were applied to individuals. Moreover, Darwin's views needed to be supplemented. The mid-century discoveries of the Austrian monk Mendel, who formulated laws of heredity, became widely known; the German Weismann disproved the inheritance of acquired characteristics; and the Dutch botanist De Vries demonstrated that sudden variations (mutations) occur rather frequently in the evolutionary process. Biological investigations deeply influenced medical research. The diseases affecting human tissues were studied in the light of the newly developed cell theory; Pasteur, Koch, and their numerous disciples made great strides in the field of bacteriology; there was notable progress in surgery, and daring operations were undertaken by Virchow and other pioneers. Public health conditions were improved in response to a growing realization of the need for sanitation. Problems of nutrition were scientifically investigated; the importance of certain vitamins was beginning to be recognized. Most significant was the study of the nervous system, which led to radical changes in the field of psychology. The Russian Pavlov described conditioned reflexes, while the Austrian Freud investigated the subconscious mind and began to utilize the techniques of psychoanalysis.

CHEMISTRY AND PHYSICS. In the field of chemistry, extensive knowledge was gained with numerous practical applications. Of far greater importance, however, was the fundamental work accomplished in physics. In rapid succession, X rays were discovered by Roentgen, electric waves were identified and analyzed by Hertz, the atomic structure of matter was investigated, and the functions of electrons were explored by Roentgen, Thomson, Millikan, and others. Becquerel discovered radioactivity. The Curies in 1898 found radium; they showed that matter disintegrates spontaneously, releasing enormous amounts of energy. The work of the Curies stimulated further studies of matter (more specifically, the structure of the atom), of radiation, and of wave systems. In 1899, Planck published his fundamental work on the quantum theory, which postulated the principle that energy is emitted by atoms not in a constant flow but in an irregular pulsating movement. Planck called the amount of energy emitted a "quantum." His theory was in turn followed in 1905 by Einstein's relativity theory. Einstein demonstrated that time and space are not absolutes, but that they are relative to the observer; and he worked out a fundamental equation $(E = mc^2)$ which stated the relationship between matter and energy. His findings, comparable in importance to Newton's discoveries more than two centuries earlier, were of great significance not merely for pure physics but also for astronomy and for new insights into the structure of the universe.

Philosophy. Scientific attitudes and methods impressed themselves so deeply on the thinking habits of Western society that the whole discipline of traditional philosophy disintegrated. Metaphysical speculations were increasingly rejected. Empiricism spread —that is, the attempt to use experience alone as a basis for an explanation of "reality." Many felt with the Austrian Mach that even though man's understanding of nature and its laws is limited by his imperfect sense perceptions, only observation and logical thought can act as trustworthy guides to knowledge. On such a premise, utilitarian concepts and a form of pragmatism, as taught by William James, were widely accepted. There were also many adherents of a rigid determinism who believed that events in history and in nature were governed by laws, such as laws of evolution, thus allowing little scope for free will. This view led many to accept a relativistic philosophy in which ethics and morals, wisdom, truth, freedom, and goodness—objects of philosophical investigation throughout the ages—were no longer significant. Such an attitude negated religious doctrines and encouraged men such as Spencer and Haeckel to develop the new subject of sociology. Few were the voices which rejected the mechanistic concepts underlying all these interpretations. One dissident, the Frenchman Bergson, reemphasized metaphysical ideas, postulating an *élan vital,* which was passed on from generation to generation and constituted the impelling force in man's evolution. More representative of the age was the German philosopher Nietzsche. Attacking the Christian creed and traditional as well as contemporaneous concepts of ethics, he called for a "transvaluation" of values. He described man's will to power, especially the exceptional man's will to power, as the source of great deeds as the standard by which man and his work should be judged ethically.

Education. The extension of man's knowledge and the acceptance of pragmatic and democratic attitudes created a need for changes in education. Elementary education became a necessity, and compulsory schooling was introduced widely on the Continent. In 1911, England followed with the necessary legislation. Simultaneously, the United States, Russia, Brazil, and other countries of great size and multinational composition were seeking solutions befitting their special situations. But elementary education did not suffice; to disseminate new ideas and discoveries, revisions had to be made in the material taught in higher schools and universities. Knowledge was no longer, as in the Middle Ages, one body of data based on one set of premises. With the secularization of learning, a multiplicity of subjects and concepts had appeared, and specialization increasingly marked the intellectual world. Disciplines such as chemistry, literature, and history had to be subdivided into numerous branches. As a result, the universities began to organize specialized "institutes," while the secondary schools were divided into two groups: one stressing natural sciences, the other emphasizing humanistic studies. Instruction in religion was left largely to separate church schools; and art and music, once an integral part of man's higher education, were slighted or eliminated. Attempts of outstanding scholars to achieve a new unity broke against the wall of necessity which the development of economic, scientific, and political endeavors had created.

Literature, Art, and Music. The *Zeitgeist* (or intellectual climate of the era) influencing science, philosophy, and education left its imprint on the world of literature and the arts. By 1870, the "Victorian style" (named after the English Queen Victoria) had become dominant. Pervading all cultural fields, it was most clearly exemplified in architecture. Solid and pretentious, and lacking in originality, architecture symbolized the way of life and the aspirations of the most successful members of the well-to-do bourgeoisie. Only slowly did a reaction develop against the ideology underlying the Victorian style, and only at the turn of the century did this critical attitude begin to show itself in works of an experimental nature—leading to "modernism" in literature, painting, and music, as well as architecture.

LITERATURE. The literary developments between 1870 and 1914 clearly evinced this changing intellectual climate. During a first period, the Victorian style was represented by a poet such as Tennyson; and the traditions of the great French *romanciers* in the age of Balzac and Stendhal were continued by a Romantic novelist such as the younger Dumas. However, gifted younger writers turned increasingly to penetrating analysis of human nature, to naturalism and criticism of society. Most prominent were the French novelist Zola, the outstanding Norwegian playwright Ibsen and his disciples, the Swede Strindberg, the Irishman Shaw, and the German Hauptmann. Their influential social descriptions and their interpretations, which retain permanent meaning, are in contrast with the pessimism, and frequent cynicism, which characterize the works of others representative of the *fin de siècle*. To a certain extent, Strindberg himself, but perhaps more so the French novelist Maupassant—and also Anatole France—represented this later trend. The Russian Chekov belonged also to the group which marked the "end of the century," and perhaps even Mark Twain, despite his earlier inclinations toward affirmation of life and humor. They overshadowed other authors, such as Lagerlöf (Swedish), Kipling (English), and Conrad (Polish-English), who continued the great tradition of writing imaginative fiction and gave—sometimes within a Romantic atmosphere—a sharp and sober picture of man's character, longings, and weaknesses.

More experimental was a third group of authors, who began to win fame shortly before World War I. Partly under the influence of Dostoevsky and Tolstoy (who, producing *Brothers Karamasov* and *Anna Karenina,* respectively, remained after 1870 the towering figures on the literary stage), they sought for entirely new forms to express their deep, psychological investigations of man's predicament, of his inner contradictions and the tragedy of life. Probing into the last recesses of his soul, into his feelings of anxiety, fear, and guilt, writers such as Kafka (*Metamorphosis*) and Proust (*Remembrance of Things Past*) attempted a new approach in what came to be known as the "surrealist" manner. But it was hardly appreciated for at least a generation.

PAINTING, SCULPTURE, AND ARCHITECTURE. Comparable changes took place in the fine arts. After 1870, the work of the impressionist school with its emphasis on light and color continued. Then, toward the end of the century, there emerged the neo-impressionists and the "Fauvists" (van Gogh, Gauguin, Seurat, Cézanne, and Matisse) and, following them, the "expressionists," such as Kandinski and Klee. It has been said that during the period 1870 to 1914, contrary to the democratic trend of the age, "a split occurred between artists and public" and that only an "elite" could grasp the meaning of many of the new paintings and their symbolism. But such splits and such limitations are, perhaps, in the nature of all works of art. In all times, many facets of artistic endeavor have been grasped first, if at all, by only a few people. No new situation was created when some of the greatest painters at the turn of the century found little appreciation among the public. In fact, by turning away from classical as well as nineteenth-century traditions and by seeking, with revolutionary fervor, to give expression to emotion and to reveal intrinsic meanings rather than merely depicting the visible environment, the expressionists seem to have anticipated a world of which subsequent generations would become more fully aware. They left a more lasting impression and exerted a deeper influence than other fine artists, such as the Americans Whistler and Homer, who proceeded along more conventional paths.

In sculpture, France produced the extraordinary artist Rodin. In architecture, the Victorian style was challenged by numerous innovators who paved the way for modernism and to whom proportions and lines meant more than detail and ornamentation. The newly appearing skyscraper gave a special character to the American environment.

MUSIC. Similarly, in symphonic and chamber music, the reaction against the Romantic spirit and against sentimentalism brought a sequence of masters, consisting of impressionist, then neoimpressionist, and eventually—in the last few years before the war—expressionist composers. Romanticism was still evident in the works of the Austrian Bruckner and later in those of the Bohemian Mahler and the Norwegian Grieg. Impressionism was represented by the Frenchmen Debussy and César Franck, while expressionism, with its new concepts of "polytonality" and atonality, came to the fore with the Germans Schönberg and Hindemith and the Russian Stravinsky. The last named was only one in a long line of extraordinary Slavic (most of them Russian) composers, including Dvořák, Mussorgsky, Rimsky-Korsakov, and the Westernizing Tchaikovsky. The opera continued in the meantime along traditional lines. In Russia, significant works such as *Boris Godunov,* were created; in Italy, the best-known operas were composed by Puccini, and in

Germany the outstanding works were contributed by Richard Strauss.

Religion. In the face of the secularization of Western culture, the churches found their hold on their members (especially the youth) increasingly difficult to maintain. The "conflict between science and religion" had begun to manifest itself in many directions. Some of the foremost contributors to the natural and social sciences sharpened the conflict by characterizing religion as a mere survival of old superstitions. Actually, the process of secularization occurring in the West did not imply a denial of the ethical demands of Christianity or of the need for inspirational and charitable functions exercised by the churches. On the contrary, so deeply were the basic humanitarian sentiments and moral principles of Christianity embedded in the Western world, after almost two thousand years of its history, that they became automatically a function of the now all-powerful states. It became the task of secular authorities to provide social legislation (in lieu of Christian charity), to spread education, and to support the arts.

STATE AND CHURCH. In this process of transition from religious to secular sponsorship and supervision, many conflicts arose—especially with Catholics, who proved less willing than the Protestants or the adherents of the Greek Orthodox Church to subordinate themselves to national political institutions. Examples included the *Kulturkampf* in Germany, the struggle between Catholics and atheists in France, the controversies between the papacy and the new regime in Italy, and other less open conflicts between materialists and the Roman Catholic Church, such as those in Spain and Latin America. In some instances the secular authorities consented to compromises favorable to a church, but even then they achieved their objectives on many points of disagreement. The materialistic trend generally assured them of victory in the battles against a church hierarchy. In Germany, the *Kulturkampf* brought church property under lay control, legalized marriages performed by civil authorities, and placed the training of the clergy under governmental control. In France, a comparable struggle led to the expulsion of the Jesuits in 1880, to the elimination of religion from primary schools a few years afterward, then to taxation of all ecclesiastical wealth, and, finally in 1905, to separation of state and church. In Italy, despite the prevalence of strong nationalistic and atheistic tendencies, attempts to separate church and state failed, but the government retained possession of the city of Rome, insisted on the legality of civil marriages, and asserted its right to determine the relationship between state and church. Unilaterally, it decreed the neutrality of the Vatican and guaranteed the possessions of the Roman Catholic Church.

SPIRITUAL REVIVAL. These new relationships between state and church enabled religious institutions, and particularly the Catholic Church, to get rid of political responsibilities and to devote all their attention to spiritual matters. Consequently, a religious revival got under way as the Catholic hierarchy, while reaffirming traditional doctrines, concentrated on improving the education of the clergy and extending their missionary activities. In the encyclical *Rerum novarum* the Church espoused social progress on the basis of Christian, as opposed to merely utilitarian, principles. The Protestant churches experienced a similar spiritual revival, which was reflected in the formation of numerous fundamentalist groups or organizations such as the Christian Science Church and the Salvation Army. There was also intensified religious activity within the Orthodox Church. In Russia the state-dominated church was opposed not only by numerous atheist Marxists, but also by so-called "Old Believers," some ten to twenty million strong, whose fervor for a dedicated Christian life only increased with discrimination and persecution. The works of outstanding Russian philosophers bore a strong religious imprint; thus, Tolstoy, Vladimir Soloviev, and Berdyaev imbued Russian thought with the spirit of Christian love and Christian wisdom.

EXPANSION OF WESTERN CULTURE

Despite ideological conflicts and the multiplicity of its problems, Western culture was diffused so widely during the half-century from 1870 to 1914 that adoption of Western scientific thought, Western technology, and Western institutions became necessary for the survival and freedom of every civilization. Nevertheless, Westernization occurred voluntarily nowhere except in Japan; everywhere else, as in China, Persia, Africa, the Arab countries, and the Latin-American hinterland, Western ways were imposed upon the native populations, who became either completely or partially subservient to European nations.

Western Influences on Outside Cultures. Wherever it penetrated, Western civilization brought new patterns of culture through the preaching of Christianity, the introduction of humanitarian laws and European educational views, the teaching of European languages, and the dissemination of Western political ideologies. Its contributions were numerous and varied—ranging from new inventions, techniques, and products (in transportation, manufacturing, agriculture, and mining) to improvements in health and medicine and even to new modes of dress. Modern concepts of sanitation were widely introduced and a supply of trained doctors proved a blessing to millions. The Westerners eliminated many savage customs and superstitions and checked tribal warfare; and slavery—though it survived for some time in Dutch and Belgian colonies and was used to obtain labor for building the Suez Canal—was abolished by law and eventually disappeared. On the other hand, Westernization also had its negative side for the native populations. Thus, some of their useful customs were often disrupted; the Westerners helped to wipe out old diseases but also brought new ailments with them; hasty changes in long-established habits of life and work wiped out some native populations; even in political affairs, new methods were not an unmixed blessing, for the old forms of human exploitation by native rulers were often merely replaced by equally cruel alien ones.

Western Exposure to Outside Influences. Owing to its inherent dynamics, Western civilization, while spreading to all parts of the world, was itself subject to the influence of foreign cultures and was compelled to solve new, challenging problems. Expansion had its disadvantages. Colonies involved the West in expenses for investments and defense. Most of them failed to drain off the surplus populations of Europe, but instead attracted mainly the most independently minded, venturesome people. The colonizing nations engaged in a constant struggle for economic and military power; often, they failed to achieve the autarchy they had expected to derive from colonization and, in fact, became more dependent than ever before upon distant sources of raw materials and income. Of course, colonization also had advantages. The mother countries were enabled to obtain needed commodities which contributed to their economic growth and profits and to a higher standard of living. Financiers and other leaders in the community made fortunes from the exploitation of colonial resources. The possession of rich colonies made it possible for small European powers, such as Holland, to attain world prestige and influence. Moreover, the expansionist drive aroused the imagination of many people who were dedicated to a cause such as "the white man's burden" of converting the heathen to Christianity. A missionary spirit went hand in hand with the mercantile spirit. Native religions, customs, art, and even food habits had an invigorating influence on Western man, for they fired his intellectual curiosity so that, often without the least consideration of possible economic advantage, he followed his inner drive to explore the unknown.

New Western Horizons. Thus, after exploring various regions for material profits, Western man turned to those which offered only intellectual or emotional rewards—satisfaction of his urge to know, his vanity, or his national ambition—his desire to plant his nation's flag on untouched soil. For such reasons, Livingstone searched for the source of the Nile; Stanley sailed to face terrible hardships in the Congo; Sven Hedin explored the arid inner regions of Asia and Tibet and visited Lhasa. English, German, and Austrian mountain climbers scaled the icy peaks of the Alps and Himalayas. Extraordinary exploits were undertaken in the Arctic and Antarctic regions. Peary reached the North Pole in 1909. And a whole group of intrepid Scandinavians achieved what for centuries had seemed impossible; the *Fram,* a ship equipped by Nansen, drifted from Norway to Labrador, almost by way of the North Pole; Nordenskjöld accomplished the first Northeast passage; Amundsen discovered the first Northwest passage; and in 1911 Amundsen, in a most brilliant achievement, reached the South Pole.

CHAPTER XIX

THE ROAD TO WORLD WAR I
(1890–1914)

WHEN BISMARCK RETIRED from the political scene in 1890, the Western world entered a new stage in international relations. Prophets of supernationalism had long been at work. In England, the writer Carlyle, the journalist Bagehot, and the statesman Joseph Chamberlain had been fervent advocates of England's imperialistic role; the historian Lecky had gone so far as to proclaim that "real liberty is for supermen and opposed to democracy." France, stung by her defeat of 1870, was inflamed to reassert her national pride by men such as General Boulanger, Delcassé and Poincaré, and even Renan, author of the *Life of Jesus*. In Germany, national passions and a longing for national glory were incited by historians such as Treitschke and Droysen, military men such as Bernhardi, and even Wagner, master of a new style in opera. In Russia, Pan-Slavists agitated for a great Slavic empire under Russian leadership, and many extolled a future Messianic role for "Holy Russia." Italy nursed her Irredentist dreams. Polish chauvinists demanded the restoration of their medieval multinational dominion. In the United States, too, repercussions of supernationalism were felt; the Spanish-American War and the policy of the Big Stick were evidences of the all-encompassing trend. Unfortunately for the peace of the world, the West possessed not only the spirit but, with its science and technology, also the means to make its nationalistic creeds an instrument of international policy and expansion. Competition among the supernationalist Western powers led to new alliances and eventually to conflict.

229

INTERNATIONAL REALIGNMENTS

The first ominous step in the direction of war came at the expiration of the German-Russian Reinsurance Treaty. The lapse of the treaty in 1890 enabled France to end her isolation and to conclude a political, and subsequently a military, alliance with Russia. In this way the large Bismarckian coalition system in Europe was gradually replaced by two competitive and opposed alliance systems —the "Triple Alliance" of Germany-Austria-Italy, and the "Triple Entente" of France-England-Russia. Bismarck, who was dismissed in 1890, watched these developments with growing concern. He died eight years after his dismissal, embittered over the ingratitude of his emperor. Actually, the dismissal was the result not of ingratitude or merely of disagreements over certain external and internal policies. It reflected rather the gulf always existing between old and new and the changing temper and ambitions of succeeding generations.

New Course. The "New Course," which brought about the change, was the result, in part of a shift in economic conditions, in part of personal influences. Bismarck's successors and Emperor William II believed that friendship with Austria was indispensable, but that it was incompatible with an alliance with Russia. They therefore risked giving up Russia, hoping to compensate for the broken Russian alliance by establishing closer ties with England; for William was the beloved grandson of Queen Victoria, and both England and Germany had already made overtures for closer cooperation. They overlooked numerous adverse factors: differences of political systems and ideologies, personal animosities, commercial rivalries, colonial disputes, and lack of popular support for common policies. They overlooked the fact that the parliamentar system of England did not lend itself easily to the making of a bin ing alliance. Moreover, the Germans trusted injudiciously in an irre concilability between French and English, as well as between Russian and English, interests—especially in colonial questions; and they therefore overestimated England's desire to ally herself with Germany. They risked offending England in a most sensitive spot— her domination of the seas; and ambitious to play a leading role on the sea, they started during the 1890's a large navy-building program under the able leadership of Admiral Tirpitz. This led to bitter competition, costly to the taxpayer, a burden to strategists, and an impediment to friendship.

Dual Entente and Entente Cordiale. Resulting coolness toward Germany encouraged England at the turn of the century to lend a favorable ear to French suggestions for renewed amity. By then, France was already strengthened through her new alliances with Russia. These two nations had exchanged courtesy visits of statesmen and military units, made a number of agreements, concluded an offensive and defensive alliance disclosed in 1895, and—most important—had negotiated huge French loans to Russia. Now France began, under the capable, single-minded Foreign Minister Delcassé, to court England. In 1898 a clash between France and England occurred in the Sudan, which England coveted in order to build her African north-south connections from Cairo to the Cape, and which France wanted to occupy for the purpose of building her west-east connections from the Atlantic to the Red Sea. Troops bent on their respective missions collided at Fashoda. Delcassé shrewdly used the occasion for a friendly settlement. He had the French troops called back; and in exchange for renouncing plans in the Sudan, he settled for a free hand in Morocco. This led to further rapprochement. When Edward, Prince of Wales, became king of England, he paid a visit to Paris; and other state visits were exchanged. These events brought understanding and political agreements regarding North Africa, East Asia, and Newfoundland; and finally, an "Entente Cordiale" emerged which, without constituting a firm alliance, laid the basis for frequent consultation and occasional exchanges of military plans.

Triple Entente. Yet, Franco-English relations remained insecure so long as France wanted to preserve an alliance with Russia in spite of English-Russian competition. (Such had previously been the dilemma of Germany in the face of Austrian-Russian rivalry.) Circumstances, however, favored France, for in 1905 Russia was defeated by Japan and weakened by revolution at home. This paved the way for a settlement of Anglo-Russian misunderstandings, for her reverses forced Russia to give up her plans of expansion in the Far East and in the direction of the English life lines through the Mediterranean; they also changed the psychological climate. Revolution brought a parliamentary system to Russia—to the great satisfaction of English public opinion. No more than one area of possible conflict now remained—the Middle East—and con-

THE CHANGING PRE-WORLD-WAR-I ALLIANCE SYSTEM

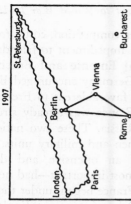

1887

(1) Re-insurance Treaty: Germany-Russia
(2) Triple Alliance: Germany-Austria-Italy
(3) Alliance Austria-Rumania
(4) France Isolated

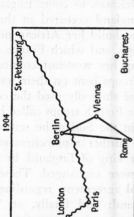

1882

(1) Three Emperors' League: Germany-Austria-Russia
(2) Triple Alliance: Germany-Austria-Italy
(3) Friendly Relations: Germany-England
(4) Alliance Austria-Rumania
(5) France Isolated

1873

(1) Three Emperors' League: Germany-Austria-Russia
(2) France Isolated

1907

(1) Triple Alliance: Germany-Austria-Italy
(2) Triple Entente: France-England-Russia

1904

(1) Triple Alliance: Germany-Austria-Italy
(2) Entente: France-Russia
(3) Entente Cordiale: France-England

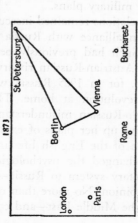

1894

(1) Triple Alliance: Germany-Austria-Italy
(2) Entente: France-Russia
(3) Alliance Austria-Rumania

flict there was smoothed over by a peaceful agreement in 1907. The agreement allowed England a free hand in Afghanistan and divided Persia into spheres of influence, with the northern part reserved for Russia and the southern part for England. With the Russo-English feud thus settled, France could proceed with her alliance system. Political and military missions were exchanged among all three countries, and the Dual Entente grew gradually into the Triple Entente of France-England-Russia. Germany, limited to her Triple Alliance with weak Austria and doubtful Italy, no longer possessed the position of strength she had enjoyed in Bismarck's times.

NATIONAL READJUSTMENTS

In most countries, questions related to foreign affairs, to which "primacy" was accorded by statesmen, were given priority over domestic problems. All the Western nations experienced economic growth and with it an increase in social problems. All of them developed democratic and humanitarian institutions, albeit with the handicaps of burdensome bureaucracies and, frequently, powerful military groups which gained undue influence in the shaping of national policies. Inasmuch as the extent and the speed of these changes varied in the different countries, there occurred subtle shifts in the strength of the nations which were to have grave consequences for the individual citizen as well as for the peace of the world. Yet, this aspect of modern society, involving the relationships between domestic and foreign affairs, was seldom appreciated by people in positions of responsibility and authority.

The Continental Countries. Among the European nations, Germany was the first to adjust domestic economic and social policies to modern requirements. Within limits imposed by size and population, the Scandinavian countries, Holland, and Switzerland followed. The Romance countries adapted themselves more slowly to the industrial age. In political matters, however, adjustment did not proceed from north to south, as in the case of economic and social change, but rather from west to east and southeast. The Atlantic nations were ahead of the Central European powers on the path of democracy, and the Central Europeans were in advance of the Eastern and Balkan nations.

GERMANY. During the twenty-five years before the outbreak of

World War I, few improvements were made in Germany's political institutions. Notwithstanding attempts by socialists to inaugurate radical changes and efforts by liberals to democratize government, widespread complacency persisted. Little was done in the direction of broader constitutional rights, reduction of military influences, extension of secondary education, or improvement in the procedures of the efficient and honest, but sometimes harsh and overbearing, government officials. Class stratification remained strong; the northern and eastern landholding nobility retained its hold on many offices and simultaneously opposed land reforms which might have given agriculture the same basis for stability and progress as that enjoyed by industry. On the other hand, the country gained rapidly in strength as exporter, financier, and importer. Her role in international affairs steadily increased. Social insurance legislation was perfected.

FRANCE. A similar conservatism prevailed in large areas of France, especially in the provinces, where many people owned small landed properties or had adequate savings and led a quiet and comparatively easy life. The leaders of industry were also conservative, lacking the progressive spirit dominating German economic affairs. Investments with safe returns were preferred to such speculative financing of new enterprises as the times demanded. But among the inhabitants of the towns, radicalism and unrest were strong. Various issues and incidents kept political reform movements alive and prevented complacency. First of all, there was the ever-gnawing memory of military defeat which stirred up nationalistic movements affecting political alignments. Second, there was the religious issue. Liberal, positivist, and atheist groups carried on a constant struggle against the Catholic majority. This conflict led to the suppression of monastic orders in 1903, and, after a quarrel with the Vatican over France's political relations with Italy, to the separation of church and state in 1905. Third, there was the issue of socialism. Social legislation had followed the German model, but dissatisfaction persisted among the industrial workers, especially in the foundries of northern France and in the textile mills; and numerous strikes occurred. These were brutally suppressed on several occasions with the help of the army; but the socialist movement grew and, even though radical "syndicalism" eventually receded, the socialist faction steadily gained influence in parliament and challenged the conservative forces. Fourth, there was a revitalization of the progressive forces. This was sparked in 1894 by an anti-Semitic outbreak when the Jewish army captain Dreyfus was falsely accused of treason and, after an unfair trial, was condemned to exile on Devil's Island; it took twelve years and the fervent protests of true patriots, such as the famous writer Zola and the politician Clemenceau, to secure a reversal of the judgment and public amends to Dreyfus. The "Dreyfus Affair" deeply stirred French emotions and eventually brought a purge of a corrupt militaristic clique. It led to improved legal procedures and, indirectly, to the strengthening of national security. Lastly, there was the issue of foreign policy involving the alliance with Russia, the entente with England, the penetration into Morocco, the enlargement of the African empire in regions adjoining the Sahara, and the conquest of Madagascar. Liberals and socialists pointed out the inherent dangers of France's expansionist policy and the iniquity of France's agreements with autocratic, backward tsarist Russia; yet, the nation as a whole approved and found stimulation in its recovery of prestige in world affairs.

ITALY. During the twenty-five years preceding World War I, Italy gained in stability and prestige. In the north of the country, important textile and machine industries were founded. Railway and shipbuilding programs progressed. Educational standards were improved; and legislation helped to mitigate at least some of the worst social iniquities. Both the national government and the local political representatives gained in administrative experience; notwithstanding a number of financial scandals involving members of the government, corruption diminished; and slowly an adequate bureaucracy was trained. After 1900, the political situation improved. Anarchistic activities, which in that year led to the assassination of the king, Humbert I, abated; and even though dire poverty continued to prevail and class differences remained (not only in urban but also in rural areas) Marxist and other socialistic movements took on the same peaceful constitutional forms as in other European countries. Moreover, Italy's foreign and colonial policies were conducted wisely. Ventures like the ill-fated expedition of 1896 for the conquest of Ethiopia were not repeated; instead, feasible aims were pursued, and the conquest of Tripoli in 1911 helped to satisfy the nationalistic ambitions of the people.

THE SMALLER NORTHERN COUNTRIES. Western civilization being an entity, similar political and social problems beset large and small powers alike. Problems and solutions varied, of course, with geographic factors, traditions, and available leaders. The undisturbed development of democratic political and social institutions could be witnessed in the Scandinavian countries and in Holland, Belgium, and Switzerland. In all these areas, military ambitions continued to be negligible; international agreements guaranteed a neutral status to Switzerland and Belgium. A peaceful settlement solved one of the thorniest problems—the fight of the Norwegians for national independence; for, in 1905, Sweden voluntarily recognized Norway's independence. (At the Congress of Vienna control over Norway had been granted to the Swedish king, but Norway had never reconciled herself to this arrangement.) Intellectual activities flourished especially in Scandinavia, where writers such as Ibsen, Strindberg, Hans Christian Andersen, and Lagerlöf, the literary critic Brandes, and the composer Grieg gained fame, and where excellent school systems were built up. Progress was made in the development of industries wherever natural resources were available—iron and lumber in Sweden, electricity in Switzerland, coal in Belgium, colonial products in Holland. On the other hand, the major social problems of the age—socialistic movements and clericalism—brought strife to many small countries and were eventually assuaged as elsewhere. In Scandinavia, co-operative institutions, which came to encompass a large part of the national economy, contributed to economic peace and stability.

SOUTHERN AND EASTERN EUROPEAN COUNTRIES. Less promising was the development of the "second-rate powers"—Austria-Hungary, Spain, and Turkey—and of the new Balkan nations. They possessed few of the economic and social resources needed for modernization, and they showed little initiative or progressive thought. Wealthy landlords, who often controlled political and economic affairs, were opposed to modern trends. Industrial development lagged; colonial expansion, owing to geographical conditions, was not a solution available to any of these nations except Spain; trade was insignificant; agriculture continued under antiquated methods and under feudal institutions. Yet, nationalistic ambitions were often manifest. Spain, Turkey, and Austria had memories of past grandeur; the new Balkan states dreamed of future luster. In Austria, the situation was complicated by tensions between Germans and Magyars, on the one side, and subjected Slavic minorities, on the other. The Balkan nations were troubled by minority questions and frontier problems. Spain, with a large part of her population living in abject poverty, was the victim of repeated revolutionary activity; monarchical and republican forms alternated, parliamentary and democratic institutions proved futile, and governments ruled with the help of army and Church. As to Turkey, not even the recognition of the independence of Serbia and Rumania, nor the subsequent establishment of Bulgaria, solved the nationality question. Revolts within the ruling cliques surrounding the throne contributed to a state of permanent political disorder without achieving the aim of abolishing the despotic powers of the sultan and rejuvenating the state apparatus.

England and the British Empire. Under capable statesmen—the aged Gladstone and after him Salisbury, Balfour, Joseph Chamberlain, Asquith, and Lloyd George—England continued along her established lines. Even though she lost her position as the leading industrial power to Germany and the United States and also lost some of her markets in Latin America and elsewhere which she had dominated in previous decades, conditions remained favorable and the population looked with satisfaction upon the material progress of the country. Numerous political and social improvements were made. The judiciary was reorganized, "board" schools were formed to improve lagging educational standards, and by 1891 free elementary schooling was introduced. Social insurance was broadened to cover unemployment, which (as poverty once had been) was still often considered the result of laziness rather than of industrial conditions beyond the power of the individual workingman. A reform in the agricultural system, advocated by Gladstone, was eventually carried out. The House of Lords (which demonstrated its lack of understanding of modern conditions by opposing such legislation and by advocating the use of force to break up strikes) was in 1911 deprived of much of its power; its right to veto legislation was sharply restricted. A Parliamentary Salary Act was passed to enable men without private means to become representatives in Parliament.

As to the British Empire, it was kept intact, even though relations of the mother country to some of the larger and more important colonies had to be liberalized. In 1900, 1907, and 1910, "dominion" status, introduced earlier for Canada, was granted successively to

Australia, New Zealand, and South Africa. However, no timely
solution was found for India, which despite most vigorous protests
remained subjugated.

Russia. While the Continental European nations and England
underwent constitutional and slowly progressive development between 1890 and 1914, a combination of internal and external forces
worked revolutionary changes in Russia. Pressure of radical groups
from within, and of Western thought from without, undermined
existing institutions.

INDUSTRIALIZATION AFTER 1870. For at least two decades prior to
1890, it had been clear that Russia, if she wanted to maintain her
power and independence, would have to build modern industries.
The change was begun around 1870 with the initiation of a large
railroad building program. After 1890, the process of industrial and
technical modernization was speeded by the efforts of Count Witte,
who had started his public career as minister of railways, then
became minister of finance, and, finally, Russia's first prime minister. It was he who secured loans from abroad and especially from
politically interested France. During the period 1891 to 1903, many
new industrial enterprises were founded in western Russia, in the
Don river region, and in the Urals; a Trans-Siberian railroad to
Vladivostok was built and a Trans-Caspian and Trans-Caucasian
railroad net was started. Witte also introduced protective tariffs,
furthered social legislation, and established the gold standard.

REVOLUTIONARY ACTIVITY. Russia was thus well on the way to
improved living conditions and industrial greatness; but for lack
of corresponding political concessions, the total situation deteriorated and the gulf between rulers and subjects widened. Although,
as elsewhere, anarchist violence diminished while the co-operative
movement and moderate socialism gained strength, the revolutionary temper grew and was intensified by the continued lack of
representative and constitutional government. The revolutionary
spirit was evinced not only by workers and peasants, but also by
the increasingly important bourgeoisie and by the intellectuals—
scientists, professors, writers, and artists, all of whom were highly
responsive to Western influence. The situation became more critical
still when, after 1900, an unfavorable business cycle in Europe
affected Russia. Disturbances once more spread in the industrial
centers and among the peasantry, and a new move toward radicalism occurred. The extremists among the socialists (rejecting evolu-

tionary means such as education, propaganda, and constitutional procedures) gained new adherents and won a majority at a Congress of Russian socialists and their emigré comrades held in 1903 in London. Hence they called themselves "Bolsheviks" (the "larger"; the "majority") as opposed to "Mensheviks" (the "lesser"; the "minority").

RUSSO-JAPANESE WAR (1904–1905). At this crucial moment, the government became involved in a dangerous foreign enterprise. Stimulated by the imperialistic policies of other European nations, the Russians had already entered the race for colonies, and were especially eager to obtain concessions in China. Following the repression of a Chinese independence movement, the so-called "Boxer Rebellion," Russia had demanded a lease on the Chinese harbor of Port Arthur and had occupied Manchuria. England and Japan, themselves coveting economic and military predominance in China, had reacted to this advance by concluding an alliance in 1902; and thus backed, Japan attacked Russia in 1904. Unprepared industrially, Russia suffered severe defeats on land near Mukden and on the sea near Tsushima. In 1905, she sued for peace, and a treaty was concluded that year at Portsmouth, New Hampshire. She ceded Port Arthur and half of Sakhalin to Japan and recognized Korea as a Japanese sphere of interest.

REVOLUTION OF 1905. In the meantime, revolution had broken out at home. For years, the Russian government had played a dangerous double game. Through its police and spies, it had often co-operated with the rebellious labor class, hoping that by supporting economic demands and even strikes against capitalists, it might deflect attention from the political shortcomings of the regime. But it had succeeded only in forfeiting the support of the bourgeoisie without gaining that of the workers. And when—led by one of the dupes of this system, the priest Gapon—workers of a large munitions factory in St. Petersburg used the wartime opportunity to press their demands for political rights, their illusion about the government came to an end. Singing hymns and marching upon the imperial palace to submit a petition, the workers were received by their "little father," the tsar, with a volley; "Bloody Sunday" of January, 1905, ended with thousands of victims dead or wounded. This incident welded the antigovernmental forces into one. In vain did the tsar attempt to calm the opposition by halfhearted promises. Peasant uprisings spread; strikes occurred in all industries; the various subjected nationalities prepared for a final blow; and patriots, outraged by the loss of the war, failed to rally around the throne. In October a general strike was called, and violence in the countryside forced the government to make radical concessions. A "Manifesto" was published, by which the tsar promulgated a constitution and granted autonomy to the Finns. Thus autocracy in Russia finally ended; it was to be replaced by constitutional government.

THE BEGINNINGS OF CONSTITUTIONAL GOVERNMENT. The manifesto instituted a nationwide representative body or *Duma* with legislative powers, elected by the various classes of the population. Only financial and military decisions remained in the hands of the tsar. Political parties became legal: Conservatives; Cadets, or Constitutional Democrats; Social Revolutionaries, or right-wing evolutionary socialists; Mensheviks; and Bolsheviks. By its concessions, the tsarist government split the revolutionary opposition as had been done in France in 1848. The liberal bourgeoisie, relying on the Duma to press for further reforms, abandoned its alliance with the working class and the socialists, when these struck once more in December, 1905. This time, the uprising was bloodily suppressed, and the tsarist government proceeded with its reform plans. Actually, it twice went back on its promises to the liberals, twice dissolved the Duma, and arbitrarily changed the constitution. Without consulting the Duma, it also wrote, on its own initiative, the final chapter of "peasant emancipation." It annulled, at the suggestion of Prime Minister Stolypin, all remaining restrictions on the peasants and abolished the *mir*. Peasants from then on were no longer bound to village communities, but gained personal property rights to their lands, which they could now sell and leave at will. But once all this had been accomplished, a Third Duma was convened. With it began a real measure of constitutional government.

The United States. The year 1890 did not mark any drastic break in American history, such as had occurred in European history. Social progress was steadily but slowly achieved, though to many the administrations of Theodore Roosevelt and Woodrow Wilson seemed, because of their innovations, to represent for the Western Hemisphere, too, the dawn of a new era.

INDUSTRIALISM AND SOCIAL LEGISLATION. Economically, the United States continued to benefit from the work in fundamental sciences carried on in Europe. Thousands of her citizens went there to study philosophy, mathematics, natural sciences, and medicine; but technological application of scientific discoveries, owing to the inventive genius of men like Edison, was more rapid than in Europe. Industries, deriving the necessary supply of laborers from the flow of immigrants, grew at an astounding pace and early standardization of tools and parts made mass production possible. The small businessman was often unable to compete with entrepreneurs such as Morgan, Rockefeller, and Ford who built huge industrial empires, and not even antitrust legislation could check their power. Nevertheless, socialism did not gain as in Europe. Threatened by depressions and unemployment, workers did fight for better conditions and wages, did organize strikes, and did form unions; but they did not adopt the concept of the "class struggle." In agriculture, the recurrence of major depressions did not lead to political radicalism among the farmers, who did not have to rely, as did the Europeans, on intensive cultivation of the soil but had enough land available for extensive cultivation and who benefited from the rapid growth of the national economy. Moreover, democratic institutions made the government and the two main political parties sensitive to popular needs; and the challenge of third (reform) parties, such as the Greenback and the Populist parties, contributed to the timely passage of progressive social legislation. During the administrations of Theodore Roosevelt and Woodrow Wilson, many such laws were passed, and effective programs for the conservation of natural resources were instituted.

IMPERIALISM. If socialist doctrine (one of the great issues of the Western world) and various other economic and political problems of Europe were of less significance for the United States, the issue of imperialism did not remain alien to America. English interference in Venezuelan affairs released violent emotions until in 1899 the British submitted the question to arbitration. The United States went to war against Spain, later annexing Puerto Rico and the Philippines and sponsoring Cuba as an independent state subject to American economic imperialism and political protection. The United States annexed Hawaii in 1898 and established naval stations in that area. Colombia was forced to renounce part of her territories, and an American Zone was established where the Panama Canal was dug across the Isthmus. The United States participated in the international action against China during the Boxer Rebellion and insisted on a subsequent economic "open-door" policy in the Far East. The Monroe Doctrine was reinterpreted to allow for possible United States interference in Latin-American affairs.

PEACE AND WAR

Social institutions and aspirations, which had prevailed ever since Napoleonic times and had been accepted as typifying the entire nineteenth century, came to an end in 1914 when World War I broke out. With our knowledge, gained in retrospect, that war did come in 1914, we are inclined to see in the nationalistic developments before 1914 a path inexorably leading to this conflict and to violence. But the forces against war were also strong, and the view cannot be maintained that war was the only means of solving the existing international problems.

International Movements to Prevent War. One of the major aspects of the nineteenth-century liberal creed was its humanitarianism—a heritage from the Age of Enlightenment. And one of the most important humanitarian aims was the abolition of war. As technology created ever more deadly weapons and as the spirit of the peoples was steadily poisoned by nationalistic propaganda and rivalry, the forces seeking to preserve permanent peace became increasingly active, and numerous steps were proposed, and some taken, to avoid a catastrophe.

PRIVATE INITIATIVE FOR THE ORGANIZATION OF PEACE. Most of the peace movements were initiated and promoted by private individuals, not by governments. Some of these individuals advocated Christian precepts rejecting violence, others adhered to Marxist views rejecting nationalism; some were pacifists, others in search of an international legal order; some wished for peace in order to conserve existing conditions, others wanted it in order to reform society. Similarly diverse were the means by which the workers for peace proposed to maintain it: political alliances, international law, arbitration, congresses, disarmament, or education. They founded organizations to investigate the causes of war and explore the possibilities of avoiding it; some of them tried to influence political leaders and electorates in the direction of peace by emphasizing the dangers and all-embracing character of modern warfare. Prizes were offered to men who contributed to the promotion of peace; "benefactors" established funds, such as the Nobel Peace Prize and

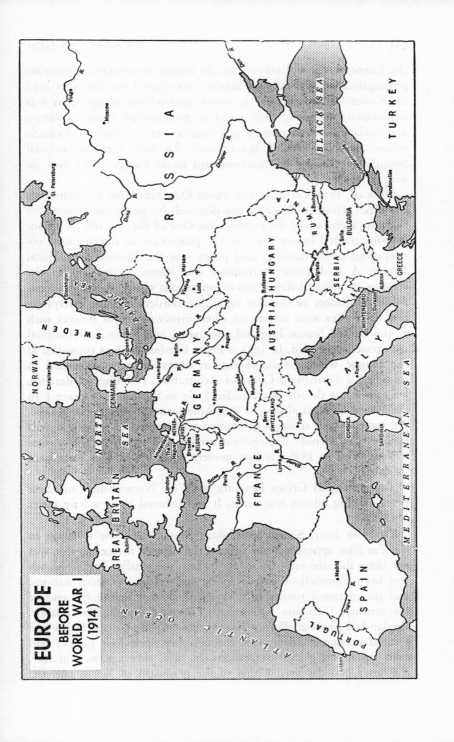

EUROPE
BEFORE
WORLD WAR I
(1914)

the Carnegie Peace Endowment. In numerous countries, vigorous propaganda against military service was carried on. Socialists held their own "Internationals" at which nationalistic competition was denounced; at home, they voted in parliaments against military appropriations. Businessmen and bankers set up trusts and cartels whose profits depended upon peace, for they ignored national boundaries, divided up markets, and made foreign loans and investments.

OFFICIAL INTERNATIONAL AND PEACE ORGANIZATIONS. Governments could not afford to disregard the demands for peace put forward by so many segments of the populations. One of the first official organizations created before 1914 for the promotion of international cooperation, understanding, and peace was the International Postal Union. A Red Cross convention was signed which led to the creation of national Red Cross organizations subject to international rules. A number of disputes regarding borders and the interpretation of treaties were arbitrated, often involving major powers such as the United States, England, Germany, and Spain. International congresses were held. In 1899, a Peace Conference was convoked at the Hague which, while failing in many respects, succeeded in founding a Permanent Court of Arbitration. (Another conference, held almost a decade later, added little to the cause of peace.) In the Western Hemisphere, the Pan-American Union was established. An international sports organization was formed to provide opportunities for friendly competition among the youth of the several nations; and in 1896 the first modern Olympic Games were held in Athens.

International Crises Leading to War. Notwithstanding these peace-making efforts, war came. It was ushered in by a long series of crises.

THE FAR EAST. Significantly, dangerous though the situation in the Far East appeared to be toward the turn of the century, it was not there that the real threat lay. In fact, the smaller Pacific islands had been peacefully divided among the various Western nations, and international rivalry in China had abated. Before the end of the century, Germany had seized Tsingtao, Russia Port Arthur, England Weihaiwei, France Kwangchowan; the United States had secured economic advantages through her open-door policy; and even Japan had gained concessions. In 1895, after a successful war, the latter had deprived China of the peninsula of Korea and the island of Formosa, and had received economic privileges in China proper. A few years later, she had concluded an anti-Russian alliance with England and had then secured from Russia some Chinese spoils. Yet, international rivalry stopped her, too, from extending too far; and thus the critical situation in the Far East was relieved. After 1910, a reform party emerged in China, the old dynasty was deposed, and under the leadership of Sun Yat-sen first steps were taken toward the building of a modern state.

AFRICA. More threatening were the developments in Africa. Toward the end of the century, Italy invaded Ethiopia, where she was defeated; France and England clashed in the Sudan at Fashoda; the Egyptians and Sudanese under the Mahdi staged a desperate revolt against the British, which cost the brutal Governor Gordon his life and subjected the British to a damaging defeat at Khartoum. Not until 1898 was the Mahdi defeated at Omdurman and was native resistance ended. Finally, the French began to penetrate into Morocco. Each of these events caused serious upsets among the Western nations. Then a critical disturbance, the Boer War, broke out in South Africa. Subsequent to the discovery of gold in the Dutch territories of Transvaal, an unofficial English expedition, backed by Cecil Rhodes (the imperialistic British prime minister of the Cape Colony), tried to gain control over the area. This "Jameson Raid" failed, but it led to war between England and the Dutch settlers, the Boers. The outbreak of war shocked not only Holland but all other European nations, yet (despite protests even from within Britain) it was vigorously pursued and it quickly demonstrated the inherent dangers of all colonial issues for the peace of the West. Ill-will between England and Germany was provoked when the German emperor tactlessly congratulated Kruger, leader of the Boers, for his valiant defense. The war itself continued until Boer resistance was crushed. Even though a moderate peace was made and eventually (in 1910) the creation of the Dominion of South Africa indirectly gave a measure of autonomy to the Boers, animosity (not only between England and the Boers, but also among the European powers) persisted.

BERLIN-BAGHDAD RAILWAY. Another crisis arose, in connection with a German railroad project. Everywhere, railroads served both economic and strategic purposes. The Russians built their famous Trans-Siberian road, the English planned a railroad from the Cape through the length of Africa to Cairo, and the Germans proposed one connecting Berlin with Baghdad via Constantinople. Lacking the capital needed for this enterprise, Germany suggested international participation, but England and, subsequently, France refused co-operation. The English feared for their Middle Eastern connections and did not wish to see Germany penetrate into areas at all near to India, and the French sided with their newly won British allies. The German proposal also antagonized the Russians, who had envisaged their own domination over Turkey and, ever since Bismarck's dismissal, had watched German policies with distrust. A rapprochement, attempted in 1905 in a conference at Björkö between Emperor William II and Tsar Nicholas II, was not brought about; for, because of existing alliances, the agreement concluded by them was ratified by neither party. Eventually, the Germans appeased Russian apprehensions, but they never reconciled England to the Baghdad railroad plan. Nor were Russian and British fears lessened when closer German-Turkish collaboration was evinced by the appointment of a German general to be the sultan's military adviser (a position comparable to that of his English naval adviser).

MOROCCO. The Fashoda crisis had brought an agreement between France and England which favored French expansion in Morocco, but had disregarded possible interests of other nations. As a result, considerable difficulty ensued for Morocco, which was rich in lands well suited to agriculture and grazing and constituted a valuable strategic asset. In 1905, the Germans demanded concessions in Morocco and began to support Mohammedan nationalists opposed to French rule; William II paid a demonstrative visit to the Moroccan ruler at Tangier. This Moroccan development led to a serious crisis which was only precariously settled by an international conference at Algeciras (1906). There, the Entente Cordiale with England brought its fruits; France was almost unanimously supported; and Germany, which had undiplomatically provoked the issue, had to be satisfied with insignificant gains. Five years later, she reopened the issue through an equally undiplomatic provocation, sending a naval unit to the port of Agadir. This time a settlement was reached only with great difficulty, and the international atmosphere was further poisoned.

BOSNIA. Despite the gravity of all these colonial disputes and the dangers of war which they involved, it was ultimately the situation in the Balkans which led to an irreparable crisis. Next to the issue of Alsace-Lorraine, Bismarck had always feared most the dangers of Balkan nationalism because of its implications for all Europe. All great powers collided there: Russia, who wanted to win the Straits and dominate her Slavic sister nations; Germany and Austria, who wanted to expand southeastward; France, who wanted to preserve long-standing economic and cultural investments; and England, who wanted to keep other great powers away from the eastern Mediterranean, chief link to India. In addition, Turkey sought to retain the rest of her European possessions, while the various Balkan nations (Serbia, Rumania, and Bulgaria—excited by their recently won independence—as well as Montenegro and Greece) were pitted against Turkey, against Austria, and against one another. No arrangement since the Congress of Berlin had achieved more than a temporary respite. Early in the twentieth century, a nationalistic revival in Turkey occurred. The Young Turks introduced a constitutional monarchy under Sultan Abdul-Hamid. Had their reform succeeded, the great European powers would have lost the influence they were accustomed to exercise in the Balkans. In view of such a prospect, the two nations most affected decided to act: in 1908, the foreign ministers of Russia and Austria met at Buchlau. Following a program which had been outlined in the 1870's, the Russians agreed not to interfere with an Austrian occupation of Bosnia, and the Austrians not to interfere with Russian plans regarding the Straits. Promptly, the Austrians helped themselves to their share of the bargain; but Russia, faced by other nations with vital interests in the region assigned to her, found herself stalled. Extremely bitter resentment at Austrian "duplicity" developed in Russia; Serbia, with claims of her own on Bosnia, was not less incensed. The flames of Pan-Slavism were fanned, and what had been intended as a compromise turned into an additional controversy that brought Europe to the brink of war.

BALKAN WARS. A major disaster was temporarily avoided, but the crisis hastened a local conflagration in the Balkans. In 1912, when Italy's annexation of Turkish Tripolitana had demonstrated the continued military weakness of the Turkish Empire, the Balkan nations deemed the moment ripe for rebellion against the sultan. The war was fought in two sections. First, Bulgars, Serbs, Montenegrins, and Greeks invaded Turkey and forced her to make a peace depriving her of all European possessions except Constantinople. Second, these victorious rebels, plus Rumania, fought one another, and, as one result, Bulgaria lost most of her spoils. The Balkan wars foreshadowed future patterns of warfare. International law was violated by every belligerent; terrible devastations and massacres occurred; and peace brought only additional sources of misery, such as forced migration of peoples and population exchanges, subjugation of aliens, economic disruption, and general impoverishment in many lands. Nothing was settled; indeed, another splinter nation—Albania—was created. Dissatisfaction was general; a festering wound was to poison areas far beyond the Balkans.

SARAJEVO AND THE OUTBREAK OF WORLD WAR I. In June, 1914, the final crisis occurred. In Sarajevo, Bosnia, a Serbian nationalist assassinated the successor to the Austrian throne, Archduke Francis Ferdinand. Enraged at the connivance of some members of the Serbian government and at the encouragement given by Russian Pan-Slavists to Serbian nationalism, the Austrians sent an ultimatum to Serbia such as would have put a virtual end to Serbian independence. Assured that Russia could not and would not desert her as in previous instances, Serbia refused full compliance; and Austria, counting on German support, lacked the wisdom to modify the conditions of her ultimatum. In vain did some of the great powers set their diplomatic machinery in motion at the last moment to stop an outbreak which, because of treaty obligations, was bound to bring France into the war as an ally of Russia and which was likely to engulf England, Italy, and, once more, most of the Balkan nations. On August 1, 1914, World War I broke out.

Internal Factors. It is often forgotten that internal political and party considerations in major countries sharpened international crises. Internal difficulties were not insurmountable, but in order to maintain themselves in power, governments had to make concessions to right-wing forces everywhere—in Britain to the anti-Irish, imperialists, and capitalists; in Germany to agrarian reactionaries and industrialists; in France to chauvinist politicians and army officers; in Austria-Hungary to the backward nobility and the enemies of Slav national aspirations; and in Russia to those bent on maintenance of the dated social structure. Also in the United States, party considerations eventually contributed to war policies.

CHAPTER XX

WAR, PEACE, AND REVOLUTION
(1914–1919)

THE YEARS 1914 to 1919 brought changes so deep and so evident that it may well be that some day the period of World War I will be considered a breaking point in history no less decisive than that of the Reformation years 1517 to 1521. During the first quarter of the twentieth century, new points of view concerning nature and society transformed science, religion, and the arts, and led to the evolution of new social and political structures. Three fundamental changes are discernible: (1) The European state system, completed with the peace of Westphalia in 1648 and modified in 1815 and 1870, broke down without being replaced by a new tenable system. Instead, the nationalistic objectives of every nation were acknowledged, with the consequence that instability prevailed throughout the world. (2) The European Balance of Power, a *modus operandi* established around 1713 (when the wars of Louis XIV ended), was destroyed. A regrouping took place, requiring the participation of an additional power—the United States of America—to assume the function of balancing the divergent groups. (3) The dominant influence of liberalism, which had been the aim of the most progressive forces of society since the Enlightenment, came to an end. Collectivism gained everywhere, and in one area— Russia—it achieved complete victory in its extreme socialistic form.

WORLD WAR I

The conflict which broke out on August 1, 1914, brought "total" warfare such as previous ages had not known. To be sure, other

wars had affected all aspects of life, had engulfed military and
civilian populations, and had inflicted "total" destruction. Such
were the War of Liberation of the Netherlands, the Thirty Years'
War, and the American Civil War. But "total" destruction applied
only to those localities in which armies actually operated. By the
time of the World War, division of labor and use of modern
communications had increased the interdependence of large areas
so much that the effects of war touched ever-widening circles. War
embraced nations in their entirety; mobilization meant the muster-
ing of all productive forces at home, as well as of armies; and the
destruction of the enemy's industries, manpower, and morale became essential objectives. Thus, the blockade of Germany brought
untold privation to her civilian population, and only fundamental
discoveries (such as Haber's discovery of the process of synthesizing
ammonia and producing fertilizer artificially) enabled the country
to continue the war. German submarine warfare had a comparable
effect upon the English people. The war stimulated the inventive
powers of nations. Many new weapons and techniques were devised or perfected, such as combat planes, armored tanks, poison
gases, and air bombing.

Origins of World War I. Historical events and processes are
too complex to allow an enumeration of "causes." At the most, a
few tentative conclusions can be made concerning the relationships
between events and some specific occurrences, and general trends preceding them. In the case of World War I, a number of basic contributing factors merit consideration. (1) The force of nationalism,
which led to numerous crises involving overseas lands as well as
European territories. (2) The existing system of competing alliances, which, less the result of aggressive intentions than of fear,
pitted nations against each other. (3) The secrecy of diplomatic
intercourse, which made the various nations suspect that sinister
agreements were being made against their interests and which
brought universal distrust and therewith a threat to peace. (4) The
absence of a "balance of power," which proved as fraught with
danger to peace as formerly the existence of such a balance had
proved to be; for the old system was not replaced by international
co-operation, but rather by an anarchical state of international
affairs rooted in nineteenth-century liberalism. (5) The feeling of
the "unavoidability" of war, which was partly brought about by

irresponsible and sensational journalism. (6) The instability of the economic system, which caused business cycles of booms and depressions and made large segments of the population lose their sense of security, thus heightening dissatisfaction with the existing economic order. (7) The scientific spirit and scientific inventions, which upset sociological patterns and mores and, in addition, changed the economic balance between nations and led to new jealousies. (8) The lack of foresighted leadership, which contributed to instability. To be sure, some statesmen, politicians, military men, and educators prepared for an armed conflict; others, with equal determination, devoted their lives to avoiding one. But the majority of leaders, though well-meaning, were weak and vacillating. The foremost statesmen lacked originality as well as independent judgment and allowed themselves to be swayed by irresponsible advisers, by political parties, by the mob, or simply by the general course of events. Thus, as Lloyd George once said, the nations "backed into war."

War Preparations. The world situation and historical trends pointed in the direction of war; yet, the actual outbreak of World War I was made possible only by the maintenance of large military establishments and by the development of careful strategic plans.

ARMAMENTS. Compulsory military service was in effect in most Continental countries, and everywhere military budgets were extremely burdensome. France was most heavily armed, with almost 2 per cent of her population in her land forces. Germany had a proportionately smaller, but more efficient army. England had a small army, a large navy. Russia had the greatest number of battalions, the poorest equipment. Austria had enough troops, but the diversity of their natural origins detracted from their dependability.

STRATEGY. Germany's position in the center of Europe was the most precarious, in view of the possibility of attack from two sides— a constant threat that developed after the destruction of Bismarck's carefully built system of alliances. Consequently, her strategic preparations were the most elaborate. For allies, she could count only on the Austrians; Italy, although temporarily committed to Germany, eventually joined the other side. The Germans had therefore worked out the Schlieffen plan (named after a chief-of-staff) according to which, in case of attack from two sides, a holding-off action in the east against Russia was to be undertaken while efforts were to be made to reach a quick decision in the west against France. Troops were to march through neutral Belgium in order to attack the French from the north, occupy the coast line, cut off possible help from England, and force Paris to surrender. This plan was not unknown to the Triple Entente of France, Russia, and England. The British had not yet promised unconditional adherence to the Entente, but they participated in military preparations which included strategic talks with "neutral" Belgium. Entente plans called for a Russian thrust, first into Austria, then into East Prussia, and a French attack along the Rhine.

War Guilt. Analysis of the events which led to World War I shows that it would be unjust to conclude that the conflict was instigated by any one of the belligerents. The victorious nations later required Germany to acknowledge responsibility; they hoped to gain practical advantages thereby, which, however, ultimately did not materialize. An objective appraisal indicated that all the participants shared in the responsibility. Austria-Hungary and France were guilty because they followed policies of expansion and of revenge, respectively. Russia fostered a war atmosphere, nurtured Pan-Slavism, and allowed too much latitude to ambitious statesmen. England and Germany were animated by the generally prevailing imperialistic spirit; they could have refused to participate in such a war and thereby made it impossible; but they failed to do so. Among the German (as among the French) military and political circles were many who were not averse to the idea of a war; Germany's extensive naval-building program had contributed much to the tension and to ultimate disaster.

The Course of the War. The first two years of the war witnessed startling victories by Germany. As a result, almost the entire war was fought on the soil of Belgium, France, northern Italy, and Polish Russia. (Minor action took place in the German colonies.) The war was fought mostly on land by armies consisting of millions of conscripts on each side. Naval and air engagements were of comparatively little significance. Germany won many important battles but failed to turn these into a decisive victory. As the struggle continued, Japan, Italy, Rumania, and various small nations joined the Allies, while the Central Powers gained the support of Turkey and Bulgaria. Participation by the United States ultimately decided the issue, for then not even the collapse of Russia (which relieved Germany of the necessity to fight on two fronts) could prevent the defeat of the Central Powers. In November, 1918, they asked for an armistice.

CAMPAIGNS OF 1914 TO 1916. In a sense, the first three months of the war were the most critical. According to plan, the Germans invaded Belgium, whereupon England promptly declared war on Germany. Nevertheless, they conquered Belgium and pushed deep into France. But the Schlieffen plan was not consummated, for they did not gain control of the Channel coast and therefore could not prevent British aid from reaching France. At the end of August, apprehensive of Russian penetration into Germany, they reduced their forces on the Western front, with the consequence that early in September their advance was stopped short at the Marne River (First Battle of the Marne). What was planned as a short lightning war turned into an interminably grim war; throughout the year 1915 millions of soldiers faced each other in trenches, unable to strike a decisive blow. In 1916, the Germans attempted to break the deadlock. Two terrible battles were fought, one at Verdun, the other on the Somme River, bringing unprecedented losses to both sides; and an important naval engagement took place off the shores of Jutland. But the situation was not changed. Only in the east, where the fronts were mobile, was a decision reached. The Russian armies early in the war, had invaded both German East Prussia and Austrian Galicia. But defeated in 1914 at Tannenberg, they were pushed out of German territory. Soon Austria was also liberated, and by 1916 the Germans had penetrated deep into Russian territory.

CAMPAIGN OF 1917. The year 1917 began with no change in sight. Yet, that year proved to be decisive, for two major events completely altered the situation. The first event was the Russian revolution, overthrowing the tsarist government and establishing a liberal democratic regime (the "Provisional Government") in February, 1917. Although Russia remained in the war for a time and even staged a mighty summer offensive, the failure of this effort merely hastened the disintegration of the Russian army. The second event was the entry of the United States into the war. Strong pro-English leanings, democratic idealism, American investments in Allied countries, effective English propaganda (coupled with the interruption of news reports from German sources) and, finally, Germany's unrestricted submarine warfare which cost the United States heavily in lives and goods—all these factors contributed to abandonment of American neutrality. As matters turned out, although active participation by American armed forces (comparatively few of whom saw action in battle) helped the Allies and gave them renewed hope, American reserves in manpower and weapons, economic resources, and food supplies were far more decisive in swinging the tide of war against the Central Powers. Actually, American aid did not make itself fully felt before a second phase of the Russian revolution occurred. In October, 1917 (November according to the Western calendar), the Provisional Government was overthrown by the Bolsheviks, who promptly concluded an armistice with Germany.

 END OF WORLD WAR I (1918). Early in 1918, the armistice between Russia and Germany was supplemented by a peace treaty, which was concluded at Brest-Litovsk. (Germany insisted on the separation of Livonia, Poland, the Ukraine, and other territories from Russia, posing as an advocate of self-determination for all peoples but actually hoping to impose her own control upon these areas.) But Germany's victory in the east could not make up for the increased danger threatening her from the west. In the course of the spring and summer of 1918, the German armies were forced to retreat, and by September, it had become evident that, despite Brest-Litovsk, the war was lost for Germany. Her military position had become untenable, and internal unrest was brewing. To avert trouble at home, various steps were undertaken to democratize the country, such as granting universal, equal suffrage in Prussia. But this failed to placate Germany's enemies (bent on a complete overhauling of the German government) and her own liberals and socialists. Desperately, in the fall of 1918, the imperial government offered to negotiate peace along lines laid down in "Fourteen Points" proposed by President Woodrow Wilson. Germany's allies (Bulgaria, Turkey, and Austria-Hungary) also sued for peace, and their rulers abdicated. Although England and France made numerous reservations regarding Wilson's war aims, the German government could hold out no longer and an armistice was concluded in November.

ABDICATION OF GERMAN EMPEROR. By this time, revolution had broken out in Germany, the emperor had fled to Holland and, like other kings and princes of the individual German states, had given up his throne. A republic was instituted. There was some street fighting in Berlin and elsewhere, soldiers and sailors deserted, and communists attempted to seize power, but the socialists, supported by the liberal democratic parties, took over the government. Thus, simultaneously with the end of the war, the imperial structure created forty-seven years previously by Bismarck fell to pieces. Under trying circumstances, democrats and socialists assumed the heritage.

PEACE OF VERSAILLES (1919)

About one hundred years intervened between the Congress of Vienna and the Treaty of Versailles. During this period, the temper of the times had changed fundamentally. At Vienna the defeated nation had taken part in the settlement, but at Versailles the voice of the vanquished was rarely heard. The prompt return of the defeated to the family of nations had been the aim of the victors in 1815, but the postponement of such a result was the objective of the victors in 1919. A balance of power was sought after Napoleon's downfall, whereas a permanent weakening of the Central Powers was desired by the Allies at Versailles. Statesmen at Vienna drew frontiers in conformity with historic dynastic rights and interests, whereas the spirit of nationalism and revenge dictated boundary arrangements in 1919. Moreover, for the first time, a non-European power, the United States, played a leading part in a European peace settlement, while Russia, which had been so prominent in the negotiations of 1815, did not even participate.

Terms of the Treaties. The decisions made at Versailles (spelled out in the treaty signed there with Germany and, subsequently, in the separate treaties made with Austria, Bulgaria, and Turkey) were, as is usual in such matters, the result of numerous compromises. Early it became clear that the victors were pursuing divergent aims. Although President Wilson was a leading figure in the negotiations, his Fourteen Points were brushed aside whenever they seemed favorable to the interests of the defeated nations. Wilson's principles called for freedom of the seas, removal of economic barriers, disarmament, impartial distribution of colonies, evacuation by Germany of all territories occupied during the war, self-determination of subjected peoples, and the establishment of a League of Nations. Instead, the ideas of President Clemenceau of

France, who presided at sessions of the peace congress, prevailed. He advocated harsh terms, and in this he was generally supported by Prime Minister Lloyd George of England.

TERMS FOR GERMANY. The final treaty stipulated that Germany surrender all her colonies and special rights overseas, cede Alsace-Lorraine to France, and give France the right to control and exploit for a period of fifteen years the rich industrial area of the Saar. Germany was forced to give up her fleet—some units of which were scuttled by the crews—and a large part of her merchant marine. She had to cede territories in the east to newly formed Poland and, after a plebiscite, some lands to Denmark. Danzig was made a "free state," and a Polish "corridor," separating German East Prussia from the main territory of the German republic, was created. Germany's army was reduced to 100,000 men, and conscription was prohibited; the production of many types of armament was either forbidden or limited. Germany had to accede to occupation of her western lands and agree not to maintain military forces in the Rhineland. In addition, she was ordered to pay, as reparations, a war indemnity the amount of which was indefinite; yet, payments were to begin immediately. Finally, she was forced to sign a clause acknowledging that she had caused the war.

TERMS FOR OTHER DEFEATED COUNTRIES. Separate treaties were concluded with Bulgaria, Turkey, and Austria-Hungary. Bulgaria lost Thrace, had to limit her armaments, and, like Germany, was ordered to pay reparations. Turkey lost practically all her non-Turkish empire in Asia and Africa; most of this area either was taken over by France and England or, wherever separate states were created, was brought within the orbit of French or British influence. Turkey also agreed to the freedom and demilitarization of the Straits. Austria-Hungary was split into pieces, a denouement which disrupted the economic unity that had been slowly forming in the middle Danube area. The territory was allocated to five nations as follows: to Austria, the German-speaking areas (except some which were handed over to Italy, Hungary, or Czechoslovakia); to Yugoslavia (newly formed out of Serbia), Bosnia and other provinces; to Poland, Cracow and parts of Austrian Galicia; to Czechoslovakia (formerly Bohemia), Moravia and parts of Galicia; and to Hungary, the Magyar areas, except Transylvania, which was ceded to Rumania.

FOUNDING OF THE LEAGUE OF NATIONS. In a world rent by hatreds

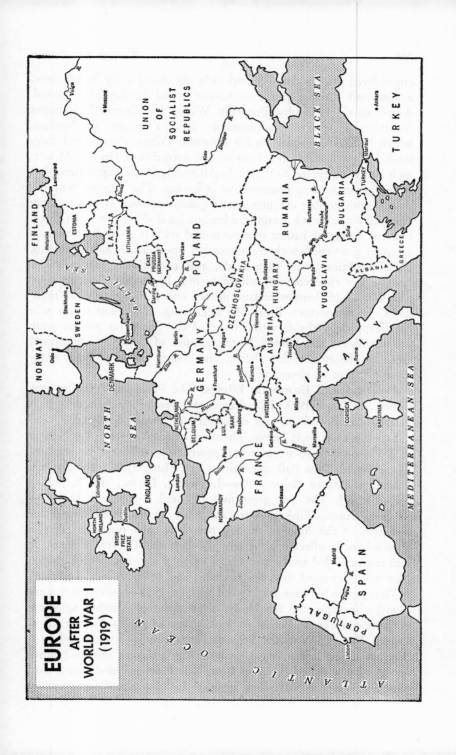

EUROPE
AFTER
WORLD WAR I
(1919)

engendered during the war and radically changed by its outcome, a just and durable peace settlement could hardly be expected. Aware of this difficulty, President Wilson had fastened his hopes for necessary peaceful adjustments upon a League of Nations, which he had advocated in his Fourteen Points. France and England did not favor such a League, but agreed to it (just as Metternich had once agreed to the Holy Alliance), in the expectation that it might serve as a conservative influence. The League was endowed with neither executive nor legislative power. It was to serve essentially as an open forum for international discussions. An International Court of Justice was connected with it, as well as various agencies concerned with humanitarian questions, health problems, labor conditions, the slave trade, and educational matters. The League was charged with administering the former German colonies, but all of them were surrendered either outright or as "mandates" to the victors. From the beginning, the organization was handicapped by the fact that three of the five great powers were not members: the United States because of domestic opposition, Germany because of her defeat, and Russia because of her communistic form of government.

Political and Economic Effects. The Peace of Versailles was signed in June, 1919. It reflected the profound changes which nationalism, liberalism, and socialism had already initiated.

THE INTERNATIONAL SCENE. There were fifteen states in the Europe of 1815; now there were twenty-seven fully independent nations. These included the Balkan countries and Hungary, Czechoslovakia, Poland, the three Baltic states—Lithuania, Latvia, and Estonia—and Finland. The last great multinational empires of Europe—Austria, Russia, Turkey—were shrunken or destroyed. Self-determination of the nations, though promised, was put into practice only where it affected adversely the defeated Central Powers. It was not accorded to the peoples of colonial nations, such as India. Nor was it granted to Austrians who had voted to join Germany, to Germans who were transferred to Italy, to Yugoslavs who were likewise incorporated into Italy, or to Alsatians, Irishmen, Macedonians, Slovaks, and other minorities. It was totally disregarded in eastern Europe. With the help of France, and notwithstanding a decision by an international group fixing Poland's eastern boundary along a so-called "Curzon Line," the Poles invaded Russia and annexed White Russia; they invaded Lithuania and incorporated the capital Vilna; they seized almost all of Germany's industrial Upper Silesia, after the people, in a plebiscite, had decided 14 to 9 against them. Because the principle of self-determination was disregarded, minority problems also persisted in Turkey, Greece, Czechoslovakia, and elsewhere, and poisoned international relations even in cases where population exchanges were undertaken.

POLITICAL TRENDS WITHIN NATIONS. The war experience and the outcome of the war had the effect of swinging public opinion and political institutions sharply to the left. Few of the European monarchies survived. Nearly all the new states were established as republics; the defeated countries were so re-established. The republics had either democratic or socialist governments. Socialists were the dominant minority in various central European countries; they also gained many votes and constituted strong opposition parties in many Western and Eastern nations. Communists ruled Russia.

THE WORLD ECONOMIC PICTURE. As in politics, so in economics, World War I upset the status quo. Capitalism had to adapt itself to a new constellation. War conditions had imposed many restrictions on it, and nowhere in Europe did it regain its former strength. One of the Fourteen Points had called for removal of economic barriers. It was ignored. Except for Germany, which was forced to open her borders to imports, European countries put up higher barriers than those existing before the war against the free exchange of goods. Russia shut herself off economically almost entirely from the Western world. Everywhere, autarchic trends increased. There was a shift in financial strength, as London lost her leading financial position to New York, and America changed from a debtor to a creditor nation. European currencies depreciated. War reparations upset the international balance of payments and necessitated redoubled export efforts on the part of Germany; this hurt other exporting nations. Russia repudiated the debts contracted by tsarist governments. Having granted Russia huge loans, France was the chief victim of repudiation, but England, Belgium, and the United States also lost substantial investments. Moreover, a sharp line of demarcation was drawn between the capitalistic and the communistic worlds. Some of the new nations in eastern Europe were built up by the Western nations as a *cordon sanitaire* against Bolshevism because of its anticapitalistic organization. On the whole, the first steps in building a "world safe for democracy" seemed none too promising.

THE RUSSIAN REVOLUTION

While the Western nations were busy rearranging the political map of Europe, the attention of the Russians was directed toward constructing an entirely new social order. The significance of the Russian Revolution far surpasses the effect it had on the outcome of World War I. It was the first revolution in Western history to give the industrial workers political power and leadership in a major nation, and to introduce a socialistic system. It constituted a substantial defeat of the bourgeoisie and of the liberal-democratic system for which the middle classes generally stood. It engendered forces which became world-wide in scope.

February Revolution (1917). Ever since the Revolution of 1905 and Stolypin's agrarian reform, radicalism in Russia had decreased. Terrorist activities had ceased; and within its narrow limits the parliament or Duma had come to gain influence and had started to build a constitutional system. The chief leaders of the radicals, notably Lenin, lived in exile; the times appeared unfavorable to them. But after 1910 and especially after the outbreak of war, the situation changed. Inasmuch as social progress had been slow, the strain of war proved disastrous. Moreover, the war governments were managed by reactionaries, the court was filled with intriguers, and the tsar was personally incapable as a ruler. He and his wife fell under the spell of Rasputin (a monk who with apparent success had administered to their ill son). The very fact of the influence of this greedy and dissolute man, even if he possessed rare common sense, indicated the corruption of the whole tsaristic system. Military defeats, manpower losses, widespread famine, and political graft hastened its disintegration. Revolutionary activities were resumed. In the winter of 1916, Rasputin was murdered; in January, 1917, strikes broke out, and mutinies occurred in the army and navy. The moderate parties in the Duma thereupon asked the tsar to yield wider powers to the parliament and to dismiss his government. Instead, the tsar dissolved the Duma. Thereupon, the liberal parties joined the socialists in the demand for his abdication. More strikes broke out; soldiers deserted; and, threatened from all sides, Nicholas II abdicated. The monarchy fell with him, and in February (March, according to the Western calendar), 1917, a Provisional Government was instituted by the Duma.

Provisional Government (1917). The new government was administered mainly by representatives of the liberal parties. It established freedom of religion, women's rights, and the legal equality of all citizens. It attacked the disturbing nationality problem by starting the Poles on the road to independence and by helping other national groups make a beginning in self-government. It passed laws to provide for social welfare, and it promised the peasants redistribution of the land along lines to be decided by a popular assembly after the end of the war. But in all its actions, the government was hindered by "soviets" (or councils) of workers and soldiers, which the socialists had set up and in which the communists dominated. The Soviet of St. Petersburg actually, if not legally, came to constitute a second governmental agency in the country, interfering with the decisions of the regular government and supervising, countersigning, or rejecting its acts. In April, 1917, Lenin returned from exile, followed soon thereafter by Trotsky. Under their leadership, the strength of the socialist opposition grew rapidly. Lenin's simple, easily understood slogan of "Peace, land, and bread" appealed to the war-tired, hungry population, especially to the peasantry; radicalism spread, and the establishment of the dictatorship of the proletariat was demanded by ever-widening circles. Soon, the more moderate members of the government, who had tried and failed to break the stranglehold of the soviets, resigned; a new offensive against the Germans collapsed and then, in July, a Bolshevik uprising occurred which was crushed with difficulty. The liberal government was replaced by one under the Social-Revolutionary Kerensky. He, too, was unwilling to accept the primary demand of the soviets—to end the war. The situation thereupon deteriorated further and led to a coup by one of the generals, who hoped to replace Kerensky's government with a military dictatorship. Kerensky was obliged to turn for help to the soviets, to free their leaders who had been arrested after the July revolts, and to call a "pre-Parliament."

October Revolution (1917) and Introduction of Communism. But it was too late. In October, Lenin, who had fled to Finland in July, returned and called for another armed uprising. The soldiers followed his lead, and at the end of October (Western November), the Provisional Government was driven out. Kerensky fled and most of his colleagues were arrested. Thus began the rule of the communists.

BOLSHEVIK LEADERS. The new government was formed by Lenin. Son of a superintendent of schools, who belonged to the lower nobility, he had, out of idealism, engaged early in revolutionary activities. Single-mindedly, he had devoted his great intellectual and organizing abilities solely to the preparation and implementation of the revolution. He had spent most of his life in exile, had edited various communist newspapers, had published books and pamphlets, and had welded the nucleus of the Russian Bolshevik party into a centralized, efficient, and devoted group. His most important collaborator after the overturn of the tsarist government was Leon Trotsky, of a fairly well-to-do Jewish family, a man as fervent in his idealism and as willing to sacrifice as Lenin himself, but more erratic, more individualistic, and less able in matters of organization. Trotsky had been one of the leaders of the 1905 revolution; he had suffered years in prison and banishment, and not until May, 1917, had he been able to return to Russia from exile in America. He became Lenin's commissar for foreign affairs. Notable among other members of the new Bolshevik government was Stalin, a revolutionary from Georgia, whose parents were a shoemaker and a washerwoman. He studied at an Orthodox seminary, from which he ran away to devote himself to the Bolshevik cause. Less intellectual than either Lenin or Trotsky, he proved himself an efficient, ruthless, practical revolutionary. By 1912 he had become editor of *Pravda,* the Bolshevik newspaper in St. Petersburg, but was subsequently exiled to Siberia and did not return until 1917. Lenin made him commissar for nationality questions.

INITIAL BOLSHEVIK RECONSTRUCTION OF RUSSIA. Lenin's government did not hesitate to carry out the Bolshevik program. Without regard for international consequences, Lenin fulfilled his promise of peace. Even though Russia's allies refused to recognize the necessity, rejected the Bolshevik proposal of a peace without annexation and indemnification, and sought to force her to continue the war, he began negotiations with the Germans and within a month concluded an armistice and, in March, 1918, negotiated the peace treaty of Brest-Litovsk. With equal determination he initiated the work of socialist reconstruction. Private property and church property were confiscated; banks and bank accounts were nationalized; factories were handed over to the workers (and later nationalized); and the lands of the nobility and of the rich were seized by the peasants. All trading activities, except those of small businesses owned and operated by individuals, were taken over by the state; the employment of one person by another was forbidden; a new police force of ardent Bolsheviks was organized; and control over the army was assumed by party commissars. Every citizen was instructed to go to work for the new government. The peasants were ordered to deliver fixed quotas of their crops. As to Russia's international role, Lenin paid little attention to traditional values. He based his policies on the expectation of world revolution, which he envisaged as the inevitable result of the war. In the meantime, he concentrated on one task only: the maintenance of communist rule in Russia.

CHAPTER XXI

TWILIGHT OF LIBERALISM (1919-1929)

WITH WAR AND DEVASTATION, any widespread feeling of security and complacency faded; but its very fading made possible the blossoming of vigorous new intellectual activity in Western culture. In the 1920's, scientific and technological work broadened in scope and significance; literature, painting, and architecture flourished, bringing to maturity the revolutionary art concepts that had been in a pioneer stage before the war; and political experiments (in democracy, socialism, and communism) engendered much idealism. The New World, having come of age, now contributed in the same way as the European nations to the cultural accomplishments of the West.

CULTURAL TRENDS

Physical and social sciences were the chief expressions of twentieth-century culture. Scientific interests continued to spread rapidly, and scientific method was applied to the new disciplines of psychology and sociology. Science affected the work of philosophers, historians, and economists. It stimulated education in which a new approach to the study of the process of learning was sought and experiments in new types of schools were undertaken. It influenced literature, which became less concerned with the character, ideas, and behavior of the exceptional individual and more concerned with the average person and with the collective behavior of the masses. Its effects can be traced in painting, architecture, and music, which gave expression to modern psychological and sociological approaches. Even

264

religious thought came to be more and more reconciled to modern science.

Science and Technology. The work of twentieth-century scientists increased man's realization of the complexities of the cosmos. In all scientific fields, further specialization became necessary.

PHYSICAL SCIENCES. The most spectacular advances were made in the physical sciences, in research concerned with the world of the atom. Physicists such as Rutherford, Bohr, and Schrödinger achieved fundamental progress in man's understanding of the structure and the processes operating in the atom. Heisenberg proposed an uncertainty principle, which postulated final limits to human possibilities of observation and thus restricted, on the atomic level, the area in which scientific verification is possible. Astronomers developed a hypothesis of a constantly expanding universe to explain many puzzling phenomena in this field. Einstein elaborated his relativity theory and ultimately undertook a search for a formula that would be as all-inclusive in explaining the relationship of natural forces as Newton's law of gravitation had once seemed to be.

CHEMISTRY. New information about the molecular structure of matter enabled chemists to broaden their efforts to produce synthetic materials, with the result that rare or expensive natural products, such as rubber and silk, could be replaced increasingly by artificial materials. This development of synthetics had effects beyond the realm of science by affecting economic, social, and political life. New products changed the habits and work of the average people, and simultaneously redirected the policies of whole nations. They reduced the dependence of great powers upon their colonies for raw materials and led to the creation of new industries, and this, in turn, eased some international tensions, engendered others, encouraged nationalism, affected independence movements among colonial peoples, and eventually contributed to recurring shifts in the balance of power.

BIOLOGY AND MEDICINE. Notable advances, aside from physics and chemistry, were also made in most other areas of science. Biologists reached fundamental achievements in their study of heredity (including the phenomena of mutations) and cell physiology. New therapies for a wide variety of diseases were discovered; hormones and antibiotics were added to the physician's arsenal. Progress in public health brought new methods for combating epidemics traced to mosquitoes, lice, rats, and other carriers of bacteria. Improved practices in sanitation also contributed to better health and a longer life for millions of people. This led to an unheard of increase in populations, which crowded into urban or rapidly growing suburban areas. Nevertheless, material standards of living could improve, since science, and particularly advances in chemistry, plant pathology, veterinary medicine, and agronomy made possible a vast increase in agricultural production so that the food supply was more ample than ever before.

PSYCHOLOGY AND SOCIOLOGY. Lastly, the two new fields of scientific psychology and of sociology made rapid progress. Psychologists applied the theories expounded by Freud and his disciples and evolved new data in normal and abnormal psychology. Sociologists applied the research techniques of psychologists and arrived at interesting, though necessarily tentative, conclusions regarding collective behavior—conclusions which had considerable influence on the fields of philosophy and political science.

Philosophy and Economic Theory. In a world dominated by scientific endeavors, philosophy continued to occupy itself largely with rational, materialistic, and social questions, rather than with transcendental or metaphysical problems. Such outstanding thinkers as Russell, Whitehead, and Dewey interested themselves in science and its method, as well as in the effects of science on human society. Pragmatic tendencies were strong, and symbolic logic and "logical positivism" were developed. Logical positivists followed the example of the nineteenth-century positivists in excluding transcendental concerns from the domain of philosophy, but they went further by devoting themselves primarily to the technical analysis of language and to the methodology of science. The question of "progress" was re-examined and, in line with evolutionary theories, the facts of history and experience rather than abstract concepts were adopted as the basis for most interpretations of the evolution of human society. Some philosophers, such as Spengler in his *Decline of the West,* came to view human history altogether as a biological process subject to natural laws and insisted that every culture passes through a cycle of youth, maturity, and old age.

Scientific, historical approaches also marked the work of economists. In the nineteenth century, Karl Marx had turned to history in order to understand economic developments; many twentieth-century economists adopted the same method. After studying the evolutionary social process in history, they reviewed and criticized the propositions of the classical economic theorists. In general, they came to reject all idealistic and utopian views and, like many philosophers, accepted "utility" as their standard. Some economists concluded that utility governed "value" and thereby, within the changing historical setting, the major phases of the economic process. They developed extensive statistical methods and, with the help of statistics, investigated business cycles, price movements, and all other characteristics of capitalism. Keynes and Schumpeter were two of the most stimulating economic theorists among them.

Education. Growing attention was paid to mass education in order to prepare the average Western man for the tasks facing him in the modern world: for handling machinery and living with it, for exercising his newly won civil rights, and for using his constantly increasing leisure time. Therefore in the decade after World War I, when literacy was becoming nearly universal (spreading to the remotest regions of the United States and Russia), educational goals underwent a radical transformation. Studies of the classics—a foundation of modern civilization—were curtailed in order to allow more time for the study of the natural sciences; instruction emphasized experience and practice rather than memorization, which had long been regarded as an indispensable tool of knowledge; discipline was relaxed and students were given greater freedom to achieve "self-expression." With mass education, a leveling process began whereby uniformity in thinking habits was promoted. Numerous experimental schools were founded. Social adjustment to the mechanized modern world was considered a major task for "democratic" education. To be sure, opposition arose against the new trends in education; critics of the idea of "progressive education" held that lack of rigid intellectual training and discipline would lead to a return to barbarism. Even in communist Russia, a foremost advocate of progressive education, a reaction occurred during the 1930's.

Literature and the Fine Arts. The 1920's stand out as a time particularly rich in writers and artists of ability and significant accomplishment. It was then that the trends, which had been developed under the leadership of the expressionists during the last decade and a half before World War I, came into full flowering. With the upheaval of war, revolution, and postwar adjustment, many of the former restraints were broken and men of genius were able to allow free rein to their inclinations and to proceed

with important experimental work. It is still too early to judge
the lasting values achieved by them, but there is little doubt about
the broad historical and social significance of their works.

LITERATURE. No specific new form of literary expression came to
the fore. The novel still offered that artistic frame which seemed
most appropriate to the temper of the time, lending itself to realistic description and to criticism of the social scene. Among the
large number of writers representing the prevailing tendencies in
fiction were the Frenchmen Rolland, Gide, and Malraux, the
Englishmen Hardy (famous also for his drama *The Dynasts*),
Galsworthy, and D. H. Lawrence, and the Russians Gorky, Alexis
Tolstoy, and Mayakovsky (who were actually products of the pre-
revolutionary days). A special place belongs to the Frenchman
Proust and the Irishman Joyce. Their works, *Remembrance of
Things Past* and *Ulysses,* became foremost examples of that type
of psychological study and penetrating observation of human instincts and behavior which have since become known as "stream-
of-consciousness" writing. Unusually vigorous and important literary production came out of the United States and Germany and
included works by Lewis, Dreiser, Dos Passos, Sinclair, and Hem-
ingway, in America, and the Mann brothers, Werfel, and Zweig,
in Germany. Compared to prose, creative work in drama and
poetry was of lesser import. The American O'Neill and the Englishman George Bernard Shaw (who despite advancing age still
remained one of the most productive authors and critics) excelled
in the drama. In lyric poetry, the most prominent writers were the
Irishman Yeats, the American T. S. Eliot, and the Frenchman
Valéry, and the two German masters, George and Rilke. Of course,
the largest audiences were not reached by the great writers, but by
newspapers, journals, and novels of sensational character.

It is noteworthy though that, just as literacy was rapidly advancing everywhere in the West, means of communication were being
invented which could dispense with the written word. Radio,
cinema, photographs, cartoons, and illustrated advertisements (i.e.,
"audio-visual" media) were used to disseminate information, entertainment, and propaganda on an unprecedented scale. Though they
often contributed to the corruption of man's taste, they also contributed to his education and elevation.

PAINTING AND SCULPTURE. In the fine arts, "expressionism" reached
its climax and brought forth a movement known as "surrealism."

Many outstanding painters and sculptors concentrated on man's psychology rather than on his visual imagery. They sought to express an inner reality: a view of twentieth-century man as being torn by the multiplicity of modern problems which he had to face without the confidence that a feeling of harmony with nature or with a world spirit had given him in other times. They revealed their concern with the social patterns of their age, which they sought to explain or criticize. Outstanding contributors were the painters Picasso, who began a new phase of creativity in his life, and Rivera, who was influenced by communist ideology; and the sculptors Epstein, Mestrovic, and Maillol. Since these painters and sculptors often preferred an abstract type of expression, it was difficult for the average person to understand their works, and most people were drawn to other, more conservative artists using a simpler, more direct language. Especially in countries with communist and fascist regimes, intellectualized, abstract trends were ridiculed and rejected, whereas artistic creations rooted in folkways and serving, if possible, the ideologies of the regimes were promoted.

ARCHITECTURE. Vigorous and artistically meaningful developments also occurred in architecture. Functionalism, which had begun to dominate during the period before World War I, now spread rapidly. It emphasized simplicity, the utmost restraint in ornamentation, and clear, geometric lines. It sought to bring aesthetic values into harmony with the practical demands of life in an industrial age. City planning and apartment-, factory-, and office-building projects engaged the attention of the architect, and social needs gave direction to his creative endeavors. The *Bauhaus* in Dessau, Germany, a school of painters and architects, became a center for modern concepts in building. Similarly, in the Netherlands, France, and the United States, the functional style with its characteristic aesthetic values made rapid progress. Owing to masters such as Gropius, Miës van der Rohe, Frank Lloyd Wright, and Le Corbusier, town landscapes in Europe and in America began to change. Uncluttered lines and a variety of color began to give many of them an impression of beauty which the nineteenth-century towns, in their grayness and with their imitative styles, their over-ornamentation, and their slums, had sadly lacked.

MUSIC. In music, traditional harmonic concepts survived in most of the popular compositions, and folklore continued to inspire their creators. But composers such as Schönberg, Stravinsky, Hindemith,

Bartók, and Sibelius went on with experimental work and the creation of "atonal" music. Like expressionist painting, atonal music failed to have an immediate appeal for the uninitiated; nevertheless, it attracted a growing audience of intellectuals. The Soviet Union produced Prokofiev and Shostakovich. America's chief contribution consisted in popular and often "intellectualized" jazz which was originated by her gifted Negroes and which influenced many leading composers. Few operas of importance were written. Classical and modern concert music came to be enjoyed by ever widening audiences. Numerous excellent orchestras were founded, especially in America, and improved radio reception and better phonographs contributed to an unprecedented awareness of man's great musical heritage.

Religion. It is significant that the rapid progress of science, technology, and secular education did not intensify the conflict between science and religion, dating back to the preceding century. Scientists began to appreciate the limitations and relativity of their knowledge, while the churches allowed a broader place for science in the mind of rational man. Atheism no longer made converts as in preceding decades, except in Russia where Marxist aims called for condemnation of all religion as a form of superstition. The challenge of science impelled the churches to re-assess their teachings and ultimately to strengthen their spiritual forces; even in Russia the church gained rather than lost by this challenge and by the withdrawal of many who had adhered to it only out of convention. Relations between church and state became more peaceful, and, with the spread of separation between church and state, governments exercised less control over religious institutions. A spiritual revival led, especially among Protestants, to a "Neo-Orthodoxy," which had its roots in ideas expounded by the nineteenth-century Danish theologian Kierkegaard. Neo-Orthodoxy asked for a reaffirmation of the Christian doctrine and a resolute acceptance of the fundamental tenets of Christianity, which demanded of each individual a "painful abandonment" of himself to his faith.

INTERNATIONAL TRENDS

Like most wars, World War I settled fewer problems than it created. The international arrangements made at Versailles were quickly shattered; the League of Nations proved ineffective; and the gulf widened between the views of capitalist countries and those of Russia and between the interests of colonial powers and those of their dependencies. The fact that mechanized civilization, with its manifold pressures, required new attitudes was comprehended by few statesmen.

Major International Problems. The two problems most disturbing to international relationships after World War I were communism and reparations. At first, the victorious Western powers sought to solve these problems by force, trying to suppress communism with armed might and to collect reparations under threats. When this method failed, they slowly settled down to the task of making compromises. Unfortunately for the peace of the West, they delayed too long.

COMMUNISM. At the end of the war, the communist system seemed to be only weakly established in Russia. Hoping, therefore, to be able to restore a capitalistic, liberal-democratic regime, four powers—America, England, France, and Japan—decided to crush the Soviets. They invaded Russia in 1918 in order to force her back into the war against Germany, and, when the war ended, continued to support the old tsarist forces in order to oust the Bolshevik government. This "intervention" led to catastrophe. After two bitter years, foreign troops were forced to quit Russian soil. Simultaneously, Russian monarchists and anticommunists, led by Denikin, Wrangel, Kolchak, and other tsarist officers, either surrendered or fled the country. By 1922, the Bolsheviks were in full control of most of Russia. Regions which had attempted to establish independent regimes, such as Siberia, parts of the Caucasus, and parts of the Ukraine, were reunited with Russia proper. They became components of the Soviet Union. Thus, within four years, communist power had firmly established itself. From then on, it became more and more of a force in the world. Even when absent from international conferences, the Soviet Union had to be considered in all political settlements. It secured recognition from most European nations and gradually expanded its influence abroad through the Comintern, the Third (*Com*munistic) *Intern*ational which Lenin had sponsored in 1919.

REPARATIONS. Some of the French leaders at Versailles had insisted upon the imposition of extremely burdensome reparations, in the hope that reparations not only would help in the reconstruction of war-damaged France, but also would make possible the permanent subjugation of Germany. These expectations were not realized. It quickly became clear that reparations were a two-edged weapon. By forcing Germany to increase her industrial capacity and to bend her efforts toward exports in order to earn the means for making reparation payments, the insistence on reparations caused a dislocation of the Western economy. By leading to a German currency inflation of a degree never before experienced, the victors made it possible for the German government to pay its internal debt in inflated currency and thereby gain strength, while other countries experienced unemployment and a limited inflation. Moreover, unemployment and inflation led to a new radicalism everywhere, as mortgage holders, bondholders, and other creditors suffered, rentiers were impoverished, and millions of people lost interest in the preservation of the capitalistic system. Finally, a wedge was driven between the Allies themselves, especially between France and England (who desired economic stability) and between the United States and her European partners (who refused to pay war debts to the United States so long as they could not collect from Germany). In 1927, an economic conference called to find a solution to the problem failed to achieve its purpose. Thus, reparations served neither the Allied interests nor the cause of world peace and reconstruction.

International Solutions. As time went on, the task of finding a basis, different from the Versailles Treaty, for rebuilding the Western community of nations became more urgent; but a solution was delayed as long as the aims of the Western states remained at variance. France desired hegemony on the European continent and therefore insisted on strict fulfillment of the stipulations of Versailles. Simultaneously, by entering into bilateral arrangements with Poland, Czechoslovakia, and Yugoslavia, she sought to build up in eastern-central Europe an alliance system which would serve the double purpose of erecting a *cordon sanitaire* against communist Russia and a counterweight against German might. England, however, wanted the re-establishment of a balance of power, whereby not only would France be prevented from becoming a menace to her but whereby also communism could be held in check. The United States, who refused to become a party to the Versailles Treaty, followed a policy of isolationism wherever possible. Germany sought a revision of the treaty and the re-establishment of her prewar position. Russia, who ranked fifth among the great powers and, like the United States, was not a signatory to the Versailles Treaty, detached herself completely from the West; she saw her aim in building a socialist society at home and spreading communism abroad.

RAPALLO (1922). The divergent aims of the great powers presaged a long period of negotiation. Since the League of Nations failed to fulfill the role intended for it, conference after conference had to be called. Various meetings took place in 1920. In 1921, a Naval Conference was held in Washington for the purpose of promoting disarmament. The only thing achieved, however, was a redistribution of naval strength. The arrangement was significant inasmuch as England, formerly the greatest power on the seas, had to accept a place of equality with the United States; Japan ranked third; and Italy and France shared fourth and fifth places. A year later, a more important conference was held at Genoa, to which both Germany and the Soviet Union were invited. It led (owing to the failure of the victors to make concessions to the two outcasts) to a German-Russian treaty. This treaty, made at nearby Rapallo, changed the existing distribution of power as much as the Franco-Russian alliance had done in 1890. Germany and Soviet Russia, both isolated and weak since the war, agreed upon formal political recognition and economic cooperation and thereby became powerful factors on the international stage. France reacted bitterly. In the following year, 1923, she used Germany's inability to pay reparations as an excuse for occupying the great German industrial region of the Ruhr. Both the United States and England refused to associate themselves with such a punitive measure and even withdrew occupation troops. As a result, the French invasion of the Ruhr gained little and further complicated the international situation.

LOCARNO (1925). Under the circumstances, the need for a realistic attack upon Western economic and political problems became more urgent. Steps were finally taken at the initiative of the United States. In 1924, with the realization of the close relationship between political and economic problems, a reparation plan (the Dawes plan) was worked out. It fixed German reparations at a sum apparently commensurate with Germany's ability to pay, and American loans were put at Germany's disposal so that she might provide for her new obligations. Once adopted, the Dawes plan opened the way for a settlement of political disputes. This was achieved by a conference held in Locarno in 1925. Owing to the efforts of the

French and German foreign ministers, Briand and Stresemann, an agreement concerning the disputed German-French border was consummated, which guaranteed the maintenance of Germany's western boundaries established by the Versailles Treaty. In the following year Germany joined the League of Nations. Simultaneously, the military supervision of Germany was ended.

BRIAND-KELLOGG PACT (1928). Further steps toward preservation of peace were taken in the next year. Inasmuch as regional meetings and disarmament conferences among the victors had failed and inequality in military strength continued to endanger world peace, the American Secretary of State, Kellogg, proposed a pact providing for compulsory arbitration of future political differences. The pact was signed by the United States and the leading European powers in 1928.

Solutions to Colonial Problems. World War I marked the end of an era of Western civilization, not only in Europe, but also in the colonies. Under the pressure of world opinion, of humanitarian views, and of socialist propaganda, European political domination began to recede while national movements led by native upper classes gained in strength. Germany and Russia dropped out of the colonial picture altogether. Germany, by virtue of the Versailles Treaty, had lost her colonies everywhere; Russia, in line with communistic ideology, voluntarily renounced treaty advantages secured (by tsarist governments) in China, Afghanistan, Persia, and Turkey. Other nations also had to modify their relations with colonial areas. The United States eased her controls in Central America and reformed the government of the Philippines. France, Japan, and England (though attempting to preserve their empires and even to enlarge them) also had to make concessions. France was obliged to give up some of her control of the Near East and to liberalize her policies in North Africa. Japanese troops were forced to leave Siberia, where they had made acquisitions during the intervention of 1918–1920. England, the largest colonial power, conceded the widest adjustments. In 1923, she accorded her dominions the right to make independent treaties with foreign powers; in 1926, she created the "British Commonwealth," which provided for the equal status of dominions and mother country within the Empire, and for independent management of internal and external affairs; and in 1930, she confirmed the new status of the colonies by means of the Statute of Westminster. She resigned her protectorate over Egypt in 1922 and broadened that country's independence in 1936. But in order to safeguard British investments and the supply of oil, she insisted on continued control of the Arab States, which had been founded within the area of the dissolved Turkish Empire. She also refused to withdraw from India. As a result, she became involved in a desperate struggle against Indian nationalists led by Mahatma Gandhi, who advocated passive resistance to all English authority and defiance of Western civilization through readoption of traditional Indian production methods. Even though Gandhi's economic precepts could not survive in an industrialized world, his moral stand gained wide recognition and laid the basis for India's independence; this objective was achieved in 1947, after his death. All Western countries lost their privileged status and their extraterritorial rights in China; further colonialism there was forestalled by the continued reform work of Sun Yat-sen and his party, the Kuomintang. In most colonies where European political power had to withdraw, European techniques were taken over by native forces.

NATIONAL TRENDS

Internal political developments in the Western nations after World War I were marked by the progressive introduction of democratic institutions and social legislation; women, for instance, came to take an increasingly important part in national affairs.

England. Reforms in her empire, loss of her place as the leading financial power, and the redoubled competition, not only of the United States but also of a rapidly recovering Germany, forced England to make numerous internal adjustments. The Liberal party declined. For three years after 1919, Britain's wartime leader, Lloyd George, continued to preside over a coalition cabinet. But a business recession, following, as so often, upon the end of hostilities and reconversion to peacetime production, restored the Conservatives to power. Thereafter the Liberal party was eclipsed by the Labor party, and in 1924 the first Labor cabinet in British history was formed. It lasted, however, only a few months (during which it effected the formal recognition of the Soviet Union) and then had to yield again to the Conservatives. Under their leadership, England benefited from the general revival which ensued after the reparations problem had been successfully attacked through the Dawes plan and the political climate improved through the Locarno agreements. Her trade balance and financial position became better, she enacted social legislation to alleviate the plight of the unemployed, she modernized her industries, and she achieved further political democratization in 1928 by granting equal suffrage to women. But grave problems remained to be solved: persistent unemployment, distress in some industries, and numerous acrimonious strikes. The Irish, dissatisfied with England's wartime promises (they received only dominion status in 1922 and they resented especially the separation of Ulster from the Irish Free State), fought desperately for complete independence. But all of these issues were overshadowed when, in 1929, a world-wide economic crisis interrupted what progress had been achieved and opened a new phase in England's history.

France. Another victor of 1918, France, faced problems of a very different kind. Her people still led (as the literary critic, André Siegfried, had observed before 1914) a more contented life than her progressive and dynamic neighbors. Favored by traditions, character, and resources, life in France had not changed as it had in the highly industrialized countries. Her economy was more balanced and self-sufficient, her political position satisfied the nationalists after the victory of 1918, and her prosperity was aided by German reparations and American debt cancellations. However, underneath the surface, French conditions were precarious. Demographically, the prewar trend of stagnating population figures remained. Politically, the individualism of the French reasserted itself, split the parties into numerous groups, and impeded nation-wide co-operation. Constant changes of government prevented the passing of timely legislation needed to adapt the economic structure to modern requirements. Inflation haunted the country and increased instability; initiative was lacking; and corruption scandals were not infrequent. In contrast to the situation in other great nations, the right of women to vote was withheld, living standards of the poor were raised but little, and class differences remained unreconciled. Thus, despite military victory, the prospects for the nation to retain its international position were substantially diminished.

Germany. Having been defeated in war, shaken by the revolution which had brought the imperial government to an end, and deprived of valuable industrial regions in the east and the west,

Germany faced the future under grave handicaps. At Weimar, in central Germany, a democratic constitution for the new German republic, which later became known as the "Weimar Republic," was drawn up in 1919 by bourgeois and socialist liberals. It provided for parliamentary government, ministerial responsibility to the diet, equal suffrage of all citizens (including women), and guarantees of other civil rights. But it found little support or respect. Bitter partisan recriminations divided the country; Bolshevists hoped to turn it into a communistic state, while reactionaries sought to re-establish old monarchical forms. Individualism, as in France, led to a large number of splinter parties which hindered the formation of effective governments and necessitated constantly changing coalitions. Although the civil service remained intact and government officials worked faithfully and honestly, disorder and violence marked the political scene. Several ministers and party leaders were assassinated, the nationalists generally being the perpetrators. The middle class, ruined by war and inflation, listened to demagogic promises of the extreme right or the extreme left. Resentment was kept alive by the Peace of Versailles with its frontier stipulations and its reparations and war-guilt clauses. Political disorders occurred: on the one hand, disappointed, chauvinistic war youths, assisted by officers of the old army clique, tried to overthrow the democratic government and staged in 1920 the "Kapp Putsch" and in 1923 the "Bierhall Putsch"; on the other hand, leftist parties sought the destruction of the government by organizing several general strikes. Nor did the Treaty of Rapallo with Russia insure internal stability, though it did restore Germany to her place as a great power; for the treaty was followed by inflation in its worst form and soon thereafter the French and Belgians marched into the Ruhr district. Hopes for constructive progress reawakened only after the currency was stabilized in 1924, reparations were reduced by the Dawes plan, a successful foreign policy was initiated by Stresemann, foreign occupation troops were withdrawn, and the Locarno Treaty brought a measure of reconciliation with the West. Even then, however, sufficient difficulties remained and national extremists as well as Bolshevists exploited them by pointing to the weakness of the national economy and to the restrictions imposed at Versailles. Thus, widespread disrespect was kept alive for a government which was trying to be liberal and to adapt itself to democratic forms. As long as economic conditions improved, these extremists had little chance; but when depression came in 1929, the nihilistic forces triumphed.

Russia. While England, France, Germany, and other Western countries adhered to moderately liberal democratic (and occasionally mildly socialistic) institutions, Russia set about building a communist society.

PERIOD OF WAR COMMUNISM (1918–1921). The Soviet constitution of 1918 established a dictatorship of the proletariat; all parties except the Communist disappeared. The former ruling classes were disfranchised; the nobility, capitalists, rich peasants, priests, and noncommunist intelligentsia were persecuted, exiled, or condemned to death. The government was put into the hands of a Central Committee of the soviets and its executive organ, the Politbureau. It was supported by a new, well-trained "Red Army" and a new Bolshevik police force, which ruthlessly used terroristic methods. The state controlled all banks, industries, large businesses, and foreign trade, and thus combined political with economic power to a degree unparalleled in any Western country.

PERIOD OF NEP (1921–1927). Nevertheless, owing to foreign war, civil strife, famine, and dissatisfaction among the peasants (who, unlike the industrial workers, had gained little influence in the government) communism might not have survived in Russia had not Lenin changed his tactics in 1921. Facing a serious crisis (the peasants refused to fulfill their quotas for delivery of foodstuffs, production came to a standstill, and a contingent of sailors revolted) he reintroduced, notwithstanding opposition within his own ranks, a number of capitalistic institutions. Small-scale private enterprise in trade and agriculture again was allowed; the policy of food levies was replaced by taxation of peasants, the terror was reduced, aid from capitalistic countries was accepted, a stable currency was restored, schools were reopened, and pre-Revolutionary scientists were re-employed. Also, a *modus vivendi* with the Orthodox Church was found. Lenin's new policy, known as "NEP" (*New Economic Policy*), brought internal improvements at the very time that Russia gained external prestige through the Rapallo Treaty and won formal recognition from the leading European powers.

PERIOD OF FIRST FIVE-YEAR PLAN (1928–1932). In July 1923, a new constitution was published. It established the Union of Socialist Soviet Republics (USSR), composed of Great Russia, Siberia, Ukraine, and the Caucasus. Shortly thereafter, Lenin died. But his work survived, despite a bitter struggle for party leadership between his two chief co-workers, Trotsky and Stalin. With the help of the Party apparatus which he controlled, Stalin, the great organizer, triumphed over Trotsky. Stalin held the view that communism had to be built on firm ground in Russia before it could be spread abroad; he rejected the individualistic tendencies of Trotsky and insisted on strict Party discipline and central direction; and ideologically he steered a middle road. Under him, the NEP (which had served well as a temporary expedient) was given up and communistic planning was resumed. A first Five-Year Plan, promulgated in 1928, provided for the central direction of all economic activities by government and party. It stipulated production quotas for all sectors of the economy: for factories, agriculture, and individual workers. It aimed at developing the resources of the country and at improving backward regions—especially the arctic areas of Siberia. It co-ordinated the activities of the various industries and controlled channels of domestic and foreign distribution. Prices and wages were fixed. The Plan promoted the collective farm, called "kolkhoz," a large farm, with land belonging to the state, but its activities managed autonomously in accordance with the Plan, its cultivation attended to in common by its members, and its products sold by state or kolkhoz stores. The individual retained for himself no more than a house and garden, but shared according to his work in a possible surplus of the collective. Mechanical help was rendered by government-run tractor stations. The Plan, which provided also for public education, for theaters, and for other cultural activities, led to a rapid increase in Russia's productive apparatus, but its rigorous enforcement caused the population untold suffering. Especially in the country, kulaks (prosperous peasants with individual holdings) whose activity had been allowed during the NEP, were sacrificed to communistic aims and hundreds of thousands of them perished either from starvation or as the result of exile and persecution.

The United States. In the United States, World War I had left fewer traces than in Europe, and, consequently, her social change was less extreme. A Republican administration, which replaced the Democrats in 1921, adopted many of the policies of political and economic liberalism. The nation prospered as business expanded, national production increased rapidly, and standards of living improved. There was substantial progress in education, science, literature, and the arts. An indication of such progress was the large number of foreign students attracted to American universities, the development of inventions, the organization of excellent orchestras, the founding of numerous museums, and the great variety of works of literature which gained world-wide reputation. In foreign affairs, the United States, notwithstanding popular isolationist sentiments, took a more active part than ever before, contributing to the solution of world problems. A rash of political corruption and crime accompanying the "noble experiment" of national prohibition failed to impede economic and cultural progress of the nation. But serious social maladjustments and problems were ignored. Little heed was given to warnings about the difficulties of the farmers and the overextension of credit. Not until the stock market crash of 1929, marking the end of the era of prosperity, did the government begin to work on solutions for some of the fundamental problems confronting the United States and other Western nations.

Other Western Countries. The smaller countries of the West, with the exception of Italy, did not suffer so much as the major powers from the war and the difficulties caused in its aftermath by revolutions, inflation, impoverishment, and social disorganization. None adopted communism; most of them made considerable progress in the development of industrial production, educational standards, and political democracy (although in some countries, such as Poland and Hungary, feudalistic institutions benefiting the owners of large landed estates continued to prevail, and in others dictatorships prospered, as in Latin America). In all Western nations, nationalism persisted as a dominant influence. It was evinced in Poland by armed aggression against her various neighbors; in Czechoslovakia, Italy, and various Balkan nations by attempts at building national industries which were motivated primarily by nationalistic aspirations; in Latin America by struggles against foreign economic domination, such as waged by Mexico when nationalizing the oil companies owned by business interests in the United States. When the depression began in the later 1920's, the nationalistic trends reflected in these events created problems among the smaller nations similar to those confronting the major powers of the Western world.

CHAPTER XXII

DEPRESSION, FASCISM, AND WAR
(1929–1945)

THE THREE WORDS, *depression, fascism,* and *war,* in this sequence, indicate a causal relationship; but they do not suffice to explain the pattern of major historical events in the 1930's. The decline of liberalism, the strength of nationalism, the achievements in science and technology, the failures of education, the shortsightedness of politicians and economists, the weakness of people in responsible positions, and the contradictions within man's nature—all these contributed to the complex events of this period. In retrospect, however, the consideration of three forces—depression, fascism, and war, to which might be added a fourth, Bolshevism—may serve as an adequate guide to analysis of the major developments.

DEPRESSION

According to some economists, in a capitalistic society cycles of prosperity and depression are inevitable. A cycle of this kind occurred after World War I. The war boom lasted until 1919. There was a brief depression in 1920, which was followed by a long period of prosperity from which all countries (neutrals as well as those directly involved in the war) benefited. The universal prosperity engendered overconfidence both in political and in economic affairs; overoptimism and excessive speculation resulted in the production of more goods than the market could absorb. From 1925 to 1929 the gap was bridged through an expansion of credit, but when debts reached dangerous limits, banks became reluctant to make more loans. Prices dropped, production fell, and confidence was undermined.

The "Crash" (1929). By 1929, a depression had begun to develop in the Western economy. Ensuing unemployment brought a chain of reactions inasmuch as even reduced production could no longer be absorbed, and further unemployment resulted. In October the so-called "crash" on the New York Stock Exchange occurred, ruining many leading business enterprises. The close relationship between domestic business and foreign trade meant that a depression in any one major country (especially the United States) inevitably affected all others, not excluding communist Russia which was compelled to accept reduced prices for her exports. In 1931 the collapse of one of the great international banks, the Kreditanstalt in Vienna, intensified the downward turn of business in all countries.

Social Consequences of Depression. The consequences of economic disaster were felt in all areas of public and private life. Many people who had considered themselves financially secure lost their means of livelihood. Farmers, unable to find a market for their products, lost their lands. Millions of factory workers were idle. Unemployment figures climbed to incredible heights in leading industrial countries, such as the United States, Germany, and England. Even in Russia, the only large Western country which did not have an unemployment problem, the depression prevented any substantial improvement of living standards. Insecurity, demoralization, and impoverishment changed man's outlook and, in a world that seemed to be disintegrating, made man ready, everywhere, to seek salvation through radical correctives.

Political Consequences. Naturally, governments tried to take remedial action; in so doing, they contributed to a further weakening of liberal, laissez-faire institutions. In the United States, the Republican President Hoover introduced "farm relief" measures, and he also advocated new forms of social legislation. In 1933, the United States devalued the dollar and instituted a program of social insurance. The governments in all European countries provided subsidies for manufacturers and exporters and found it necessary to establish extensive controls over business. Tariffs were raised and the exchange of currency was restricted. The export of gold and other funds was forbidden. In 1931 England gave up the gold standard; as in previous emergencies, she had recourse to a national coalition cabinet, this time with a Labor party premier. In 1932 she abandoned her free-trade policy, introducing new protective tariffs, though providing "preference tariffs" for members of her empire. In Germany, the government claimed, under an emergency clause of the constitution, almost dictatorial powers. Then, backed only by a minority against the opposition of a large but ideologically divided majority, it followed the example of other Western governments, enacting laws to relieve distress. But, also like the others, it found itself unable to solve the basic unemployment problem. The effects of the depression were less severe in France and Italy, which were not so dependent upon highly developed industries, and in the agricultural countries of the East. Nevertheless, even in these countries, suffering was widespread and long-established political systems were imperiled as the radical parties of right or left gained adherents. Repercussions also developed in the Far East, whereever European economic methods and influence had made headway. Japan, in particular, experienced reverses owing to the loss of her foreign markets and was tempted to utilize the drastic remedies of war and territorial expansion.

International Consequences. The undermining of national economies destroyed the international balance of power. Statesmen sought in vain to restore it. The League of Nations (which, notwithstanding adverse criticisms, had succeeded in settling numerous minor international disputes and in arranging various international contracts) proved unfit for such a major task. Again, the world had to rely on traditional diplomacy. Firstly, diplomats turned their attention to the reparations problem. As early as 1929, a new plan (named after the American industrialist Young) had been drafted, which had substantially reduced the balance to be paid by the Germans. In 1932, the remaining reparations debts were practically cancelled. Next, the former Allies held a disarmament conference in futile attempts to economize by reducing military expenditures. Furthermore, to improve the international economic situation Germany and Austria proposed a "Customs Union," whereby a free central-European trading area could have been created, but their plan, which had political implications, was vetoed by the victorious nations. Finally, in 1933, a general World Economic Conference was held in London to discuss concerted remedial action. By that time, however, the various nations had initiated individual programs to deal with the crisis, and none of them was ready to accept international measures which might impede domestic relief programs. The United States, in particular, was reluctant to agree to proposed international economic ties, and the conference failed. In 1934, a disarmament conference revealed further disintegration of the international community, owing to the triumph of the fascistic form of government in the key country, Germany.

FASCISM

As a political ideology, fascism had had a comparatively long history before the 1930's. Its roots lay in the economic developments and nationalistic trends of the late nineteenth and early twentieth centuries. Like socialism, fascism embraced a variety of ideas, objectives, and programs, differing in radicalism. In some of its aspects fascism was heralded by writers hostile to the major political developments of the liberal age; among them were sociologists, such as the Italian Pareto, who felt that contemporary social thought was based mainly on the rational views derived from the Age of Enlightenment and that it neglected the irrational element in human behavior. With the onset of a depression, which many people attributed to the inefficiency of the democratic and capitalistic systems, fascism gained millions of proselytes. For, fascism appeared to offer an alternative to those who rejected democracy but who, owing to their nationalistic attitudes, could not accept the Bolshevik doctrines. The political and economic implications of fascism made it a decisive influence in countries such as Germany and Italy which, as a consequence of World War I, had to endure, in addition to economic difficulties, the frustration of their nation ambitions.

Characteristics of Fascism. Fascism was consistent with the trend of opposition to nineteenth-century liberalism, but its opposition was far more radical than that of any other political movement except communism. The type of fascism which developed in the 1920's and 1930's relegated the individual to a minor role in society. It subordinated him entirely to the state, which was extolled as an all-embracing source of authority. The state was to become the ultimate judge of right and wrong, "right" being whatever served its interests. In fascist countries, no party but that of the state was to be allowed; parliamentary activity was to be reduced to a mere formality. Instead of freely elected governments, fascism would provide a single leader to whom primarily all allegiance was owed and who would have such authority as despots had exercised in earlier times. It would not countenance other loyalties The fascists claimed the right to regulate or direct economic activities; they sought to free their country economically as well as politically from dependence upon other countries. They undertook to restrict civil liberties and to censor the radio, books, the cinema, and newspapers—suppressing any opinions that might encourage opposition to the leader of the nation. It was their aim to control the work of scholar and artist, whose endeavors were to be judged on the basis of utility to the nation. In most cases, fascism conflicted with religion and promoted atheism: inasmuch as it wanted to avoid any double allegiance, it sought to reduce church influence. Its moral creed was generally opposed to Christian beliefs and to many concepts of ethics evolved in the West during two thousand years of its historical development. It sought to gain support from the masses—support which it needed in view of its illegitimate origin—by emphasizing the socialistic aspects of its creed. Extolling the role of laborer and peasant, the fascists promised to introduce social improvements, provide work through public projects, and raise wages. But they would not permit independent labor organizations, and they would safeguard private property rights and protect the business "leader." They considered it the task of the government to form public opinion by propaganda and would not hesitate, for this purpose, to twist facts, present half-truths, and blame the ills of preceding eras on minority groups—communists, Jews, and others. Eventually, having roused chauvinistic ambitions, they would embark upon an expansionist foreign policy. In general, fascists were "men of action, not doctrinaires."

Spread of Fascism (1922-1940). The first country to adopt fascism, indeed the country which gave it the name, was Italy. The fascist leader, Mussolini, established his regime in 1922. In 1923, Turkey under Mustapha Kemal, later called Atatürk, instituted a government exhibiting fascist traits. Next came Poland, in 1926, under Pilsudski; his regime (strengthened along fascist lines in 1935) was marked by more nationalistic than socialistic characteristics. In 1928, Salazar seized the government in Portugal; he established a dictatorship there in 1933. During the period 1929 to 1935, the Baltic states—Latvia, Estonia, and Lithuania—adopted some features of the fascistic state. In 1929, King Alexander arbitrarily converted the parliamentary government of Yugoslavia into a personal dictatorship. Hungary began to introduce a fascist system under Gömbös in 1932 and 1933. Hitler established his regime in Germany in 1933. In Greece, Metaxas abolished democratic institutions in 1936, and three years later Franco triumphed in Spain. These dictators permitted no opposition; their orders had to be obeyed, and their policy of aggressive nationalism prevailed. During World War II, fascist governments (usually with the help of native groups) were imposed upon several additional countries.

Fascism in Action. The regime established in Italy served as a model for other fascist states until, in the late 1930's, Hitlerian Germany was accepted as a pattern.

ITALY. In Italy, fascism began in 1919 with the formation of a political party by Mussolini who, early in his career, had been a newspaperman and socialist. He opposed the liberal trend but promised his followers social improvements along noncommunistic lines; he assured them that he would put an end to social strife, establish order, and re-establish the prestige of Italy which, he insisted, had fared badly at the hands of the Allies at Versailles. He gained support from workers, from industrialists afraid of communism, from ex-soldiers disappointed with postwar conditions, and from small-scale businessmen. Leading a number of armed bands (the so-called "Black Shirts") he marched upon the government in Rome in 1922, whereupon King Victor Emmanuel III, rather than risk civil war, assigned to him the task of forming a new government. Having gained control, Mussolini abolished all parties except his own, assembled a new parliament consisting of representatives of the various economic groups (instead of representatives of political parties) and thus introduced what came to be known as a "corporate state." Direction of policy was vested in the hands of the leader (the "Duce"); all forms of social strife, especially strikes, were outlawed; the opposition was brutally suppressed, some of its leaders being murdered; and employers and workers were called upon to work for a new order through "patriotic co-operation." The army was reorganized, programs for the drainage of swamps and for the reforestation of the denuded mountain areas were started, and improvements were made in public services. In 1929 Mussolini signed a concordat with the papacy, which provided for recognition of a tiny sovereign state (Vatican City), compensation for the territorial losses of the

Church, and designation of Catholicism as the official religion of Italy. On the whole, the population felt invigorated and hopeful; it tolerated the injustices committed by the regime and applauded Mussolini's plans for national aggrandizement.

GERMANY. The pattern set by fascism in Italy was perfected in Germany. The movement there was known as "National Socialism," indicating its twofold objective. A political party and armed bands of "Brown Shirts" were organized by Hitler. After a first vain attempt at a *Putsch* in 1923, he had applied his oratorical skill and personal magnetism to gain a following. By 1932 the "Nazi" party had become the largest in the country, and its armed organizations were a threat to internal peace. In 1933, after constitutional repressive measures against the Nazis had proved to be useless, Hitler was entrusted with the formation of a government. He thus achieved power "legally." With approval and assistance by some industrialists and the demoralized segments of the middle class and the proletariat (who had suffered the consequences of Germany's defeat in 1918 and had been impoverished by inflation and depression) he substituted an authoritarian system for the national constitution. He suppressed first the Communist, then all other parties, sent his political enemies into concentration camps or had them murdered, and established himself as dictator and "Führer." He turned the resentment of the masses against the Jews whom he pictured as the instigators of existing political and economic evils, and preached a rabid "race" doctrine which was designed to appeal to the frustrated. All activities in art, science, and business had to be co-ordinated with party doctrines, and the "leadership principle" was extended to all areas of national life. Hitler attacked the unemployment problem, first by initiating public-works projects and a compulsory national-labor service, then by building an armament industry, and, finally, by reintroducing compulsory military service. Simultaneously, he inaugurated measures to assist farmers, relieving them of their mortgage burdens and protecting inherited farms against continued indebtedness. These measures helped to revive economic life. Private enterprise benefited and re-employed millions. Within a few years unemployment had disappeared and a shortage of labor had developed which forced wages to rise. A Four-Year Plan was initiated which mobilized all the economic forces in the country. Its financing was helped by the confiscation of property owned by Jews (and by many non-Jews) who were ex-

pelled from public life and business. Steps were taken to make
Germany less dependent upon foreign imports and to develop new
internal resources instead; for example, many new oil wells were
dug, and artificial rubber production was undertaken on a large
scale. The resulting national revival impressed both Germans and
foreigners to such an extent that the injustices of the system and its
neglect of the concepts embodied in Western laws and ethics were
too readily overlooked. Whatever feeble opposition could be offered
—by individuals, by conservative groups, by old staff officials of the
bureaucracy, by army officers or clergymen—was defeated by de-
famatory propaganda and by violence.

SPAIN. Spain became the third great center of fascism. Unlike
Germany and Italy, she refrained, primarily because of her internal
weakness, from imperialistic enterprises; and again, unlike the two
others, she did not combat traditional religious forces, but augmented her strength by allying herself with the Catholic Church.
As early as 1923, a dictatorship had been established in Spain under
Primo de Rivera. He had not succeeded, however, in composing
factional strife in the country. Old ills persisted: the domineering
influence of a small landowning class faced by an impoverished
peasantry; the division of interests between the industrialized north
and the agricultural south; the aggressiveness both of clerics and
of large atheistic groups; the agitation of monarchists opposed to
fervent republicans; and the weakness of a moderating and mediat-
ing middle class. Having failed to solve the problems, Rivera
resigned in 1930. In the following year the king, potentially an
effective unifying influence for the country, was forced into exile.
An election put into office a republican government (at first moderately liberal, later strongly socialistic) which aroused the bitter
resistance of the conservatives by passing extensive anticlerical and
anticapitalistic legislation. As a result, civil war broke out in 1936.
In brutality, it was perhaps unequaled by any other modern war.
Foreign interventionists soon participated—communists, fascists,
and volunteers from democratic countries. For years, the triangular
struggle raged between these three groups, until in 1939 Franco,
leader of the Falange—as the Spanish Fascists came to be known—
emerged victorious. He achieved internal peace by rewarding his
adherents and by crushing all opponents, but like Pilsudski—and
unlike Hitler and Mussolini—he introduced few, if any, social

reforms. His personal dictatorship solved hardly any of Spain's domestic problems.

Democracies Versus Fascism. Fascist doctrines and their apparent successes (particularly in the economic sphere, as in dealing with unemployment) won many adherents in the traditionally democratic countries. But since these countries had not experienced the frustration of national ambitions, most people remained loyal to their well-established governments and avoided fascist experiments—despite economic difficulties.

EUROPE. France, most of all, was in great danger. Fascists gained much ground there and in 1937 upset a "popular front" government which had been trying to save the country both from the rightist and from equally strong leftist extremists; however, the traditional forces succeeded in meeting the threat and preserving democratic institutions. In Holland, Norway, and other nations, fascist parties also gained influence; yet, there, too, established institutions prevailed. The small fascist party in England had even fewer opportunities to make headway, for the government gradually introduced measures improving social conditions, modernized its foreign-trade policy, and adjusted its methods of administration to contemporary needs; and the English electorate proved its traditional aversion to radical changes. A crisis, such as the one arising from the abdication of King Edward VIII, could be settled without disturbing the political structure. In the member nations of the Commonwealth (especially in Australia and New Zealand) the governments, opposed to all radicalism and prepared to preserve capitalism, prevented the triumph of fascism by far-reaching social legislation in the interests of the workers.

THE UNITED STATES. The influence of fascist groups in the United States was kept at a negligible level as social and economic changes similar to those in Europe were inaugurated during the "New Deal" administrations of Franklin D. Roosevelt. Social-security laws were passed (such as those providing for old-age and unemployment insurance and minimum wages in industry); the gold standard was abandoned; debtors were granted a moratorium; huge government projects (e.g., the electrification of the Tennessee Valley) were undertaken; and some national planning was also attempted. Private enterprise was brought under partial regulation by government and thus a system of subsidies was used in order to influence the farmer's decisions regarding the types of crops and the acreage to be planted. To be sure, more radical attempts at regimentation, such as Roosevelt's proposal for "packing" (adding new judges to) the United States Supreme Court, were defeated; but even in the United States, emphasis was placed upon "leadership," and a bureaucracy dependent upon a strong central government grew rapidly. Eventually public confidence was restored, and, although a great deal of unemployment persisted, the American economy recuperated and standards of living improved.

Internal recovery was reflected in United States foreign policies. Despite the continued opposition of isolationists, interest and participation in European affairs increased. The Bolshevik government in Russia was formally recognized, and closer cooperation with nonfascist nations was promoted. A conciliatory attitude toward Latin-American nations was adopted, as a "Good-Neighbor Policy" was proclaimed, long-standing quarrels were settled, and, through the Pan-American Union, political and economic collaboration was advanced. Thus, owing to timely action, fascism was given no chance to develop in the United States.

Communism versus Fascism. While fascism was making headway in central Europe and while a modified liberal-democratic system was being introduced in the western areas of the Continent, communism increased its hold in Russia and made the appearance of any other ideology impossible.

RUSSIAN PLANNING. By 1930, the first Five-Year Plan, which was to lay the economic foundation for the new society, was well on its way toward successful accomplishment. Production in heavy industries began to surpass the levels of tsarist Russia; the transportation system was repaired, and grew rapidly, with such vast undertakings as the railway connection between Turkestan and Siberia (Turksib Railroad) and the improvement of inland waterways. Domestic commerce and foreign trade could again be expanded; the prices of consumer goods were reduced. Stability returned to the lives of the ordinary workers, and collective farming became the dominant system in agriculture. The threat of external interference receded with the strengthening of the armed forces. In 1932 a second Five-Year Plan provided for a continuation of the same domestic policy. Collectivization was pushed until most private farms had disappeared, and heavy industries were given preference over those producing consumer goods.

RUSSIAN GOVERNMENT. In 1936, a new constitution was adopted for the Soviet Union. By then the nation consisted of thirteen republics, each enjoying local autonomy but subject to central political direction and central economic planning. The executive power remained in the hands of the Politbureau, with Stalin at its head. Civil rights were formally extended to all Russians; thus, after twenty years of discrimination, constitutional inequities directed against various "bourgeois" groups of the population were abolished. As before, only one party—the Communist—was allowed to function. However, communist practice differed from theory. The Party and its functionaries exercised strict supervision over all economic and social enterprises. Promised civil rights were disregarded; dissenting voices were silenced; hundreds of thousands, possibly millions, of citizens were banished to Siberia. Workers and peasants, notwithstanding the existence of labor unions and collective-farm councils, had little chance to make their voices heard, and freedom of movement was sharply restricted. Scholars, physicians, authors, teachers, and artists who tried to act independently found their works censored and their lives imperiled. Labor camps were filled with political prisoners. One wave of purges followed another. The struggle for supreme power which had begun with Stalin and Trotsky soon engulfed all supporters of Trotsky, who had been banished in 1929. (He was assassinated in Mexico in 1940.) His adherents were brought to trial for treason and exiled or executed. By 1938, Stalin, defending himself against "right" and "left" opposition, had disposed of most of the leading Bolshevists. The terror also embraced the supreme command of the army, whose chief-of-staff and other high-ranking officers were executed. Purges of political opponents became an integral part of the Bolshevik system.

RUSSIAN SOCIETY. Despite sacrifices, the ideal communistic society promised by the regime was slow in developing. As those who had constituted the upper classes in pre-Revolutionary times and those who had risen with the Revolution were overthrown, a constant tendency toward new class formations and elites became apparent. The Party hierarchy and officials in the state bureaucracy enjoyed numerous privileges and maintained a living standard far higher than that of the masses. In addition, intellectuals loyal to the Stalin system and an elite group of workers rose above the level of the masses. In order to speed up production, the government offered special rewards and prizes to workers who surpassed in productivity the norms demanded of them. In industry such workers were known as "Stakhanovites" in honor of Stakhanov, a miner who had shown extraordinary inventiveness and efficiency in raising production. Nevertheless, although industrial output increased rapidly, the speed-up system eventually aroused dissatisfaction among ordinary workers. Nor were the recipients of the high wages greatly served, for investment possibilities were lacking and costs of luxuries were fixed so as to channel the extra income quickly back into the state treasury.

WORLD WAR II

With three vigorous ideologies—fascism, remodeled democracy, and Bolshevism—competing during the 1930's, suspicion and hatred spread throughout the world. Sharpened by continued economic difficulties, they led to a rapid worsening of international relations. This happened despite the fact that the pressures of the Versailles settlement had been reduced and treaties based on equality had been made. Eventually, Germany rearmed and laid claim to adjoining territories. Germany's actions met with appeasement until her demands, increasing with every success, imperiled the western European powers and they decided to take up arms again. In 1939, World War II broke out.

International Tension. The first significant step on the road to war came with the withdrawal, in 1933, of Hitler's Germany from the League of Nations. In itself this action had no great effect upon the international scene, inasmuch as the League had only recently proved anew its political impotence by its inability to cope with a Japanese invasion of Chinese territory and the subsequent establishment of Manchuria as a separate state subject to Japanese influence. But Hitler's exit was a psychological shock, for it highlighted the League's weakness and demonstrated the rebirth of extreme nationalism. His action was answered by the initiation of a policy of so-called "collective security." Co-operation between the Allies of 1914 was resumed. In 1935, France concluded a special defensive agreement with Russia; the Soviet Union was drawn into the League of Nations; pacts were made between Russia, France, and some of the smaller East European countries, such as Czechoslovakia and Rumania; and England assumed a friendlier attitude toward Russia. These moves were used by Germany to justify military preparations of her own. Denouncing prohibitory stipulations of the Versailles Treaty, Hitler, in 1935, ordered the rearmament of Germany and the reintroduction of compulsory military service—pacifying England by a naval agreement which guaranteed British superiority on the seas. He then proceeded to send troops into the demilitarized Rhineland—without encountering serious opposition from the Allies, who realized that Germany would eventually have to be granted her full sovereign rights and who were divided in their political aims and in their assessment of the role of Hitler as a counterweight to Bolshevik power. Moreover, the Allies had become involved in another difficulty. In 1935 fascist Italy had invaded Ethiopia and the League of Nations had decreed economic sanctions against her. Since they did not wish to offend the Italian dictator, whom they regarded as a potential opponent of Hitler's expansionist schemes, neither England nor France applied the sanctions vigorously. In this way they failed to stop Mussolini and succeeded only in alienating him. He turned to Hitler, with whom in 1936 he concluded an alliance, the "Rome-Berlin Axis." This was supplemented by an "Anti-Comintern Pact" between Germany and Japan; and thus, the West was once again split into two camps. The United States remained outside both camps, in a position to swing the balance of power in either direction.

Appeasement (1938). In this triangular situation, the democratic countries of the West were at a disadvantage. Relying on slow parliamentary procedures, they were faced with ruthless and determined men, whose arbitrary will could at any moment be transformed into deeds. So long as they were militarily weak, Western diplomats were compelled to appease their fascist opponents and, while trying to come to terms with them, seek support from enemies of fascism outside the democratic camp. But they failed to pursue whole-heartedly the negotiations which they had initiated with the only nation able to give them powerful support—the Soviet Union. Consequently, Hitler was free to resume his expansionist schemes. Early in 1938 he united Austria and Germany—a union Austrians and Germans had long desired. Austria had voted for Anschluss soon after the end of World War I, but had been forbidden to take such action. An objective hitherto denied to Germany's democratic governments was now granted to the Nazis. Encouraged by this achievement Hitler next demanded the incorporation of the Sudetenland, a part of Czechoslovakia settled by Germans. Again, a pretext for the Nazi claim was offered—the idea that the Germans in that area had a right of self-determination. Unprepared for war, the Western powers agreed to a series of conferences and at Munich, in 1938, handed the Sudetenland over to Hitler. The Soviet Union, though affected by whatever position France would take, had not even been invited, and the French alliance system in the East therewith collapsed.

Outbreak of War (1939). Peace was not promoted by appeasement, for, contrary to his assertions, Hitler annexed the rest of Czechoslovakia in the following year. This time, not even the incorporation of German populations desirous of joining the Reich could be used as an argument, inasmuch as it was an alien Czech population, proud of its independence and achievements, that was forced under Nazi domination. The Western powers refused to give their sanction to this annexation and speeded up military preparations. They also revived the dragging political negotiations with Soviet Russia. It was too late. In April, 1939, Italy invaded and subjugated Albania. Germany forced Lithuania to surrender Memel, and reclaimed Danzig, two areas which had been separated from Germany by the Treaty of Versailles. Next, Poland was asked to return other former German possessions, but, with the backing of the Western countries, refused to do so. This time the Western powers were unwilling to make any compromise. Not only had they become convinced of the untrustworthiness of Hitler but in the meantime they had also witnessed the growing radicalism of nazism and its social implications. The extreme brutality of the Nazis was fully exposed by their treatment of opponents (especially the Jews, who were plundered, tortured, forced into exile, imprisoned in labor camps, or murdered). Appeasement ceased; no further concessions were made to Hitler—not even when suddenly, in August, the conclusion of a trade and nonaggression pact between Germany and the Soviet Union was announced and the pro-Western diplomat Litvinov was replaced by the anti-Western Molotov as Soviet foreign minister. Thus ended all hopes for "collective security." In September, German armies marched into Poland. World War II began.

Early Campaigns (1939–1941). Polish resistance collapsed within a few weeks. Just before the end came, Russian armies from the east marched into the country, and Poland underwent her fourth partition. This development was followed by a half-year lull (the so-called "Phony War") on the Western front; Russia, however, continued her military action, first by attacking Finland, and then by incorporating and sovietizing the Baltic states. The Finns put up a surprisingly long and successful resistance, but eventually had to submit and cede some of their eastern territories. The Finnish-Russian war had scarcely ended when hostilities were resumed in the West. In April, German forces attacked neutral Norway, Denmark, Holland, and Belgium. Aided by native fascists, the so-called "quislings" (named after the chief fascist in Norway), they quickly forced these countries to surrender. They then turned on France, whose government was weakened by indecision, confusion, and corruption, and whose general staff was overconfident about France's main defense system along the western border, the so-called "Maginot Line." This Maginot defense system was built on the basis of experiences in World War I, but proved inadequate to cope with new techniques of mobile warfare and aerial support. It was bypassed in the north and collapsed within a few days. The Nazis overran the entire northern coastal area of France as well as Paris; the British auxiliary corps narrowly escaped to England; and on June 22, 1940, France capitulated. France's catastrophe was the signal for Mussolini to enter the war; he promptly seized areas in southern France which once had been under Italian rule. A pro-German French government led by Marshal Pétain was soon organized at Vichy. Despite the collapse of France, England, however, did not yield. Under the leadership of a new prime minister, Winston Churchill, the British took effective defense measures and continued the desperate struggle. Neither prolonged Nazi air attacks nor intensive submarine warfare sufficed to prepare the ground for an invasion. Consequently, the Germans eventually shifted their attention southeastward, in the direction of Egypt and the Suez Canal and, joined by the Italians, opened a new front in Africa. Still another area was engulfed by war when in October, 1940, Mussolini failed in an attack upon Greece, and the Germans rushed to his aid. By the end of May, 1941, all the Balkan countries either had surrendered or, after installing fascist governments, had concluded alliances with the Axis powers.

Global War (1941-1943). The remaining months of 1941 proved to be a turning point in the war. The first decisive event occurred in June, when Hitler suddenly turned upon his Russian ally and invaded the Soviet Union. This move radically changed the balance of power, for what the negotiations of England and her allies had failed to achieve, Hitler's megalomania brought about: a common front for the Bolshevik and democratic nations and a two-front war for Germany. At first, the Germans showed great superiority over the Soviet forces. Within a few months, they reached the outskirts of Leningrad, Moscow, and Sevastopol, and they conquered the industrially valuable Don basin and the rich agricultural lands of the Ukraine. But they failed to capture Moscow; instead, heavy losses and severe weather forced them to retreat. Just then, the second decisive event took place. On December 7, 1941, Japan made a surprise attack against the American naval base at Pearl Harbor in the Hawaiian Islands, and Hitler promptly declared war on the United States. These developments brought the enormous resources of the United States fully into the war. From the beginning the American people had been on the side of England. Disregarding neutrality, they had supported her, and supplies and arms had been shipped to her under a "Lend-Lease" plan. Moreover, the United States had introduced peacetime conscription which paved the way for eventual military intervention. Hatreds against Germany were more and more inflamed as the Nazis disregarded all international treaties and moral concepts, attacked neutrals, impressed labor from conquered countries into their war industries, looted art depositories, established everywhere their concentration camps for political opponents, and began on the Continent a fearful extermination campaign against Jews. America now became an active belligerent on the Anglo-Russian side. Notwithstanding numerous further victories of the Axis powers, the fate of these aggressors was sealed from then on. Japan conquered much of the Chinese coast, overwhelmed French Indochina and "impregnable" British Singapore, invaded Burma and Dutch Indonesia, and drove the Americans out of the Philippines; and Germany penetrated still deeper into Russia, reached the Caucasus and Volga, took an enormous toll of Allied shipping with her submarines, and, together with Italy, gained North Africa up to the Egyptian border. But the objective—to win the war—was not achieved.

Defeat of Italy, Germany, and Japan (1943–1945). Early in 1943, Germany's military reversals began. At Stalingrad, the Nazis suffered a terrible defeat; an entire army was captured by the

Russians. In Africa, the Germans and Italians had to retreat before invading Allied armies, and by May, 1943, all Axis forces had been either driven out of Africa or captured. The submarine menace had been overcome through speedy production of shipping in America and the invention of new defensive devices. Continuous, heavy bombardment of German cities brought ruin to that country, which had previously been almost untouched by direct action. Japan's drive was halted. In July, the Allies invaded Italy; Mussolini's government fell, and thus the first fascist regime disappeared. In June, 1944, a long-planned Allied invasion of the Continent began as American and Allied troops landed in Normandy and quickly drove the German forces back. By September they had reached the frontier and had started their invasion of the German homeland. Rather than submit to the Allied demand for "unconditional surrender," the Germans obeyed the order of the Nazi leaders to fight to the bitter end. The most desperate resistance was put up against the Russians who, having liberated their own and neighboring countries from the Nazis, had crossed the German borders from the east. Only when American and Russian troops had joined in the center of Germany and when Berlin was in flames did Hitler take his own life, and only then did the country capitulate. Promptly, the Allies turned their full force against Japan. The Japanese had already lost most of their conquests and had been forced into a steady retreat on land and sea. Their fate was sealed when, in August, 1945, the Americans dropped an atomic bomb (the first one ever used in war) on Hiroshima, destroying the town, and shortly thereafter launched another such attack on Nagasaki. Simultaneously, the Russians entered the war against Japan; and the country was forced to surrender.

End of World War II. No peace treaty was concluded at the end of the war because the disagreements among the Allies multiplied during the last year of hostilities. In fact, they agreed unanimously on only one point—to destroy the power of Germany and Japan; and this task was undertaken.

OCCUPATION AND CONFERENCES. Germany and Japan were occupied and governed by the victors. In Japan, this procedure was comparatively easy, for, though deprived of all overseas possessions, she retained her home territory intact, and the United States took full charge of the administration. The situation was different in Germany, which was divided into four zones of occupation. Millions of inhabitants were driven out of their homes, and countless people perished. Workers were abducted, factories were dismantled, and production was brought to an almost complete standstill so that a terrible famine resulted; and moral laws were ignored on all sides. No constructive plans for Germany's future existed since the victors (Russia, England, and the United States) had failed to provide for them. In 1943, in a conference at Teheran, they had been concerned only with the conduct of the war. Early in 1945, when victory was in sight, they had planned in a second conference, held at Yalta, the division and occupation of Germany, and a drastic reduction in its economic, industrial, and military power. During the summer of 1945 (after Germany's capitulation), when a third conference was held at Potsdam, the task of determining a common future peace policy should have been undertaken. But the Potsdam meeting disclosed the sharp fundamental disagreements between the democratic West and the communist East. Russia had quickly established a communist regime in eastern Germany, such as had already been established in Poland, Hungary, Rumania—in fact, wherever Soviet Russia maintained occupation troops. On the other hand, the Western Allies sought liberal-democratic forms of government, such as had been re-established in Italy and France.

THE UNITED NATIONS. Nor did the founding of a new world organization, the United Nations, further co-operation. The United Nations was created in order to provide an international forum comparable to the defunct League of Nations and to organize humanitarian agencies concerned with economics, agriculture, health, and education. But, like the League, it received no military or police force. Although control over the organization was vested in a Council and a General Assembly, the three principal victors in the war (England, Russia, and the United States), as well as France and China, each were given a veto power over decisions in the Council.

New Beginnings. The two world wars differed fundamentally in respect to their causes, conduct, and consequences. In 1914, nations had been trapped in the nets of their diplomacy and had "backed into" the war. But World War II had been unilaterally provoked by the fascist countries. Ideological differences had been slight before World War I; they played a major role in the era of World War II. Warfare was much more savage during the later conflict than the earlier one, for women and children of victors and vanquished alike were engulfed by the holocaust. Civilians and soldiers were equally involved. Whole population groups were murdered. After the war many statesmen, industrialists, military leaders, and other citizens in the defeated countries (including those who were helpless tools as well as those who had wittingly perpetrated atrocities) were tried and punished as criminals. Nevertheless, World War II did not constitute so sharp a break in the course of history. The war of 1914 shattered the social and cultural patterns of the nineteenth century, a society based upon the ideas of enlightenment and dedicated to the aims of national freedom and progress under a capitalistic system dominated by the bourgeoisie. World War II brought no such social change. As part of the adjustment to the new world emerging, it left fewer gulfs and (except among some of the smaller countries) fewer permanent resentments. Moreover, it left Europe, if not all of Western civilization, weaker and with a deeper feeling of interdependence than had existed during the period after the Treaty of Versailles.

CHAPTER XXIII

THE POSTWAR ERA (1947 TO PRESENT)

IN WESTERN CIVILIZATION three trends, which had developed to some extent after World War I, rapidly gained headway after World War II. These trends were: the use of mechanization in production and in everyday living; the increasing equalization of social classes; and the decline of Europe's power and prestige in international affairs. Human society—even though still divided into classes, into nations, and into "two worlds" with opposing ideologies —was moving in the direction of one interrelated, interdependent world.

INTELLECTUAL AND CULTURAL DEVELOPMENTS

Too short a time has elapsed since World War II to justify broad generalizations about postwar intellectual trends. Yet, a few facts are apparent. Men have devoted themselves increasingly to science and technology and have achieved remarkable progress in these fields. There has been a growing realization that—contrary to the hopes of the ages of Enlightenment and Liberalism—"progress," though undeniable in material achievements, does not necessarily encompass the moral side of man. Preoccupation with personal "security" has acted as a check on daring original thinking and has led to a measure of conservatism and desire for conformity. This has been true for the communistic as well as the democratic parts of the world, both of which have sought to maintain the *status quo* regardless of its manifold shortcomings.

Science. Wars have always stimulated science and technology.

Danger has always forced men to invent tools and processes which could save their lives and preserve their freedom; and the insight into the mechanics of nature gained during wars has furthered the progress of science in times of peace. World War II was no exception. Radar, guided missiles, and atomic fission were developed for military purposes in the period 1939 to 1945. They afterwards became important for peacetime use. Aviation in particular was greatly advanced during the war. Whereas in 1927 Lindbergh had made a lonely first transatlantic flight to Paris, twenty-five years later (when the war was over) tens of millions of passengers were crossing continents and oceans by airplane each year. Countries of vast expanse and poor transportation systems, like Brazil, could now plan to skip the "railroad age" and immediately enter the "air age." In chemistry and nuclear physics, discoveries, made under pressure of war by both victors and vanquished, were exploited to serve new peaceful purposes. With the help of newly discovered vaccines and drugs, the incidence of many diseases—pneumonia, tuberculosis, infantile paralysis—could be diminished. Increasingly, nations put their faith in scientists; the Soviet Union trained scientists by the hundred thousand, and the United States showed an unaccustomed appreciation of "pure" science and mathematics (fields in which she had long relied upon European work). Wartime experiences had an effect on production methods. Automation —i.e., mechanization of parts of the industrial process which so far had required supervision by human minds—was introduced in large enterprises. It involved the use of machines to replace technical, clerical, and even scientific personnel.

Religion and Philosophy. After World War II the memory of the horrors and uncertainties of war had the apparent effect of impelling man to intensify his search for security and comfort. Many who were fearful of the dangers inherent in man's growing mastery of natural forces (as evinced by the development of atomic weapons) and who were disturbed by the use of subtle weapons which physiological and psychological studies made available for purposes of propaganda, indoctrination, and mental persuasion (drugging and "brainwashing"), turned anew to the consolations of religion. The consequent religious renaissance brought a re-emphasis upon dogma, as evinced by the spread of Neo-Orthodox beliefs; it led to the acceptance of long submerged ecumenical ideas promoting co-operation among the various faiths; and it caused a

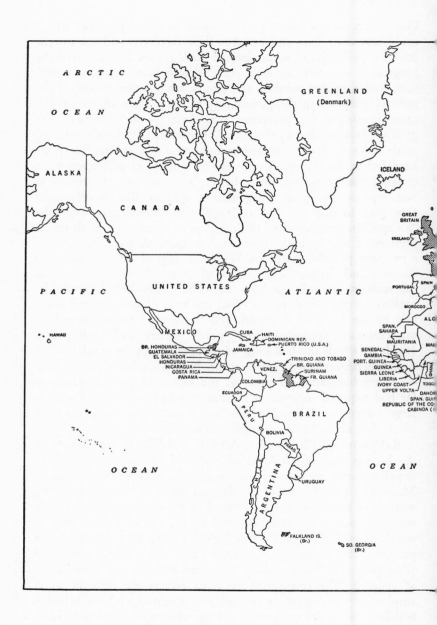

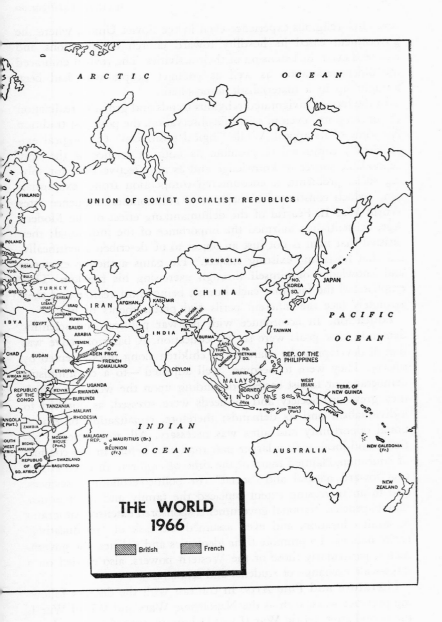

ARCTIC OCEAN

OCEAN

FINLAND

UNION OF SOVIET SOCIALIST REPUBLICS

POLAND
CZECH
HUNG.
ROM.
YUG.
BULG.
ALB.
GREECE
TURKEY
SYRIA
LEBAN.
ISRAEL
IRAQ
JORDAN
KUWAIT
IRAN
AFGHAN.
KASHMIR
NEPAL
SIKKIM
BHUTAN
IBYA
EGYPT
SAUDI
ARABIA
YEMEN
PAKISTAN
PAK.
INDIA
BURMA
CHAD
SUDAN
ADEN PROT.
OMAN
FRENCH
SOMALILAND
SOMALI REP.
CENT.
AFRICAN REP.
ETHIOPIA
CEYLON
REPUBLIC
OF THE
CONGO
UGANDA
KENYA
RWANDA
BURUNDI
TANZANIA
MALAWI
RHODESIA
ANGOLA
(Port.)
ZAMBIA
MALAGASY
REP.
MAURITIUS (Br.)
RÉUNION
(Fr.)
OUTH
WEST
AFRICA
BECHU-
ANALAND
MOZAM-
BIQUE
(Port.)
REPUBLIC
OF
SO. AFRICA
SWAZILAND
BASUTOLAND

MONGOLIA

CHINA

NO.
KOREA
SO.

JAPAN

LAOS
THAI-
LAND
NO.
VIETNAM
CAMBODIA SO.

TAIWAN

PACIFIC

OCEAN

REP. OF THE
PHILIPPINES

MALAYSIA
SUMATRA
BORNEO
I N D O N E S I A
JAVA
BRUNEI
TIMOR
(Port.)

WEST
IRIAN

TERR. OF
NEW GUINEA

PAPUA

INDIAN

OCEAN

AUSTRALIA

NEW CALEDONIA
(Fr.)

NEW
ZEALAND

THE WORLD
1966

British   French

revival of religious experience even in the Soviet Union, where the government eased its hostility toward church organizations and tolerated even the extension of their activities. The revival embraced the older generation as well as younger people who had been brought up in a materialistic atmosphere.

In the face of invigorated religious trends and growing realization of "uncertainty" even in scientific observation, the positivist tradition lost some of its appeal. While "logical positivism" (or "logical empiricism") continued to promote its faith in science as the only dependable source of knowledge and as an effective basis for solving social problems, it encountered competition from "existentialism," which constituted a major new philosophical influence after World War II. Fearful of the dehumanizing effect of the Modern Age, existentialists affirmed the importance of the individual; they insisted that man is not just an object to be described scientifically, but that he is an "existing subject." He gains authentic existence and knowledge of himself through exercising his freedom. They emphasized the fact that each human being must realize and then resolutely face the inherent perils and predicaments of life.

Education. In accordance with postwar political and scientific demands, new goals were set for education. A basic objective was that of developing the character of children along lines accepted by society. They were to become "well adjusted"—to a communistic, democratic, or fascist society, depending upon the world in which they grew up. Society and its needs were stressed, as opposed to individualism and its demands; therefore, equalization of educational opportunity and aims was necessary. All governments, national and local, took a larger part than ever before in the conduct of education, claimed more of the time of children, directed education toward natural and "social" (or politico-economic) sciences, and to an increasing extent replaced the family and other educational agencies. National governments sponsored extensive programs of adult education, and even assumed the task of "re-educating" entire nations. To promote their ideologies and policies, the governments, particularly those of the Western powers, also carried on a large-scale exchange of students and scholars.

Literature and Fine Arts. In contrast with the decades following previous wars, such as the Napoleonic Wars and World War I, the period after World War II was lacking in outstanding works of literature and the fine arts. The outbreak of World War I marked the end of one age in Western civilization. Authors in the 1920's had entered upon a new age, had utilized great new artistic and social problems as their themes. In the 1940's and the 1950's, however, authors did not find new issues of like dimension. Nor did artists face a challenge such as the preceding postwar periods had posed. Solid work was done by scholars, writers, musicians, painters, and architects; but no individual name of surpassing glory immediately appeared. In an age of material progress and socio-political preoccupations, Western man lived on his great cultural heritage, which he carefully cultivated, but without adding (through originality, beauty of form, or depth of content) much that was likely to enlarge the permanent store of his achievements.

ECONOMIC, SOCIAL, AND POLITICAL DEVELOPMENTS

The dominating issue on the international stage was the rivalry between the United States and the Soviet Union. This rivalry was reflected first in the failure to reach a German settlement, next in a struggle over communist penetration of other European nations, and eventually in the struggle over influence in the Far East, the Middle East, and Africa. It embraced political, economic, cultural, and military issues. Its intensity varied with temporary conditions, as well as with long-range developments over which the rivals themselves had no control. Thus, it depended upon factors such as the rapidly rising population figures in Europe and in overseas areas. New population pressures occurred; yet, unemployment along prewar lines did not reappear despite the fact that within a decade consumer goods were, at least in the Western countries, once more abundant. Soon production totals surpassed—even in the defeated nations—the highest prewar figures, making possible an improvement of prewar living standards. Whether for reasons of a better understanding of economic processes or of more extensive state planning, or of other—uncontrollable—factors, a prolonged period of economic growth began.

Postwar Economic Situation. It had been the plan of the victors to provide for the rebuilding of their own national economies and for the permanent economic subjugation of Germany. This plan was initiated by the dismantling of German industries, by the expropriation of German ships, freight cars, locomotives, and other rolling stock, by seizure of her patents and production secrets, and by the forced recruitment of scientists as well as laborers and prisoners into the service of the victors. Consequently, for more than a year after the cessation of hostilities, this additional source of terrible suffering affected Germany—though without benefit to the victors, most of whom had to continue enforcing sharp austerity measures. At this juncture, a drastic change occurred in the relationship between the victorious and the defeated nations.

REBUILDING OF THE WESTERN ECONOMY. By 1947 it had become clear that the intense struggle between the communist East and the democratic West required a new approach to the task of rebuilding the Western economy. The United States took the initiative. The nation had quickly "returned to normalcy" after the war. Rationing had been abolished, farm incomes had risen, a measure of controlled inflation had led to an increase in prices and wages, and a feeling of confidence and, with it, new incentives for further production and broader employment had been created. Successful reconversion of production facilities made it possible for the United States to propose (in 1947) the "Marshall Plan"—named after the then current American Secretary of State—which made financial aid available to European countries. Ideological, humanitarian, and economic purposes were simultaneously served thereby. England and France received most of the aid; but lest impoverished peoples should fall prey to communist doctrines, help was extended also to other Western nations including former enemies. This program enabled almost all the European democracies to rebuild their production apparatuses within a decade; by the middle of the 1950's their economies flourished as never before. Germany, though deprived of the industries in her eastern zones, regained her position as the leading industrial power of Europe. Italy, too, made a good start toward economic recovery and stability.

REBUILDING OF THE EASTERN ECONOMY. In the East, Russia took the lead. New Five-Year Plans were drafted and co-ordinated with the industrial plans of regions which the Soviet Union directly or indirectly controlled. Important new centers of industry were built in Siberia. Production in heavy industries increased rapidly. Within less than a decade the Soviet Union attained the rank of the second largest industrial power in the world, being surpassed only by the United States, and was enabled to export surplus goods and to make investments abroad. However, since hard and long labor was needed to create the production apparatus, little could be done to develop the industries manufacturing goods for civilian consumption. Consequently, standards of living remained at a low level. In agriculture, productivity did not increase sufficiently; new experiments with collective farms, which were combined into larger units, did not bring the expected results.

Political Situation. Political readjustment came more slowly than economic recovery. No final war settlement was achieved, no all-inclusive peace treaty negotiated.

EASTERN EUROPE. Russia enlarged her territories by incorporating parts of Finland, Poland, Germany, and Rumania. The formerly independent Baltic states were forced to remain within the jurisdiction of the USSR. Bolshevik governments were established in Poland and in occupied Balkan countries, and all were bound closely to Russia. Eastern Germany was assigned to Polish administration, and its inhabitants were being driven out while Poles were settled there. In 1945 Czechoslovakia was reconstituted under a democratic government (her borders approximately those of 1937) and the Germans living there were likewise brutally expelled; but through a *coup,* the democratic government was replaced in 1948 by a communist regime closely allied to Russia. A special role in world affairs was played by Yugoslavia under the communist Tito, who insisted on independent policies. "Titoism" revealed tensions and dissensions among the communist powers. Tito rejected the right of the Soviet Union to dictate policies to other communist nations—notwithstanding the fact that Marxism had preached the identity of the interests of the workers in all countries and that the Soviet Union had theretofore been considered the leader and spokesman of true Marxism.

CENTRAL AND WESTERN EUROPE. In the center of Europe, Germany —except for Polish-occupied territories—was divided, first, into four zones, but later, into two zones. The latter zones became separate German states, a Western and an Eastern republic, both of which within a decade achieved virtual sovereignty, though each remained politically affiliated with its original occupying powers. This enforced duality reflected the continued shrinkage of the area of Western civilization and tradition, and it symbolized the division of the world into Eastern communist and Western democratic areas. Austria was re-established as a small, and eventually independent, nation—a neutral buffer between East and West. Italy regained most of her European territories but had to accord a measure of autonomy to the German population under her rule and to Sicily. The other Western countries underwent no drastic territorial changes. *Be*lgium, the *Ne*therlands, and *Lux*embourg combined in a common customs area ("Benelux") to obtain mutually beneficial trade advantages. Western Germany, France, and Benelux, with the blessing of the United States, formed a "coal and steel community" which provided for predetermined production quotas, a common market, and the elimination of tariff barriers for these products. Plans for a broader customs union, possibly including Great Britain, were formulated. A "Council of Europe," constituting a consultative assembly of the western European nations, was established in Strasbourg, at the very border between Germany and France; a bank to ease mutual convertibility of European funds and currencies was founded; and plans were made by the member states for co-operative atomic research and exploitation of atomic energy. Even though a unified military force, as once considered, was not organized, a military alliance which joined the United States of America and England to the Continent was concluded. This alliance ("NATO") had a central headquarters and an American supreme commander. As a whole, the idea of European unity made considerable progress among the Western peoples, and cultural contacts and exchanges were augmented by political co-operation.

AMERICA. In America the political impact of World War II was felt much more than that of World War I. Isolationism did not return to the United States as after 1918. Instead, she took a leading part in almost all international decisions. Not only European countries, but also former European colonies came to be her concern. The members of the British Empire, especially Canada and Australia, oriented themselves increasingly toward America; and economically "backward" countries appealed to her and received aid designed to prevent them from turning to communist Russia. Military bases were installed in France, England, Germany, Spain, Turkey, and other European countries, in Asia, and also in the Arctic and Antarctic. New treaties were made with Latin-American nations, which were granted financial aid for economic development. Extensive programs for the exchange of teachers and students were inaugurated, and the unprecedented scale of travel of Americans abroad helped to establish numerous relationships with the Western nations.

COLONIAL AREAS. World War II speeded the decline of colonialism. After Japan's defeat, China gained control over most of her former territories, including Western-held Shanghai and Russian-dominated Manchuria. Indochina rebelled against and defeated France, who lost more than half of her former colony, and granted wide independence to the remainder. Rebellious Indonesia separated from Holland and became an independent state. The Philippines were peacefully granted independence by the United States. The Gold Coast in Africa was given statehood by England. India abolished British rule and, though staying formally within the Commonwealth, built a republic which envisaged neutrality in the East-West struggle. Iran quarreled with European powers over the possession and management of her oil industries, and forced substantial concessions upon the Western owners. Arab states likewise asserted their independence in the conduct of their foreign policies and obtained a greater share in the profits from their oil. Cypriotes rose against England, as did native tribes in Africa. Egypt forced the British to withdraw their military forces from the Suez Canal, and nationalized the Canal Company in 1956. This led to a Franco-British invasion, which, owing to American and Russian opposition, miscarried; within a few months, the invading forces had to be withdrawn and Egypt gained her objective. A particularly bloody struggle occurred in France's North African possessions. The Arabs in Tunisia and Algeria rebelled, and Tunisia gained especially far-reaching concessions. But, as Arab nationalism demanded complete separation from France, the struggle went on. It was sharpened by the fact that in 1948 a Jewish state, Israel, had been founded on Arab territory in Palestine. As early as 1916, such a state had been promised to the Jews by the English, but only after Hitler's pogroms and World War II had demonstrated the urgency of finding a refuge for the Jews, the pledge was finally honored. The establishment of Israel roused bitter resentment among all Arabs; intermittent border clashes threatened the peace of the entire West.

On the whole, the revolt of Asia and of the culturally advanced areas of Africa was the result of the successful Westernization of former colonial regions. European ideologies of democracy and communism, European sciences, medicine, and technology, European habits, dress, and living modes, and European-born nationalism had penetrated to all parts of the world. The time was approaching when the masters were no longer needed; the division of the Western world into democratic and communist segments gave the former colonies the opportunity to assert their independence.

Governmental Institutions and Ideologies. No new political ideology was developed as a result of World War II. Fascism in its extreme forms was abolished, but not entirely eradicated. Fascist regimes continued to function in countries such as Spain, and fascism was introduced in a few other countries (such as Argentina, where Perón held power until 1955). Fascist principles also found their way into some of the democratic countries: in France and even in the United States there was fear that certain fascist tendencies might gain headway.

Communism persevered in most of eastern Europe. In Russia where the enforcement of communist doctrines had to be relaxed during the war (so that it would not interfere with the war effort), the government resumed the drastic applications of its socialistic policies. Devaluation of the currency deprived people who had accumulated profits of their gains. Land which the peasants had alienated from collective farms and used for private gardens had to be returned. Writers and scientists were compelled to follow the party line strictly. But outside of the Soviet Union, communism after the end of World War I did not win the allegiance of Europeans despite the widespread impoverishment and Russia's prestige as one of the principal victors. Except for Czechoslovakia, European countries did not establish a communistic government unless they were occupied by Russian military forces. Only in Asia, notably in China, did communism spread under native leadership.

Democracy continued to be the predominant form of government in Western countries. Democratic types of government were reintroduced in West Germany and Italy. Most democratic institutions, however, were affected by socialistic ideas. In the United States, social reforms which had been assailed as "creeping socialism" in the 1930's were accepted as a matter of course in the postwar period. Labor unions grew in influence, and employers had to make ever-increasing concessions to their workers. In England, the Labor party, which obtained power immediately after the war, socialized the steel and coal industries, nationalized the railways, and introduced a most comprehensive public health program. Subsequent conservative governments could not abandon all the new programs of socialization and reform, although they did prevent

CULTURAL FLUCTUATIONS

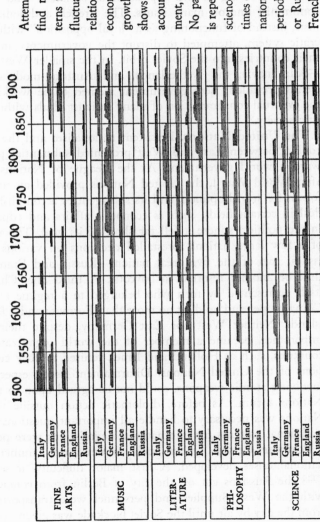

Attempts have been made to find regular evolutionary patterns for cultural growth and fluctuations, and also to trace relationships between political-economic conditions and cultural growth. However, the chart shows that creative genius, which accounts for cultural achievement, appears almost at random. No pattern set by one country is repeated by another; no art or science flourished exclusively in times of either national stress or national prosperity. (Note the periods of Italian art, German or Russian music or literature, French or English science, etc.)

the nationalization of the steel industry. In West Germany, where a strong democratic government took office, socialists constituted the largest opposition group in the diet, and workers in the great coal and steel industries gained the right to share with the owners in the functions of management. In France and Italy, democratic governments remained in control, but they faced grave difficulties owing to the opposition of socialists who followed a communist line on many issues. The French and Italian communists, instead of functioning as a "loyal opposition" within a democratic system, attempted to disrupt the governments and to swing their countries into the Soviet orbit. In the smaller Western nations —Scandinavia, the Netherlands, and Austria—moderate socialist trends prevailed; here government seemed to be working toward the eventual consummation of many socialist ideals within a capitalistic society.

The United Nations. Persistent nationalism and the ideological conflict between East and West prevented substantial progress toward a world government. As the League of Nations had done after World War I, the United Nations provided an international forum for world opinion, and its sub-agencies accomplished a great deal in certain fields, such as economic affairs and education; but in the political sphere it fell far short of its goal. The veto power of a few large nations forestalled decisions on various important issues; two of the five great nations—Russia and France—at one time or another resorted to boycotts. A third one, China, found itself represented by men who belonged to a regime ousted from China proper and holding no more than Formosa and a few smaller islands. Neither West nor East Germany, despite their economic importance, became a member of the world organization. Small countries, such as Holland and Israel, refused to obey certain decisions of the United Nations. Disarmament issues, especially those involving atomic weapons, could not be agreed upon in the United Nations forum. As before, diplomatic action outside the United Nations was necessary to handle all important questions; and thus traditional patterns for international negotiations were perpetuated.

Postwar Crises. Under such circumstances, numerous international crises developed. A first major difficulty arose when in 1948 the Russians cut off the city of Berlin from contact by land with the West. Supplies and personnel were transported to and from the city by air until the Soviet blockade was given up. In 1950 a new major crisis arose when communists in North Korea invaded South Korea, which had been under American occupation. This time, war resulted; various members of the United Nations, including the United States, participated on the South Korean side, while North Korea had the backing of Russia and active military help from Communist China. This conflict, entailing heavy casualties on both sides, led to an uneasy truce whereby the country was divided into two areas—a communist and a Western-supported state. Hardly had hostilities ended than a similar war developed in French Indochina, which led to a parallel result. The North became communist and separate; the South gained considerable independence from France but remained in the Western camp. In the meantime, crises developed in other regions—in Iran over its decision to nationalize the foreign oil companies there, in the Near East over the Suez Canal, Syria, and Israel, and in North Africa over the question of freedom from French dominion. Behind all these issues loomed the greater struggle—the "cold" war between the Western democracies, under American leadership, and the Eastern communist nations, under Russian leadership. Both sides built their military potential and acquired vast stocks of atomic bombs and weapons. And while they avoided an open break, they waged a bitter struggle over the allegiance of the "neutral" areas, such as India, Persia, and the Arab states, and of the colonies where Russia had become a factor by aiding indigenous national movements.

Coexistence and New Conflict. Stalin died in 1953. During his administration, he had concentrated upon the reconstruction of the Soviet Union so that it became the second greatest industrial power of the world, and he had with an iron hand preserved the communist institutions of the nation. He had imposed his will on scholars, scientists, artists, and the masses of the Russian people. Under his regime, Soviet scientists made enormous strides, including discoveries in the field of atomic energy and guided missiles. But owing to his arbitrariness and dictatorial ways he had alienated even close collaborators and owing to his ruthlessness and guile he had forfeited the confidence of his European allies and aroused misgivings among even the communists of other nations. His death therefore marked a turning point—the more so as dissensions among his political heirs introduced a further element of weakness into the position of the Soviet Union. Promptly, the Russian policy of the cold war was modified. Friendly words were addressed to the West, amnesties were proclaimed in Russia, travel restrictions were eased, and a meeting between Eastern and Western statesmen at Geneva in 1955 seemed to herald an era of "peaceful coexistence." However, when after a sudden denunciation of Stalin's personal dictatorship, Stalin's successors had consolidated their position, the cold war proved not to have ended but to have entered a new stage. Practical concessions were few. Although Russia agreed to a peace with Austria and established diplomatic relations with West Germany, no progress was made in regard to the crucial problem of German reunification. Soviet dissensions with Tito's Yugoslavia were temporarily composed, but Soviet control of satellites was not yielded, despite revolts in eastern Germany, Poland, and Hungary. Western nations were invited to establish closer ties with the communist world, especially in the economic field; nevertheless, opposition to their policies was invariably encouraged. Still, on the positive side, open hostilities were avoided. In 1956 the cause of world peace was imperiled by events such as Anglo-French aggression in Egypt and the brutal Russian suppression of a revolt in Hungary. Other crises occurred in the following years. In 1958, the overthrow of the monarchy in the Arab state of Iraq threatened the political and economic position of the Western powers in the Near East and the safety of their oil interests there. Uprisings in the Congo upon the withdrawal of the Belgians in 1960 and the establishment of an independent nation there; attacks by Communists on Laos in 1961; Indian aggression in Portuguese Goa; and in particular the persistent refusal of Soviet Russia to agree to supervised reduction of atomic armaments and her efforts to force the Western powers to give up their position in Berlin contributed further to the dangers of the political situation. The United Nations organization, challenged in its undertakings by its own members, lost more and more of its prestige and usefulness. Atomic testing was resumed in 1962, and new dissensions arose from continued Soviet demands with regard to Berlin, from simmering warfare in Laos and Vietnam, and ultimately from Soviet arms deliveries to Cuba. Only Western firmness in the face of this last challenge and the subsequent Soviet withdrawal, quickened perhaps by fears of a growing rift within the Soviet orbit between China and Russia, led to a certain easing of the international tension and, in the course of 1963, to a tentative agreement on suspension of testing of atomic weapons and to an increase in East-West trade.

NEW CHALLENGES

By the middle 1960's many of the hopes held by the generation that had fought the two world wars were not realized, although in some ways progress in that direction had been made. As always in the course of human affairs, the changes which had been brought about had created a new situation where old solutions no longer served; and new problems had arisen which demanded a new response and a fresh start.

A Young Generation. By the middle sixties, a generation had grown up which had lived through neither depression nor World War II. The old issue of capitalist-communist ideological rivalry had lost much of its meaning for this generation. Russian communism had become more liberal, capitalistic, and ultra-nationalistic, Western capitalism more socialistic and authoritarian. The Soviet hold on its satellite countries had weakened, while United States leadership was challenged by France under President de Gaulle, as well as subsequently by Germany, England, and, despite the economic and military aid given to them, by Asian and African nations. These political issues faced by the young generation were enhanced by economic and cultural change. By 1967 the "economic miracles" of the post-war period had apparently come to an end; rivalries over markets, problems of inflation and stability of currencies (especially the dollar and the pound), and struggles over tariffs reappeared. Subtly, power had begun to slip from the hands of leaders and their bureaucracies into those of small groups of scientifically trained experts—the technologists and economists who advised governments. A barrage of propaganda and advertising, seeking to hammer in ideas or sell goods, sought in vain to convince a new generation of the desirability of the *status quo*. Witnessing persisting social, national, and racial inequalities, continuing war preparations, and depersonalization of society through technological advances, the young generation began to challenge prevailing morality, reject hypocrisy, and attack materialism and pragmatism.

Demography. The outstanding event of the post-World War II period was the enormous population increase—not only in countries where, until then, lack of medical knowledge and care had checked population growth, but also among the highly developed countries. Once more the question which Malthus had posed at the end of the eighteenth century—whether or not population increases would outrun the available food supply—was raised. To meet the issue, a twofold attack was begun. To serve immediate needs, new scientific methods for improving agriculture were developed; food, grown in advanced countries, was distributed to hungry populations; and technical knowledge was disseminated so that these would be able to increase their own production. And to provide a long-term solution, steps were taken to reduce, through birth control, the increase in birth rates, especially high in Latin America. Even governments and churches, traditionally opposed to such measures, began to support controls, reflecting thereby a change in fundamental Western attitudes. Actually, a decrease in birth rates, at least in the advanced countries, was noted by 1966.

Science. A second occurrence of overwhelming importance was scientific progress. Physics, biology, chemistry, medicine, and astronomy, while revealing undreamed-of complexities, also brought discoveries of lasting significance. Soon, borderlines between these fields were difficult to draw. Scientific thinking also permeated social fields such as economics, psychology, history, and philosophy; a fundamental approach, often using, as did the natural sciences, mathematical studies and leading, with the help of statistical methods and computer sciences, to quantification, was applied to these subjects too. New machinery speeded up the obtaining of solutions to problems and made obsolete the work of even skilled personnel.

Economy. The effect of technological evolution was felt when dealing with daily practical problems as well as when considering long-term cultural trends. Production methods were as much affected as general social conditions.

INDUSTRY. A steady growth of industrial productivity occurred and industrialization with all its consequences spread with the help of Russia and the West—in competition with each other—to "underdeveloped" countries. In continental Europe, owing to mutual assistance and cooperation, Common Market countries at least for a decade showed high rates of economic growth and stimulated ideas of organization of a Common Market even in Latin America. The unemployment of prewar years was replaced by an employment shortage in many trades—especially in areas of technological services. Significantly, this occurred despite progress in "automation" in industry and apparently it was made possible by state economic planning which did not reject deficit financing and which did provide for constant and coordinated economic growth in the sectors of production, wages, and prices. Social security was steadily extended. While this policy heightened the dangers of monetary inflation, currency regulations diminished and tariffs were lowered. These developments were accompanied by a rapid rise of living standards, of "prosperity," in Western Europe and the United States; in the Soviet Union and Japan, considerable improvements in living conditions were also made. In the Soviet Union, challenged not only by Western skills but also by a China that succeeded in 1965 in producing atomic bombs, special attention was paid to the rapid refinement of industrial processes. Marked advances in space technology enabled the Soviet Union, in 1957, to launch the first *sputnik*, in 1961 to orbit a human being in outer space, and in 1966 to achieve a soft landing of a missile on the moon; nevertheless, other countries, notably the United States, were also making great strides in space achievements.

AGRICULTURE. Outwardly less spectacular but equally fundamental were the changes in agriculture. Agricultural organization, whether of the nature of collective farms in Communist-ruled areas or individually-owned farms in the West, moved toward consolidation of land holdings and abolishment of small farms. The peasantry as a class began to merge with the middle class. Production was influenced, if not directed, by governmental policies, price supports, setting of standards, international agreements, and mechanization in all branches. In the West, these measures brought overproduction despite a rapid population increase, and only the distribution of the products between areas with overproduction and the underdeveloped parts of the world remained a serious problem.

Education. Changed, sophisticated production methods and resulting social transformation necessitated radical adjustments in education. The demand for unskilled laborers, who had made up the proletariat, declined; their children swelled the ranks of the middle class, since office workers in vast bureaucracies and technicians, expert at operating and servicing machines, were needed. For all these positions, training was required. School systems were therefore extended; and universities, teaching specialized knowledge, had to adjust to the influx of overwhelming numbers of students. For the few creative thinkers, the establishment of additional institutes became ever more urgent. In order to meet the new tasks, society had to become aware of the issue and, through taxes, provide new funds. The results were rewarding. Medical advances lengthened the life span, and many diseases were successfully combatted. Studies of genetics and astronomy, of the weather and of human behavior patterns, were promoted, and economic and historical scholarship profited thereby. An intellectual approach, often using mathematical methods, helped to solve formerly unsolvable problems. Engineering benefitted especially. A superabundance of paperback books and pictorial magazines, films, and television spread knowledge and entertainment, and scientific journals proliferated.

Individualism. In a world so dependent on intricate scientific methods and technology and so subject to mass production and mass domination, the individual encountered ever greater difficulties in maintaining his individuality and escaping the pressures of society with its set of values and tastes. Workers in factories, on the land, in the universities, and in research were dependent on others and had to pool their knowledge or skills, and much of the individual's efforts was absorbed by collective projects. Even the creative arts—architecture, literature, music—were affected. Tastes tended toward equalization; mass communication media, newspapers, films, and television set the tone. Sociological aspects rather than problems of the individual fascinated the writer and the historian. Theater and concerts, and other artistic or scientific programs, furthered by public and private support, envisaged "educational" effects upon the masses. Urban living and urbanization, whether in cities or suburbs, or in settlements erected uniformly by builders, contributed to the equalization trends, as did government policies in capitalistic as well as communistic countries. Perhaps as a reaction, abstract tendencies in painting and music, early medieval and Byzantine studies in history, Zen and other oriental religions gained the interest of those who tried to remain outside the collective pattern. And even though, in the middle 1960's, a certain rejection of abstract art became noticeable, the protest was continued by a young generation which, in a certain parallel to the *jeunesse dorée* of 1795, insisted on defying tradition in sexual behavior, dress, and taste.

Nationalism. Not only the individual man, but also the individual nation found itself exposed to the impact of the new attitudes and economic forces. It, too, began to be submerged.

TRENDS TOWARD INTERNATIONAL ORGANIZATION. While nationalism (in the sense in which it had developed in the Western world) was still increasing in areas where earlier colonial domination had hindered its growth, it began to wane in some respects among Western nations. The emphasis on national boundaries and on closed national economic units disappeared—as evinced by coordination of foreign policies, pooling of armed forces, partial disappearance of economic borders and customs barriers, mutual currency policies, institution of common scientific projects, easing of passport regulations, and increased tourism and exchange of labor forces. The division of Germany, the disintegration of the British Empire (in 1961, a dominion, South Africa, and in 1965, a colony, Rhodesia, left the Commonwealth), and the separation of Algeria from France in 1962 did not disturb the core of these leading nations as would have happened only a few decades earlier. The European Common Market under French-German leadership was, despite attacks, a working reality. Communist Eastern Europe, through emphasis on interdependence among its members, likewise contributed its share to the progressive decline of an older type of nationalism. Even such an institution as the Catholic Church felt the impact of the more cosmopolitan trends. In an Ecumenical Council, which was convened by Pope John XXIII in 1961 and which lasted until 1965, rules were passed designed to "update" Church life, adjust to modern patterns, and ease long existing antagonisms between Catholics and other Christian churches as well as Eastern religions, Jews, and pagans.

TRENDS TOWARD REVIVAL OF NATIONALISM. As the two World Wars receded farther into history, an opposite movement reappeared. In France, where a fifth republic with vast powers for its President de Gaulle was instituted in 1958, nationalism resurged. Appealing to the old concepts of "national sovereignty," de Gaulle insisted on completely independent rights for his country and did not hesitate to weaken such cooperative institutions as the Common Market or NATO which the Western world had created in response to the bitter lesson of the World Wars. Struggling England tried to keep alive ideas of her "special" position and vacillated about entering a European community in which she could play no privileged role. Italy, ignoring her fascist past, applauded nationalistic aims, and in the Communist orbit, not only the Soviet Union and Yugoslavia pursued policies of national self-interest but, by 1966, Rumania, Bulgaria, Poland, and Hungary also began to assert their national interests and to struggle for emancipation from Russian domination. In defeated Germany, surrounded by increasingly nationalistic sentiments, national aspirations were ever more strongly reaffirmed despite resolute support of all forms of European and Atlantic cooperation. The United States was no less concerned with the national question; it played a leading role, involving "national prestige," in a bitter war in Vietnam against revolting, socialist forces supported by Communist China. By 1966, the Vietnam war constituted, indeed, the foremost international problem. Nationalism contributed also to the rift which rent the socialist worlds of Russia and China, and it threatened the peace in India, Pakistan, Indonesia, Malaysia, the Arab states, and in various parts of Africa.

Democracy. The meaning of the term "democracy" changed. Communist countries used the word in a sense entirely opposed to that in Western countries; and these, while holding on to the theory of the age of enlightenment, gave democracy in practice an entirely new content. Democratic forms taken over from Anglo-Saxon countries—with free elections and powerful popular representative assemblies, and with systems of checks and balances protecting the "rights of man," including the right of private property—were maintained in the West and the countries adhering to Western ideas. Democratic forms belittling these concepts and stressing a classless society, subordination of the individual to the common good, economic equality, and the conduct of affairs by a government and single party organization representative of the interests of all the workers in society, were continued in the East and its dependencies. But everywhere, "leadership," if not in the extreme form of Nazi patterns, was extolled. In Russia, the leadership principle predominated at least until 1964, during the years of Khrushchev's premiership which had followed a two-year struggle for power after Stalin's death. In Germany, Chancellor Konrad Adenauer, though checked by democratic procedure, gave the country vigorous and capable leadership from 1954 to 1964. From 1958 on, France was led by Charles de Gaulle. The United States, where racial unrest threatened the traditional democratic fabric, looked to steadily enhanced authority, influence, and direction by its presidents. In Cuba, a Communist-supported leader, Castro, made himself the spokesman of the democratic forces and soon expropriated foreign—principally United States—property. Leadership rather than liberal democratic patterns was accepted also by new African nations, while army dictatorships survived, or were reintroduced, in countries such as Brazil or some of the Central American nations. Threatened by totalitarian patterns, a changed democracy thus struggled to preserve for the individual those fundamental freedoms for which Western civilization had striven for centuries.

Outlook. Soon after the end of World War I, Oswald Spengler had stated in his famous work *The Decline of the West* that Western civilization had outlived its allotted time and was now facing dissolution—to be succeeded by a new, fresh civilization. Twenty years later, in his *Study of History,* Arnold Toynbee agreed with some of Spengler's views but insisted that an early end of Western civilization was not inevitable. Toynbee suggested that a religious surge revivifying the latent strength of its culture could prolong the life of Western civilization. Almost another twenty years later, Karl Jaspers, dealing with the same question in his *Origin and Goal of History,* concluded that, even though a dangerous transition period must be anticipated, a new order—not necessarily a "Western," but a "world" civilization—would be evolved. World unity is necessary and is, he felt, coming as wars and revolutions become less and less feasible under the impact of scientific and technological developments; and in a united world, man's soul and spirit, his aspiration and institutions, will be changed. A world civilization such as Jaspers envisioned, seems, however, still far off. Political divisions (such as those between East and West Germany, Arabs and Jews, Pakistan and India, Northern and Southern Vietnam, China and Formosa, Northern and Southern Korea) exemplify conflicting ways of life, concepts of justice, economic organizations, and political ideologies. Technical developments (such as those connected with spacecraft and atomic research) indicate not a diminishing but a growing gap between the potentials of underdeveloped countries, developed nations, and the two super-industrialized giants, the United States and the Soviet Union. Persistent social differences, whether of racial or economic origin, portend continued revolutionary trends; and educational opportunities in the industrially advanced societies, enhanced by manifold attempts to bring cultural achievements to masses of people, accentuate the advantage of these nations, notwithstanding the benefits which mass media of communication make available to less developed countries. Under such conditions, Western civilization still has a major task to accomplish. Even though its political strength may be declining after centuries of ascendancy, its modes of thinking, its inventive and driving spirit, its arts and sciences, its whole approach to life still constitute the most important force.

The issues which, as described, faced the Western world, the attacks on its ideological foundations, and the rift between the generations (none of these was brand new or more foreboding than that which had plagued earlier generations) were reflected, as usual, in the disturbing events of the time. Among them was the war between the Israelis and Arabs in June, 1967, which was marked by fanaticism and led to conquest but not to peace; the bloody struggle in Vietnam, which involved the United States and defied efforts at peacemaking until the spring of 1968; and the 1968 invasion of Czechoslovakia by the Soviets who, "for the sake of socialism and the protection of socialist countries," subdued the Czechs and imposed their armies on them. Amidst such conflicts, international diplomacy achieved little. A nuclear non-proliferation treaty was ratified in 1969, cooperation in the European Common Market diminished, and a monetary crisis broke out in 1968, forcing Western countries to adopt restrictive arrangements for covering their paper currencies. In the Far East, Japan was moving toward third place among all industrial powers, while a Western country like Italy could find no means to build up the economy of her backward areas.

Nor was the spiritual health of the West furthered. Despite the reform attempts of the Second Vatican Council, the Catholic Church in 1969 still rejected many proposed changes, including those regarding birth control and clerical celibacy. There were serious student riots—in Paris (May, 1968), Madrid, Berlin, New York, Mexico City. Occasionally, students allied themselves with groups of workers (as in France) or with racial minorities (as in the United States). In America, the Negro civil-rights leader, Dr. Martin Luther King, Jr., was murdered in 1968. The racial struggles increasingly aspired not so much to the attainment of common and equal rights but to separatism; many blacks seemed to be striving for a civilization at variance with the traditional Western one.

Yet, in spite of the world's difficulties, living conditions among Western peoples seemed to be improving: wages were generally rising faster than prices, social insurance systems were being broadened, and the average life span was increasing. In 1967, the first transplant of a human heart was achieved by doctors in South Africa. All together, the balance of Western achievements and setbacks did not seem entirely adverse; in many respects, the West continued to fulfill the promise that its civilization has held out since Renaissance times.

EXAMINATIONS

The following questions have been asked in examinations in various universities. Similar problems (formulated in various ways) are taken up in examinations at most universities. Therefore, careful study of precise answers to the following questions will prove helpful in preparing for examinations in almost any Western Civilization course.

NOTE: Numbers in parentheses refer to pages on which pertinent information can be found.

Sixteenth Century:

1. Describe the significance of the geographic discoveries of the fifteenth and sixteenth centuries for the economic and intellectual life of Europe. (24–28)

2. What is meant by "humanism" in the sixteenth century and to what extent are "humanistic" tendencies expressed in the art, literature, and science of the sixteenth century? Refer to specific examples. (29–31)

3. A. Describe the conditions in the Catholic Church which led to the Reformation. B. Discuss the spread of the Reformation, giving specific examples. C. How did the Catholic Church react to the Reformation? (39–40; 43–48; 49–50)

4. Trace the changes in the international scene of Europe and in the distribution of power from the beginning of Charles V's rule in 1519 to the end of the rule of his son Philip II in 1598. (36–37, 43–44, 51–61)

5. Compare the political organization of Philip II's Spain and Elizabeth I's England. (53–54, 57–59)

6. Define, give the approximate date, and explain the significance of each of the following:
   1. First circumnavigation of the globe (24)
   2. Joint stock companies (25)

   3. Enclosure movement (28)
   4. Renaissance concept of "virtù" (22)
   5. Copernican Theory (30)
   6. Luther's 95 theses (41)
   7. Peace of Augsburg (47)
   8. "Thirty nine articles" (58)
   9. Edict of Nantes (57)
  10. Council of Trent (49)
  11. Night of St. Bartholomew (56)
  12. Peasant Wars (42–43)
  13. War of Liberation of the Netherlands (55–56)
  14. *Praise of Folly* (29)
  15. *Utopia* (31)
  16. *The Prince* (31)
  17. *Gargantua* (62)

Seventeenth Century:

   7. Compare the development of governmental institutions and of class stratification in England and France during the seventeenth century. With specific illustrations, show in what ways the process was similar in both countries and in what ways it was different. (73–76, 82, 84, 86–88)

   8. Discuss the role of religion in the course of the histories of (a) Germany, (b) England, (c) France, (d) Spain during the seventeenth century. (70–71, 74–76, 82, 85, 87, 91)

   9. What was the significance of the "Age of Louis XIV" for seventeenth century Europe and what heritage did it leave for subsequent centuries? (81, 92–96)

  10. Compare the colonial expansion of Spain, England, and France during the seventeenth century in America and describe the organization of their colonies. Relate the colonial activities to the governmental and economic conditions in the home countries. (66–68, 69, 72, 75–76, 84, 87, 90–92)

  11. Define, give the approximate date, and explain the significance of each of the following:
     1. Baroque (79–95)
     2. Mercantilism (27, 76, 84, 90)
     3. Navigation Acts (76, 87)
     4. Kepler's laws (77)
     5. Pantheism (93)
     6. System of "farming out" tax collection (75)
     7. "Noblesse de la robe" (76, 84)
     8. The Fronde (82)
     9. Versailles (84, 95)
    10. Huguenots (56, 76, 85, 91)

11. Peace of Westphalia (71)
12. "Restoration" in England (87)
13. Glorious Revolution (88)
14. Brandenburg (71, 90–91)
15. *Letter on Toleration* (93)
16. *Simplicissimus* (95)
17. *Tartuffe* (94)

Eighteenth Century:

12. How did government in England during the eighteenth century differ from government in Louis XV's France, Frederick the Great's Prussia, and Peter the Great's Russia? (98–100, 102–103)

13. What were the most important discoveries of the scientists of the Enlightenment, and what underlying assumptions were common to them and to the philosophers of the same age? (112–114, 135–136, 138)

14. Discuss the changes in the economic conditions of Europe during the eighteenth century and their relation to the changes in the distribution of colonies. (108–110, 112–113, 118–119, 120)

15. Rousseau, writing in the 1760's stated that "man is born free, and everywhere he is in chains." Referring concretely to the conditions of France at about the time Rousseau wrote, what actual restrictions on freedom (political, economic, social, and other) then existed? Would Rousseau have been justified in making the same statement for France at the end of the century? Or for England, the United States, Prussia, or Russia? (98–100, 102, 103–104, 126, 134)

16. One authority on the French Revolution, Louis Gottschalk, has written that all great revolutions presuppose certain conditions: (a) a widespread sense of grievance; (b) a program and leadership; (c) the failure of the existent regime to reform itself; (d) the weakening of the forces of order. Discuss the French Revolution with reference to this statement. (120–123)

17. Define, give the approximate date, and explain the significance of each of the following:
    1. Balance of power (104–105, 108)
    2. Great Northern War (105)
    3. Enlightened Despotism (97–101)
    4. Cabinet System in England (103)
    5. Physiocrats (112)
    6. Partitions of Poland (101, 124)
    7. *Spirit of the Laws* (113)
    8. *The Social Contract* (114)
    9. *The Wealth of Nations* (112)
    10. Deism (114, 125)
    11. Oath of the Tennis Court (122)

12. *Lettres de cachet* (121)
13. Jacobins (123–125)
14. *Art of the Fugue* (116)
15. *Critique of Pure Reason* (138)
16. *Faust* (141)

General: Sixteenth to Eighteenth Centuries:

18. The sixteenth century in European history was marked by religious controversy, the seventeenth by attempts to consolidate royal absolutism, and the eighteenth by the rivalry of European powers on a world wide scale. Select two countries for each century and discuss to what extent events there illustrate the above generalizations.

19. Write an essay on the economic life of Europe from 1500 to 1815, describing specifically (a) entrepreneurial activity, (b) "classes," (c) economic policies of governments, (d) economic influences exercised by overseas expansion. Give concrete examples and indicate major changes which occurred in the course of the centuries.

20. Compare and contrast the attitudes of the Renaissance, the Reformation, and the Enlightenment towards:
    A. God. B. The universe. C. Human nature. D. Reason. E. The idea of progress.
    Mention specific events, personalities, and intellectual trends in order to illustrate your generalizations.

21. Describe the state system (mentioning the major states) existing in 1500 and the "balance of power" of Europe at that time. Then, describe the changes which took place in the seventeenth, and then in the eighteenth century, and conclude by describing the state system and "balance of power" existing around 1800.

22. What achievements in the fields of art and science of the sixteenth, seventeenth, and eighteenth centuries influence our lives and thoughts today?

Nineteenth Century up to 1871:

23. "Liberalism and nationalism ordinarily went hand in hand." Discuss what liberalism and nationalism stood for and whether the above statement would hold true for the Italy and the Germany of the period between 1815 and 1871. (142–143, 148, 154, 166–168, 171–174, 177–182)

24. What are the main characteristics of the "Industrial Revolution"? Is it appropriate to speak in this connection of a "revolution"? What economic and social problems resulted from industrialization, and what were some of the possible solutions offered for these problems? (154, 155–158, 164, 177, 195–196)

25. What were the grievances underlying the French revolutions of 1830, of 1848, and of 1871? Did the revolutions accomplish what those who instigated them had hoped for? (147, 151, 165, 170–171, 174, 196–197)

26. Compare the social structure of Russia with that of France and that of the United States between 1815 and 1871. (149–151, 165, 168–170, 176–177, 183–187)

27. Define, give the approximate date, and explain the significance of each of the following:

    1. Continental System (130)
    2. "1812" (131)
    3. Holy Alliance (133)
    4. Congress of Vienna (132–133)
    5. "Young Italy" (167)
    6. Reform Bill of 1832 (152)
    7. Utopian Socialism (157)
    8. Nihilism (195, 207)
    9. Crimean War (183–184)
    10. *Impressionism* (191, 223)
    11. Syllabus of Errors (194)
    12. *War and Peace* (190)

1871–1919:

28. What were the main ideas of Karl Marx? Why did they win the allegiance of much of the working class of Europe and many of her intellectuals? (156, 158, 195–197, 200–201, 203, 206–207, 217–219, 239–240, 260–262)

29. Compare the economic growth of Russia with that of Germany and England. (200, 203, 206–207, 213–219, 234, 237, 238–239, 260–263)

30. What factors in the history of the United States made its society unlike the societies of Europe and to what extent did the United States, despite social differences, share in the general trends of Western civilization between 1850 and 1915? (186–187, 209–211, 240–242)

31. Compare the peace settlement of Vienna (1815) with that of Versailles (1919). (133, 143–145, 255–259)

32. Describe (a) efforts for the maintenance of peace between 1870 and 1914, and then (b) describe those forces which in the end prevailed and led to war. Include in your discussion a survey of the division of Europe into two opposing camps and under (b) give an account of European imperialism. (230–233, 241, 242–244, 244–246, 250–252)

33. Define, give the approximate date, and explain the significance of each of the following:

    1. *Kulturkampf* (200–201, 225)
    2. Fabian Socialism (203, 219)

3. "The prisoner of the Vatican" (182, 205)
4. Social Insurance legislation (201, 216–217, 234, 237, 240)
5. Congress of Berlin (208–209)
6. Dreyfus Affair (235)
7. *Entente cordiale* (231–232)
8. Revolution of 1905 (239–240)
9. Nobel prizes (242)
10. Cartels (214, 244)
11. Expressionism (224, 267–269)
12. "Splendid isolation" (203, 230–231)
13. Battle of the Marne (253)
14. February Revolution in Russia (253, 260–261)

1919–to Date:

34. Describe the German "Weimar Republic," comparing its institutions with those of the USA and France, and then discuss the rise of National Socialism (Nazis) and its aims. (276–278, 284–288)

35. Certain social, political, and economic problems were met in Russia, Italy, and the United States in the period between World War I and World War II. List these problems and then at some length describe the social doctrines and methods used to solve these problems. (278–280, 286–287, 289–292)

36. Discuss in detail the impact of World War I on the European economy. (259, 262–263, 266–267, 271–272, 275–277, 280)

37. Describe the international scene in the period between the two World Wars, the major aims of the foreign policies of the great powers, and the shifts in the distribution of power between 1919 and 1939. (270–275, 283–284, 290, 292–294)

38. Define, give the approximate date, and explain the significance of each of the following:
    1. Rapallo Treaty (273)
    2. Locarno Treaty (273–274)
    3. NEP (278)
    4. Comintern (271)
    5. Kolkhoz (collective farm) (279)
    6. Stalingrad (296)
    7. Collective Security (292–294)
    8. Yalta conference (298)
    9. Marshall Plan (305)
    10. Suez crisis (312, 313)
    11. Spanish Civil War (288–289)
    12. *Ulysses* (268)
    13. *The Decline of the West* (266, 313)

General: 1815–to Date:

39. What have been the main scientific and economic factors responsible for a large increase in the population of many European countries?

40. Describe the status of the balance of power in Europe (a) immediately after the Congress of Vienna; (b) after the Peace of Versailles; (c) after the Second World War.

41. Discuss the "Idea of Progress" as conceived in the eighteenth century and as seen in the nineteenth and twentieth centuries.

42. Describe the impact of science and technology on society from 1815 to the present and discuss in connection with this the so-called "conflict of science and religion."

43. Discuss the influence of Russia on Europe, politically and culturally, from the time of the Congress of Vienna until today.

44. Describe the influence of nationalism on the political and cultural life of the West since 1815.

45. Describe peace movements and peace organizations from the times of the Holy Alliance until today.

46. Arrange in chronological order and identify: (*See* Chronology and Index)

    A. Goethe, Voltaire, Montaigne, Shakespeare, Erasmus, Molière, Tolstoy, Ibsen, Milton.

    B. Newton, Copernicus, Einstein, Darwin, Lavoisier, Curie, Kepler, Freud, Pasteur, Galileo.

    C. Richelieu, Bismarck, Louis XIV, Cromwell, Cavour, Philip II, Peter the Great, Lenin, Metternich, Frederick the Great.

    D. Kant, Spinoza, Descartes, Comte, Marx, Hegel, Dewey, Locke, Leibnitz, Nietzsche.

SOME MEMORABLE THINKERS AND ARTISTS

	Philosophy	Religion	Art	Music	Literature	Social Sciences	Nat. Sciences	Exploration
XVI Century		Luther Ignatius of Loyola Calvin	Leonardo da Vinci Raphael Michelangelo Dürer Holbein Titian Brueghel El Greco	Palestrina	Erasmus Shakespeare	Machiavelli	Copernicus Galileo	Magellan Cortez Pizarro
XVII Century	Descartes Spinoza Pascal Leibnitz		Rubens Velasquez Vandyke Vermeer Franz Hals Rembrandt	Monteverdi	Corneille Racine Molière Milton	Locke	Kepler Newton	
XVIII Century	Hume Kant	Wesley	Gainsborough	Bach Handel Gluck Rameau Corelli Haydn Mozart	Pope Lessing Goethe Schiller Wordsworth	Montesquieu Voltaire Rousseau Malthus	Halley Boerhaave Linnaeus Franklin Priestley Boyle Lavoisier Laplace	Bering Cook
XIX Century	Hegel Fichte Comte Schopenhauer Nietzsche	Pius IX	Goya Manet Monet Renoir van Gogh	Beethoven Schubert Chopin Rossini Musorgski Wagner Verdi	Hugo Balzac Dickens Pushkin Dostoevsky Tolstoy Ibsen	Bentham Mill Proudhon Karl Marx	Lyell Helmholtz Darwin Pasteur Mendel Pavlov Roentgen Curie	Nansen
XX Century	Bergson Dewey	John XXIII	Picasso	Strauss Sibelius Prokofiev	Shaw Mann Joyce Gide	Lenin	Planck Einstein Freud Heisenberg	Amundsen (Sputnik)

SOME MEMORABLE STATESMEN

	France	England	Germany	Russia	Italy	USA (Presidents)
XVII Century	Sully Richelieu Mazarin Colbert	Cromwell				
XVIII Century	Turgot	Walpole Pitt the Elder		Potemkin		Washington
XIX Century	Talleyrand	Pitt the Younger Palmerston Disraeli Gladstone	Metternich Bismarck	Witte	Cavour	Jefferson Jackson Lincoln
XX Century	Clemenceau Briand De Gaulle	Lloyd George Churchill	Stresemann Hitler Adenauer	Lenin Stalin Khrushchev	Mussolini	Wilson F.D. Roosevelt J.F. Kennedy

SOME MEMORABLE RULERS

Holy Roman Empire
1519–1556	Charles V	(House of Hapsburg)
1619–1637	Ferdinand II	(" " ")
1740–1780	Maria Theresa	(" " ")
1780–1790	Joseph II	(" " ")

France
1515–1547	Francis I	(House of Valois)
1589–1610	Henry IV	(House of Bourbon)
1643–1715	Louis XIV	(" " ")
1774–1792	Louis XVI	(" " ")
1804–1814	Napoleon I, Emperor	

England
1509–1547	Henry VIII	(House of Tudor)
1558–1603	Elizabeth I	(" " ")
1625–1649	Charles I	(House of Stuart)
1653–1658	Cromwell, Lord Protector	
1660–1685	Charles II	(House of Stuart)
1760–1820	George III	(House of Hanover)
1837–1901	Victoria	(" " ")

Spain
1556–1598	Philip II	(House of Hapsburg)
1759–1788	Charles III	(House of Bourbon)

Tsars of Russia
1462–1505	Ivan III, "the Great"	(House of Rurik)
1533–1584	Ivan IV, "the Terrible"	(" " ")
1598–1605	Boris Godunov	
1689–1725	Peter I, "the Great"	(House of Romanov)
1762–1796	Catherine II, "the Great"	
1855–1881	Alexander II, "Tsar-Liberator"	(" " ")

Electors of Brandenburg, Kings of Prussia, German Emperors
1640–1688	Frederick William, "The Great Elector"	(House of Hohenzollern)
1740–1786	Frederick II, "the Great"	(" " ")
1861–1888	William I	(" " ")
1888–1918	William II	(" " ")

Popes
1492–1503	Alexander VI	(House of Borgia)
1513–1521	Leo X	(House of Medici)
1523–1534	Clement VII	(" " ")
1846–1878	Pius IX	
1878–1903	Leo XIII	
1958–1963	John XXIII	

CHRONOLOGY

1492 COLUMBUS DISCOVERS AMERICA

1492 Death of Lorenzo de Medici
End of Mohammedan state of Granada in Spain
1494 France invades Italy
TREATY OF TORDESILLAS
Hanseatic factory in Novgorod closed by Russians
1495 Leonardo da Vinci, *Last Supper* (1503: *Mona Lisa*)
1498 VASCO DA GAMA REACHES INDIA VIA CAPE OF GOOD HOPE
Savonarola hanged and burned at stake in Florence
1503 Death of Pope Alexander VI (Borgia)
1508 Michelangelo, *Ceiling of Sistine Chapel*
1513 Balboa reaches Pacific shores
Machiavelli, *The Prince*
1516 Raphael, *Sistine Madonna*
Thomas More, *Utopia*

1517 LUTHER, 95 THESES

1518 **Zwingli** begins work in Zürich
1519 **Charles V** becomes German emperor
Cortez begins conquest of Mexico
Magellan begins circumnavigation of the world
1520 Suleiman the Magnificent becomes sultan of Turkey
1521 LUTHER BEFORE DIET OF WORMS
1523 Sweden leaves Scandinavian Union: Gustavus Vasa becomes
king
1524 Peasants' Revolt in Germany
1525 Battle of Pavia: Francis I of France made prisoner of
Charles V
Death of Jacob **Fugger**
1526 Dürer, *Four Apostles*
1527 Rome sacked by troops of Charles V
1529 Turks besiege Vienna
Diet of Spires ("Protestants")

1530 AUGSBURG CONFESSION DRAWN UP
1532 Pizarro undertakes conquest of Peru
1533 Reformation begins in England **(Henry VIII)**
1534 Rabelais, *Gargantua*
1536 **Erasmus of Rotterdam dies**
     Calvin, *Institutes of the Christian Religion*
1540 Order of Jesuits founded
1541 Paracelsus dies
1543 Copernicus, *De Revolutionibus Orbium Coelestium (On the Revolutions of the Heavenly Spheres)*
     Vesalius, *De Humani Corporis Fabrica (The Structure of the Human Body)*
     Holbein dies
1547 Protestants defeated by Charles V at Mühlberg
1552 Protestants resume war: Charles V flees across Alps
1553 Servetus burned at stake in Geneva
1554 Marriage of Mary Tudor of England and Philip II of Spain

1555 RELIGIOUS PEACE OF AUGSBURG

1555 Persecution of Protestants in England
     Muscovy Company founded in England
1556 ABDICATION OF CHARLES V
1558 England loses Calais, last foothold on Continent
     Ivan the Terrible invades Livonia
1559 Publication of Prayer Book in England **(Elizabeth I)**
1562 Beginnings of religious wars in France (Huguenots)
1563 "Thirty-Nine Articles" of the Anglican Church

1563 COUNCIL OF TRENT CONCLUDED

1565 Beginning of risings against Spain in the Netherlands
1568 Mary, Queen of Scots, flees to England
     Duke of Alba in the Netherlands
1569 Union of Lublin between Poland and Lithuania
     Mercator publishes map of the world
1571 BATTLE OF LEPANTO: TURKS DEFEATED
1572 Beginnings of War of Liberation of the Netherlands **(William the Silent)**
     Massacre of the Night of St. Bartholomew in Paris
     John Knox, Scottish reformer, dies
1576 Titian dies
1580 Montaigne, *Essais*
1581 NORTHERN NETHERLANDS DEPOSE PHILIP II
     Russian penetration into Siberia

1582 Gregorian calendar introduced
1587 Mary, Queen of Scots, executed

1588 SPANISH ARMADA DESTROYED

1592 Alexander of Parma dies
1594 HENRY IV GAINS PARIS: end of civil wars in France
Palestrina dies
1595 Dutch colonization of East Indies begins
1597 Francis Bacon, *Essays*
1598 Franco-Spanish peace of Vervins: death of **Philip II**
Edict of Nantes
1600 Founding of English East India Company
1602 Founding of Dutch East India Company
1603 Shakespeare, *Hamlet*
Death of Elizabeth I of England
1604 Galileo: law of falling bodies
1605 Beginning of Times of Trouble in Russia
Cervantes, *Don Quixote*
1607 JAMESTOWN SETTLEMENT IN VIRGINIA FOUNDED
1614 Dutch settlement on Hudson
Invention of logarithms
1616 **Richelieu** becomes minister in France

1618 BEGINNING OF THIRTY YEARS' WAR

1620 Settlement in New Plymouth founded (*Mayflower*)
Francis Bacon, *Novum Organum*
1621 **Kepler's** laws
1624 English settlements in East India and Dutch settlements in
Indonesia
Decline of Portugal
1625 Grotius, *De Jure Belli et Pacis* (*Law of War and Peace*)
1628 PETITION OF RIGHTS SUBMITTED TO CHARLES I OF ENGLAND
Surrender of Huguenot-held La Rochelle to Richelieu
Harvey's treatise on circulation of blood published
1629 Edict of Restitution
1630 Theory of **mercantilism** (Thomas Mun's treatises)
Swedish intervention in Thirty Years' War (**Gustavus
Adolphus**)
1632 Battle of Lützen
Rembrandt, *Anatomy*
1634 Assassination of Wallenstein
1636 Corneille, *Le Cid* (*The Cid*)
Harvard College established

1637 Descartes, *Discours de la Méthode* (*Discourse on Method*)
1642 Civil War breaks out in England

1648 PEACE OF WESTPHALIA

1649 ENGLISH KING CHARLES I EXECUTED
1651 FIRST ENGLISH NAVIGATION ACT
     Hobbes, *Leviathan*
1653 End of Fronde
     Cromwell becomes Lord Protector
1656 Russia incorporates Ukraine
1658 Death of Cromwell
1659 Peace of the Pyrenees
1660 **Restoration** of Charles II in England
     Peace of Oliva
     Death of Velasquez
1661 Death of **Mazarin:** Colbert named controller-general
1666 Death of Frans Hals
1667 Milton, *Paradise Lost*
     Beginning of War of Devolution
1670 Pascal, *Pensées*
1672 **Newton** formulates laws of gravitation
1673 Test Act in England
1677 Spinoza, *Ethics*
1678 Peace of Nijmwegen
     Bunyan, *Pilgrim's Progress*
1681 Strasbourg annexed by France
1682 La Salle in Mississippi Valley
1683 Turks besiege Vienna
     William Penn in Pennsylvania (Philadelphia)
1684 Leibnitz publishes method of differential calculus
1685 REVOCATION OF EDICT OF NANTES
1687 Newton, *Principia Mathematica*

1688 GLORIOUS REVOLUTION

1688 Death of Frederick William, "Great Elector" of Brandenburg
1689 Act of Toleration; BILL OF RIGHTS
1690 Huyghens promulgates theory of light
     Locke, *Essay concerning Human Understanding*
1697 Peace of Ryswyck
1699 Peace of Karlowitz
1700 **Charles XII** of Sweden defeats Russians at Narva
1701 Beginning of War of Spanish Succession
1703 ST. PETERSBURG FOUNDED

1704 Newton, *Optics*
     Newcomen builds steam engine
1707 Union of England and Scotland established
1709 **Peter the Great** defeats Swedes at Poltava

1713 PEACE OF UTRECHT

1713 England gains *asiento*
1714 Peace of Rastatt and Baden
     Leibnitz, *Monadology*
1715 Death of Louis XIV: Regency of Duke d'Orléans
1716 John Law in Paris
1719 Defoe, *Robinson Crusoe*
1720 "South Sea Bubble" in England
1721 PEACE OF NYSTAD
     Montesquieu, *Lettres Persanes (Persian Letters)*
1729 Bach, *St. Matthew Passion*
1733 Beginning of War of Polish Succession
1735 Linnaeus, *Genera Plantarum*
1738 Invention of flying shuttle by Kay
1739 Hume, *Treatise of Human Nature*
1740 Maria Theresa becomes empress (Pragmatic Sanction)
     Outbreak of First Silesian War **(Frederick the Great)**
1741 Dupleix French governor general in India
     Handel, *Messiah*
1742 Thermometer of Celsius
1744 Second Silesian War
1745 LOUISBOURG CONQUERED BY BRITISH
1748 PEACE OF AIX-LA-CHAPELLE
     Montesquieu, *L'Esprit des Lois (Spirit of Laws)*
1749 Bach, *Art of the Fugue*
1752 Franklin's experiments on lightning and electricity
1754 Beginning of French and Indian War
1755 Lisbon earthquake
1756 Outbreak of Seven Years' War
1758 Quesnay, *Tableau économique*
1759 Conquest of Quebec
     Voltaire, *Candide*
1760 BATTLE OF WANDEWASH
1762 Rousseau, *Contrat Social (Social Contract)*
     Gluck, *Orfeo*

1763 END OF SEVEN YEARS' WAR: PEACE OF PARIS

1765 Stamp Act for American colonies
1768 Watt's steam engine

1770 Cook returns from trip around world
1771 Arkwright's spinning mill in England
1772 FIRST PARTITION OF POLAND
1773 Reorganization of English administration in India
Beginning of Pugachev Revolt in Russia
1774 **Turgot** becomes controller-general
Goethe, *Sorrows of Werther*

1776 AMERICAN DECLARATION OF INDEPENDENCE

1776 Adam Smith, *Wealth of Nations*
1781 Kant, *Kritik der reinen Vernunft* (*Critique of Pure Reason*)
1783 SECOND PEACE OF PARIS
1787 Mozart, *Don Giovanni*
1789 U.S. Constitution in force

1789 BEGINNING OF GREAT FRENCH REVOLUTION

1789 Fall of the Bastille
1792 War against France
Russian-Turkish Peace of Jassy
1793 Louis XVI guillotined
1794 ROBESPIERRE GUILLOTINED
1795 Peace of Basle
Third Partition of Poland
1796 Napoleon's Italian campaign
Haydn, *Emperor Quartet*
1798 Napoleon's Egyptian campaign
Wordsworth and Coleridge, *Lyrical Ballads*
Malthus, *Essay on the Principle of Population*
1799 **Napoleon** becomes First Consul
1803 Purchase of Louisiana by U.S.A.
1804 Schiller, *Wilhelm Tell*
1804 Napoleon becomes emperor
Beethoven, *Eroica Symphony*
1805 BATTLE OF TRAFALGAR
BATTLE OF AUSTERLITZ
1806 End of Holy Roman Empire
1807 Reforms in Prussia (vom Stein)
Fulton's steamship on the Hudson
INTRODUCTION OF CONTINENTAL SYSTEM
1808 Goethe, *Faust* (first part)
1812 Napoleon's Russian campaign
War between England and U.S.A.
Byron, *Childe Harold's Pilgrimage*

1813 Wars of Liberation against Napoleon
1814 Stephenson's steam locomotive built
1815 BATTLE OF WATERLOO: Napoleon exiled to St. Helena

1815 CONGRESS OF VIENNA CONCLUDED: HOLY ALLIANCE FOUNDED

1818 Chile and La Plata region declare independence from Spain
Congress of Aix-la-Chapelle
1819 KARLSBAD DECREES
Bolívar founds Republic of Gran Colombia
Scott, *Ivanhoe*
1820 Revolutions in Italy: Congress of Troppau
Missouri Compromise
1821 Weber, *Freischütz*
1822 CONGRESS OF VERONA
Independence of Brazil
1823 Monroe Doctrine
1824 Beethoven, *Ninth Symphony*
Hegel, lectures on *Philosophy of History*
Robert Owen's establishment of New Harmony, Indiana
1825 Decabrist revolt in Russia
1827 Battle of Navarino
Heine, *Book of Songs*
Schubert, *Trout Quintet*
1829 PEACE OF ADRIANOPLE
Catholic Emancipation Act in England
1830 Greek independence declared
France seizes Algeria

1830 JULY REVOLUTION IN FRANCE

1830 Pushkin, *Eugene Onegin*
Victor Hugo, *Hernani*
1831 Faraday's experiments with electromagnetism
1832 FIRST REFORM BILL IN ENGLAND
Goethe, *Faust* (second part)
Beginnings of "Young Italy" movement (Mazzini)
1833 Zollverein founded in Germany
1835 David Friedrich Strauss, *Life of Jesus*
1836 Ranke, *History of the Popes*
1837 Invention of telegraph by Morse
Dickens, *Oliver Twist*
1839 British-Chinese Opium War
Belgium established as independent neutral state

1841 STRAITS CONVENTION STIPULATING TURKISH INDEPENBENCE
Carlyle, *Heroes and Hero-Worship*
1842 **Chartist** risings in England
Comte, *Cours de philosophie positive*
1845 Texas annexed by U.S.A.
Poe, *Tales*
Dumas, *Count of Monte Cristo*
1846 REPEAL OF CORN LAWS OF ENGLAND
1847 Helmholtz, *On the Conservation of Energy*

**1848 FEBRUARY REVOLUTION IN FRANCE; REVOLU-
TIONS IN ITALY AND GERMANY**

1848 California, New Mexico, etc., incorporated by U.S.A.
First Pan-Slav Congress
Marx, *Communist Manifesto*
Balzac, *Comédie humaine* completed
Mill, *Principles of Political Economy*
1849 Frankfurt Assembly dissolved
Macaulay, *History of England*
1852 **Napoleon III** becomes emperor
Cavour becomes prime minister of Piedmont
1853 Wagner, *Ring of the Nibelungen*
1854 **Crimean War**
Kansas-Nebraska Act changes Missouri Compromise
Opening of Japan to the West
1856 PEACE OF PARIS
Bessemer process for steel manufacturing invented
1857 Indian Mutiny
1858 Treaty of Tientsin: opening of China to the West
1859 War between Austria and Piedmont
Mill, *Essay on Liberty*
Darwin, *Origin of Species*
1860 Garibaldi's expedition to Sicily
Cobden Treaty between France and England
1861 KINGDOM OF ITALY FOUNDED; death of Cavour
Outbreak of **Civil War** in U.S.A.
Emancipation of serfs in Russia
1862 **Bismarck** becomes Prussian prime minister
1863 Emancipation Proclamation by Lincoln
Revolt in Poland
1864 Danish-German War for Schleswig-Holstein
French expedition in Mexico (Emperor Maximilian)
"FIRST INTERNATIONAL" (workers' association)
Pius IX, *Syllabus of Errors*

1865 End of American Civil War; **Lincoln** assassinated
Maxwell, *Treatise on Electricity*
Tolstoi, *War and Peace*
1866 AUSTRO-PRUSSIAN ("SEVEN WEEKS'") WAR
Italy annexes Venetia
Dostoevski, *Crime and Punishment*
1867 Dual Monarchy of Austria-Hungary established
Invention of dynamite (Nobel)
Second Reform Bill in England
Marx, *Capital*
Ibsen, *Peer Gynt*
Purchase of Alaska by U.S.A.
1869 OPENING OF SUEZ CANAL

1870 OUTBREAK OF FRANCO-PRUSSIAN WAR

1870 Napoleon made prisoner by Germans, deposed by French
End of Papal States: Rome becomes Italian Capital
Dogma of Papal Infallibility
1871 FOUNDING OF GERMAN EMPIRE
Revolt of the **Commune** in Paris
Impressionist exhibition in Paris
Verdi, *Aida*
1873 Three Emperors' League (Germany, Austria, Russia)
Kulturkampf in Germany
1875 British purchase of Suez Canal shares
1877 Outbreak of Russian-Turkish War

1878 CONGRESS OF BERLIN

1879 Edison invents electric bulb
1881 Assassination of Alexander II of Russia
Tunisia under French protectorate
1882 TRIPLE ALLIANCE ESTABLISHED (Germany, Austria, Italy)
British occupy Egypt
Beginning of Bismarck's SOCIAL LEGISLATION in Germany
1884 Germany acquires colonies
Nietzsche, *Zarathustra* completed
1887 German-Russian Reinsurance Treaty
U.S.A. passes Interstate Commerce Act
1890 DISMISSAL OF BISMARCK
1891 Franco-Russian Alliance
1894 Dreyfus affair in France
1895 Jameson Raid
Discovery of X rays by Roentgen

1898 European powers occupy Chinese ports
     U.S.A. ANNEXES HAWAII; SPANISH-AMERICAN WAR
     Discovery of radium by **Curie**
     Germany builds large navy
     FASHODA INCIDENT
1899 OUTBREAK OF BOER WAR
1900 Boxer Rising in China
1901 **Planck,** quantum theory
1902 British-Japanese alliance
1903 Panama independence established
     Trans-Siberian Railway completed
     FIRST AIRPLANE FLOWN (Wright brothers)
     Shaw, *Man and Superman*
1904 *Entente cordiale* of France and England
     Outbreak of Russo-Japanese War
1905 PEACE OF PORTSMOUTH
     Revolution in St. Petersburg; a duma introduced
     Independence of Norway established
     Einstein, relativity theory
1907 Anglo-Russian treaty over Persia; TRIPLE ENTENTE COM-
     PLETED
1908 First Congress of Psychoanalysis (**Freud**)
     Young Turk revolt
1909 Expressionist school of painting started
1911 Italy annexes Turkish Tripoli
     Amundsen discovers South Pole
1912 OUTBREAK OF FIRST BALKAN WAR
1913 Second Balkan War
     Atomic structure described by Niels Bohr
1914 PANAMA CANAL OPENED
     Clayton (antitrust) Act in U.S.A.

1914 OUTBREAK OF FIRST WORLD WAR

1914 Battle of the Marne
1916 Battle of Verdun
1917 Abdication of Russian Tsar: **February Revolution**

1917 OCTOBER REVOLUTION IN RUSSIA: BOLSHEVIKS (Lenin) ESTABLISH COMMUNISM

1918 German-Russian Peace of Brest-Litovsk
     Armistice concludes First World War
     REVOLUTION IN GERMANY, Austria, Turkey: republics declared
1919 Allied Intervention in Russia; civil war in Russia

1919 TREATY OF VERSAILLES; LEAGUE OF NATIONS

1920 Polish-Russian War
1921 Disarmament Conference in Washington
    NEP IN RUSSIA
1922 German-Russian Treaty of RAPALLO
    Mussolini establishes fascist regime in Italy
    Sinclair Lewis, *Babbitt*
    Joyce, *Ulysses*
1923 French invasion of Ruhr
    USSR established
    Stabilization of German currency
1924 DAWES PLAN FOR GERMAN REPARATIONS ADOPTED
    Death of Lenin
1925 LOCARNO TREATY
1926 Nationalization of oil industry in Mexico
1928 BRIAND-KELLOGG PEACE PACT
    First Five-Year Plan in USSR initiated
1929 **Stalin's** dictatorship established: Trotsky banished
    Concordat Italy-Papacy: VATICAN CITY becomes sovereign
        Papal State
    CRASH ON NEW YORK STOCK EXCHANGE
1930 Young plan for reparations adopted
    Passive resistance against England in India **(Gandhi)**
    HEISENBERG'S indeterminacy theory
1931 England gives up gold standard
    England promulgates Statute of Westminster
    Austrian Kreditanstalt collapses
1932 Lausanne Reparation Conference
    Britain introduces protective tariffs
    Japanese expansion in Chinese territory

1933 HITLER BECOMES GERMAN CHANCELLOR

1933 F. D. Roosevelt becomes U. S. president: U.S.A. gives up
    gold standard
1934 Russia enters League of Nations
1935 Social security acts passed in U.S.A.
1936 Purges in Russia; STALIN CONSTITUTION passed
    Italy annexes Abyssinia; Rome-Berlin Axis
    OUTBREAK OF CIVIL WAR IN SPAIN
    Germany reintroduces conscription and reoccupies the
    Rhineland
1937 Constitution for Ireland (Eire)

1938 Austria united with Germany
MUNICH CONFERENCE ("appeasement")
Incorporation of Sudetenland into Germany
1939 Collapse of Czechoslovakia
Italy invades Albania

1939 OUTBREAK OF SECOND WORLD WAR

1939 Partition of Poland between Germany and Russia
Russia attacks Finland
1940 Germany occupies Norway, Denmark, Holland, Belgium
Incorporation of Estonia, Latvia, Lithuania into USSR
COLLAPSE OF FRANCE
1941 GERMANY INVADES RUSSIA
ATTACK ON PEARL HARBOR BY JAPAN: U.S.A. AT WAR
1942 Allied landing in Africa
1943 German defeat at STALINGRAD
1944 ALLIED LANDING IN NORMANDY, FRANCE
1945 Yalta Conference

1945 SURRENDER OF GERMANY AND JAPAN; UNITED NATIONS ESTABLISHED

1945 First atom bomb (dropped by U.S.A. on Japan)
1947 MARSHALL PLAN for economic rehabilitation of Europe
INDIA BECOMES INDEPENDENT from the British and is divided
1948 Berlin blockade
State of Israel founded
Independence of Ireland
1949 TRIUMPH OF COMMUNISTS IN CHINA
Establishment of a West German Republic
1950 Outbreak of Korean War
SCHUMAN PLAN for European steel and coal production
1953 DEATH OF STALIN
1955 Germany enters NATO
1956 SUEZ CANAL NATIONALIZED BY EGYPT: abortive invasion by
England, France, Israel
1957 First earth satellite ("Sputnik") launched
1961 Construction of Berlin Wall
1962 Independence of Algeria
1966–1967 Escalation of Vietnam conflict
1967 Israeli-Arab War. Defeat of Arabs (UAR)
1968 Students' and civil-rights disorders
Soviet invasion and occupation of Czechoslovakia
1969 Nuclear non-proliferation treaty

BIBLIOGRAPHY

The following bibliography is confined to the listing of a few general history books and a few others of perhaps uncommon interest. It includes only works in English which seem rather "readable" and easily available. It should be used in connection with the bibliographies given in the various textbooks which are listed in the correlating tables on pp. x–xvii; most of these bibliographies are subdivided to render orientation easy, and some also discuss the merits of the works listed.

Two excellent series of history books deal with European history:

"The Rise of Modern Europe," ed. by William L. Langer (New York: Harper and Row).

"Berkshire Studies in European History," ed. by R. A. Newhall, *et al.* (New York: Holt, Rinehart and Winston).

The volumes included in these series are not individually listed in the following bibliography, but are to be found in library card catalogues, and are highly recommended for detailed studies.

A. GENERAL:
Hughes, Henry Stuart. *Consciousness and Society*. New York, 1958.
McNeill, W. H. *The Rise of the West*. Chicago, 1963.
Ploetz' *Dictionary of Dates*. New York, 1925.
Randall, John H. *The Making of the Modern Mind*. Boston, 1940.
Shepherd, W. R. *Historical Atlas*. New York, 1964.
Steinberg, S. H. *Historical Tables*. London, 1945.
Stromberg, Roland N. *An Intellectual History of Modern Europe*. New York, 1966.

B. MEANING OF HISTORY:
Berdyaev, Nicholas. *The Meaning of History*. London, 1949.
Burckhardt, Jacob. *Force and Freedom*. New York, 1943.
Muller, Herbert J. *The Uses of the Past*. New York, 1952.
Spengler, Oswald. *The Decline of the West*. New York, 1932.
Toynbee, Arnold. *Study of History*. London, 1934–54.

C. SOME HISTORIES ARRANGED BY COUNTRIES:
England:
Lunt, William E. *History of England*. New York, 1956.
Trevelyan, George M. *English Social History*. New York, 1947.
France:
Seignobos, Charles. *The Evolution of the French People*. New York, 1949.
Wright, Gordon. *France in Modern Times*. Chicago, 1960.

Germany:

Holborn, Hajo. *A History of Modern Germany.* New York, 1958.
Pinson, Koppel S. *Modern Germany.* New York, 1959.

Italy:

Salvatorelli, Luigi. *A Concise History of Italy.* New York, 1940.
Smith, Dennis Mack. *Italy, A Modern History.* Ann Arbor, 1959.

Russia:

Clarkson, Jesse D. *History of Russia.* New York, 1962.
Kirchner, Walther. *History of Russia.* (College Outline Series)
von Rauch, Georg. *A History of Soviet Russia.* New York, 1957.

Scandinavia:

Andersson, Ingvar. *A History of Sweden.* New York, 1956.
Larsen, Karen. *A History of Norway.* New York, 1948.

Southeastern Europe:

Lukacs, John A. *The Great Powers and Eastern Europe.* New York, 1953.
Wolff, Robert L. *The Balkans in our Time.* Cambridge, 1956.

Spain:

Merriman, Roger B. *The Rise of the Spanish Empire.* New York, 1918–34.
Sedgwick, Henry D. *Spain, A Short History.* Boston, 1931.

United States of America:

Blum, John, *et al. The National Experience.* New York, 1968.
Boorstin, Daniel. *The Americans: Colonial Experience.* New York, 1958.
————. *National Experience.* New York, 1965.
Hofstadter, Richard. *The American Tradition and the Men Who Made It.* New York, 1948.
Meyers, Marvin. *The Jacksonian Persuasion.* Stanford, 1957.
Morison, Samuel E. *The Oxford History of the American People.* New York, 1965.
Persons, Stow. *American Minds.* New York, 1959.
Stamp, Kenneth. *The Peculiar Institution.* New York, 1956.

D. SOME HISTORIES ARRANGED BY FIELDS OF SPECIALIZATION:

History of History:

Nevins, Allan. *The Gateway to History.* Boston, 1938.
Shotwell, James T. *The History of History.* New York, 1939.

History of Ideas:
Brinton, Crane. *Ideas and Men.* New York, 1950.
Russell, Bertrand. *A History of Western Philosophy.* New York, 1945.

Economic History:
Ashton, Thomas S. *The Industrial Revolution, 1760–1830.* New York, 1952.
Clough, Shepard B., and Cole, Charles W. *Economic History of Europe.* New York, 1948.
Heaton, Herbert. *Economic History of Europe.* New York, 1948.
Heckscher, Eli. *Mercantilism.* London, 1934.
Kapp, K. W., and Kapp, L. L. *History of Economic Thought— A Book of Readings.* (College Outline Series)
Nussbaum, Frederick L. *A History of the Economic Institutions of Modern Europe.* New York, 1933.
Roll, Erich. *A History of Economic Thought.* London, 1938.
Sloan, H. S., and Zurcher, A. J. *Dictionary of Economics.* (Everyday Handbook Series)

Political History:
Gulick, Edward V. *Europe's Classical Balance of Power.* New York, 1955.
Langer, William L. *European Alliances and Alignments.* New York, 1931.
Smith, E. C., and Zurcher, A. J. *Dictionary of American Politics.* (Everyday Handbook Series)
Taylor, A. J. P. *The Struggle for Mastery in Europe, 1848–1918.* New York, 1954.

History of Science:
Bernal, J. D. *Science in History.* London, 1954.
Hall, Alfred R. *The Scientific Revolution, 1500–1800.* New York, 1966.
Mason, Stephen F. *The Main Currents of Scientific Thought.* New York, 1953.
Pledge, H. T. *Science since 1500.* New York, 1947.
Shryock, Richard H. *Development of Modern Medicine.* Philadelphia, 1936.

History of Art:
Gardner, Helen. *Art through the Ages.* New York, 1936.
Gombrich, E. H. *The Story of Art.* New York, 1954.
Janson, Horst. *History of Art.* Englewood Cliffs, 1962.
Upjohn, Everard M., *et al. History of World Art.* New York, 1949.
Vincent, Jean A. *History of Art.* (College Outline Series)

History of Music:
Einstein, Alfred. *A Short History of Music.* New York, 1938.
Lovelock, William. *A Concise History of Music.* New York, 1954.
Miller, Hugh M. *History of Music.* (College Outline Series)

History of Literature:
Chadwick, H. M. *The Growth of Literature.* Cambridge, 1932–40.
Macy, John A. *The Story of the World's Literature.* New York, 1925.
Magnus, Laurie. *A History of European Literature.* London, 1934.
Trawick, Buckner B. *World Literature.* (College Outline Series)

E. SOME ADDITIONAL HISTORIES ARRANGED BY PERIODS:
1492–1815:
Beloff, Max. *The Age of Absolutism, 1660–1815.* New York, 1954.
Grimm, Harold J. *The Reformation Era, 1500–1650.* New York, 1966.
Manuel, Frank E. *Age of Reason.* Ithaca, 1964.

1815–1965:
Albrecht-Carrié, René. *A Diplomatic History of Europe.* New York, 1968.
Craig, Gordon. *Europe since 1815.* New York, 1962.
Taylor, Alan J. P. *From Napoleon to Stalin.* London, 1953.
Thomson, David. *Europe since Napoleon.* New York, 1962.

Sixteenth Century:
Abbott, Wilbur C. *The Expansion of Europe.* New York, 1924.
Brandi, Karl. *Emperor Charles V.* London, 1939.
Burckhardt, Jacob. *The Civilization of the Renaissance in Italy.* New York, 1937.
Davies, R. T. *The Golden Century of Spain, 1501–1621.* New York, 1954.
Janelle, Pierre. *The Catholic Reformation.* Milwaukee, 1949.
Petrie, Charles A. *Philip II of Spain.* New York, 1963.
Ranke, Leopold von. *The History of the Popes.* London, 1847–51.
Read, Conyers. *The Tudors.* New York, 1936.

Seventeenth Century:
Friedrich, Carl J. *The Age of the Baroque.* New York, 1952.
Gipson, Laurence H. *The British Empire before the American Revolution.* Caldwell, 1936–56.
Maland, D. *Europe in the Seventeenth Century.* New York, 1966.
Schevill, Ferdinand. *The Great Elector.* Chicago, 1947.

Trevelyan, George M. *England under the Stuarts*. New York, 1933.
Wedgwood, Cicely W. *The Thirty Years War*. New York, 1939.
Wolf, John B. *Louis XIV*. New York, 1968.

Eighteenth Century:
Cassirer, Ernst. *The Philosophy of the Enlightenment*. Princeton, 1952.
Gay, Peter. *The Enlightenment*. New York, 1966.
Gershoy, Leo. *The French Revolution and Napoleon*. New York, 1961.
Gooch, George P. *Frederick the Great*. New York, 1947.
Kluchevsky, Vasily O. *Peter the Great*. New York, 1958.
Palmer, Robert R. *The Age of the Democratic Revolution*. Princeton, 1959–64.

Nineteenth Century:
Berlin, Isaiah. *Karl Marx*. New York, 1948.
Bruun, Geoffrey. *Nineteenth Century European Civilization*. London, 1959.
Croce, Benedetto. *A History of Italy, 1871–1915*. New York, 1963.
Eyck, Erich. *Bismarck and the German Empire*. London, 1950.
Hobsbawn, Eric I. *Age of Revolution, Europe 1789–1848*. London, 1962.
Nicolson, Harold. *Congress of Vienna*. London, 1946.
Woodward, Ernest L. *The Age of Reform (1815–1870)*. Oxford, 1938.

Twentieth Century:
Carr, Edward H. *A History of Soviet Russia*. New York, 1950–58.
Craig, Gordon A. *Europe since 1914*. Holt, 1966.
Fay, Sidney B. *The Origins of the World War*. New York, 1928.
Lafore, Laurence D. *The Long Fuse: An Interpretation of the Origins of World War I*. Philadelphia, 1965.

F. A FEW STIMULATING WORKS OF SPECIAL INTEREST:

Brinton, Crane. *Anatomy of Revolution*. New York, 1952.
Heilbroner, Robert L. *The Worldly Philosophers*. New York, 1953.
Kohn, Hans. *The Idea of Nationalism*. New York, 1944.
Krieger, Leonard, and Stern, Fritz. *Responsibility of Power*. Garden City, 1967.
Masaryk, Thomas E. *The Spirit of Russia*. New York, 1919.
Nef, John U. *War and Human Progress*. Cambridge, 1950.
Ropp, Theodore. *War in the Modern World*. Durham, 1959.
Stern, Fritz, ed. *The Varieties of History*. New York, 1956.

Tawney, R. H. *Religion and the Rise of Capitalism.* New York, 1926.

Zinsser, Hans. *Rats, Lice, and History.* New York, 1935.

G. SUPPLEMENTARY READINGS IN PAPERBACKS ARRANGED BY PERIODS:

Narratives:

Trevor, Aston, ed. *Crisis in Europe, 1560–1660.* Anchor, 1965.

Marsak, Leonard M. *The Rise of Science in Relation to Society.* Macmillan, 1964.

Landes, David S. *The Rise of Capitalism.* Macmillan, 1966.

Lewis, W. H. *The Splendid Century.* Anchor, 1957.

Lefevre, G. *Coming of the French Revolution.* Princeton, 1947.

May, Arthur J. *Age of Metternich.* Holt, 1963.

Hayes, Carlton J. H. *A Generation of Materialism.* Harper, 1963.

Venturi, Franco. *Roots of Revolution.* Grosset and Dunlap, 1960.

Shaffer, Harry G. *The Soviet Economy.* Appleton, 1963.

Greene, Nathaniel, ed. *Fascism.* Crowell, 1968.

Problems:

Rule, John C., ed. *The Early Modern Era, 1648–1770.* Heath, 1967.

Reid, W. Stanford, ed. *The Reformation.* Holt, 1968.

Hay, Denis, ed. *The Renaissance Debate.* Holt, 1965.

Green, Robert W. *Protestantism and Capitalism.* Heath, 1959.

Church, William F., ed. *The Greatness of Louis XIV.* Heath, 1959.

Dowd, David L., ed. *The Age of Revolution.* Heath, 1967.

Lee, Dwight E., ed. *Outbreak of the First World War.* Heath, 1958.

Snell, John L., ed. *War and Totalitarianism, 1870 to Present.* Heath, 1967.

Documents:

Bainton, Roland H., ed. *The Age of the Reformation.* Van Nostrand, 1956.

Spitz, Lewis W., ed. *The Protestant Reformation.* Prentice-Hall, 1966.

Lossky, Andrew, ed. *The Seventeenth Century.* Free Press, 1967.

Hampshire, Stuart, ed. *The Age of Reason.* Mentor, 1956.

Rudé, George, ed. *The Eighteenth Century.* Free Press, 1965.

Cairns, John C., ed. *The Nineteenth Century.* Free Press, 1965.

INDEX